# ILIAD

# Homer

# ILIAD

Translated by
## Stanley Lombardo

Introduction by
## Sheila Murnaghan

Hackett Publishing Company, Inc.
Indianapolis/Cambridge

cover photo: Into the Jaws of Death. June 6, 1944.
Reproduced by courtesy of the U.S. Coast Guard.

03  02  01                  4  5  6  7  8  9

For further information, please address
  Hackett Publishing Company, Inc.
  P.O. Box 44937
  Indianapolis, Indiana 46244-0937

Cover design by Brian Rak and John Pershing
Text design by Dan Kirklin


**Library of Congress Cataloging-in-Publication Data**

Homer.
    [Iliad. English]
    Iliad/Homer; translated by Stanley Lombardo;
    introduction by Sheila Murnaghan.
        p.      cm.
    Includes bibliographical references (p.) and index.
    ISBN 0-87220-353-0 (cloth).   ISBN 0-87220-352-2 (pbk.)
   1. Epic poetry, Greek—Translations into English.   2. Achilles
(Greek mythology)—Poetry.   3. Trojan War—Poetry.   I. Lombardo,
Stanley, 1943–    . II. Title.
PA4025.A2L66  1997                              96-53368
883′.01—dc21                                     CIP

# Contents

For Judy, my wife,
Mae, my mother,
Ben, my son
and Ursula, my daughter

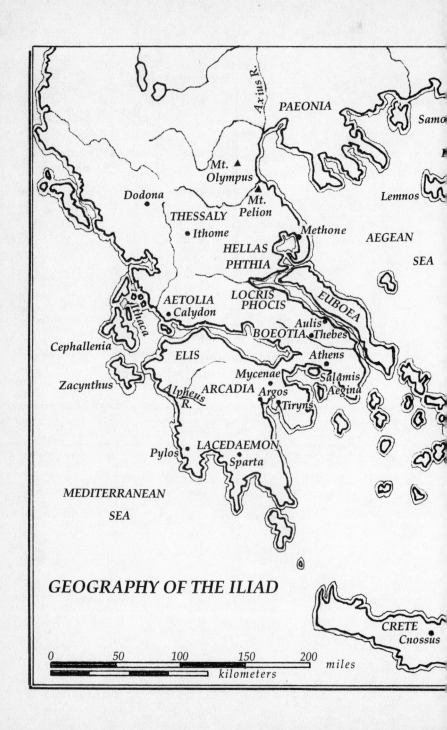

GEOGRAPHY OF THE ILIAD

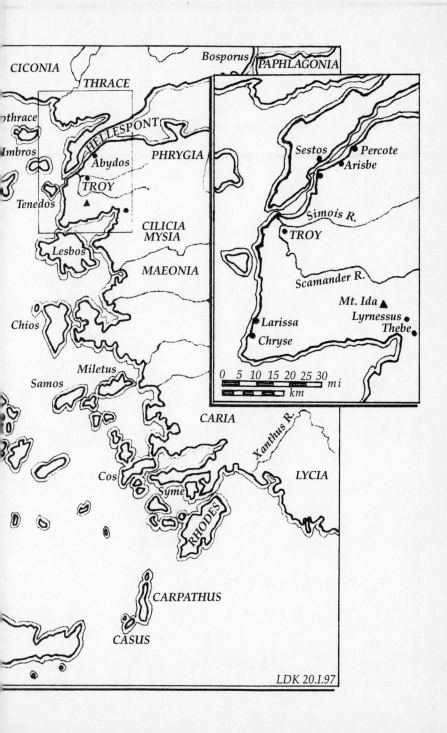

# Translator's Preface

A musician once asked Ezra Pound if there was anywhere one could get all of poetry, in the sense that one could get all of music in Bach. Pound's response was that if a person would take the trouble really to learn Greek, he could get all of it, or nearly all of it, in Homer. If Pound is right, and I think he is, then the real work of the Homeric translator is clear: to produce a version that is responsive not only to meaning and nuance but also to overall poetic effect, a version that has as much poetry as the original text, the translator's talent, and the current literary situation will yield. This requires loyalty to the essential qualities of Homeric poetry—its directness, immediacy, and effortless musicality— more than replication of the verse's technical features (although these must be at least suggested). In the end, it is the greatness and reach of Homer as a poet that the translator must confront. Accuracy and nuance are attainable through scholarship and good writing; technical problems admit of various solutions; but what we love is the poet's voice, and finding its tone, rhythm, and power is the heart of Homeric translation.

This translation of the *Iliad* began as scripts for solo performances I began giving ten years ago. In this respect, the production of the translation mirrors that period in the evolution of the *Iliad* when writing began to shape the body of poetry that had until then existed only in the mind of the composer and in live performance. We don't know exactly how writing shaped the monumental *Iliad* that we possess. Many scholars are convinced that the grand scale of the poem and its detailed, symmetrical architecture can only have been accomplished in a final written version. I am not sure that this view gives sufficient credit to the compositional and revisional powers of the human memory, especially when it is stimulated by repeated performance. Still, it does seem likely that as writing became more common, performance scripts would have been made and that these would have become the basis for texts for definitive public performance and for private reading. At some point, then, perhaps in the sixth century B.C.E., the *Iliad* became a written text. Although it

continued to be performed for hundreds of years as one of the
central documents of Greek culture, and although ancient editors
continued to quibble about this or that word or line, the *Iliad*'s
character had become essentially fixed as text. More than two
millennia later, and more than five hundred years after its reintro-
duction into western European culture as a printed book, we now
encounter the *Iliad* in Greek primarily in the *Oxford Classical Text*
edition by Monro and Allen (first published in 1902)–15,693 lines
of hexameter verse, the solid blocks of almost calligraphic text
interrupted only by the twenty-four book divisions adopted by
ancient editors. Reading it now, in the late twentieth century, is
the work of a scholar. Bringing it to life again is the work of the
scholar, the translator, and the performer. Performance is the
beginning and the end point of the *Iliad*. But a translation of the
*Iliad* cannot be simply a script; it must become, like the original
*Iliad*, a text and, finally, a printed poem. The poetics of this trans-
lation insists that it also be a performance on the page for the
silent reader. So the circle is complete. Throughout the period of
composing the translation as poetry on the page, I continued
reciting it to audiences, voicing the text as I crafted it and crafting
it to capture the voice that I heard.

This, then, is a translation that has been shaped by the alter-
nating and complementary pressures of poetic composition and
dramatic performance. Perhaps the most easily demonstrable ex-
ample of this process is my treatment of the similes. Critics have
long observed that similes in the *Iliad* tend to assume a poetic life
of their own, taking us away from the battlefield into the natural
and domestic world. In the Greek text, these passages are syntac-
tically (and typographically) integrated into the narrative, typi-
cally introduced by a phrase meaning "As when," and followed
by a phrase meaning "So also." In performance, I found myself
isolating the similes somewhat and marking them—pausing a
little before and after, changing the voice, dropping any percus-
sion I may have been using—in order to bring out their quality
as poetic events distinct from the poetry of the narrative and
speeches. I found that the narrative resumed with a kind of quiet
power after a simile had been given full attention in this way, and
that the audience's engagement with the performance was deep-

ened. I wanted to accomplish some of this on the printed page as well and settled on using italics, spaces, and indentation to mark the similes. Once the similes were typographically marked, the framing phrases "As when" and "So also" seemed less necessary, and I would often omit them or replace them with phrases inviting the imaginative participation of the reader, a practice that I then carried over into performance. The final version of the text of the translation retains traces of both the traditional Homeric style in similes and my own performing style.

The same can be said for my handling of the epithets and formulaic language in general. The Greek text meticulously preserves these stylistic features—set phrases that were fully functional only in the ancient performance tradition, which originally was at least partially improvisatory. My own performances, even when memorized, were always scripted, so there was no need for formulaic language as an aid to improvisation. Moreover, strict replication of the formulae (especially those introducing speeches) and heroic epithets would have made the performance seem less alive—stilted in style and slow in pace. Therefore, in preparing script I varied some of the formulaic phrases and cut others, especially epithets that added length but not much else to the line. I have operated on the same principles, although much more conservatively, in transforming script to poetic text and in composing the parts of the translation that I had never performed. My primary concern as a poet has been, in producing text as in performing, to represent as fully as possible the energy that comes from Homer's directness and rapidity. But I am very much a classicist also, and as such I want all of the contours of the Greek text to be present, too.

Part of the problem in translating epithets and other formulae is the difference in the genius of the languages involved. Greek hexameters can manage to be both rapid and direct while incorporating polysyllabic compound adjectives that would be deadly in English. This accounts for some of the streamlining I have done. As for the variations I have introduced, my practice is in part a response to the linguistic fact that no single word or phrase in one language ever completely translates even a simple word or phrase in another language. When the word or phrase to be translated has poetic resonance, the single translation is even less adequate. Most of the time we must be content with a single translation. But repeated epithets (and longer formulations) present the possibility of multiple translations, each of which might capture the poetic essence of the original in a different way. So, for instance, Athena's epithet *glaukopis*, traditionally rendered as either "grey-eyed" or "owl-eyed," I translate in both these ways, but I also bring in other associations to suggest the depths of the goddess's gaze: "eyes grey as slate" or (when she is betraying Hector) "her eyes as grey as winter moons" or (when she appears to Achilles in his rage) "Athena's eyes glared through the sea's salt haze." This last version exemplifies as well the technique of turning an adjective into an image or an event and integrating it into the action, a device that I use throughout the translation, although sparingly, in the interests of keeping the poem dynamic and in the moment.

In the end, then, I have retained most of the substance of Homer's formulaic language and enough of the form to give an impression of the original style, although I have pruned some phrases and selectively varied and highlighted others.

Formulaic language in Homeric epic is intimately connected with the metrics of the Greek hexameter line, in which each phrase having a fixed metrical shape fills certain positions in the line (or occupies an entire line). Although it is technically possible to write dactylic hexameter verse in English (witness Longfellow's *Evangeline*) and even to mimic the Greek's quantitative structure, in which the rhythm is based on the length of the syllables rather than the accentuation, the results are far from satisfactory. Again, it is a matter of the linguistic—and poetic— differences between the two languages. And in any case, Homer's musicality cannot be heard in any kind of English. For these reasons, I have not tried to compose hexameters, nor have I substituted any standard, regular meter, such as iambic pentameter, for Homer's dactylics. Instead, I have tried to stay true to the dominant practice of American poets in a tradition that leads from Whitman, Pound, and Charles Olson to the present: writing lines based on the cadences of natural speech, a practice that has its roots in the earliest English poetry before metrical forms from Romance languages, with their regular syllabic count, were imported into English. In this sort of verse, the sort I am using, the natural stresses of the spoken sentence establish the rhythm. The rhythmic integrity of each line is important to me (which is why I follow the tradition of capitalizing the first letter in each line), as is overall modulation of the sound to suit the sense in a line and throughout a passage. Tempo, of course, varies depending on the context, ranging from spondaic to staccato to anapests with a swing in them, but I have tried to maintain Homer's forward momentum at all times and to keep the lines crisp to reflect the clarity and sharp movement of Homer's gaze. I have occasionally used typographical effects to shape lines or whole passages— most notably the Catalogue of the Ships in Book 2—choreographing them for the eye as well as scripting them for the voice, again following contemporary poetic practice.

A few words about diction and poetic tradition. Homer's language does not correspond to any form of Greek ever spoken. It was a poetic dialect developed over generations of performance— rich, flexible, and capable of producing a wide variety of musical and semantic effects. It has often been observed that in the late twentieth century there is no longer available any traditional poetic language for translation of epic—or for writing English or American poetry for that matter—that we must content ourselves with the diction of prose cast into verse of some kind, and that we cannot therefore hope to achieve in translation the epic grandeur of Homer. I do not think there is much truth to this. What is true is that the use of an artificial poetic diction would serve to embalm Homer rather than bring him to life. But English and American poetry contains vast resources that are available to the translator; these resources include a modern poetics based on natural language that, far from being prosaic, is capable of great energy and beauty. A successful translation, especially of a work of the scale of the *Iliad*, must grow out of the poetic tradition of its own language and become one of its current embodiments. I am not the one to judge my success in producing living poetry in this translation, but the production of living poetry has been my goal. Living poetry means living speech, certainly in the speeches that account for almost half of the *Iliad*'s lines—how else could the characters be credible?—and also in the narrative and the similes. The *Iliad* is war poetry, and war poetry at the end of this century must be dead-on if it is to be done at all. If the diction of this translation is anachronistic in the broad sense—and sometimes even the narrower one—that is the condition for taking the great poem into its own future, which is where I want it to go.

Like every translator of Homer, I am indebted to those who have gone before me. I have respect for all who have toiled in these fields, and I have learned from most of them, even when our poetics differ. I have used Monro and Allen's *Oxford Classical Text* as the basis of the translation and have continually referred to the six-volume commentary published by Cambridge under the general editorship of G. S. Kirk (*The Iliad: A Commentary*, Vols. 1 and 2, G. S. Kirk; Vol. 3, J. B. Hainsworth; Vol. 4, Richard Janko; Vol. 5, Mark Edwards; Vol. 6, Nicholas Richardson). I have benefitted as well, in ways general and specific, from other Homeric scholarship, not all of which by any means is listed in the bibliography, which is intended as a short list for the general reader.

The Homerists who have helped me most directly have been Andrew Becker, who served as one of the readers for the press, and Sheila Murnaghan, who besides providing her splendid introduction also read the entire manuscript and improved it in countless details. I would also like to thank others who read early versions for the press: Georgia Nugent, Paul Woodruff, and several anonymous readers.

Brian Rak, the editor of this book at the press, has been deeply involved in every aspect of the work. He deserves and has my deepest gratitude. My thanks also to Dan Kirklin, Shannon Bahler, and Shawn Woodyard for their work in turning manuscript copy into a finished book.

Many friends have had a voice in this translation. William Levitan has been my literary coach, conscience, and comrade in this as in many previous ventures. Anne Carson has taught me as much by example as by direct comment, for both of which I am grateful. Beth Bailey, a historian of American culture with a good ear, has kept me on key in many passages. I would like to thank Karen Bell, Monica Peck, and Kathleen Whalen for critical help at various junctures. My gratitude also goes to my students at the University of Kansas, who have helped me in more ways than they know, and especially the students in a memorable undergraduate seminar: David Childers, Amy Coplan, John Lahti, Heather Lusk, Lesa Marbut, and Amy Welch. Jean Valk, besides doing most of the work in compiling the indexes, has also checked the entire manuscript for accuracy and assisted me with many revisions. Michelle Müller took care of many last-minute details, including the line numbers. My colleagues in the Classics Department at the University of Kansas have been unfailing in their moral and logistical support. And to all who have invited me to do performances in their homes, schools, and theaters, my sincerest thanks for providing the audiences who have collectively shaped the translation as much as any single person has.

Of all voices, the one I miss the most is that of Gareth Morgan, who died this past summer and who read Homer's Greek out loud more beautifully than any man on earth.

The voice I cherish the most is that of Judy Roitman, mathematician, poet, and my wife, whose humor and generosity have seen me through this long labor.

Work on the translation was supported by the University of Kansas in the form of sabbatical leaves, a fellowship from the Hall Center for the Humanities, and generous assistance from the College of Liberal Arts and Sciences.

Stanley Lombardo
University of Kansas

# INTRODUCTION

The *Iliad* is the story of a raging anger and its human toll. The poem recounts "the rage of Achilles," the greatest of the Greek heroes fighting in the war against Troy. Achilles' rage is superhuman (the Greek word translated as "rage," *mēnis*, is used otherwise only of gods) and aligned with cosmic forces: it fulfills the purposes of the supreme god Zeus and brings overwhelming destruction both to Achilles' Greek companions and to their enemies, the Trojans. This rage, the poet tells us,

> . . . cost the Greeks
> Incalculable pain, pitched countless souls
> Of heroes into Hades' dark,
> And left their bodies to rot as feasts
> For dogs and birds, as Zeus' will was done.  (1.2–6)*

And yet this far-reaching fury has its origins, not in the enmity of the Greeks and Trojans, but in the day-to-day tensions of the Greek camp, where a long-standing rivalry between Achilles and his commander Agamemnon flares up in a bitter quarrel. As it opens with this episode of internecine strife, the *Iliad* draws us into a world of warrior aristocrats for whom honor, gained and regained in the front lines of battle, is paramount. Under conditions of extreme pressure, their carefully cultivated distinctions of status give way to contention and hostility.

The story begins with a series of fateful blunders on the part of Agamemnon. Agamemnon has as a war prize a woman, Chryseis, who is the daughter of a priest of the god Apollo. When her father appeals to him to return her, invoking Apollo and offering a rich ransom, Agamemnon rudely dismisses him until Apollo sends a plague against the Greeks, which forces Agamemnon to give Chryseis back. Insisting that his loss of Chryseis must be compensated, Agamemnon decides to take a prize from another leader. He soon fixes on Briseis, the prize of Achilles, whose

---

*Line numbers in the Introduction, in the margins of the translation, and in the appendixes refer to the translation. Line numbers of the Greek text appear in the translation in brackets at the top of the page.

superiority as a fighter has been a source of friction between them and who has challenged Agamemnon's shaky authority by taking the lead in coping with the plague and by pointing out that the Greeks have no undistributed prizes to replace Chryseis with. For Achilles, Agamemnon's decision means public humiliation and an insulting disregard for his own hard-won status as the best of the Greeks, and he explodes with vicious taunts.

> You bloated drunk,
> With a dog's eyes and a rabbit's heart!
> You've never had the guts to buckle on armor in battle
> Or come out with the best fighting Greeks
> On any campaign! Afraid to look Death in the eye,
> Agamemnon? It's far more profitable
> To hang back in the army's rear—isn't it?—
> Confiscating prizes from any Greek who talks back
> And bleeding your people dry.          (1.235–44)

Achilles' anger quickly escalates as he follows his fighting words with an aggressive gesture. He slams to the ground the scepter, "studded with gold," that for generations has marked the right to speak in the Greek assembly, invoking its authority for a devastating threat.

> By this scepter, which will never sprout leaf
> Or branch again since it was cut from its stock
> In the mountains, which will bloom no more
> Now the bronze has pared off leaf and bark,
> And which now the sons of the Greeks hold in their hands
> At council, upholding Zeus' laws—
> By this scepter I swear:
> When every last Greek desperately misses Achilles,
> Your remorse won't do any good then,
> When Hector the man-killer swats you down like flies.
> And you will eat your heart out
> Because you failed to honor the best Greek of all.
>           (1.248–59)

Achilles' sense of unfair deprivation and his frustration with Agamemnon express themselves in an instinctive response that has far-reaching and unforeseeable consequences, as he turns his back on the whole community of Greeks, whose customs and traditions are embodied in the scepter he throws down, and seeks confirmation of his value in the triumph of their enemy Hector. The rest of the *Iliad* works out these consequences, charting the course of Achilles' rage as it intensifies, changes direction, and finally subsides. Achilles' self-willed estrangement from his former companions places him in unexpected situations that open up new and often painful perspectives on his role as a supremely great warrior. As it tells this story, the *Iliad* offers a full-scale examination of strife as an inescapable feature of human experience. All the characters in the poem must struggle to survive, endure, and make something of value out of conditions of constant conflict, which exist at all levels of the universe: in the clashes of divinities, in the drawn-out war between the Greeks and the Trojans, and in the tensions and rivalries of individuals.

## The Iliad and the Trojan Legend

The Trojan legend, in which the quarrel of Achilles and Agamemnon is a brief episode, concerns a central event of Greek mythology. The Greeks (or, in Homer's own term, the Achaeans) band together and cross the Aegean Sea to wage war against Troy, a gracious, prosperous city in Asia Minor (present-day Turkey). Their motive is revenge, for the Trojan prince Paris has stolen Helen, the most beautiful woman in the world, from her husband Menelaus, a major Greek chieftain. Under the leadership of Menelaus' brother Agamemnon, the Greeks fight around Troy for ten years and finally succeed in destroying the city and regaining Helen. The *Iliad* gets its title, which in Greek is *Ilias* and means the story of Troy, from one of the Greek names for Troy, *Ilios* or *Ilion*.

The *Iliad* focuses on Achilles' clash with Agamemnon, which occurs in the final year of the war. But that brief episode is presented in ways that allow it to stand for or suggest the whole of the larger story of which it is part. The events of the *Iliad* represent a decisive turning point in the war. Although Achilles remains stubbornly resistant to Agamemnon's attempts to appease him, he does eventually return to battle, drawn back by an overwhelming need to avenge the death of his closest companion,

Patroclus. Patroclus at first joins Achilles in his withdrawal from the war but is eventually overcome by pity for the Greeks. In Achilles' absence, the Greeks are dying in large numbers and the Trojans, led by Hector, are threatening to burn the Greek ships and so to cut the Greeks off from any hope of returning home, even in disgrace. Patroclus borrows Achilles' armor and returns to battle in Achilles' place. Although he fights brilliantly, killing a major Trojan hero, Sarpedon, he is eventually killed by Hector. Shamed and outraged by Patroclus' death, Achilles is filled with anger against Hector and returns to the battlefield, where he eventually meets and kills Hector.

The *Iliad* ends soon after this, with Achilles' decision to return Hector's body to his father, Priam, and with the funeral for Hector that can then take place. But it is clear that the story of the Trojan war is effectively over: by killing Hector, Achilles has eliminated Troy's indispensable defender, assuring the fall of the city and the victory of the Greeks. The story of Achilles is also over: as he learns from his mother, Thetis, who is a goddess, his own death is fated to follow soon after Hector's. The poet goes out of his way to keep us aware of these looming consequences, although he does not recount them. As they mourn over Hector, the Trojans anticipate the loss of their city and their own defeated future. The death of Achilles is expressed symbolically in the death of Patroclus, who represents for Achilles a kind of second self.

In addition to anticipating events that lie beyond the end of its story, the poem includes numerous episodes that evoke earlier stages of the war. In Book 4, a truce between the Greeks and Trojans is broken when a Trojan warrior decides to aim for personal glory and shoots at Menelaus; this recapitulates the origins of the war, which also started with an act of Trojan wrongdoing, Paris' theft of Helen. When the Greek army marches out to battle at the end of Book 2, we are given a list (known as the Catalogue of Ships) of all the commanders and how many shiploads of men each commanded, something one might expect in an initial account of the expedition. The following book includes an episode in which Helen comes out on the wall of Troy, where the Trojan elders are watching the proceedings, and identifies for them the various Greek leaders; this is hardly likely to have been necessary by this point in the war, but it offers us an introduction to some of most important participants. Because Achilles stays out of the action for most of the *Iliad*, the poet is able draw attention to the many other Greek warriors, such as Ajax, Agamemnon, Diomedes, and Odysseus, who over the course of the war also contribute to the Greek effort that Achilles ultimately dominates. As Achilles predicts to Agamemnon, his absence also provides a crucial opportunity to Hector, who emerges as a major character, as we follow his progress toward near victory over the Greeks. Beyond that, the poet weaves into his narrative the names and stories of many other, less prominent figures, striving for comprehensiveness in a way that is typical of epic, the poetic genre that, as the earliest example in the Western tradition, the *Iliad* in part defines.

Epic is a monumental form which recounts events with far-reaching historical consequences, sums up the values and achievements of an entire culture, and documents the fullness and variety of the world. While the *Iliad* uses Achilles' story as a means of organizing and concentrating its portrait of the Trojan war, it differs from the sharply focused explorations of individual experience found in many modern novels or in classical tragedy. One of its aims is to record the sheer number of people, each with his or her own history and circumstances, whose lives are decisively shaped by the war, whether by sounding their names in a virtuoso list of the participants such as the Catalogue of Ships, or by focusing in on a particular warrior's final moments on the battlefield, or by taking us into Troy, where the women and old men of the city live as anguished spectators of the war. Achilles' story gains in grandeur and significance because of the countless others who are affected by his departure from the war and his eventual return and whose individual efforts his own choices illuminate. His brilliant exploits acquire their meaning in the context of the large-scale cooperative venture of the Greek expedition. The *Iliad* is the portrait of an entire society, structured around the experience of one individual who struggles to define himself within it and against it.

## Heroic Society

The society that the *Iliad* portrays and that Achilles rejects when he slams down the scepter is a distinctive one, an aristocratic, warrior society, centered on battlefield achievement and its rewards. At the top of its hierarchical structure are heroes, superior men who are descendants of gods as well as of mortals. Heroes are born into positions of prominence, which they also reaffirm by their public actions and especially by courageous performance in combat. Their high status is expressed in social gestures (such as how they are addressed); in special privileges (where they sit at a feast); in their share of the tangible wealth of the group (in such forms as wine, meat, tripods, cattle, land, and women); and in the intangible reward of reputation or fame. The communal life of these heroes is highly ceremonious; as they eat together, worship the gods together, participate in councils together, and enter battle together, they follow prescribed forms of speech and behavior that knit them together as a group, that express the honor that they are continually granting and receiving, and that endow their harsh labors with the elegance and orderliness of civilization.

Book 12 of the *Iliad* contains a famous speech that seems to sum up the workings of this social system. It is delivered by Sarpedon, the son of Zeus himself, who is a prominent warrior from an area in Asia Minor called Lycia, fighting on the Trojan side. Here it is important to note that the Trojans and their allies are depicted as having the same values and customs as the Greeks; while the *Iliad* recounts a myth that played a major role in the formation of Greek identity, it does not present the Greeks' enemies as alien. Homeric warfare involves a great deal of talking as well as fighting, and before plunging into battle, Sarpedon turns to his friend Glaucus and offers a kind of meditation on why they willingly accept this experience of violence, chaos, and likely death.

> Glaucus, you know how you and I
> Have the best of everything in Lycia—
> Seats, cuts of meat, full cups, everybody
> Looking to us as if we were gods?
> Not to mention our estates on the Xanthus,
> Fine orchards and riverside wheat fields.
> Well, now we have to take our stand at the front,
> Where all the best fight, and face the heat of battle,
> So that many an armored Lycian will say,
> "So they're not inglorious after all,
> Our Lycian lords who eat fat sheep
> And drink the sweetest wine. No,

They're strong, and fight with our best."
Ah, my friend, if you and I could only
Get out of this war alive and then
Be immortal and ageless all of our days,
I would never again fight among the foremost
Or send you into battle where men win glory.
But, as it is, death is everywhere
In more shapes than we can count,
And since no mortal is immune or can escape,
Let's go forward, either to give glory
To another man, or get glory from him.

(12.320–42)

Sarpedon confidently outlines a series of bargains and calcula-
tions on which his society rests. People like him and Glaucus get
more honor and more material rewards than other people be-
cause they do more, fighting harder than others to further the
interests of the community as a whole and especially fighting in
the front lines, where the risk of death is greatest. They accept this
heightened risk because of those rewards and because death is
inescapable. Since life is finite, they are willing for it to be cut
short if they can enjoy honor and privileges while it lasts and if
they can win some permanent fame that will outlive them. Part of
what makes heroic combat so breathtaking is this head-on re-
sponse to mortality. Instead of evading death, heroes make it their
own, inflicting it on others and courting it for themselves.
As Sarpedon describes it, this system works smoothly, and he
does indeed follow his speech by entering the battle (although his
cheerful acceptance comes to seem more poignant in retrospect
when he is killed by Patroclus). But the *Iliad* does not just describe
this society and celebrate the achievements of its leaders; it also
reveals its flaws and weaknesses as they emerge under conditions
of severe strain. The *Iliad* is set at a time when the war has been
going on for so long that both sides have been drained of re-
sources and everyone involved is exhausted. Even if it can sur-
vive, Troy has lost the wealth and manpower that made it a great
city. The Greeks have been cut off for nine years from the rich
fields and glorious feasts that supposedly make combat worth-
while. Both sides have trouble remembering why they are fight-
ing in the first place. Helen appears in the poem as a bitterly

self-blaming spectator of the suffering she has caused, having long regretted her impulsive desertion of Menelaus for Paris. As she tells her Trojan father-in-law, Priam,

> Death should have been a sweeter evil to me
> Than following your son here, leaving my home,
> My marriage, my friends, my precious daughter,
> That lovely time in my life. None of it was to be,
> And lamenting it has been my slow death.
>
> (3.182–86)

Under these conditions, calculations like Sarpedon's break down, and the point of a warrior ethic of honor and courage is increasingly open to question. The crisis in the Greek camp, with which the plot begins, reflects the particular strains that arise when a group of heroes, who are all preeminent at home, as Sarpedon is in Lycia, have to temper their individual claims in order to work together as a unified force. This situation is further complicated by the intervention of the gods through Apollo's plague. The forced return of Chryseis disrupts the harmony achieved by the acceptable distribution of booty. With one fewer prize to go around, it is no longer possible for every hero to feel appropriately honored and there is nothing to keep the competition between Agamemnon and Achilles from flaring up in open hostility.

The desperate reactions of both heroes to the threat of losing a prize show how fully their sense of self is bound up in these external marks of honor. They know themselves in large part through their social status, which is created and expressed in public settings. Furthermore, as Sarpedon's speech makes clear, these prizes acquire added value from their supremely high price: the heroes' willingness to risk their lives every time they enter battle. The conflict between Achilles and Agamemnon also shows how hard it can be to apportion honor in a way that satisfies everyone. Agamemnon's implicit decision that if there is only one prize, it should go to him, not to Achilles, raises stubborn questions about the relative value of a great fighter and a king, questions which have clearly been causing tension in the Greek camp for some time, and which Achilles throws in

Agamemnon's face when he calls him a coward and labels himself "the best Greek of all." In contrast to Sarpedon's entrance into battle, Achilles' repudiation of Agamemnon's leadership expresses a loss of confidence in the ability of his community to reward his efforts. He then launches an attempt to find adequate compensation outside the conventional words and actions of that community and, in doing so, forces every reader of the *Iliad* to consider how and whether this is possible.

## The Homeric Gods

Achilles' withdrawal from the Greek camp is fueled by his strong sense of difference from its other members, which is manifested in his superior fighting ability and also in his birth: he has a divine mother, Thetis, a widely powerful sea goddess, as well as a mortal father, Peleus. Through Thetis he is able to appeal to Zeus, the king of the gods and the commanding figure of the universe. Zeus honors his appeal by making the Trojans succeed in the war, so that Agamemnon and the other Greeks become agonizingly aware of what Achilles' alienation is costing them.

In turning to Zeus, Achilles turns to a realm of powerful beings who are constantly involved in human affairs and who resemble human beings but who also differ from them in important ways. The Homeric gods can control all the different forces that shape human life, from the weather to emotions to social practices and institutions. The distinctness of these forces and their potential for conflict is expressed in the existence of a range of individual gods with different associations: for example, Poseidon is the god of the sea, Aphrodite of erotic love, Athena of craftsmanship and of war as an instrument of justice, Ares of war in its violence and brutality, Apollo of music and prophecy, etc. At the same time, the gods are linked as members of a single family, under the authority of its head, Zeus, whose supremacy is expressed in his control of the sky and his possession of thunder and lightning as weapons.

Because of their superior power, the gods can command the obedience and veneration of human beings, who must seek their favor through offerings, most often the sacrifice of animals, and they are constantly able to intervene in human life. In fact, all human endeavors occur under the sponsorship of the gods, and Homeric poetry frequently alludes to the divine support that underlies one human act after another. On the battlefield, a spear often meets its mark because a god makes sure that it does or falls uselessly to the ground because a god has chosen to deflect it. The gods have individual favorites whose interests they promote, and they also take sides in the war. Thus Aphrodite is on the Trojan side and Hera, Zeus' wife, and Athena, his daughter, are on the Greek side, because of an event that lies behind the story of the *Iliad*, although it is mentioned only once, toward the end of the poem, the so-called Judgment of Paris. Paris' theft of Helen—the occasion of the Trojan War—has been carried out with the help of Aphrodite as a reward for picking her over Hera and Athena in a beauty contest. As this episode reveals, the gods' superior power does not make them nobler than mortals, or less passionate in the pursuit of their individual interests.

Not only do the Homeric gods have more power than human beings, they also have greater knowledge, in particular of fate; they know what is destined to happen and act consciously to bring that about. For many modern readers, the activities of the gods and the existence of fate seem to drain the human characters of their autonomy, to turn them into puppets. It is important to recognize, however, that divine intervention is almost always in harmony with the preexisting qualities and instincts of those human characters. Divine favor may make possible displays of heroic excellence, but it is also a response to that excellence; in an unbreakably circular logic, men are heroic because the gods help them, and the gods help them because they are heroic. When gods influence events, they work through impulses that are already present in the characters, and the poet often presents events as doubly motivated, stemming both from the plans and projects of the gods and from those of the human characters.

The confluence of divine intervention and human impulse can be illustrated from an episode early in the poem. Just before Achilles insults Agamemnon and slams down the scepter, he almost kills him instead. As he reaches for his sword, he wavers:

> . . . should he
> Draw the sharp sword that hung by his thigh,
> Scatter the ranks and gut Agamemnon,
> Or control his temper, repress his rage?
>                                   (1.199–202)

At this point, Athena comes down, grabs him by the hair, and tells him not to kill Agamemnon, promising that he will get many more prizes in the end if he restrains himself. A modern reader may want to interpret Athena here as symbolizing a psychological force within Achilles, an intrinsic capacity for restraint and rational calculation. Granting her the external reality she has for Homer, we can still see that her intervention makes Achilles decide on a course of action he was already considering.

Similarly, fate does not function in the Homeric world as a force that causes characters to do what they otherwise would not. Human beings bring about what is fated through all of the individual, often short-sighted decisions they make while pursuing their various goals. Knowledge of fate, which the gods possess and occasionally share with mortals, is like advance knowledge of the plot of a novel or a film. It allows a greater appreciation of the direction of events that for most characters seem random and open-ended, but it does not alter the behavior of those characters. Certainly the human characters in the *Iliad* experience their lives as involving choices, often difficult ones, and they expect to be judged by the consequences of their choices despite the fact that those choices—like all human actions—are sponsored by the gods and bring about what is fated.

While the Homeric gods resemble humans to a striking extent in their appearance and their emotions, they differ in the crucial respect that they are not subject to permanent change, including above all death; they are immortal. This makes them profoundly different from mortals in their values and their behaviors, because they do not—and cannot—share the attachments and commitments that humans make in the face of death. This difference is pointedly illustrated early in the *Iliad,* when the conflict in the Greek camp with which the poem begins is followed by an episode of conflict among the gods. When Thetis comes to Zeus and asks him to help Achilles by making the Trojans do well in the war, so Agamemnon will recognize his mistake and restore Achilles' honor, Hera suspects what is going on and, because she herself favors the Greeks, becomes angry. When Zeus returns to the divine circle, she berates him, and the gods' habitual gaiety is threatened by discord.

But while the discord among the Greeks continues for many days and does not end until many men, both Trojan and Greek, have been killed, this divine quarrel is instantly patched up, as Hera's son Hephaestus persuades her to give up her anger. He tells her a story to remind her that there is no point resisting Zeus, who is more powerful than the rest of them, and he reminds her that a quarrel between her and Zeus will spoil the gods' fun:

> This is terrible; it's going to ruin us all.
> If you two quarrel like this over mortals
> It's bound to affect us gods. There'll be no more
> Pleasure in our feasts if we let things turn ugly.
>
> (1.606–9)

This episode brings out two key differences between divine and human society. Among the gods there is a clear hierarchy: Zeus may have had struggles in the past, and he may continue to suffer challenges, but he is the strongest god and always will be, so there is no lasting good to be gained by resisting him. Among the human characters, the power structure is less clear and more subject to change, so that Achilles does have reason to contest Agamemnon's authority. And the gods, having nothing to lose, see no point in fighting over what they care about. Hera would rather that the Greeks not do badly in the war, but their losses do not mean enough to her that she would sacrifice the pleasure of a feast because of them. Achilles, on the other hand, goes to great lengths to protest his loss of Briseis, because she represents the honor which is his only compensation for the likely loss of his life.

Only in a few rare instances are the gods shown as suffering the constraints that define human life, and those involve cases where they are bound to humans by the tie of parenthood. In a surprising episode in Book 16, Zeus himself experiences the demands of fate, with its intimate connection to human mortality, as a painful limitation. As the moment approaches when his own son Sarpedon is fated to die at the hands of Patroclus, Zeus toys with the idea of reversing fate but backs off, weeping tears of blood, when the other gods make it clear that they will not support him. Much more extensively, the *Iliad* portrays Achilles' mother, Thetis, as deeply pained by the fate of her son, whose present sufferings and future death she constantly mourns.

Despite the sympathy of his mother, when Achilles turns away from his fellow humans to Zeus in his quest for satisfaction, he is relying on a being who not only is vastly more powerful than they but who also has his own distinct purposes and values. While Achilles imagines at that point that Zeus' only intention is to restore Achilles' lost honor, Zeus' role in the events of the *Iliad* is, in fact, much more complicated and enigmatic. The aims of the human characters and the other gods, through whom Zeus works, are relatively clear, but the "will of Zeus" itself remains opaque. Although he is the ultimate source of most good things in human life, and he reacts with distaste to Hera's intransigent hatred of the Trojans, he seems mysteriously bent on the perpetuation of the war to the point of maximum destruction. As Achilles later concludes, renouncing his rage against Agamemnon and wondering at its origins: "Somehow it has pleased Zeus / that many Greeks should die." (19.291–92)

## Achilles

With Zeus' help, Achilles is able to bring Agamemnon to his knees. The Trojans are so successful that they push the Greeks back into their ships, around which the Greeks have built a defensive wall and ditch; the Trojans now camp on the plain, no longer retreating into Troy at night. Recognizing that their cause is lost without Achilles, Agamemnon sends three ambassadors to him with an offer of amends that includes the return of Briseis and a huge number of additional prizes. In a stunning response that overturns all expectations, Achilles rejects this offer. In a long and passionate speech, he announces that he is going to leave Troy and return home. While the force of this speech is unmistakable, its exact meaning has been much debated: making sense of this difficult speech is a major challenge for readers of the *Iliad*.

This speech is so challenging because Achilles' continued sense of outrage expresses itself in contradictory positions, and he shifts back and forth between them. In part he is simply still furious at what Agamemnon has done, unable to forget Agamemnon's errors and his own mistreatment:

> He cheated me, wronged me. Never again.
> He's had it. He can go to hell in peace,
> The half-wit that Zeus has made him.
> His gifts? His gifts mean nothing to me.
>
> (9.386–89)

But Achilles' loss of respect for Agamemnon, the source of the gifts through which he has experienced his own value, sparks a much more fundamental questioning of the value of those gifts themselves, gifts that for someone like Achilles, who already has plenty of possessions, have no meaning outside their ability to confer honor. As a result, Achilles' expressions of ongoing anger are set side by side with radical reconsiderations of the basic principles of heroic culture, such as the assumption that honor-bearing gifts are a worthwhile compensation for the loss of life in battle.

> Nothing is worth my life, not all the riches
> They say Troy held before the Greeks came,
> Not all the wealth in Phoebus Apollo's
> Marble shrine up in craggy Pytho.
> Cattle and flocks are there for the taking;
> You can always get tripods and chestnut horses.
> But a man's life cannot be won back
> Once his breath has passed beyond his clenched teeth.
>
> (9.415–22)

He asks as well whether a courageous death in the front lines of battle really is meaningfully different from and better than any other death.

> It doesn't matter if you stay in camp or fight—
> In the end, everybody comes out the same.
> Coward and hero get the same reward:
> You die whether you slack off or work.
>
> (9.324–27)

As when he slams down the scepter in his first impulse to quit the Greek cause, Achilles expresses simultaneously a deep attachment to the system that he has trusted in and that has betrayed him and a new detachment born from that betrayal, now elaborated into a full-scale critique of heroic values. In his continuing frustration, he asks a great deal of his culture, perhaps more than it can give. He tells the ambassadors that he will not yield until Agamemnon has "paid in full for all my grief" (9.400), holding out for a complete restitution that may not be possible. Agamemnon has certainly erred in the past, and he may be erring still in approaching Achilles through ambassadors rather than apologizing in person, but the gifts he offers are, as the wise veteran Nestor puts it, "beyond reproach" (9.168), and he cannot undo the past or stop being king. Even as he insists on these demands, Achilles also voices a new and unparalleled clarity about how little his culture has to offer, about the paltriness of the gifts and privileges with which men honor each other compared to the immensity of death.

Here too, Achilles' independence from the other Greeks and from the values that animate them is supported by his special closeness to the gods. In his speech, he brings up the privileged information that he has from his divine mother.

My mother Thetis, a moving silver grace,
Tells me two fates sweep me on to my death.
If I stay here and fight, I'll never return home,
But my glory will be undying forever.
If I return home to my dear fatherland
My glory is lost but my life will be long,
And death that ends all will not catch me soon.

(9.423–29)

Through his special access to divine foreknowledge, Achilles knows that if he fights in the war he certainly will die. This certainty sets him off from other heroes, who can always hope, against all odds, to be spared, and it gives him a sense of freedom and choice, an ability to choose against the unequal bargain of life for honor that more ordinary warriors regularly enter into.

Achilles' newfound clarity about the inadequacy of the system in which he and the other Greeks have operated brings a new perspective to the poem, allowing it to show how the heroic world may look from a position outside it. But, as with all human vision, Achilles' clarity is only partial and is accompanied by blindness. Some of what Achilles cannot see is expressed in the speeches of the ambassadors who respond to him. Horrified by Achilles' decision, which spells certain disaster for all of them, they offer answers to his complaints that are deeply embedded in their common heritage. First Phoenix, Achilles' beloved old tutor, tells him "a very old story" (9.542) about another hero, Meleager, who like Achilles becomes angry at his community and withdraws from it during a war. Like Achilles, Meleager is offered rich gifts if he will return and is solicited by his friends and family, but he remains adamant until the moment when his city is about to be destroyed and his wife, Cleopatra, begs him to save it. Meleager returns to battle and saves his city, but at that point the gifts are no longer available. Phoenix's story responds to Achilles' claim that gifts are not adequate compensation for fighting, by showing that there are other reasons why people fight besides honor. If you are going to end up fighting anyway, he points out, you might as well take the gifts when they are offered.

Ajax in his response draws, not on a traditional story, but on a shared institution, that of the blood price. He bitterly criticizes Achilles for his savage heart and lack of pity for the Greeks, who have loved and honored him, and he counters Achilles' sense of outraged superiority with another model of human behavior, one that involves self-restraint and acceptance of loss.

> A man accepts compensation
> For a murdered brother, a dead son.
> The killer goes on living in the same town
> After paying blood money, and the bereaved
> Restrains his proud spirit and broken heart
> Because he has received payment.
>
> (9.652–57)

While Achilles rejects Agamemnon's gifts because they do not seem adequate compensation for the loss of honor he has suffered or the loss of life he faces, Ajax points out that people regularly do accept inadequate recompense for the most wrenching losses. Faced with a loss that can never be made up, they let go of their attachment to the dead and are content with the only compensation there is.

These speeches answer Achilles' concerns obliquely, and his own response to them is ambiguous. In his words, he repeats both his undiminished anger at Agamemnon, telling Ajax that

> Everything you say is after my own heart.
> But I swell with rage when I think of how
> The son of Atreus treated me like dirt.
> (9.668–70)

and his sense of transcendent detachment from the Greeks, telling Phoenix that "I don't need that kind of honor. . . . My honor comes from Zeus" (9.624–25). But he does keep retreating from his announced plan of leaving Troy, first telling Phoenix that he will decide in the morning whether or not to go and then telling Ajax that he will stay out of the war until he is personally threatened, until Hector is about to burn his own huts and ships. The episode concludes with a disparity between what Achilles is able to think and say and what he is actually able to do that the rest of the poem must resolve.

The debate between Achilles and Agamemnon's ambassadors ends there and is never explicitly taken up again, but the rest of the *Iliad* tells how Achilles ends up doing what he has so adamantly insisted he will not do, fighting again for the Greeks. And, in doing so, Achilles reenacts the pattern set by Phoenix's story of Meleager: Achilles too returns to battle to save his community through the agency of the person he cares most about, in his case Patroclus (whose name inverts and echoes the name of Meleager's wife Cleopatra).

The relationship between Achilles and Patroclus involves both intense closeness (they are so close that later Greeks who idealized male homosexual relations assumed they were lovers, although there is no indication of that in the *Iliad*) and a stark contrast: while Achilles is violent, quick to anger, and jealous of his own honor, Patroclus is gentle, concerned for the bonds of friendship between members of the army, and compassionate, and he reenters the war out of pity for the many Greeks who are dying because of Achilles' absence. When he rejoins the battle, Patroclus does so as Achilles' surrogate, literally impersonating him by wearing his armor, and he represents Achilles' double as well as his opposite. Patroclus becomes consumed with the kind of rage for combat associated with Achilles, and he fights with risky brilliance, achieving glorious success by killing Sarpedon but also exposing himself to death at the hands of Hector. Conversely, Patroclus' death awakens in Achilles a sense of connectedness to other people as he experiences anguish for the loss of his beloved friend and shame for his failure to protect him. Shaken from his sense of glorious superiority, Achilles now sees himself, in his willed isolation, as worthless, "a dead weight on the earth," as he tells his mother (18.109).

For Achilles, Patroclus' death is a shattering reminder of those other reasons for fighting that he seemed to forget in his obsession with Agamemnon's faults and the insufficiency of honor. In their self-presentation and their rational calculations, heroes may stress the material rewards and status that come from fighting, as Sarpedon does in his speech to Glaucus, but they are also inspired by concern for the communities they protect and by deep bonds between each other: although Sarpedon may present their situation as a set of bargains, he does also address Glaucus as "my friend."

This is not to say, however, that Achilles in returning to battle is also returning to the Greek warrior community, with all of its rituals and customs. The rage that he has felt toward Agamemnon is now supplanted by a new rage against Hector, and he fights with a viciousness and single-mindedness that contrast sharply with the rest of the fighting described in the *Iliad*. That fighting, while brutal, is nonetheless balanced by civilized practices like pausing to eat, to sleep, or to bury the dead. As he seeks revenge for Patroclus' death, Achilles seems more like an elemental force than an ordinary warrior (in his indiscriminate violence, taking on even the river Scamander), and he stands outside the normal practices of human warfare. As he rejoins the Greek army, he has no patience for stopping to let the men eat and drink or even for receiving the gifts that Agamemnon has promised him; and Odysseus, who is much more finely attuned to the protocols of heroic society, has to insist that he go through those motions. Meeting for the second time a Trojan warrior, Lycaon, whom before he has been willing to take captive and hold for ransom rather than kill, Achilles is now unmoved by Lycaon's pleas, and, with a single cut to the collarbone, he buries his sword in Lycaon's chest.

Achilles' distance from the normal decorum of warfare is most pointed and explicit at the moment when he finally encounters the object of his fury, Hector. Hector proposes a bargain whereby the winner of their combat will return the loser's body to his family for the loving and ceremonious burial with which people attempt to cure the insult of violent death, but Achilles has no interest in that:

> Don't try to cut any deals with me, Hector.
> Do lions make peace treaties with men?
> Do wolves and lambs agree to get along?
> No, they hate each other to the core,
> And that's how it is between you and me.
> No talk of agreements until one of us
> Falls and gluts Ares with his blood.
>                    (22.287–93)

Although he is motivated to fight by his love for Patroclus, Achilles remains isolated from all other members of the human community, rightly comparing himself to the most savage animals. Still set apart by his godlike knowledge of fate—made all the clearer by Thetis when she tells him, as he decides to return, that he will die next after Hector: "Hector's death means yours," (18.101)—Achilles fights unhampered by any hope of survival, with nothing to lose.

## Hector

In rejecting Hector's proposal, Achilles distances himself from a hero who, unlike Achilles, has always remained identified with the values and rituals of his society. Throughout the *Iliad*, Hector and the other Trojans provide a different perspective on heroism from the Greeks, as they fight around and for their own city, battling for the survival of their homes and families, rather than for the glory to be won in a foreign expedition. While Hector shares the courage and fighting ability typified by Achilles, he also manifests the connection to his community associated with Patroclus, and, as he too struggles with his identity as a hero, he does so in the context of his relations with family members rather than with his commander.

Earlier in the poem, Hector, like Achilles, has been faced with a choice, although it is formulated differently and he gives a very different response. A large part of Book 6 of the *Iliad* is devoted to an episode in which Hector returns from the battlefield to Troy, the shared space of his community, and meets there a series of women: his mother, Hecuba; his sister-in-law, Helen; and his wife, Andromache. What emerges from these encounters is how fully, as a warrior, Hector is cut off from the community he is risking his life to protect. His mother offers him some wine and invites him to pour a libation to Zeus, but he points out that he is unfit for this routine religious observance:

> I have too much reverence to pour a libation
> With unwashed hands to Zeus almighty,
> Or to pray to Cronion in the black cloudbanks
> Spattered with blood and the filth of battle.
>
> (6.277–80)

Andromache has their young child, Astyanax, with her, and Hector's cherished son is terrified by his father's war helmet and shrinks from him until Hector takes it off and puts it on the ground. The possibility of lingering in the city with these women is presented as a dangerous temptation, as Hector expresses fear that Hecuba's wine will rob him of his strength and fends off Helen's seductive invitation to sit down beside her.

The most compelling temptation is presented by Andromache, who wretchedly points out that Hector's courage is bound to bring his death and with it the destruction of the city he is supposed to be saving. Dwelling in painful detail on the bitter life of enslavement and humiliation that lies ahead for her and Astyanax, she asks him to give up his commitment to fighting aggressively in the front lines, suggesting that he fall back to the wall and fight defensively. Hector expresses sympathy for her position and anguish over her fate and his, but is unable to do as she asks:

> Yes, Andromache, I worry about all this myself,
> But my shame before the Trojans and their wives,

With their long robes trailing, would be too terrible
If I hung back from battle like a coward.
And my heart won't let me. I have learned to be
One of the best, to fight in Troy's first ranks,
Defending my father's honor and my own.

(6.463–69)

Like Achilles when he rejects Agamemnon's ambassadors, Hector is sacrificing his community to his pursuit of honor, but he does so by embracing rather than by rejecting its values, and here the poem reveals a contradiction within heroic values that is in some ways more devastating than Achilles' explicit critique. Hector's words show that his own society has made him unable to respond to his wife's desperate plea, no matter how much he feels for her: his combative instincts are instilled by his training and the social pressures that control his behavior through honor and its opposite, shame. The child Astyanax creates a moment of harmony between Hector and Andromache, as they laugh together at his fear of the helmet, but Hector soon leaves with a prayer that his son may become—like him—a powerful and dedicated warrior.

When Hector finally faces Achilles, he does so as someone who has always stayed within the framework of heroic values and who embodies the blindness and self-destructiveness that are bound up with heroic glory. Buoyed up by his temporary success, Hector has recklessly ignored the good advice of his brother Polydamas and has dismissed an omen from the gods. But, when he first sees Achilles in all his force and passion, Hector's first instinct is to run. Achilles chases him three times around the city, until Athena disguises herself as Hector's brother Deïphobus and tricks him into stopping and facing Achilles by promising to support him. Hector does face Achilles, but, when he loses his spear and turns—he thinks—to Deïphobus for another, he finds no one there. Realizing at once that he is alone and doomed, he continues to fight, voicing the essential heroic determination to make something out of inevitable death: "I will not perish without some great deed / that future generations will remember" (22.332–33).

## The Enduring Heart

By killing Hector, Achilles saves the Greeks, opening the way for the taking of Troy and making it possible for them to return home at last. He also secures his own future fame, performing a deed that will be remembered and sung about forever. Having chosen, in the end, a short life, he achieves the glory that goes with it, fighting with a godlike brilliance and a bestial ferocity. With his death now imminent, his story is essentially over. But the *Iliad* does not end here: Achilles does not meet his mortal end without also rediscovering his identity as a mortal; he does not die without first recovering his connection to other human beings.

True to his word, Achilles does not honor Hector's request to return his body to his family. Instead he repeatedly yokes it to his chariot and drags it in the dust around Patroclus' tomb. This vengeful assault on the body of Patroclus' killer is the ultimate expression of Achilles' rage. That rage finally comes to an end when Hector's father, Priam, persuades him to give the body back, after all, in exchange for a rich ransom.

Like all the other events of the *Iliad*, the ransoming of Hector's body stems from both divine and human motives, beginning with the decision on Olympus that Achilles must give the body back. Although the gods are repelled by Achilles' savage behavior, they do not simply take the body away from him but, as always, work through the emotions and practices of human life. Thus Zeus summons Thetis to Olympus, and, on his instructions, she goes down to Achilles and tells him he must accept Priam's ransom. This action inverts the opening sequence of the poem, in which Thetis goes up to Zeus to get him to do what Achilles wants, and it underscores what the plot of the poem has already revealed, the limits to Achilles' special favor from Zeus.

Achilles' sense of Zeus' favor, his feeling of having honor from Zeus, has allowed him to do what no other hero can, to step outside his warrior culture and voice a detached and godlike perspective on that culture. But Achilles' detachment has a high price, in the lost lives of the many Greeks and Trojans who die while he stays out of the war, and it does not, in the end, protect him from either the danger or the grief of a warrior's life. He experiences the ambiguity of Zeus' favor most bitterly with Patroclus' death, in his stunned realization that he has gotten what he asked for, recognition from the Greeks through Trojan success, but at an intolerable cost that he never envisioned. In his dealings with Zeus, Achilles confronts the painful lessons—the gap between what humans can imagine and long for and what they can actually have, the difficulty of learning except too late and by suffering—that were later to be explored in classical tragedy, and he has experiences that we have come to label "tragic." Like many later tragic characters and like many of the heroes of the *Iliad*, most notably Hector before his death, Achilles performs his most memorable and most valued actions when he feels the gods have abandoned him.

After Thetis' communication, Achilles' return of Hector's body is renegotiated on the human level as Priam makes his dangerous journey into the enemy camp and pleads with Achilles to give up his son's remains. In responding to Priam's plea, Achilles displays and affirms a form of human achievement that is far removed from the energetic initiatives of the battlefield: the patient endurance of suffering. This is the quality that Ajax speaks of in Book 9, when Achilles is unready to hear him, and Ajax's sentiments are recalled in Book 24 by Apollo as he and the other gods condemn Achilles' mistreatment of Hector's body.

> A man may lose someone dearer than Achilles has,
> A brother from the same womb, or a son,
> But when he has wept and mourned, he lets go.
> The Fates have given men an enduring heart.
>
> (24.50–53)

As Apollo's words make clear, the enduring heart is a peculiarly human virtue, a response to the suffering that human beings experience and gods do not. It is a harsh virtue, in that it demands a certain hard-heartedness, a willingness to let go of the most precious attachments, but it is, after all, an adaptation to harsh conditions. And that eventual letting go makes possible the consolations that human beings are able to find in the face of suffering. In that sense it is, as Apollo describes it, a gift from the gods.

In the final episode of the *Iliad*, both Priam and Achilles command our admiration for their extraordinary endurance, and, as a result, they are each able to gain something of value from even the doomed and heartbreaking situations in which they find themselves. As he makes his appeal to Achilles, kneeling before him as a suppliant and asking him to think of his own father, Peleus, Priam has to give up his hatred of Achilles as the killer of Hector, and he speaks of his action in a way that shows how endurance can be itself a form of heroism:

> I have borne what no man
> Who has walked this earth has ever yet borne.
> I have kissed the hand of the man who killed my son.
>
> (24.541–43)

Doing so, he gains Achilles' awed respect ("You have a heart of iron," 24.560) and the release of his son's body.

To return the body and accept the ransom, Achilles has to let go of his overwhelming attachment to Patroclus, to stop feeling the bitter outrage that has kept him uselessly punishing Hector even after he is dead, but he is able to experience the solace of shared grief as he and Priam mourn together. He is able then to move beyond grief as they eat and drink together and, for a moment, gaze with admiring delight at one another. That Achilles is now able to grant Priam's one desire shows how endurance is a humane as well as a harsh virtue, linked, as Ajax suggests, to pity. Achilles' detachment from the dead Patroclus, for whom he can now do nothing more, allows him to do something meaningful for Priam, who, while his enemy, is still living and can benefit from his action.

As he opens himself up to pity for Priam, Achilles finally comes to terms with his identity as a mortal, bound to other mortals by the common experience of incurable loss. He voices a sense of what it means to be mortal, in an account of Zeus and his role in shaping mortal life that is very different from his earlier vision of Zeus as his particular supporter. He tells Priam that Zeus gives every man gifts from two jars, one of good things, one of evils. To some he gives all evils, to some a mixture a good and evil; to no one does he give all good. To exemplify the life of good mixed with evil that is the best one can hope for, he develops the comparison between Priam and Peleus, to which Priam has appealed. Both are men who have known great prosperity, but have had their lives darkened by the loss of a beloved son. These examples draw our attention to war in particular as a source of human misery. It is through war that mortality is made even more painful than it has to be, as young men die deaths that are early and violent, and parents must bury their children.

In honoring Priam's appeal to remember Peleus, Achilles finally resolves the issue of his mixed parentage. He becomes identified with his mortal father rather than with the divine mother who once made him feel different and freer than other mortals. As he recognizes that Thetis can no longer help him, he no longer shares his sorrows with her, but with another mortal who, even though he is an enemy, meets him on common ground. And by agreeing to accept Priam's ransom, he also resolves the issue of the insufficiency of material rewards that has haunted the entire *Iliad.*

This issue emerges at the very beginning of the poem with Agamemnon, who sets the plot in motion when he refuses to take ransom from the old priest Chryses for his daughter Chryseis; with Priam's successful ransoming of Hector's body, the end of the poem recalls and corrects its beginning. Agamemnon refuses the ransom offered him by Chryses because it does not seem to him adequate to the value he places on Chryseis, who is to him not just an exchangeable sign of honor but a woman he cares for. As we have seen, the same issue comes up with far more urgency in Achilles' rejection of the embassy, when he refuses Agamemnon's gifts because they are not commensurate with the value of his only life. When Achilles takes Priam's ransom, he finally gives up the stubborn insistence on equal compensation that has caused both him and Agamemnon so much grief; he accepts and values that ransom as the only compensation there is.

Both Agamemnon and Achilles show how characteristic it is of human beings to long for and fantasize about complete restitution for whatever they have lost. But that fantasy is ruled out by the very nature of mortal life, in which gifts come from other human beings who are always, like Agamemnon, flawed and in which time is irreversible, choices are finite, and death is incurable. There is in the end no better way than to take whatever meager recompense is offered. At the same time, the *Iliad* reveals and celebrates the value that people can give to mere material objects, as they embellish their clothes and their armor, as they strip a stick of its leaves, stud it with gold, and turn it into a symbol of communal order, or as they consent to equate robes, cauldrons, and tripods with the life of a beloved friend.

At the end of the *Iliad*, Achilles is in an extraordinary situation, having asserted his superiority to all other living heroes and having secured immortal glory, but not yet dead. Yet he has no more meaningful way of experiencing his greatness than by accepting the ordinary, limited consolations of everyday human life, finding fellowship in the company of others, taking gifts and the honor they convey, eating food, making love, and going to sleep. Nothing brings this home more clearly than the final image of Achilles with which the poem leaves us—asleep in his shelter, with Briseis at his side.

## The Iliad as a Poem of War

The achievement of accord between Achilles and Priam brings the *Iliad* to a moving and surprisingly peaceful conclusion that is made all the more powerful by its lack of sentimentality. There is no suggestion that either Achilles or Priam has been miraculously transformed by his experiences.

> Achilles called the women and ordered them
> To wash the body well and anoint it with oil,
> Removing it first for fear that Priam see his son
> And in his grief be unable to control his anger
> At the sight of his child, and that this would arouse
> Achilles' passion and he would kill the old man
> And so sin against the commandments of Zeus.
>
> (24.627–33)

Both men retain the passionate sense of honor that motivates heroic behavior and can lead in a flash to violent conflict. Furthermore, as they negotiate a truce to allow for Hector's burial, both take it for granted that the war will continue. No lasting change has been brought about by their amazing encounter.

Consistent with its view of conflict as a defining feature of human life, imposed on mortals by the gods, the *Iliad* presents its characters as thinking about ending the war, or even trying to end it, but never actually being able to do so. Early in the poem, both sides agree to settle their differences through a single combat between Paris and Menelaus, but their truce breaks down because an unimportant Trojan warrior (egged on by Athena, who, like the other gods, seems bent on keeping the war alive) makes a bid for glory and aims an arrow at Menelaus. As he waits to face Achilles, Hector fantasizes about disarming and approaching Achilles with terms for peace, but then reminds himself of Achilles' unstoppable rage:

> . . . Achilles
> Will cut me down in cold blood if I take off
> My armor and go out to meet him
> Naked like a woman. (22.139–42)

In the course of the *Iliad*'s plot, Hector and Achilles between them confront various good reasons to stay out of the war, but neither is able to do it. Rather, that plot is structured in such a way as to separate out and explore the range of motives that are usually tangled up with one another and that keep warriors returning to battle: revenge for a lost companion, a stolen wife, or a terrible insult; the preservation of a threatened community; the drive for glory; surrender to "the joys of war" (4.238).

In telling this story, the poet too remains in the world of war, never depicting peace as part of the present reality of his characters. When peacetime scenes are evoked, they come in the context of the home the Greeks long to return to, or the past that the Trojans have lost—as when we are told that Achilles chases Hector past a pair of springs outside the walls of Troy.

> There were broad basins there, lined with stone,
> Where the Trojan women used to wash their silky clothes
> In the days of peace, before the Greeks came.
>
> (22.175–77)

Some of the most sustained descriptions of peacetime come in similes, comparisons that illuminate the world of warfare for the poem's audience but that are not part of the experience of the characters. These similes often take us away from the battlefield to a very different setting, as in this description of what it was like when the entire Greek army marched out against the Trojans:

*Innumerable throngs of buzzing flies*
*Will swarm all over a herdsman's yard*
*In springtime, when milk wets the pails—*

Likewise the throngs of long-haired Greeks
Who stood on the plain facing the Trojans . . .
                                    (2.505–9)

Sometimes the activity of combat itself is compared to the productive labor and craftsmanship of the peacetime world, as in this account of the tug-of-war that takes place over Patroclus' body after he has been killed by Hector.

The day was passing. Men hacked slowly at each other
In pain, the sweat from their labor coating
Their thighs and knees, pooling under their feet,
Spattering from their arms into their glazed eyes,
As the two armies fought over Achilles' surrogate.

*A tanner gives his men an oxhide to stretch,*
*Having first drenched it in oil. They stand in a circle*
*And pull at it until its moisture is squeezed out*
*By all of their tugging and the oil has a chance*
*To penetrate the taut leather's pores.*

So too the tight circle of men on either side
Tugging at the corpse . . .                    (17.393–404)

This comparison alters a reader's perception of combat in complicated, even contradictory ways. In part, it makes combat seem more familiar and natural by equating it with an ordinary activity that someone who has never seen war can easily understand. At the same time, by removing us momentarily from the battlefield, it promotes a more distanced perspective, from which the contrast between the wasteful work of killing and dying and the productive labor of making something useful may make combat seem alien and horrific.

At times the similes seem themselves to build in the presence of a different perspective, from which war has another aspect than it

does to its participants, as in this comparison of troops of soldiers
to banks of storm clouds:

As they were strapping on their helmets
Behind them a cloud of infantry loomed.

> *A goatherd standing on a rocky lookout*
> *Sees a cloud moving in over the purple sea.*
> *As a westerly gale sweeps it closer to land*
> *It looks blacker than pitch. The sea ruffles*
> *Beneath it, the air suddenly turns cold.*
> *And the goatherd drives his flock to a cave.*

So the dark battalions behind the two Ajaxes,
Squall lines of young men nurtured under the sky
Bristling with shields and spears.

                              Agamemnon
Was glad to see them . . .          (4.292–304)

But, like Achilles, who briefly achieves a detached, Olympian
perspective on warfare but never loses the allegiances that draw
him back into battle, the poet of the *Iliad* seems committed to
combat by the project he shares with his characters of turning
violence into a work of art, a project in which the similes play an
important part, as this description of Menelaus wounded by Pan-
darus makes explicit.

The arrow's tip just grazed the human skin,
And dark blood started to flow from the wound.

> *In Maeonia and Caria women stain ivory*
> *With scarlet, to be cheek pieces for horses.*
> *Such a piece will lie in a treasure chamber,*
> *And though many horsemen pray to use it*
> *As an ornament for the horse and glory*
> *For the driver, it lies there as a king's prize.*

That, Menelaus, was how your thighs were stained
With blood, and your fine shins and ankles beneath.
                              (4.152–61)

The poet of the *Iliad* says little directly about himself and his own attitudes, but he does seem at moments to identify himself with the viewpoint of the warrior heroes who dominate the world of the poem. Since poetry itself is one of the prime vehicles for conferring fame and transmitting heroic achievements to future generations, the poet may be committed by his very medium to the heroic assumption that fame is worth killing and dying for. At the beginning of the list of Greek troops in Book 2, he states that there were too many men there for him to name them all and so he will name only the leaders, seeming to associate himself with the aristocratic bias of heroic culture. Just before that, he describes with seeming approval an episode in which a low-ranked soldier, Thersites, tries to challenge his leaders and is quickly silenced. Strikingly, Thersites asks many of the same questions Achilles does about why the Greeks should be risking their lives for the sake of Agamemnon and his brother Menelaus, but Thersites' speech is met with violent rejection. Odysseus essentially beats him into submission, and the other Greeks are united in uproarious approval of this punishment.

And, yet, the poet is by no means limited to the perspective of the powerful. This episode involving Thersites does bring Thersites' voice and point of view into the poem, and it does make visible the brutality with which the hierarchy of the Greek camp is enforced. Elsewhere as well, the poem incorporates other voices than those of the warrior-heroes who occupy center stage, notably those of women like Andromache, who, as we have seen, questions the point of courting death in battle. While it tells the story of how neither Achilles nor Hector can stay out of battle, the *Iliad* does close with the laments of the women whom Hector leaves behind, which stress the costs rather than the glory of warfare.

In his portrayal of combat, the poet seems to share his characters' acceptance of warfare as unavoidable and thus to be embraced as the arena of glorious action, but also their aching awareness of war as the source of suffering beyond what is necessary. While the narrative is structured around the story of Achilles, on which this discussion has also focused, large sections of it are dedicated to extended scenes of fighting, from which Achilles is mostly absent, as the poet details the exploits of the many other heroes who fight at Troy and whose experience Achilles illuminates. These passages evoke the heady excitement of battle, its bracing atmosphere of power and risk, as well as its terror and pain. Hundreds of accounts of individual successes express a limitless appreciation of the skill that turns killing into an art form. For example,

> Meges took out Pedaeus, Antenor's son.
> Though he was a bastard, Theano raised him
> As one of her own, to please her husband.
> Now Meges got close enough to him
> To send his spear through the tendon
> At the back of his neck and on into his mouth,
> Cutting away the tongue at its root. He fell
> Into the dust, his teeth clenched on cold bronze.
>
> (5.78–85)

Here the poet draws us into Meges' triumph, evoking the exhilarating danger of coming close to the enemy, and relishing the power and precision with which Meges zeroes in on Pedaeus' neck and pierces it. But, at the same time, he reveals Pedaeus' death as a sickening reduction of a person to a single vulnerable body part. And he takes the time to interject a fragment of biography for even this insignificant hero, creating some record of the life that is being lost, making some mention of the people whose lives will be darkened as a consequence, opening up a wider perspective on this quick death than that of either the gloating victor or the gasping victim. Attending in this way to the fates of warrior after warrior, the *Iliad* becomes a monumental work of commemoration, which is neither a lament, although the poem draws on and incorporates traditions of poetic lamentation, nor an expression of unqualified glorification, although it is the principal means by which these heroes' glory is preserved.

The ways in which the poem remains caught up in war, even as it offers a broader, more tempered view of it than simple celebration, is reflected in the *Iliad's* several internal depictions of works of art. One is a weaving that, like the *Iliad* itself, depicts the battles around Troy. Its maker is Helen, who, far from being a detached observer, is herself the cause of those battles, so that she is "designing into the blood-red fabric / The trials that the Trojans and Greeks had suffered / For her beauty under Ares' murderous hands" (3.128–30).

The most extensively described work of art in the poem is itself a weapon, the shield that Achilles carries into battle on his return. Achilles' shield is decorated with a series of images that seem to comprise the whole of human experience, presenting in a systematic arrangement the various activities that are evoked in a scattered way throughout the poem: farming, hunting, settling disputes, celebrating weddings, dancing, and singing, as well as fighting. Strikingly, only a relatively small portion of this is devoted to warfare, which occurs in one scene surrounded by images of mostly peaceful pastimes. Here the *Iliad* seems to offer a kind of alternative to itself, a work with the scope of epic in which war is only one aspect of human experience, but also to underscore its own deliberately restricted focus. When the characters in this poem see that shield, they think of war. For Achilles' comrades, it is a source of awesome terror. For Achilles it is a source of aesthetic pleasure; he feels "pangs of joy at all its intricate beauty" (19.29); but it also intensifies his rage for battle: "But Achilles, / When he saw it, felt his rage seep / Deeper into his bones . . ." (19.22–24).

These depictions link art like the poet's own to the realm of warfare, narrowing the separation between the activity of combat and the work that represents it. For the poet of the *Iliad*, poetry and war are bound up with one another, and, in one of his most direct comments on his momentous and terrible subject, he presents warfare as already itself a beautiful spectacle: "It was glorious to see—if your heart were iron, / And you could keep from grieving at all the pain" (13.355–56).

## The Historical Context

In considering the self-presentation of the *Iliad*'s poet and his stance toward the story he tells, it would obviously be helpful to know something about the person who composed the poem and the circumstances under which it was produced. In fact, we know much less than we would like to about how and when the *Iliad* came into being. Ancient tradition attributed the poem to Homer, who was also considered responsible for another epic about the

Trojan legend, the *Odyssey*, which tells about the return of the Greeks from Troy, and several shorter poems about the gods; but we have no reliable information about Homer that can contribute to an understanding of these works.

Where questions of chronology are concerned, it is not really possible to pin the poem to a single historical period. There is a strong—but far from complete—scholarly consensus that the *Iliad* was first written down in something like the form in which we now have it in the last half of the eighth century B.C.E., the time at which the Greeks acquired the art of alphabetic writing and written literature thus became possible. At the same time, we know the *Iliad* to be the result of a long tradition of earlier poetry, stretching back over many centuries, to which we have no direct access, because it was never written down, and which we can approach only through the traces it has left on the *Iliad* and other early Greek literature. The immense scholarly effort devoted to Homeric poetry over the last several centuries has made it clear that the *Iliad* reflects several historical periods, in a complicated amalgam whose layers we can only approximately distinguish.

First, it is important to recognize that the *Iliad* is itself a work of history, that it presents its story as a recollection of long-past events taking place in a time very different from that in which those events are being recalled. The characters in the story are seen as belonging to a superior, even semidivine breed that no longer exists, and they perform actions that no living person could duplicate. This sense of a gap between the world of the poem and the poet and his audience surfaces in occasional comments, as when the poet describes how Diomedes in the middle of combat "levered up in one hand a slab of stone / Much too large for two men to lift— / As men are now . . ." (5.328–30). It also informs the poem's frequent use of similes, which assimilate the distant world of heroic combat to a more ordinary, everyday world familiar to the poem's audience.

The Trojan legend is a story of large-scale destruction. It includes not only the annihilation of Troy, but the many disruptions, almost as devastating as what they have inflicted on the Trojans, experienced by the Greeks as they return: they are blown off course and lost at sea, or they make it back, only to find their homes in turmoil and their own positions there under attack. For the ancient Greeks, this legend recorded the passing of an age of heroes that was understood to precede the drearier world of the present. To a modern historian, it reflects the end of the first stage of ancient Greek history, which is known as the Bronze Age, after the widespread use of bronze during that time, or the Mycenaean period, after the city of Mycenae, one of the main power centers of that era.

Mycenaean civilization developed in the centuries after 2000 B.C.E., which is approximately when Greek-speaking people first arrived in the area at the southern end of the Balkan peninsula that we now know as Greece. Those Greek-speakers gradually established there a rich civilization dominated by a few powerful cities built around large, highly organized palaces. These palaces were at once fortified military strongholds and centers for international trade, in particular trade with the many islands located in the Aegean Sea, to the east of the Greek mainland. On the largest of those islands, the island of Crete, there was already flourishing, by the time the Mycenaeans arrived in Greece, the rich and sophisticated Minoan civilization, by which the Mycenaeans were heavily influenced and which they came ultimately to dominate.

From the Minoans the Mycenaeans gained, along with many other crafts and institutions, a system of writing: a syllabary, in which each symbol stands for a particular syllable, as opposed to an alphabet—like the Roman alphabet now used to write English—in which each symbol stands for a particular sound. The Mycenaeans adapted the syllabary which the Minoans used to write their own language (a language which, although we have examples of their writing, still has not been deciphered) and used it to write Greek. This earliest Greek writing system is known to present-day scholars as Linear B, and archaeologists excavating at the mainland centers of Mycenae and Pylos have recovered examples of it incised on clay tablets. These tablets contain not— as was hoped when they were found—political treaties, mythological poems, or accounts of religious rituals—but detailed accounts of a highly bureaucratic palace economy: inventories of grain or livestock and lists of palace functionaries assigned to perform such specialized roles as "unguent boiler," "chairmaker," or "bath-pourer."

Mycenaean civilization reached its height at about 1600 B.C.E. and was essentially destroyed in a series of natural disasters and political disruptions about four hundred years later, around 1200 B.C.E. We do not really know what happened, but all of the main archaeological sites show some evidence of destruction, burning, or hasty abandonment at about that time, and a sharp decline thereafter in the ambition and complexity of their material culture. Among these is the site of Troy itself, which was discovered in the late nineteenth century by Heinrich Schliemann, who followed the topographical details given in the *Iliad;* through this discovery, Schliemann both vindicated the historical validity of Homer and helped to found the field of archaeology.

Related in some way to the disruptions that ended the Bronze Age was the emergence of a new group of Greek speakers as the dominant people on the mainland. The Classical Greeks referred to these people as the Dorians and believed that they had invaded Greece from the north. Modern historians are uncertain whether they were new migrants or people already present in Greece who newly came to power in the upheavals of this period. In any case, many people left the mainland as a consequence and moved east, settling on various islands of the Aegean and along the coast of Asia Minor, in the area that is now western Turkey but which then became, in its coastal region, as much a part of the Greek world as was the mainland itself.

Both the Greeks who remained on the mainland and those who migrated to Asia Minor lived in conditions that involved less material prosperity and less highly organized concentrations of political and military power than had been characteristic of the Mycenaean period, and their period is traditionally known as the Dark Age, both because their physical remains suggest a less magnificent level of civilization and because we know relatively little about it. One result of the transition to the Dark Age was that writing, which was probably practiced in the Mycenaean period only by a small class of professional scribes, fell out of use, and the Greeks became once again a culture without writing. On the other hand, they had always relied, and they continued to rely, on oral communication as their central means of recalling, preserving, and transmitting the historical memories, religious beliefs, and shared stories that in our culture would be committed to writing—or now to various forms of electronic media. In particular, the Greeks of Asia Minor, known as the Ionians, developed a tradition of heroic poetry through which they recalled their own history, looking back and recounting the experiences of that earlier, lost era. This poetry centered on certain legendary figures and events, among them the events surrounding the Trojan war, which, as mentioned above, appear to reflect the final moments of Mycenaean civilization.

The so-called Dark Age came to an end during a period roughly corresponding to the eighth century—the 700s—B.C.E. The cultural shift that we label the end of the Dark Age and the beginning of the Archaic Period involved, not a series of upheavals, as with the end of the Bronze Age, but the emergence of new activity in a variety of fields. A growth in population led to a wave of colonization, with established Greek centers sending out colonies to such places as the Black Sea, Sicily, southern Italy, and southern France. There was also greater contact among the various Greek communities, which were politically distinct and remained so for centuries. This led to the development of institutions designed to unite those communities culturally and to reinforce a shared Greek, or Panhellenic, heritage, such as the oracle of Apollo at Delphi and the Olympic Games (founded in 776 B.C.E.). Around this time, the Greeks began to build large-scale temples and to make large-scale statues and a new kind of pottery decorated with elaborate geometric patterns. Many of the features of Greek culture that we associate with the Classical Period—the period that loosely corresponds to the fifth and fourth centuries B.C.E.—had their origins in the eighth century.

In addition to colonization, this was also a time of renewed trade and thus of encounters with other Mediterranean cultures. One consequence of this trade was that the Greeks came into contact with the Phoenicians, a Semitic people whose culture was centered in present-day Lebanon, and learned from them a system of writing—not a syllabary like Linear B, but an alphabet, the alphabet which, with some modification, is still used to write Greek and which eventually was adapted to become the Roman alphabet, now widely used for many languages, including English.

This new way of writing Greek quickly became much more widespread than Linear B had been, and it was put to a greater variety of uses, among them the writing down of poetry. Thus the *Iliad* and other early Greek poems (including the other Homeric epic, the *Odyssey;* two poems by Hesiod, the *Theogony* and the

*Works and Days;* and a group of hymns that were also attributed to Homer in antiquity) came into being in the written form in which we know them. But, as mentioned already, while these poems were written down in the eighth century, they claimed to describe events that had taken place approximately five hundred years before. For the Greeks of the eighth century and afterward, these were works of history, authoritative records of their own past. A modern historian might be more inclined to label them historical fiction, thinking that whatever conflict lies behind the story of the Trojan War is more likely to have been fought over trade routes to the Black Sea than—as Homer tells it—over the Trojans' theft from the Greeks of the world's most beautiful woman, Helen of Troy. In any case, like most works of historical fiction—or indeed of history—the *Iliad* and the *Odyssey* reflect the time (or, in this case, the times) of their telling at least as much as the time in which they are set.

Historians and archaeologists who have tried to match the culture described in the Homeric epics to what we know of Greek history from other sources have found that that culture unselfconsciously combines elements of the Bronze Age with elements of the Dark Age: memories of the earlier time in which the Trojan legend is set have been woven together with circumstances borrowed from the period during which the legend evolved. This can be seen in the depictions of combat that are a major feature of the *Iliad*. While it is repeatedly mentioned that the weapons being used are made of bronze—which fell out of use for weapons after the Bronze Age, being replaced by iron—some of the specific implements and fighting practices belong to a later time. Some of the fighting practices described there seem not to be fully understood by the poet—for example, the use of chariots, which are mentioned mainly as transportation to and from the battle, when they must in fact have been used in the actual fighting.

The peacetime world, described more fully in the *Odyssey* than in the *Iliad*, centers on kingdoms that are much smaller and much less highly organized than those of the Mycenaean Period, and many details of their material culture and social organization accord more closely to what we know of Dark Age life. There are also ways in which the world of Homer reflects the emerging concerns and conditions of the eighth century: for example, some scholars draw a connection between the fact that the Homeric

poems omit certain religious practices that were tied to particular
localities and the unifying, Panhellenic impulses reflected in the
Delphic Oracle and the Olympic Games. There is surely a connec-
tion to be made between the *Iliad*'s focus on the hard-won success
of the Greeks in overcoming internal dissension to achieve the
common goal of taking Troy and that period's concern with the
development of a shared cultural identity. It is also clear that
some of the practices of Homeric culture are entirely artificial,
conditioned by the aims of the poem itself; for example, the habit
that the *Iliad's* heroes have of pausing in the middle of battle to
talk, reflecting, as Sarpedon does, on the meaning of what they
are doing—a fatal lapse in real combat, but an effective strategy
for a poem.

## The Poetic Tradition

Just as the society described in the Homeric epics reflects the
centuries-long period during which the Trojan legend evolved, so
the poems themselves—in their language, their style, and their
modes of narration—also reflect that period and that process of
evolution. The *Iliad* is manifestly the product of a long tradition
within Greek culture and follows on many previous tellings of
the same legendary material. Beyond that, the poem has roots in
the traditions of the ancient Near East, which we can recognize
but not trace precisely. This can be seen in the parallels between
episodes in the *Iliad* and many Near Eastern myths, such as the
story told in the Sumerian *Epic of Gilgamesh,* which also concerns
a hero who is the son of a goddess and who causes the death of
his dearest companion, for whom he passionately grieves.

The *Iliad*'s debt to tradition is revealed in the way in which it
tells its story, plunging into the quarrel of Achilles and Agamem-
non with confidence that its audience will already be familiar
with these characters and the legends to which they belong. Simi-
larly, the characters in the poem—especially older characters like
Nestor and Phoenix—habitually refer to other similar legends,
apparently drawing on a related fund of inherited stories. The
traditional character of Homeric poetry is also deeply embedded
in the language and style of the original Greek text, as the schol-
arship of the last century has made increasingly clear. In particu-
lar, it has been demonstrated that the diction and phraseology of

Homeric Greek are not those of written literature, but rather of the kind of orally composed and recited poetry that preceded our written *Iliad* and that still exists in some cultures today. Generally speaking, rather than reciting a fixed, memorized text, an oral poet composes a new telling of the story while speaking, always fitting the words into the patterns of a metrical scheme. To do this requires a different and larger set of verbal resources than those of writing or ordinary speech. A major achievement of Homeric scholarship—and especially of an American scholar of the 1920s and 1930s, Milman Parry, who did comparative work with the practicing oral poets of the Balkan region—has been to identify the peculiarities of Homeric Greek, which include an expanded vocabulary and a huge repertory of repeated phrases and lines, with the resources of the oral poet.

The identification of Homeric style as that of oral poetry has solved some of the problems that students of Homer wrestled with for centuries, as they tried to make sense of the ways in which the Homeric epics are unlike later written poems, in particular their continual use of repetition and their occasional rough edges and narrative inconsistencies. But it does not, of course, explain the *Iliad* we have, which is not an oral recitation, but a written text, although it should be stressed that, even after the *Iliad* was written down, it continued to be recited for centuries, at least into the Classical Period, and oral performance continued to be the medium through which this poem reached its primary audience, despite the existence of a written text.

Certain characteristics of the *Iliad* cannot easily be referred to the poem's oral origins, particularly its monumental scale. A performance of the *Iliad* would take at the absolute minimum about twenty hours, whereas the bards studied by modern scholars, like the several bards who are portrayed in the *Odyssey* as entertaining groups of people at banquets, all sing songs lasting about an hour. It is difficult, even impossible, to imagine an occasion when the *Iliad* could have been sung through for an audience from beginning to end. Clearly, it is significant that the final stages of the poem's composition coincide with the reintroduction of writing in the eighth century, but the exact role of writing in shaping the poem that we have remains mysterious, especially since marks of oral composition such as those found in Homer tend to disappear quite quickly once poets begin to use writing as an aid to composition.

Homeric scholars also have to deal with a further mystery, which is the relationship between the versions of these poems that we hypothesize were written down in the eighth century and the first written versions we have any evidence for: versions that were produced in the mainland city of Athens in the sixth century B.C.E. Just as we cannot disentangle the layers of previous history that merged in the written poems of the eighth century, we cannot altogether distinguish the further transformations that those poems underwent before they became the medieval manuscripts on which the texts we currently use—and ultimately this translation—are based. We do know, for example, that the division of the poems into books belongs to the third century B.C.E., when the poems were edited by scholars attached to the library of Alexandria in Egypt. But we are not sure what features may have been introduced, for example, when the poems were recorded in sixth-century Athens. The *Iliad* contained in this book is the product of four millennia—from the remembered experiences of the Mycenaean period to the English words and phrases chosen by a late-twentieth-century translator.

Perhaps the greatest challenge posed by our awareness of the oral background of Homeric poetry is the issue of how to integrate the role of tradition into an appreciation of a poem that we view as an accomplished masterpiece. This is the problem that most excites present-day critics of Homer, who may find there an echo of the questions about the relative values of individual insight and inherited wisdom, or of personal achievement and collective action, that are central to the *Iliad* itself. Readers of the *Iliad* have to decide to what extent they are able to see it as the group effort of many generations, as opposed to the original creation of an individual.

It is notable in this context that the poet-narrator of the *Iliad* does not present himself as original, but rather as the mouthpiece, not of human tradition, but of divinities, the Muses. In doing so, he claims a far greater value for his work than he could if he presented it as his own invention, for the Muses' inspiration allows him to give a truthful account of past events that he has not witnessed, to produce a work of authoritative history. Nonetheless, most modern readers have found it difficult to view the *Iliad* and the *Odyssey* as anything other than the creations of an individual (or a pair of individuals). To many it is impossible to imagine that the qualities that make these poems so great—their fundamental coherence of design and theme, their profound and particular vision—could be anything other than the achievement of an unusually creative individual.

In attributing the *Iliad* to an individual, modern readers are also, of course, aligning themselves with ancient tradition. But the information we are given about Homer is quite unhelpful, consisting essentially of legends about a blind bard from an Ionian city (several claimed him) who wandered from place to place, having adventures suspiciously similar to those of his hero Odysseus. Modern critics tend to discount these legends and to find their version of Homer in the person responsible for whatever strikes them as the most impressive features of the epics: their monumental scale, their coherence of design, their written form, their reinterpretation of traditional material.

Much recent critical and scholarly work on the *Iliad* and the *Odyssey* has been devoted to this last feature, the reinterpretation of traditional material, showing how these poems employ traditional elements, but in purposeful, particular, and even untraditional ways. The fundamental decision to tell the Trojan legend through the brief episode of Achilles' rage is clearly one example of this: it not only allows the poet to bring concentration and intensity to what might otherwise be a sprawling narrative, but it helps him to ask fundamental questions about how the stories of individuals like Achilles fit into the larger projects of their communities.

Many studies have been devoted to showing how typical episodes that clearly reflect long-standing conventions of epic narrative are reworked in the *Iliad*, with striking and novel effects. For example, the typical scene of a hero arming for war is used with pointed significance to tell the story of Achilles. When Patroclus prepares for battle by putting on Achilles' armor, this is described in completely conventional terms, until the point at which the hero regularly picks up his spear, when we are given the ominous information that Patroclus did *not* pick up Achilles' spear, because he was, in fact, unable to lift it. When Achilles finally arms himself to avenge Patroclus' death, the momentousness of this entry into battle is expressed in the way in which the description of the decoration on a hero's shield—usually only a matter of several lines—is elaborated into a panorama of human activity that encompasses and subsumes the world in which the *Iliad*'s plot takes place.

Making use of what spotty evidence they have, scholars have attempted to reconstruct earlier versions of the stories or types of stories told in the *Iliad*, in order to show how they have been adapted to the *Iliad*'s distinctive purposes. Other versions of the Meleager story told by Phoenix in Book 9 allow us to see that there it has been reworked to provide a pointed parallel to the story of Achilles. Some critics have speculated that there may have been many traditional accounts of powerful heroes who felt dishonored and withdrew from their armies until their honor was restored, but that the surprising development of Achilles' continued withdrawal even after Agamemnon's embassy may have been unique to the *Iliad*. Our evidence suggests that other poems in the tradition out of which the *Iliad* and the *Odyssey* emerged contained many more supernatural and miraculous elements, including the achievement of immortality by the most successful heroes. By contrast, the Homeric epics seem distinctive in their unremitting insistence on the constraints of mortal existence and the inescapability of death.

In making this translation, Stanley Lombardo has located Homer in the performer or performers through whom the *Iliad* existed primarily as a spoken work, even after it was written down. Lombardo's version highlights the living connection that the poet builds between himself and his audience and his evocation of the spontaneous and idiosyncratic accents of the individual speakers whom he impersonates. In doing so, Lombardo brings out yet another way in which the concerns of the poet intersect with those of his characters, for in his recreation of heroic warfare, Homer has made it a realm not only of forceful action, but also of powerful speaking. The characters of the *Iliad* use speech constantly, to further their competitions through insults, to confer honor on one another through praise, to reflect on what they are doing, to bring the traditions of the past to bear on their present dilemmas, to lament their dead. In this way they fulfill the vision of heroism that Phoenix instilled in Achilles on the instructions of his father, Peleus: "To be a speaker of words and a doer of deeds" (9.455).

Sheila Murnaghan
University of Pennsylvania

# ILIAD 1

R<small>AGE:</small>
   Sing, Goddess, Achilles' rage,
Black and murderous, that cost the Greeks
Incalculable pain, pitched countless souls
Of heroes into Hades' dark,
And left their bodies to rot as feasts
For dogs and birds, as Zeus' will was done.
   Begin with the clash between Agamemnon—
The Greek warlord—and godlike Achilles.

*(who is speaking here?)*

W<small>hich</small> of the immortals set these two
At each other's throats?
                              A<small>pollo,</small>                              10
Zeus' son and Leto's, offended
By the warlord. Agamemnon had dishonored
Chryses, Apollo's priest, so the god
Struck the Greek camp with plague,
And the soldiers were dying of it.
                              Chryses
Had come to the Greek beachhead camp
Hauling a fortune for his daughter's ransom.
Displaying Apollo's sacral ribbons                              20
On a golden staff, he made a formal plea
To the entire Greek army, but especially
The commanders, Atreus' two sons:

"Sons of Atreus and Greek heroes all:
May the gods on Olympus grant you plunder
Of Priam's city and a safe return home.
But give me my daughter back and accept
This ransom out of respect for Zeus' son,
Lord Apollo, who deals death from afar."

A murmur rippled through the ranks:                          30
"Respect the priest and take the ransom."
But Agamemnon was not pleased
And dismissed Chryses with a rough speech:

"Don't let me ever catch you, old man, by these ships again,
Skulking around now or sneaking back later.
The god's staff and ribbons won't save you next time.
The girl is mine, and she'll be an old woman in Argos
Before I let her go, working the loom in my house
And coming to my bed, far from her homeland.
Now clear out of here before you make me angry!"           40

The old man was afraid and did as he was told.
He walked in silence along the whispering surf line,
And when he had gone some distance the priest
Prayed to Lord Apollo, son of silken-haired Leto:

"Hear me, Silverbow, Protector of Chryse,
Lord of Holy Cilla, Master of Tenedos,
And Sminthian God of Plague!
If ever I've built a temple that pleased you
Or burnt fat thighbones of bulls and goats—
    Grant me this prayer:                                   50
Let the Danaans pay for my tears with your arrows!"

Apollo heard his prayer and descended Olympus' crags
Pulsing with fury, bow slung over one shoulder,
The arrows rattling in their case on his back
As the angry god moved like night down the mountain.
He settled near the ships and let loose an arrow.
Reverberation from his silver bow hung in the air.

*[handwritten margin notes: Greek Gods easily angered and displeased when one of their own is dishonored.]*

He picked off the pack animals first, and the lean hounds,
But then aimed his needle-tipped arrows at the men
And shot until the death-fires crowded the beach.  60

Nine days the god's arrows rained death on the camp.
On the tenth day Achilles called an assembly.
Hera, the white-armed goddess, planted the thought in him
Because she cared for the Greeks and it pained her
To see them dying. When the troops had all mustered,
Up stood the great runner Achilles, and said:

*Gods control what happens, where is free will?*

"Well, Agamemnon, it looks as if we'd better give up
And sail home—assuming any of us are left alive—
If we have to fight both the war and this plague.
But why not consult some prophet or priest  70
Or a dream interpreter, since dreams too come from Zeus,
Who could tell us why Apollo is so angry,
If it's for a vow or a sacrifice he holds us at fault.
Maybe he'd be willing to lift this plague from us
If he savored the smoke from lambs and prime goats."

Achilles had his say and sat down. Then up rose
Calchas, son of Thestor, bird-reader supreme,
Who knew what is, what will be, and what has been.
He had guided the Greek ships to Troy
Through the prophetic power Apollo  80
Had given him, and he spoke out now:

"Achilles, beloved of Zeus, you want me to tell you
About the rage of Lord Apollo, the Arch-Destroyer.
And I will tell you. But you have to promise me and swear
You will support me and protect me in word and deed.
I have a feeling I might offend a person of some authority
Among the Greeks, and you know how it is when a king
Is angry with an underling. He might swallow his temper
For a day, but he holds it in his heart until later
And it all comes out. Will you guarantee my security?"  90

Achilles, the great runner, responded:

"Don't worry. Prophesy to the best of your knowledge.
I swear by Apollo, to whom you pray when you reveal
The gods' secrets to the Greeks, Calchas, that while I live
And look upon this earth, no one will lay a hand
On you here beside these hollow ships, no, not even
Agamemnon, who boasts he is the best of the Achaeans."

And Calchas, the perfect prophet, taking courage:

"The god finds no fault with vow or sacrifice.
It is for his priest, whom Agamemnon dishonored          100
And would not allow to ransom his daughter,
That Apollo deals and will deal death from afar.
He will not lift this foul plague from the Greeks
Until we return the dancing-eyed girl to her father
Unransomed, unbought, and make formal sacrifice
On Chryse. Only then might we appease the god."

He finished speaking and sat down. Then up rose
Atreus' son, the warlord Agamemnon,
Furious, anger like twin black thunderheads seething
In his lungs, and his eyes flickered with fire            110
As he looked Calchas up and down, and said:

                          "You damn soothsayer!
You've never given me a good omen yet.
You take some kind of perverse pleasure in prophesying
Doom, don't you? Not a single favorable omen ever!
Nothing good ever happens! And now you stand here
Uttering oracles before the Greeks, telling us
That your great ballistic god is giving us all this trouble
Because I was unwilling to accept the ransom
For Chryses' daughter but preferred instead to keep her    120
In my tent! And why shouldn't I? I like her better than
My wife Clytemnestra. She's no worse than her
When it comes to looks, body, mind, or ability.
Still, I'll give her back, if that's what's best.
I don't want to see the army destroyed like this.
But I want another prize ready for me right away.

I'm not going to be the only Greek without a prize,
It wouldn't be right. And you all see where mine is going."

And Achilles, strong, swift, and godlike:

"And where do you think, son of Atreus,　　　　　　*130*
You greedy glory-hound, the magnanimous Greeks
Are going to get another prize for you?
Do you think we have some kind of stockpile in reserve?
Every town in the area has been sacked and the stuff all divided.
You want the men to count it all back and redistribute it?
All right, you give the girl back to the god. The army
Will repay you three and four times over—when and if
Zeus allows us to rip Troy down to its foundations."

The warlord Agamemnon responded:

"You may be a good man in a fight, Achilles,　　　　*140*
And look like a god, but don't try to put one over on me—
It won't work. So while you have your prize,
You want me to sit tight and do without?
Give the girl back, just like that? Now maybe
If the army, in a generous spirit, voted me
Some suitable prize of their own choice, something fair—
But if it doesn't, I'll just go take something myself,
Your prize perhaps, or Ajax's, or Odysseus',
And whoever she belongs to, it'll stick in his throat.

But we can think about that later.　　　　　　　　*150*
　　　　　　　　　　　　Right now we launch
A black ship on the bright salt water, get a crew aboard,
Load on a hundred bulls, and have Chryseis board her too,
My girl with her lovely cheeks. And we'll want a good man
For captain, Ajax or Idomeneus or godlike Odysseus—
Or maybe you, son of Peleus, our most formidable hero—
To offer sacrifice and appease the Arch-Destroyer for us."

Achilles looked him up and down and said:

"You shameless, profiteering excuse for a commander!

How are you going to get any Greek warrior                      160
To follow you into battle again? You know,
*I* don't have any quarrel with the Trojans,
They didn't do anything to *me* to make me
Come over here and fight, didn't run off *my* cattle or horses
Or ruin *my* farmland back home in Phthia, not with all
The shadowy mountains and moaning seas between.
It's for *you*, dogface, for your precious pleasure—
And Menelaus' honor—that we came here,
A fact you don't have the decency even to mention!
And now you're threatening to take away the prize         170
That I sweated for and the Greeks gave me.
I never get a prize equal to yours when the army
Captures one of the Trojan strongholds.
No, I do all the dirty work with my own hands,
And when the battle's over and we divide the loot
You get the lion's share and I go back to the ships
With some pitiful little thing, so worn out from fighting
I don't have the strength left even to complain.
Well, I'm going back to Phthia now. Far better
To head home with my curved ships than stay here,          180
Unhonored myself and piling up a fortune for you."

The warlord Agamemnon responded:

"Go ahead and desert, if that's what you want!
I'm not going to beg you to stay. There are plenty of others
Who will honor me, not least of all Zeus the Counselor.
To me, you're the most hateful king under heaven,
A born troublemaker. You actually *like* fighting and war.
If you're all that strong, it's just a gift from some god.
So why don't you go home with your ships and lord it over
Your precious Myrmidons. I couldn't care less about you    190
Or your famous temper. But I'll tell you this:
Since Phoebus Apollo is taking away my Chryseis,
Whom I'm sending back aboard ship with my friends,
I'm coming to your hut and taking Briseis,
Your own beautiful prize, so that you will see just how much
Stronger I am than you, and the next person will wince
At the thought of opposing me as an equal."

Achilles' chest was a rough knot of pain
Twisting around his heart: should he
Draw the sharp sword that hung by his thigh,                    200
Scatter the ranks and gut Agamemnon,
Or control his temper, repress his rage?
He was mulling it over, inching the great sword
From its sheath, when out of the blue
Athena came, sent by the white-armed goddess
Hera, who loved and watched over both men.
She stood behind Achilles and grabbed his sandy hair,
Visible only to him: not another soul saw her.
Awestruck, Achilles turned around, recognizing
Pallas Athena at once—it was her eyes—                    210
And words flew from his mouth like winging birds:

"Daughter of Zeus! Why have you come here?
To see Agamemnon's arrogance, no doubt.
I'll tell you where I place my bets, Goddess:
Sudden death for this outrageous behavior."

Athena's eyes glared through the sea's salt haze.

"I came to see if I could check this temper of yours,
Sent from heaven by the white-armed goddess
Hera, who loves and watches over both of you men.
Now come on, drop this quarrel, don't draw your sword.                    220
Tell him off instead. And I'll tell you,
Achilles, how things will be: You're going to get
Three times as many magnificent gifts
Because of his arrogance. Just listen to us and be patient."

Achilles, the great runner, responded:

"When you two speak, Goddess, a man has to listen
No matter how angry. It's better that way.
Obey the gods and they hear you when you pray."

With that he ground his heavy hand
Onto the silver hilt and pushed the great sword                    230
Back into its sheath. Athena's speech

*[handwritten marginal note:]* Either the humans are incapable of settling things themselves OR... the Gods like to remain in control. And their subjects in order to do so.

Had been well-timed. She was on her way
To Olympus by now, to the halls of Zeus
And the other immortals, while Achilles
Tore into Agamemnon again:

"You bloated drunk,
With a dog's eyes and a rabbit's heart!
You've never had the guts to buckle on armor in battle
Or come out with the best fighting Greeks
On any campaign! Afraid to look Death in the eye,                240
Agamemnon? It's far more profitable
To hang back in the army's rear—isn't it?—
Confiscating prizes from any Greek who talks back
And bleeding your people dry. There's not a real man
Under your command, or this latest atrocity
Would be your last, son of Atreus.
Now get this straight. I swear a formal oath:
   By this scepter, which will never sprout leaf
Or branch again since it was cut from its stock
In the mountains, which will bloom no more                       250
Now that bronze has pared off leaf and bark,
And which now the sons of the Greeks hold in their hands
At council, upholding Zeus' laws—
By this scepter I swear:
When every last Greek desperately misses Achilles,
Your remorse won't do any good then,
When Hector the man-killer swats you down like flies.
And you will eat your heart out
Because you failed to honor the best Greek of all."

Those were his words, and he slammed the scepter,             260
Studded with gold, to the ground and sat down.

Opposite him, Agamemnon fumed.
Then Nestor
Stood up, sweet-worded Nestor, the orator from Pylos
With a voice high-toned and liquid as honey.
He had seen two generations of men pass away
In sandy Pylos and was now king in the third.
He was full of good will in the speech he made:

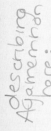

describing Agamemnon here ::

"It's a sad day for Greece, a sad day.
Priam and Priam's sons would be happy indeed,                    270
And the rest of the Trojans too, glad in their hearts,
If they learned all this about you two fighting,
Our two best men in council and in battle.
Now you listen to me, both of you. You are both
Younger than I am, and I've associated with men
Better than you, and they didn't treat me lightly.
I've never seen men like those, and never will,
The likes of Peirithous and Dryas, a shepherd to his people,
Caineus and Exadius and godlike Polyphemus,
And Aegeus' son, Theseus, who could have passed for a god,    280
The strongest men who ever lived on earth, the strongest,
And they fought with the strongest, with wild things
From the mountains, and beat the daylights out of them.
I was their companion, although I came from Pylos,
From the ends of the earth—they sent for me themselves.
And I held my own fighting with them. You couldn't find
A mortal on earth who could fight with them now.
And when I talked in council, they took my advice.
So should you two now: taking advice is a good thing. *duh.*
     Agamemnon, for all your nobility, don't take his girl.    290
Leave her be: the army originally gave her to him as a prize.
Nor should you, son of Peleus, want to lock horns with a king.
A scepter-holding king has honor beyond the rest of men,
Power and glory given by Zeus himself.
You are stronger, and it is a goddess who bore you.
But he is more powerful, since he rules over more.
Son of Atreus, cease your anger. And I appeal
Personally to Achilles to control his temper, since he is,
For all Greeks, a mighty bulwark in this evil war."

And Agamemnon, the warlord:                                     300

"Yes, old man, everything you've said is absolutely right.
But this man wants to be ahead of everyone else,
He wants to rule everyone, give orders to everyone,
Lord it over everyone, and he's not going to get away with it.
If the gods eternal made him a spearman, does that mean
They gave him permission to be insolent as well?"

And Achilles, breaking in on him:

"Ha, and think of the names people would call me
If I bowed and scraped every time you opened your mouth.
Try that on somebody else, but not on me.                          310
I'll tell you this, and you can stick it in your gut:
I'm not going to put up a fight on account of the girl.
You, all of you, gave her and you can all take her back.
But anything else of mine in my black sailing ship
You keep your goddamn hands off, you hear?
Try it. Let everybody here see how fast
Your black blood boils up around my spear."

So it was a stand-off, their battle of words,
And the assembly beside the Greek ships dissolved.
Achilles went back to the huts by his ships                        320
With Patroclus and his men. Agamemnon had a fast ship
Hauled down to the sea, picked twenty oarsmen,
Loaded on a hundred bulls due to the god, and had Chryses'
    daughter,
His fair-cheeked girl, go aboard also. Odysseus captained,
And when they were all on board, the ship headed out to sea.

Onshore, Agamemnon ordered a purification.
The troops scrubbed down and poured the filth
Into the sea. Then they sacrificed to Apollo
Oxen and goats by the hundreds on the barren shore.
The smoky savor swirled up to the sky.                             330

That was the order of the day. But Agamemnon
Did not forget his spiteful threat against Achilles.
He summoned Talthybius and Eurybates,
Faithful retainers who served as his heralds:

"Go to the hut of Achilles, son of Peleus;
Bring back the girl, fair-cheeked Briseis.
If he won't give her up, I'll come myself
With my men and take her—and freeze his heart cold."

It was not the sort of mission a herald would relish.

*Achilles'*
*men*

The pair trailed along the barren seashore                          *340*
Until they came to the Myrmidons' ships and encampment.
They found Achilles sitting outside his hut
Beside his black ship. He was not glad to see them.
They stood respectfully silent, in awe of this king,
And it was Achilles who was moved to address them first:

"Welcome, heralds, the gods' messengers and men's.
Come closer. You're not to blame, Agamemnon is,
Who sent you here for the girl, Briseis.
                              Patroclus,
Bring the girl out and give her to these gentlemen.          *350*
You two are witnesses before the blessed gods,
Before mortal men and that hard-hearted king,
If ever I'm needed to protect the others
From being hacked to bits. His mind is murky with anger,
And he doesn't have the sense to look ahead and behind
To see how the Greeks might defend their ships."

Thus Achilles.
                  Patroclus obeyed his beloved friend
And brought Briseis, cheeks flushed, out of the tent
And gave her to the heralds, who led her away.              *360*
She went unwillingly.
                       Then Achilles, in tears,
Withdrew from his friends and sat down far away
On the foaming white seashore, staring out
At the endless sea. Stretching out his hands,
He prayed over and over to his beloved mother:

"Mother, since you bore me for a short life only,
Olympian Zeus was supposed to grant me honor.
Well, he hasn't given me any at all. Agamemnon
Has taken away my prize and dishonored me."                *370*

His voice, choked with tears, was heard by his mother
As she sat in the sea-depths beside her old father.
She rose up from the white-capped sea like a mist,
And settling herself beside her weeping child
She stroked him with her hand and talked to him:

"Why are you crying, son? What's wrong?
Don't keep it inside. Tell me so we'll both know."

And Achilles, with a deep groan:

"You already know. Why do I have to tell you?
We went after Thebes, Eëtion's sacred town,            380
Sacked it and brought the plunder back here.
The army divided everything up and chose
For Agamemnon fair-cheeked Chryseis.
Then her father, Chryses, a priest of Apollo,
Came to our army's ships on the beachhead,
Hauling a fortune for his daughter's ransom.
He displayed Apollo's sacral ribbons
On a golden staff and made a formal plea
To the entire Greek army, but especially
The commanders, Atreus' two sons.            390
You could hear the troops murmuring,
'Respect the priest and take the ransom.'
But Agamemnon wouldn't hear of it
And dismissed Chryses with a rough speech.
The old man went back angry, and Apollo
Heard his beloved priest's prayer.
He hit the Greeks hard, and the troops
Were falling over dead, the god's arrows
Raining down all through the Greek camp.
A prophet told us the Arch-Destroyer's will,            400
And I demanded the god be appeased.
Agamemnon got angry, stood up
And threatened me, and made good his threat.
The high command sent the girl on a fast ship
Back to Chryse with gifts for Apollo,
And heralds led away my girl, Briseis,
Whom the army had given to me.
Now you have to help me, if you can.
  Go to Olympus
And call in the debt that Zeus owes you.            410
I remember often hearing you tell
In my father's house how you alone managed,

Of all the immortals, to save Zeus' neck
When the other Olympians wanted to bind him—
Hera and Poseidon and Pallas Athena.
You came and loosened him from his chains,
And you lured to Olympus' summit the giant
With a hundred hands whom the gods call
Briareus but men call Aegaeon, stronger
Even than his own father Uranus, and he                    420
Sat hulking in front of cloud-black Zeus,
Proud of his prowess, and scared all the gods
Who were trying to put the son of Cronus in chains.
    Remind Zeus of this, sit holding his knees,
See if he is willing to help the Trojans
Hem the Greeks in between the fleet and the sea.
Once they start being killed, the Greeks may
Appreciate Agamemnon for what he is,
And the wide-ruling son of Atreus will see
What a fool he's been because he did not honor          430
The best of all the fighting Achaeans."

And Thetis, now weeping herself:

    "O my poor child. I bore you for sorrow,
Nursed you for grief. Why? You should be
Spending your time here by your ships
Happily and untroubled by tears,
Since life is short for you, all too brief.
Now you're destined for both an early death
And misery beyond compare. It was for this
I gave birth to you in your father's palace              440
Under an evil star.
                    I'll go to snow-bound Olympus
And tell all this to the Lord of Lightning.
I hope he listens. You stay here, though,
Beside your ships and let the Greeks feel
Your spite; withdraw completely from the war.
Zeus left yesterday for the River Ocean
On his way to a feast with the Ethiopians.
All the gods went with him. He'll return

To Olympus twelve days from now,                                     450
And I'll go then to his bronze threshold
And plead with him. I think I'll persuade him."

And she left him there, angry and heartsick
At being forced to give up the silken-waisted girl.

Meanwhile, Odysseus was putting in
At Chryse with his sacred cargo on board.
When they were well within the deepwater harbor
They furled the sail and stowed it in the ship's hold,
Slackened the forestays and lowered the mast,
Working quickly, then rowed her to a mooring, where           460
They dropped anchor and made the stern cables fast.
The crew disembarked on the seabeach
And unloaded the bulls for Apollo the Archer.
Then Chryses' daughter stepped off the seagoing vessel,
And Odysseus led her to an altar
And placed her in her father's hands, saying:

"Chryses, King Agamemnon has sent me here
To return your child and offer to Phoebus
Formal sacrifice on behalf of the Greeks.
So may we appease Lord Apollo, and may he                    470
Lift the afflictions he has sent upon us."

Chryses received his daughter tenderly.

Moving quickly, they lined the hundred oxen
Round the massive altar, a glorious offering,
Washed their hands and sprinkled on the victims
Sacrificial barley. On behalf of the Greeks
Chryses lifted his hands and prayed aloud:

"Hear me, Silverbow, Protector of Chryse,
Lord of Holy Cilla, Master of Tenedos,
As once before you heard my prayer,                                480
Did me honor, and smote the Greeks mightily,
So now also grant me this prayer:
                                        Lift the plague

From the Greeks and save them from death."

Thus the old priest, and Apollo heard him.

After the prayers and the strewing of barley
They slaughtered and flayed the oxen,
Jointed the thighbones and wrapped them
In a layer of fat with cuts of meat on top.
The old man roasted them over charcoal                    *490*
And doused them with wine. Younger men
Stood by with five-tined forks in their hands.
When the thigh pieces were charred and they had
Tasted the tripe, they cut the rest into strips,
Skewered it on spits and roasted it skillfully.
When they were done and the feast was ready,
Feast they did, and no one lacked an equal share.
When they had all had enough to eat and drink,
The young men topped off mixing bowls with wine
And served it in goblets to all the guests.                *500*
All day long these young Greeks propitiated
The god with dancing, singing to Apollo
A paean as they danced, and the god was pleased.
When the sun went down and darkness came on,
They went to sleep by the ship's stern-cables.

Dawn came early, a palmetto of rose,
Time to make sail for the wide beachhead camp.
They set up mast and spread the white canvas,
And the following wind, sent by Apollo,
Boomed in the mainsail. An indigo wave                     *510*
Hissed off the bow as the ship surged on,
Leaving a wake as she held on course through the billows.

When they reached the beachhead they hauled the black ship
High on the sand and jammed in the long chocks;
Then the crew scattered to their own huts and ships.

All this time Achilles, the son of Peleus in the line of Zeus,
Nursed his anger, the great runner idle by his fleet's fast hulls.
He was not to be seen in council, that arena for glory,

Nor in combat. He sat tight in camp consumed with grief,
His great heart yearning for the battle cry and war.                    *520*

   Twelve days went by. Dawn.
The gods returned to Olympus,
Zeus at their head.
                    Thetis did not forget
Her son's requests. She rose from the sea
And up through the air to the great sky
And found Cronus' wide-seeing son
Sitting in isolation on the highest peak
Of the rugged Olympic massif.
She settled beside him, and touched his knees                    *530*
With her left hand, his beard with her right,
And made her plea to the Lord of Sky:

"Father Zeus, if I have ever helped you
In word or deed among the immortals,
   Grant me this prayer:
Honor my son, doomed to die young
And yet dishonored by King Agamemnon,
Who stole his prize, a personal affront.
Do justice by him, Lord of Olympus.
Give the Trojans the upper hand until the Greeks                    *540*
Grant my son the honor he deserves."

Zeus made no reply but sat a long time
In silence, clouds scudding around him.
Thetis held fast to his knees and asked again:

"Give me a clear yes or no. Either nod in assent
Or refuse me. Why should you care if I know
How negligible a goddess I am in your eyes."

This provoked a troubled, gloomy response:

"This is disastrous. You're going to force me
Into conflict with Hera. I can just hear her now,                    *550*
Cursing me and bawling me out. As it is,
She already accuses me of favoring the Trojans.

Please go back the way you came. Maybe
Hera won't notice. I'll take care of this.
And so you can have some peace of mind,
I'll say yes to you by nodding my head,
The ultimate pledge. Unambiguous,
Irreversible, and absolutely fulfilled,
Whatever I say yes to with a nod of my head."

And the Son of Cronus nodded. Black brows          560
Lowered, a glory of hair cascaded down from the Lord's
Immortal head, and the holy mountain trembled.

Their conference over, the two parted. The goddess
Dove into the deep sea from Olympus' snow-glare
And Zeus went to his home. The gods all
Rose from their seats at their father's entrance. Not one
Dared watch him enter without standing to greet him.
And so the god entered and took his high seat.
                                    But Hera
Had noticed his private conversation with Thetis,          570
The silver-footed daughter of the Old Man of the Sea,
And flew at him with cutting words:

"Who was that you were scheming with just now?
You just love devising secret plots behind my back,
Don't you? You can't bear to tell me what you're thinking,
Or you don't dare. Never have and never will."

The Father of Gods and Men answered:

"Hera, don't hope to know all my secret thoughts.
It would strain your mind even though you are my wife.
What it is proper to hear, no one, human or divine,
Will hear before you. But what I wish to conceive          580
Apart from the other gods, don't pry into that."

And Lady Hera, with her oxen eyes wide:

"Oh my. The awesome son of Cronus has spoken.
Pry? You know that I never pry. And you always

*[handwritten margin note: are women seen as lesser even as Goddesses?]*

Cheerfully volunteer—whatever information you please.
It's just that I have this feeling that somehow
The silver-footed daughter of the Old Man of the Sea
May have won you over. She *was* sitting beside you
Up there in the mists, and she did touch your knees.          590
And I'm pretty sure that you agreed to honor Achilles
And destroy Greeks by the thousands beside their ships."

And Zeus, the master of cloud and storm:

"You witch! Your intuitions are always right.
But what does it get you? Nothing, except that
I like you less than ever. And so you're worse off.
If it's as you think it is, it's my business, not yours.
So sit down and shut up and do as I say.
You see these hands? All the gods on Olympus
Won't be able to help you if I ever lay them on you."          600

Hera lost her nerve when she heard this.
She sat down in silence, fear cramping her heart,
And gloom settled over the gods in Zeus' hall.
Hephaestus, the master artisan, broke the silence,
Out of concern for his ivory-armed mother:

"This is terrible; it's going to ruin us all.
If you two quarrel like this over mortals
It's bound to affect us gods. There'll be no more
Pleasure in our feasts if we let things turn ugly.
Mother, please, I don't have to tell you,          610
You have to be pleasant to our father Zeus
So he won't be angry and ruin our feast.
If the Lord of Lightning wants to blast us from our seats,
He can—that's how much stronger he is.
So apologize to him with silken-soft words,
And the Olympian in turn will be gracious to us."

He whisked up a two-handled cup, offered it
To his dear mother, and said to her:

"I know it's hard, mother, but you have to endure it.

I don't want to see you getting beat up, and me          *620*
Unable to help you. The Olympian can be rough.
Once before when I tried to rescue you
He flipped me by my foot off our balcony.
I fell all day and came down when the sun did
On the island of Lemnos, scarcely alive.
The Sintians had to nurse me back to health."

By the time he finished, the ivory-armed goddess
Was smiling at her son. She accepted the cup from him.
Then the lame god turned serving boy, siphoning nectar
From the mixing bowl and pouring the sweet liquor        *630*
For all of the gods, who couldn't stop laughing
At the sight of Hephaestus hustling through the halls.

And so all day long until the sun went down
They feasted to their hearts' content,
Apollo playing beautiful melodies on the lyre,
The Muses singing responsively in lovely voices.
And when the last gleams of sunset had faded,
They turned in for the night, each to a house
Built by Hephaestus, the renowned master craftsman,
The burly blacksmith with the soul of an artist.         *640*

And the Lord of Lightning, Olympian Zeus, went to his bed,
The bed he always slept in when sweet sleep overcame him.
He climbed in and slept, next to golden-throned Hera.

# ILIAD 2

The gods slept soundly that night,
And the men, by their warhorses.

But Zeus lay awake in the dark,
Thinking of how to honor Achilles
And destroy Greeks by the shipload.
His thoughts parted like stormclouds,
And in the clear space between them
He saw what seemed to be the best plan:
To send to Agamemnon, son of Atreus,
A wooly menace, a Dream,                                      10
And to it he spoke these feathery words:

"Go, deadly Dream, along the Greek ships
Until you come to the hut of Agamemnon,
And deliver this message to him exactly:
Order him to arm his long-haired Greeks.
Now is his time to capture Troy.
The Olympian gods are no longer divided;
Hera has bent them all to her will
And targeted the Trojans for pain."

The Dream listened and went. Shadows flew             20
Around the Greek ships. It found Agamemnon
Wrapped in deep, starlit slumber.

20                                                                              [1–19]

The Dream stood above his head. It looked
Like Nestor, the old man that Agamemnon
Respected the most, looked just like Nestor,
And this dream that was a god addressed the king:

"Asleep, son of Atreus, horsebreaker,
Wise man? You can't sleep all night.
All those decisions to make, so many people
Depending on you. I'll be brief.                    30
I am a messenger from Zeus, who is
Far away, but loves you and pities you.
He orders you to arm your long-haired Greeks.
Now is your time to capture Troy.
The Olympian gods are no longer divided;
Hera has bent them all to her will
And targeted Troy for sorrow from Zeus.
Think it over. Keep your wits about you,
And don't forget this when sleep slips away."

And the voice trailed off, leaving him there       40
Dreaming of things that were never to be.
He thought he would take Priam's city that day,
The fool. He didn't know what Zeus had in mind,
The pain and groans for both Trojans and Greeks
In the unendurable crush of battle.
He woke from sleep, the god's voice
Eddying around him. He sat upright,
Pulled on a silky shirt, threw on a cloak,
Laced a pair of sandals on his shining feet,
And hung from his shoulder a silver-worked sword.   50
And he held his imperishable, ancestral staff
As he walked through the ships of the bronze-kilted Greeks.

Dawn had just reached the peak of Olympus,
Speaking light to Zeus and the other immortals.

Agamemnon ordered the heralds
To call the Greeks to assembly.

The call went out, and the people gathered.
Agamemnon seated the elders first
By Nestor's ship and unfolded his plan:

"Listen, my friends. A dream from Zeus                    *60*
Came to me last night in my sleep. It looked
Just like Nestor, same face, same build,
And it stood above my head and spoke:
'Asleep, son of Atreus, horsebreaker,
Wise man? You can't sleep all night.
All those decisions to make, so many people
Depending on you. I'll be brief.
I am a messenger from Zeus, who is
Far away, but loves you and pities you.
He orders you to arm your long-haired Greeks.         *70*
Now is your time to capture Troy.
The Olympian gods are no longer divided;
Hera has bent them all to her will
And targeted Troy for sorrow from Zeus.
Think it over.' The dream said all this
And off it flew, and I awoke from a sweet sleep.
We'd better move if we're going to get the men in armor.
But I'm going to test them first with a little speech,
The usual drill—order them to beat a retreat in their ships.
It's up to each one of you to persuade them to stay."     *80*

He had his say and sat down. Then up rose
Nestor, king of sandswept Pylos.
He was full of good will in the speech he made:

"Friends, Argive councillors and commanders:
If any other Greek told us this dream
We would call it a lie and turn our backs on him.
But this is a man with a claim to be
The best of the Greeks. We'd better move
If we're going to get them in armor."

And he headed out. The other commanders stood up,     *90*
Convinced he was right.

The troops were moving now,

*Swarming like insects over the beach, like bees*
*That hum from a hollow rock in an endless line*
*And fly in clusters over flowers in spring,*
*Grouping themselves in aerial throngs.*

The Greeks made like that as they swarmed
Out of the ships and the huts clutched beneath them,
Filing through the deep sand into assembly,
Swept along by Zeus' emissary,                                   100
Wildfire Rumor. They milled about
In the assembly ground, and the earth
Groaned as the unruly crowd eased itself down,
And nine bawling heralds tried to stop their shouting
And get them to listen to their Zeus-spawned kings.
They settled down finally and kept their seats
And stopped all the noise.

       Up stood Lord Agamemnon,
Holding a staff.
       Hephaestus had crafted this staff            110
And Hephaestus had given it to Cronion Zeus.
Zeus in turn gave it to quicksilver Hermes
And Hermes to Pelops, the charioteer.
Pelops handed it on to Atreus,
And when Atreus died he left it to Thyestes.
Thyestes left it for Agamemnon to bear
And rule over the islands and all of Argos.
Leaning on it now he addressed the Greeks:

"Danaan heroes and soldiers,
          Zeus                       120
Is a hard god, friends. He's kept me in the dark
After all his promises and nods my way
That I'd raze Ilion's walls before sailing home.
It was all a lie, and I see now that his orders
Are for me to return to Argos in disgrace,
And this after all the armies I've destroyed.

I have no doubt that this is the high will
Of the god who has toppled so many cities
And will in the future, all glory to his power.
But it will be shame for generations to come,                    130
That such a large and powerful army of Greeks
Has fought this futile war against a few puny men.
There is no end in sight, nor has there ever been.
Look, if the Greeks and the Trojans
Agreed to a truce, and both sides counted off—
All of the Trojans who live in the city
And all of the Greeks—and if we Greeks formed up
In platoons of ten, and each platoon picked a Trojan
To pour our wine, there would be many platoons
With no one to pour. That's how much our Greek forces      140
Outnumber the Trojans who live in the city.
It's their allies, reinforcements from other cities,
Who keep hitting me hard and won't let me capture
Ilion's serried fortress no matter how hard I try.
Nine years of great Zeus have passed.
Our ships' timbers are rotten and their tackle loose.
Our wives and little children are no doubt
Sitting at home waiting for us. And here we are,
The job that we came to do unfinished.
Now this is what I say, and I want us all to obey:          150
Let's clear out with our ships and head for home.
There's no more hope we will take Troy's tall town."

This speech roused the spirits of the rank and file,
The masses who had not been in on the council.

The army started to move on the shore.

> *Long waves form*
> *On the Icarian Sea when winds East and South*
> *Explode from the clouds of patriarch Zeus;*
> *Or the West Wind rapes a field of deep wheat,*
> *Rippling and tassling the ears as it blows.*                 160

So too these troop lines.
                    Then the shouting began,

And the mad rush to the ships, dust rising
In plumes from their feet as confused yells—
To fasten boathooks, clear out launchways
And drag the ships down to the shining sea—
Rose to the sky. They were going home.

They had already begun to remove the chocks
From under the hulls, and there might have been
An unordained homecoming then for the Greeks          170
If Hera had not had a word with Athena:

"This is awful. Child of Zeus, Mystic Daughter
Of the Aegis-Holder, are we going to allow
The Greeks to go home just like that, run away
To their own country over the sea's broad back?
They're just going to hand Priam and the Trojans
The glory, not to mention Helen of Argos,
For whose sake many a Greek has perished in Troy,
Far from his homeland. Go down there now
Along the ranks of the bronze-shirted Greeks,          180
And with your mild words restrain each man.
Don't let them haul their curved prows to the sea."

And Athena streaked down from Olympus' crags,
Her eyes like owls', grey in the blue air,
And came quickly to the ships in the beachhead camp.
She found Odysseus there, his mind like Zeus' own,
Standing in thought. He had not laid a hand
On his benched, black ship, and his heart was heavy.

The owl-eyed goddess stood close to him and said:

"Son of Laertes in the line of Zeus, wily Odysseus,          190
Are you Greeks going to run away just like that,
Home to your fatherland over the sea's broad back?
Are you just going to hand Priam and the Trojans
The glory, not to mention Helen of Argos,
For whose sake many a Greek has perished in Troy,
Far from his homeland? Now go down along
All the ships of the bronze-shirted Greeks,

And with your mild words restrain each man.
Don't them haul their curved prows to the sea."

Odysseus knew that voice, and he set off at a run,　　　200
Throwing his cloak behind him—Eurybates
The herald, his man from Ithaca, gathered it up—
And he went up to Agamemnon and got from him
His ancestral staff, that splinter of eternity,
And with it went along the ships of the Greeks.
Whenever he encountered a chieftain or the like,
He tried to restrain him with gentle words:

"What's gotten into you? I don't mean to frighten you
As if you were a coward, but sit down here yourself
And make your men sit down. You don't really know　　210
Agamemnon's mind. He's just testing us now,
But before long he's going to come down on us hard.
Didn't we all hear what he said in council?
If he gets angry the whole army had better watch out.
Kings are bred by Zeus and have tempers to match."

But if he caught any of the ordinary soldiers yelling,
He would belt him with the staff and bawl him out:

"You there, who do you think you are? Sit still
And listen to your betters. You're a weakling,
Unfit for combat, a nothing in battle and in council.　　220
Do you think every Greek here can be a king?
It's no good having a carload of commanders. We need
One commander, one king, the one to whom Zeus,
Son of Cronus the crooked, has given the staff
And the right to make decisions for his people."

And so Odysseus mastered the army. The men all
Streamed back from their ships and huts and assembled
With a roar.

　　　*A wave from the restless, churning sea*
*Crashes on a beach, and the water seethes and thunders.*　　230

They had all dropped to the sand and were sitting there,
Except for one man, Thersites, a blathering fool
And a rabble rouser. This man had a repertory
Of choice insults he used at random to revile the nobles,
Saying anything he thought the soldiers would laugh at.
He was also the ugliest soldier at the siege of Troy,
Bowlegged, walked with a limp, his shoulders
Slumped over his caved-in chest, and up top
Scraggly fuzz sprouted on his pointy head.
Achilles especially hated him, as did Odysseus,                    240
Because he was always provoking them. Now
He was screaming abuse at Agamemnon.
The Achaeans were angry with him and indignant,
But that didn't stop him from razzing the warlord:

"What's wrong, son of Atreus, something you need?
Your huts are filled with bronze, and with women
We Achaeans pick out and give to you first of all
Whenever we take some town. Are you short of gold?
Maybe some Trojan horse breeder will bring you some
Out of Ilion as ransom for his son                    250
Whom I or some other Achaean has captured.
Maybe it's a young girl for you to make love to
And keep off somewhere for yourself. It's not right
For a leader to march our troops into trouble.
You Achaeans are a disgrace, Achaean women, not men!
Let's sail home in our ships and leave him here
To stew over his prizes so he'll have a chance to see
Whether he needs our help or not. Furthermore,
He dishonored Achilles, who's a much better man.
Achilles doesn't have an angry bone in his body,                    260
Or this latest atrocity would be your last, son of Atreus!"

That was the abuse Agamemnon took
From the mouth of Thersites. Odysseus
Was on him in a flash, staring him down
With a scowl, and laid into him:

"Mind your tongue, Thersites. Better think twice

About being the only man here to quarrel with his betters.
I don't care how bell-toned an orator you are,
You're nothing but trash. There's no one lower
In all the army that followed Agamemnon to Troy.          270
You have no right even to mention kings in public,
Much less badmouth them so you can get to go home.
We have no idea how things are going to turn out,
What kind of homecoming we Achaeans will have.
Yet you have the nerve to revile Agamemnon,
Son of Atreus, the shepherd of his people,
Because the Danaan heroes are generous to him?
You think you can stand up in public and insult him?
Well, let me tell you something. I guarantee
That if I ever catch you running on at the mouth again          280
As you were just now, my name isn't Odysseus
And may I never again be called Telemachus' father
If I don't lay hold of you, strip your ass naked,
And run you out of the assembly and through the ships,
Crying at all the ugly licks I land on you."

And with that he whaled the staff down
On Thersites' back. The man crumpled in pain
And tears flooded his eyes. A huge bloody welt
Rose on his back under the gold stave's force,
And he sat there astounded, drooling with pain          290
And wiping away his tears. The troops, forgetting
Their disappointment, had a good laugh
At his expense, looking at each other and saying:

"Oh man! You can't count how many good things
Odysseus has done for the Greeks, a real leader
In council and in battle, but this tops them all,
The way he took that loudmouth out of commission.
I don't think he'll ever be man enough again
To rile the commanders with all his insults."

That's what they were saying in the ranks.          300

Then Odysseus, destroyer of cities, stood up
Holding the staff. Owl-eyed Athena transformed herself

Into a herald and silenced the troops
So that every last man in the Greek army
Would listen closely to what he had to say:

"Son of Atreus, the Greeks are out to make you,
My lord, the most despised man on earth,
And they have no intention of keeping the promise
They made to you when they set out from Argos—
Not to return until you pulled down Ilion's walls.          310
They are like little children or widow women,
The way they whine to each other about going home.
God knows it's hard enough to make a man give up
And go back. A man gets discouraged when he spends
Even one month away from his wife on his ship,
Battling winter winds and the surging sea.
For us, it's nine years we've been here now.
I can't blame our men for getting discouraged
As they wait beside their beaked ships. But still,
It would be a disgrace to go home empty-handed          320
After all this time. So bear up, friends,
And let's stay long enough to find out whether
Calchas has prophesied truly or not.
Everyone here—and I'm talking about all of us
Not carried off by the wings of death—remembers it.
It seems like just yesterday when the ships
Were mustered at Aulis with their cargo of sorrows
For Priam and the Trojans. We were gathered
Around a spring, offering sacrifice on sacred altars,
Perfect hecatombs, beneath a beautiful plane tree          330
From under which the shining water flowed.
Then we saw it: a serpent, its back blood-red,
Horrible—the Olympian himself
Must have brought it into the daylight.
It slithered out from the altar and up the plane tree.
A sparrow's fledglings were nested
On the topmost branch, eight little birds
Trembling under the leaves, or nine, counting
The mother who hatched them, and the serpent
Devoured them all as they cheeped pitifully.          340
The mother fluttered around, mourning her nestlings,

But he coiled and got her by the wing as she shrieked.
After he had eaten the sparrow and her young,
The very god who revealed him turned him to stone,
An unmistakable portent from Zeus, son of Cronus.
We stood there in awe of what had happened,
This prodigy that crept into our sacrifice.
Calchas was quick to pronounce its prophetic meaning:
'Why are you silent, all you long-haired Greeks?
This great portent is a message from Zeus,                    350
Whose glory shall never die—a portent late in coming,
And late to be fulfilled. As this serpent devoured
The sparrow's children and the bird herself,
Eight hatchlings, nine, counting the mother,
So will we for as many years wage this war,
But in the tenth year we will capture the city.'
That was his prophecy, and it has all come true.
So let's have every Greek who ever strapped on armor
Stay put, until we capture Priam's great city!"

He finished. And the Greeks cheered, so loud              360
That the wooden hulls of the ships boomed
With their approval of godlike Odysseus' speech.

Then Nestor, the Gerenian rider, addressed them:

"Bah, you're carrying on like silly boys
Who have no business at all fighting a war.
What will become of our compacts and oaths?
Into the fire with our resolutions and plans,
The pure wine we poured out, the handclasps
We trusted in! We are wrangling with words now
And will not find thereby the ways or means              370
To stay the course for long.
                          Son of Atreus,
Assert yourself, and resume your command
Of the Greek forces in all their grueling battles.
To hell with those one or two Achaeans
With private plans—which will come to nothing—
To return to Argos before we know for sure
Whether Zeus' promise was a lie or not.

I say that the Aegis-Holder nodded his assent
On that day when the Argives came in their ships                    *380*
With their cargo of carnage and death for the Trojans.
Lightning on the right, favorable signs revealed.
No man here should be in a hurry to go home
Until he has spent the night with some Trojan's wife
As revenge for Helen's struggles and groans.
But if anyone is so almighty eager
To go back home, let him touch his black ship—
So he can seal his fate before the whole army.
But now, my lord, be prudent and take the advice,
Hardly negligible, that I am about to give.                    *390*
Divide the men by tribes and clans, Agamemnon,
So that clans and tribes can support each other.
If you do this and the army complies,
You will know which of your captains is a coward
And which is brave, and so too with the soldiers,
For they will fight as units. You will know too
Whether it is heaven's will that you not take the city
Or that your men are cowards and witless in war."

He spoke, and Lord Agamemnon answered:

"Once again, Nestor, the best speech of all.                    *400*
Father Zeus, Athena, and Apollo, give me
Ten such counsellors, and Priam's city
Would lay her head in our lap, taken and ravaged.
But Zeus, son of Cronus, has given me grief,
Embroiling me in pointless quarrels.
Yes, Achilles and I argued over a girl,
And it was I who grew angry first.
If we two could agree, there would not be
The slightest postponement of evil for Troy.
But go eat now, so we can get this battle together.                    *410*
Sharpen your spears and dress your shields,
Lay out fodder for your horses,
And inspect your chariots. We're going to war.
We're going to fight all day and hate every minute
Without any breaks until it's too dark to see.
It's going to be chests sweating under shield straps,

Hands sore from gripping spears, horses sweaty
From pulling us around in our polished cars.
And if I catch anyone even thinking about
Staying out of the fight back here with the ships,          420
The dogs and birds will have him by nightfall."

The cheer that followed this speech came on like a wave

*That pounds a high cliff, a wave swollen by wind*
*Against a jutting crag that is constantly worried*
*By wind-driven waves from every direction.*

The men stood up and scattered to their ships,
Made fires in their huts and took their meal.
And each made sacrifice to his favorite god,
Praying to escape from battle alive.
The warlord Agamemnon sacrificed a fat bull,             430
Five years old, to Cronus' almighty son,
And he summoned the elders, the best of the Achaeans,
Nestor first of all, and the warlord Idomeneus,
Then the two Ajaxes, and Tydeus' son, Diomedes,
And as the sixth, Odysseus, Zeus' match in wisdom.
Menelaus, the rallier, came on his own,
Knowing what his brother was up against.
They stood 'round the ox and took up the barley grains,
And the warlord Agamemnon led them in prayer:

"Zeus, most glorious, most great,                          440
Dark Cloud that art in heaven,
May the sun not set nor darkness gather
Until I have cast Priam's roof beam
Smoldering to the ground, and burned
His doorways with consuming fire.
And may I tear Hector's heart out with bronze,
And may many of his comrades
Fall headlong around him,
Face down in the dust."

But Zeus would not grant his prayer,                      450
Not yet. He accepted Agamemnon's sacrifice

But blew upon his woes and increased them.

After the prayers and the strewing of barley
They cut the ox's throat and flayed it,
Jointed the thighbones and wrapped them
In a layer of fat with cuts of meat on top.
These they roasted over split kindling wood.
When the thigh pieces were charred and they had
Tasted the tripe, they cut the rest into strips,
Skewered it on spits, and roasted it carefully.                 460
When they were done and the feast was ready,
Feast they did, and no one lacked an equal share.
When they had eaten and drunk to their heart's content,
Nestor the Gerenian horseman spoke:

"Son of Atreus, my lord Agamemnon,
Let us remain gathered here no longer
Nor delay the work that the gods have given us.
Have the heralds of the bronze-armored Greeks
Make proclamation all through the ships
And muster the army. We will patrol camp                        470
In a group, to waken Ares more quickly."

He spoke, and the warlord Agamemnon
Ordered the heralds to muster the troops
In battle formation. They gave their skirling cry,
And all the commanders around Atreus' son
Hurried to have their men fall in.
And in their midst Athena, eyes like slate,
Carried the aegis, priceless and out of all time,
Pure gold tassels flying in the wind, each
Woven strand worth a hundred oxen.                             480
And the goddess herself, glowing like moonlight,
Rushed over the sand, sweeping them on
And stiffening their hearts, so that for each of them
To die in battle was sweeter than going home.

*A fire raging through endless forests*
*In a mountain range can be seen far away*
*As a distant glow.*

Likewise the glare
From the advancing army's unimaginable bronze,
An eerie light that reached the stratosphere.     490

*Migratory birds—cranes, geese, or long-necked swans—*
*Are gathering in a meadow in Asia*
*Where the river Caystrius branches out in streams.*
*For a while they fly in random patterns*
*For the pure joy of using their wings,*
*But then with a single cry they start to land,*
*One line of birds settling in front of another*
*Until the whole meadow is a carpet of sound.*

Likewise from the ships and huts, tribe after tribe
Poured out onto the Scamander's floodplain,     500
And the ground groaned and reverberated
Under their feet and the hooves of their horses.
And they stood in the flowering meadow there,
Countless as leaves, or as flowers in their season.

*Innumerable throngs of buzzing flies*
*Will swarm all over a herdsman's yard*
*In springtime, when milk wets the pails—*

Likewise the throngs of long-haired Greeks
Who stood on the plain facing the Trojans,
Intent on hammering them to pieces.     510

*And as goatherds easily separate out*
*Wide flocks of goats mingled in pasture,*

So the commanders drew up their troops
To enter battle, and Lord Agamemnon
Moved among them like Zeus himself,
The look in his eyes, the carriage of his head,
With a torso like Ares', or like Poseidon's.

*Picture a bull that stands out from the herd*
*Head and horns above the milling cattle—*

Zeus on that day made the son of Atreus                        *520*
A man who stood out from the crowd of heroes.

Tell me now, Muses,
Who live on Olympus—for you are
Goddesses, and are present,
And know all things, while we
Hear only reports and know nothing—
Who were the Greek captains and lords?
The rank and file I could never name,
Not even if I had ten tongues, ten mouths,
A voice that never broke, and a bronze heart,           *530*
Unless the Olympian Muses, daughters
Of Zeus, called to my mind
All those who came under Ilion's walls.

Now I will call the roll of the ships.

The Boeotians were led by PENELEUS and LEITUS,
With Arcesilaus, Protoenor, and Clonius.

Their towns were Hyria,
                    rocky Aulis,
                              and Schoenus,
Scolus,                                                            *540*
          ridged Eteoneus,
                    Thespeia,
                              Graea,
Broad Mycalessus,
                    Harma,
                              Eilesion,
Erythrae,
          Eleon,
                    Hyle,
                              Peteon,                              *550*
Ocalea,
          Medeon,
                    Copae,
                              Eutresus,

Dovecoted Thisbe,
            Coroneia,
                        grassy Haliartus,
Plataea,
            Glisas,
                        Lower Thebes,                          *560*
                                    Onchestus,
Posideon, with its grove,
                        and Arne, its vineyards,
Mideia,
            sacred Nisa,
                        and on the coast, Anthedon.

Fifty ships, and aboard each ship,
One hundred and twenty young men of Boeotia.

            The Minyans from Aspledon and Orchomenos
            Were led by ASCALAPHUS and IALMENUS,                *570*
            Sons of Ares, born to Astyoche, then a virgin,
            In the palace of Actor, son of Azeus,
            When she had the god in her upstairs room.

            Their thirty vessels were drawn up in rows.

            The Phocians were led by SCHEDIUS and EPISTROPHUS,
            Sons of Iphitos, grandsons of Naubolus.
            Their towns were Cyparissus
                                    and rocky Pytho,
            Sacred Crisa,
                        Daulis,                                 *580*
                                    Panopeus,
            Anemoria,
                        Hyampolis,
                                    on the river Cephisus,
            And Lilaea,
                        by the springs of Cephisus.

Forty black ships formed their contingent,

And their leaders marshalled their ranks
Left of the Boeotians as they readied for war.

The Locrians were led by swift AJAX,                          590
Son of Oïleus, not as great as Telamonian Ajax,
Not nearly, a small man who wore a linen corselet
But with a spear the best soldier in Greece.

They lived in Cynus
                    and Ophus and Calliarus,
In Bessa and Scarphe
                    and lovely Augeiae,
In Tarphe and Thronion
                    by the streams of Boagrius.

Ajax led forty black ships, manned by Locrians               600
Who dwell over against sacred Euboea.

    The Abantes, who hold Euboea and Chalcis,
    Eretria and the vineyards of Histiaea,
    Seaside Cerinthus and the steep stronghold of Dios,
    And those in Carystus and also in Styra,
    Were led by ELEPHENOR, a scion of Ares
    And son of Chalcodon. He was chief of the Abantes,
    A spirited people, swift and hot-tempered,
    Their hair long in the back, spearmen eager
    With outstretched spears to rend enemy corselets.        610

    Forty black ships followed Elephenor.

Those who held Athens—the well-founded citadel
And the land of Erechtheus, whom Athena fostered
After the grain field bore him, and made him live
In her own rich precinct, where Athenian youths
Still propitiate him yearly with rams and bulls—
These were led by MENESTHEUS, Peteos' son.
This man had no equal anywhere on earth
At marshalling chariots and infantry,

Rivalled only by Nestor, who was his elder.                    620

Fifty black ships followed Menestheus.

  AJAX led from Salamis twelve ships
  And stationed them by the Athenian contingent.

Those who held Argos and walled Tiryns
And Hermione and Asine, on the deep gulf,
Troezen and Eionae and vine-clad Epidaurus,
And the Achaean youths in Aegina and Mases—
All these were led by DIOMEDES and STHENELUS,
Son of Capaneus, with EURYALUS as a third.
But the commander in chief was Diomedes,                    630

And eighty black ships followed him.

  Those who held Mycenae's citadel,

  And wealthy Corinth,
              and those in Cleonae
  And in Orneiae
              and lovely Araethyrea,
  And in Sicyon,
              where Adrastus first was king,
  And those in Hyperesia
              and steep Gonoessa,                    640
  And in Pellene,
              and around Aegium,
  Throughout all Aegialus
              and around wide Helice—

  All these were commanded,
              a hundred ships,
  By Lord AGAMEMNON,
              son of Atreus.

  His contingent was far the largest and best,
  And among them he put on his gleaming bronze,              650
  Glorying, preeminent among all,

And the army he led was largest of all.

Those who lived
        in Lacedaemon's gulches,
In Pharis and Sparta,
        in dove-haunted Messe,
And those in Bryseiae
        and lovely Augeiae,
And Amyclae and Helus,
        a citadel by the sea,                        660
And those in Laas
        and the environs of Oetylus—
These were led
        by Agamemnon's brother,
MENELAUS,
        whose voice carried in battle,
In sixty ships
        marshalled separately.

And he moved among them with confidence,
Urging them into war. He wanted most of all      670
Requital for Helen's struggles and groans.

Those who lived in Pylos and lovely Arene,
In Thyron, ford of Alpheius, and Aipy,
In Cyparisseis and Amphigeneia,
In Pteleos and Helus and Dorium, where
The Muses met Thamyris and stopped his song
As he journeyed from Eurytus' house in Oechalia
Boasting he would win even if the Muses,
Daughters of Zeus, were to sing against him,
And in anger they maimed him, took away          680
His melody and silenced his lyre—

All these Gerenian NESTOR led, and had
Ninety hollow ships drawn up in rows.

Those who held Arcadia in Cyllene's shadow
Beside Aepytus' tomb, where men fight hand to hand,
And those in Pheneos and Orchomenos,

In Rhipe and Stratia and windy Enispe,
Those who held Tegea and Mantinea,
Those who held Stymphalus and lived in Parrhasia—

All these AGAPENOR led, Ancaeus' son,                    *690*
Fifty ships, and each ship had on board
Many Arcadians who knew how to fight.
Agamemnon himself had given them ships
To cross over the sea's grey wine,
For the Arcadians knew nothing of sailing the sea.

    Those from Buprasium
        and shining Elis,
    And the land that Hyrmine
        and Myrsinus enclose
    On the coast,                                      *700*
        and between Olen rock and Alesium—

All those had four leaders, each with ten ships
With many Epeians aboard. The captains were
AMPHIMACHUS and THALPIUS, both of Actor's line,
One Cteatus' son, the other of Eurytus;
Third was mighty DIORES, son of Amarynceus;
Fourth was godlike POLYXEINUS, Augeias' son.

    Those from Dulichium
      and the holy islands,
    The Echinaes,                                      *710*
      that lie in the sea offshore from Elis,

Had MEGES as leader, peer of Ares,
Whom Phyleus dear to Zeus had begotten,
The horseman Phyleus who once upon a time
Had moved to Dulichium angry with his father.

Forty black ships followed Meges to Troy.

    ODYSSEUS led the proud Cephallenians
    Who held Ithaca
        and forested Neriton,

And those in Crocyleia                                    *720*
      and rugged Aigilips,
In Zacynthus and Samos,
         and all those who lived
Along the mainland coast
         opposite these islands.

Odysseus led them, peer of Zeus in counsel,
And twelve vermillion prows followed him to Troy.

The Aetolians were led by Adraemon's son,
THOAS. They lived in Pleuron, Olenos, Pylene,
In seaside Chalcis and rocky Calydon.                     *730*
For great-hearted Oeneus' sons were gone,
And he himself was dead, and blond Meleager,
Who once was told to rule all Aetolia.

Forty black ships followed Thoas to Troy.

The Cretans were led by IDOMENEUS.

Their cities were Cnossus
         and walled Gortys,
Lyctus and Miletus
         and lime-white Lycastus,
Phaestus and Rhytium,                                     *740*
         well-peopled cities,
And all who dwelled in Crete's hundred towns.

Idomeneus, famed for his spear, was captain,
As was MERIONES, who could kill like Ares.

Eighty black ships sailed with them to Troy.

Heracles' son TLEPOLEMUS, a good man, and big,
Led nine ships from Rhodes. The Rhodians
Were divided into three contingents:
Lindos, Ialysus, and lime-white Cameirus.
They were led by the warrior Tlepolemus,                  *750*
Born to great Heracles by Astyocheia,

Whom he had taken out of Ephyre
And away from the river Selleis, after
Pillaging the cities of many a hero.
But when Tlepolemus came of age in the palace,
He killed his father's dear uncle, Licymnius,
A scion of Ares, then getting on in years.
He quickly built a fleet, gathered a following,
And took flight on the sea, threatened by the other
Sons and grandsons of mighty Heracles.                    760
He came to Rhodes in his painful wanderings,
And his people settled in three regions by tribes.
They were loved by Zeus, who rules gods and men,
And the son of Cronus showered them with wealth.


    NIREUS led three trim ships from Syme.


    Nireus was the son of Aglaia and Charops,
King of Syme, and was the handsomest man
Of all the Danaans who came to Troy,
After the flawless son of Peleus.
But he was weak, and few men followed him.              770


  Those who held
Nisyrus and Carpathus,
  Casus and Cos,
Eurypylus' city,
  And the Calydnian islands,


Were led by PHEIDIPPUS and ANTIPHUS,
The two sons of Thessalus, Heracles' son.


Their thirty vessels were drawn up in rows.


Those who inhabited
                Pelasgian Argos                    780
And lived in Alos,
            Alope, and Trachis,
And held Phthia and Hellas,
                land of fair women,

And were known as MYRMIDONS,
    Hellenes,
    Achaeans—

ACHILLES commanded their fifty ships.

But none of them now thought of gruesome war,
Since there was no one to lead them into the ranks.   *790*
The great sprinter lay idle in their beachhead camp,
Nursing his wrath because of the girl,
Fair-haired Briseis, whom he had taken,
After great effort, out of Lyrnessus
When he sacked that town and levelled Thebes' walls
And cut down Mynes and Epistrophus,
King Evenos' sons, great warriors both.
Heartsick for her, and angry, Achilles lay idle,
 But he would rise again soon.

  Those in Phylace          *800*
    and flowering Pyrasus,
  Demeter's sanctuary,
    and those in Iton,
  Mother of flocks,
    in Antron, by the sea,
  And in the grasslands
    of Pteleos—

All these were led by PROTESILAUS,
While he still lived. The black earth now held him.
His wife, cheeks torn, was left in Phylace,   *810*
His house half-built. A Dardanian killed him
As he leapt from his ship, the first Greek ashore.
His men were not leaderless—though they missed
Their leader—for PODARCES marshalled them,
Son of Ipichlus Phylacides, rich in flocks, and
Protesilaus' brother. But Protesilaus was older
And a better man, a hero, and though his men
Did not lack a leader, they yearned for him.

Forty black ships followed Protesilaus to Troy.

Those in Pherae beside Lake Boebeis,                          *820*
And in Boebe,
        Glaphyrae,
              and well-built Iolkos,

Were in eleven ships led by EUMELUS,
Admetus' son by a glorious woman,
Alcestis, loveliest of Pelias' daughters.

  Those in Methone and Thaumacia,
  In Meliboea and rugged Olizon,
Came in in seven ships led by PHILOCTETES,
The great archer, and aboard each ship                       *830*
Were fifty oarsmen skilled with the bow.
But Philoctetes now lay in pain on an island,
Sacred Lemnos, where the Achaeans stranded him,
Afflicted with a wound from a deadly snake.
He lay there in anguish, but the Greeks at Troy
Would soon remember Lord Philoctetes.
Nor were these men leaderless. MEDON
Marshalled them, Oïleus' bastard son,
Whom Rhene bore to the pillager Oïleus.

  Those in Tricca and craggy Ithome,                      *840*
  And those in Oechalia, Eurytus' city,
Were led by the two sons of Asclepius,
PODALEIRIUS and MACHAON, good healers both,

With thirty vessels drawn up in rows.

Those who held Ormenios and the spring Hypereia,
And Asterion and Titanos' white peaks,
Were led by EURYPYLUS, Euaemon's great son.

Forty black ships sailed with him to Troy.

Those who held Argissa,
                              and lived in Gyrtone,                    *850*
In Orthe,
                Elone,
                          and white-bricked Oloöson,

Were led by POLYPOETES, staunch in battle,
Son of Peirithous, whom deathless Zeus begot.
Gloried Hippodameia conceived Polypoetes that day
When Peirithous punished the shaggy centaurs,
Drove them from Pelion and to the Aethices.
Leonteus shared the command, Caeneus' grandson.

Forty black ships sailed with them to Troy.                           *860*

  GOUNEUS led twenty-two ships from Cyphus,
  And with him came the Enines and Paraebi,
  Who had settled around wintry Dodona
  And in the fields around the stream Titaressus,
  A tributary of the Peneius. Its lovely water
  Does not mingle with Peneius' silver eddies
  But glides on its surface like olive oil,
  A branch of Styx, the dread water of oaths.

    The Magnetes, who lived around Peneius
    And forested Pelion, were led by swift PROTHOUS,                   *870*
    Son of Tenthredon, in forty black ships.

These were the leaders of the Danaans.

But tell me now, Muse, who were the best
Of men and of horses in the Atreides' army?

The best horses were the mares of Eumelus,
Swift as birds, of the same age, with matching coats,
And their backs were as even as a levelling line.
Apollo Silverbow had bred them in Pereia,

A team of mares who bore Panic in battle.

     The best warrior was Telamonian Ajax—                              *880*
While Achilles was in his rage. For Achilles
Was second to no one, as were the horses
That bore Peleus' flawless son. But now he lay idle
Among his beaked, seagoing hulls, furious
With Agamemnon, the shepherd of the people,
The son of Atreus. Achilles' men
Amused themselves on the shore, throwing
The discus and javelin and shooting their bows.
The horses stood beside their chariots
Champing lotus and marsh parsley.                                      *890*
The chariots lay covered in their owners' huts.
The men missed their leader. They tramped
Through the camp and had no part in fighting.

     The army marched, and it was as though the land
Were swept with fire. Earth groaned beneath them,

     *As beneath Zeus when in his wrath he thunders*
     *And lashes the country of the Arimi with lightning*
     *Where men say Typhoeus lies in the ground.*

So the earth groaned under their feet
As they pressed on quickly over the plain.                             *900*

     Zeus notified the Trojans of all this
By sending Iris streaking down to Ilion.
She found the citizens assembled in one body,
Young and old alike, near Priam's gate, talking.
Iris positioned herself nearby
And made her voice sound like Polites'—
A son of Priam who, trusting his speed,
Often sat as lookout on top of the barrow
Of old Aesytes, watching for any movement
Of Greek troops from their ships.                                      *910*
Using his voice, the goddess said to Priam:

"Sir, you are as fond of endless speeches now
As you were in peacetime. But this is war.
I have been in a battle or two, but never
Have I seen an army like this,
Covering the plain like leaves, or like sand,
As it advances to attack the city.
Hector, you're in charge of this operation.
But because there are so many allies here
With different languages from points abroad,                    920
Each captain should give the word to his own men
And lead them out marshalled by cities."

Hector knew this was a goddess's speech
And dismissed the assembly. They rushed to arms.
All the gates were opened, and the troops
Poured through them, on foot and in war cars.

In front of the city there is a steep hill
Out in the plain, level terrain all around it.
Men call this hill Batieia. Immortals call it
The barrow of Myrine the Dancer.                    930
It was here that the Trojans and their allies
Drew up their troops in companies.

The Trojans were led by great HECTOR,
Son of Priam, in his shining helmet.
His contingent was far the largest and the best,
Arrayed for battle, resolute with their spears.

The Dardanian troops were led by AENEAS,
Whom bright Aphrodite bore to Anchises,
A goddess lying with a mortal man
In the foothills of Ida. Sharing the command                    940
Were Antenor's two sons, Archelochus
And Acamas, skilled in all forms of combat.

The Troes, who lived in wealthy Zeleia
At Ida's foot, and drank the Aesepus' dark water,
Were led by the glorious son of Lycaon,
PANDARUS, whose bow was a gift from Apollo.

Those who held Adrasteia and the deme Apaesus,
And Pityeia and the steep Mount Tereia,
Were led by ADRASTUS and AMPHIUS,
With linen corselets, sons of Merops and Percote.          950
This man knew divination, and forbade his sons
To go to war, but they would not listen,
For Death's black birds were calling them on.

Those who lived around Percote and Practios,
Who held Sestus and Abydus and bright Arisbe,
Were led by ASIUS Hyrtacides, a born leader,
Asius, whom his great chestnut horses
Had drawn from Arisbe and the river Selleis.

The Pelasgian tribes, ferocious spearmen
From fertile Larisa, were led by HIPPOTHOUS          960
With his brother PYLAEUS. They were sons
Of Pelasgian Lethus, grandsons of Teutamus.

ACAMAS and PEIROUS led all the Thracians
Beyond the strong current of the Hellespont.

EUPHEMUS captained the Ciconian spearmen,
Son of Troezenus and grandson of Ceas.

PYRAECHMES led the distant Paeonians,
With curved bows, from Amydon and the river
Axius, whose water flows fairest over the earth.

PYLAEMENES, shaggy heart, led the Paphlagonians          970
From the land of the Eneti, where the mules run wild.
Their cities were Cytoros and Sesamos,
And they lived around the river Parthenios
In Cromna, Aegialos, and high Erythini.

ODIUS and EPISTROPHUS led the Halizones
From distant Alybe, ancient source of silver.

The Mysians were led by CHROMIS
And ENNOMUS, who foretold the future

From the flight of birds, but could not ward off
The black birds of death. They would be slain in the river      *980*
By the terrible sword of swift Achilles,
Aeacus' grandson, when he killed many there.

PHORCYS and ASCANIUS led the Phrygians
From distant Ascania, battle-hungry troops.

The Maeonians were led by MESTHLES and ANTIPHUS,
Talaemones' sons, whose mother was the nymph
Of Lake Gygaea, under Mount Tmolus.

NASTES led the Carians, who spoke a foreign tongue.
Their strongholds were Miletus, and Mount Phthires,
The streams of Maeander, and Mycale's steep crests.            *990*
AMPHIMACHUS shared the command with Nastes,
Who came to the war wearing gold like a girl,
The fool, but it could not save him from death.
Achilles killed him in his rush through the river
Without a second thought, and bore off the gold.

SARPEDON and GLAUCUS captained the Lycians
Who came from the faraway, swirling Xanthus.

# ILIAD 3

Two armies,
The troops in divisions
Under their commanders,

The Trojans advancing across the plain

*Like cranes beating their metallic wings*
*In the stormy sky at winter's onset,*
*Unspeakable rain at their backs, their necks stretched*
*Toward Oceanic streams and down*
*To strafe the brown Pygmy race,*
*Bringing strife and bloodshed from the sky at dawn,*                    10

While the Greeks moved forward in silence,
Their breath curling in long angry plumes
That acknowledged their pledges to die for each other.

*Banks of mist settle on mountain peaks*
*And seep into the valleys. Shepherds dislike it*
*But for a thief it is better than night,*
*And a man can see only as far as he can throw a stone.*

No more could the soldiers see through the cloud of dust
The armies tramped up as they moved through the plain.

And when they had almost closed—                                        20

50

Was it a god?—no, not a god
But Paris who stepped out from the Trojan ranks,
Leopard skin on his shoulders, curved bow, sword,
And shaking two bronze-tipped spears at the Greeks
He invited their best to fight him to the death.

When Menelaus, who was Ares' darling, saw him
Strutting out from the ranks, he felt

> *As a lion must feel when he finds the carcass*
> *Of a stag or wild goat, and, half-starving,*
> *Consumes it greedily even though hounds and hunters*          30
> *Are swarming down on him.*

                          It was Paris all right,
Who could have passed for a god,
And Menelaus grinned as he hefted his gear
And stepped down from his chariot. He would
Have his revenge at last. Paris' blood
Turned milky when he saw him coming on,
And he faded back into the Trojan troops
With cheeks as pale as if he had seen—
Had almost stepped on—a poisonous snake          40
In a mountain pass. He could barely stand
As disdainful Trojans made room for him in the ranks,
And Hector, seeing his brother tremble at Atreus' son,
Started in on him with these abusive epithets:

"Paris, you desperate, womanizing pretty boy!
I wish you had never been born, or had died unmarried.
Better that than this disgrace before the troops.
Can't you just hear it, the long-haired Greeks
Chuckling and saying that our champion wins
For good looks but comes up short on offense and defense?          50
Is this how you were when you got up a crew
And sailed overseas, hobnobbed with the warrior caste
In a foreign country and sailed off with
A beautiful woman with marriage ties to half of them?
You're nothing but trouble for your father and your city,
A joke to your enemies and an embarrassment to yourself.

No, don't stand up to Menelaus: you might find out
What kind of a man it is whose wife you're sleeping with.
You think your lyre will help you, or Aphrodite's gifts,
Your hair, your pretty face, when you sprawl in the dust?          60
It's the Trojans who are cowards, or you'd have long since
Been dressed out in stones for all the harm you've done."

And Paris, handsome as a god, answered him:

"That's only just, Hector. You've got a mind
Like an axe, you know, always sharp,
Making the skilled cut through a ship's beam,
Multiplying force—nothing ever turns your edge.
But don't throw golden Aphrodite's gifts in my face.
We don't get to choose what the gods give us, you know,
And we can't just toss their gifts aside.                          70
So all right, if you want me to fight, fine.
Have the Trojans and the Greeks sit down,
And Menelaus and I will square off in the middle
To fight for Helen and all her possessions.
Winner take all.
And everyone else will swear oaths of friendship,
You all to live here in the fertile Troad,
And they to go back to bluegrass Argos
And Achaea with its beautiful women."

Hector liked what he heard.                                        80
He went out in front along the Trojan ranks
Holding a spear broadside and made them all sit down.
Greek archers and slingers were taking aim at him
And already starting to shoot arrows and stones
When Agamemnon boomed out a command
For them to hold their fire. Hector was signalling
That he had something to say, and his helmet
Caught the morning sun as he addressed both armies:

"Listen to me, Trojans, and you warriors from Greece.
Paris, on account of whom this war began, says this:          90
He wants all the Trojan and Greek combatants
To lay their weapons down on the ground.

He and Menelaus will square off in the middle
And fight for Helen and all her possessions.
Winner take all.
And everyone else swears oaths of friendship."

Utter silence,
Until Menelaus, who was good at the war shout, said:

"Now listen to me, since my pain is paramount
In all this. It may be that the Greeks and Trojans          100
Can at last call it quits. We've had enough suffering
From this quarrel of mine that Paris began.
Whichever of us is due to die, let him die.
Then the rest of you can be done with each other.
Bring a pair of lambs, a white one and a black,
For Earth and Sun. Our side will bring another for Zeus.
And have Priam come, so he can swear oaths himself,
In person, since his sons are arrogant perjurers
Who would just as soon trample on Zeus' solemn word.
Younger men always have their heads in the clouds.          110
An old man looks ahead and behind, and the result
Is far better for both parties involved."

You could see their mood brighten,
Greeks and Trojans both, with the hope
That this wretched war would soon be over.
They pulled their chariots up in rows,
Dismounted, and piled up their weapons.

There was not much space between the two armies.

Hector dispatched two heralds to the city
To fetch the lambs and summon Priam.                        120
Agamemnon sent Talthybius back to the ships
With orders to bring back a lamb.

While these human heralds were off on their missions,
Iris, the gods' herald (who is also the rainbow),
Came to white-armed Helen disguised as Laodice,
Her sister-in-law and Priam's most beautiful daughter.

She found Helen in the main hall, weaving a folding mantle
On a great loom and designing into the blood-red fabric
The trials that the Trojans and Greeks had suffered
For her beauty under Ares' murderous hands.                    130
Iris stood near Helen and said:

"Come and see, dear lady, the amazing thing
The Greek and Trojan warriors have done.
They've fought all these years out on the plain,
Lusting for each other's blood, but now
They've sat down in silence—halted the war—
They're leaning back on their shields
And their long spears are stuck in the sand.
But Paris and Menelaus are going to fight
A duel with lances, and the winner                    140
Will lay claim to you as his beloved wife."

The goddess's words turned Helen's mind
Into a sweet mist of desire
For her former husband, her parents, and her city.
She dressed herself in fine silvery linens
And came out of her bedroom crying softly.
Two maids trailed behind, Aethrê,
Pittheus' daughter, and cow-eyed Clyménê.
They came to the Western Gate,
Where a knot of old men sat—                    150

Priam, Panthous, Thymoetes,
Lampus, Clytius, Hicetaon
(Who was in Ares' bloodline)
Ucalegon and Antenor,
Who lived and breathed wisdom—

These veterans sat on the wall by the Western Gate,
Too old to fight now, but excellent counsellors.

  *Think of cicadas perched on a branch,*
  *Their delicate voices shrill in the woods.*

Such were the voices of these Trojan elders                    160

Sitting on the tower by the Western Gate.
When they saw Helen coming
Their rasping whispers flew along the wall:

"Who could blame either the Trojans or Greeks
For suffering so long for a woman like this."

"Her eyes are not human."

"Whatever she is, let her go back with the ships
And spare us and our children a generation of pain."

But Priam called out to her:

"Come here, dear child, sit next to me                    170
So you can see your former husband
And dear kinsmen. You are not to blame
For this war with the Greeks. The gods are.
Now tell me, who is that enormous man
Towering over the Greek troops, handsome,
Well-built? I've never laid eyes on such
A fine figure of a man. He looks like a king."

And Helen,
The sky's brightness reflected in her mortal face:

"Reverend you are to me dear father-in-law,                180
A man to hold in awe. I'm so ashamed.
Death should have been a sweeter evil to me
Than following your son here, leaving my home,
My marriage, my friends, my precious daughter,
That lovely time in my life. None of it was to be,
And lamenting it has been my slow death.
But you asked me something, and I'll answer.
That man is Agamemnon, son of Atreus,
A great king and a strong warrior both.
He was also my brother-in-law—shameless bitch          190
That I am—if that life was ever real."

The old man was lost in reverie and wonder:

"The son of Atreus. Born to power and wealth.
Blessed by the gods. Now I see
How many Greek lads you command.
I thought I saw it all when I went
To Phrygia once and saw thousands
Of soldiers and gleaming horses
Under the command of Otreus and Mygdon
Massed by the banks of the Sangarios,                    200
An army in which I myself served
On that fateful day when the Amazons
Swept down to fight against men.
They were nothing compared to these wild-eyed Greeks."

Then he saw Odysseus and asked:

"Now tell me about this one, dear child,
Shorter than Agamemnon by a head
But broader in the shoulders and chest.
His armor is lying on the ground
And he's roaming the ranks like a ram,                   210
That's it, just like a thick-fleeced ram
Striding through a flock of silvery sheep."

And Helen, Zeus' child:

                    "That is Laertes' son,
The master strategist Odysseus, born and bred
In the rocky hills of Ithaca. He knows
Every trick there is, and his mind runs deep."

Antenor turned to her and observed astutely:

"Your words are not off the mark there, madam.
Odysseus came here once before, on an embassy           220
For your sake along with Menelaus.
I entertained them courteously in the great hall
And learned each man's character and depth of mind.
Standing in a crowd of Trojans, Menelaus,
With his wide shoulders, was more prominent,
But when both were seated Odysseus was lordlier.

When it came time for each to speak in public
And weave a spell of wisdom with their words,
Menelaus spoke fluently enough, to the point
And very clearly, but briefly, since he is not                    230
A man of many words. Being older, he spoke first.
Then Odysseus, the master strategist, rose quickly,
But just stood there, his eyes fixed on the ground.
He did not move his staff forward or backward
But held it steady. You would have thought him
A dull, surly lout without any wit. But when he
Opened his mouth and projected his voice
The words fell down like snowflakes in a blizzard.
No mortal could have vied with Odysseus then,
And we no longer held his looks against him."                    240


The third hero old Priam saw was Ajax.


"And who is that giant of a Greek over there,
Head and shoulders above the other Achaeans?"


And Helen, shining in her long trailing robes:


"That is big Ajax, the army's mountain.
Standing beyond him is Idomeneus,
Like a god, with his Cretan commanders.
He used to come often from Crete
And Menelaus would entertain him
In our house. And now I can make out                    250
All the other Greeks, those I know
And whose names I could tell you.
But there are two commanders I do not see,
Castor the horse breaker and the boxer
Polydeuces, my brothers, born of one mother.
Either they didn't come here from lovely Lacedaemon,
Or else they did come in their seagoing ships
But avoid the company of the fighting men
In horror of the shame and disgrace that are mine."


But they had long been held by the life-giving earth                    260
There in Lacedaemon, their ancestral land.

A̲nd now the heralds came up to the town
With the sacrificial victims, the two rams,
And as fruit of the fields, hearty wine
In a goatskin bag. The herald Idaeus
Held a gleaming bowl and a golden chalice
And roused the old man with this speech:

"Rise, son of Laomedon.
The best men of Troy and Achaea summon you
Down to the plain to swear solemn oaths.                          270
Paris and Menelaus will fight
A duel for the woman, and she will
Follow the winner with all her possessions.
Everyone else will swear oaths of friendship,
We to live here in the fertile Troad,
And they to go back to bluegrass Argos
And Achaea with its beautiful women."

The old man stiffened.
He ordered his companions to yoke his horses,
Then mounted himself and took the reins.                          280
Antenor rode with him in the beautiful chariot
And they drove out through the Western Gate
And onto the plain. They pulled up in the space
Between the two armies and stepped down to the earth.

Agamemnon rose,
And Odysseus, deep in thought.

Heralds brought the animals for the oaths
And mixed wine in the great bowl.
They poured water over the kings' hands,
Then Agamemnon drew the knife                                     290
That hung by his sword scabbard
And cut hairs from the rams' heads.
The heralds gave these to the leaders on both sides,
And Agamemnon lifted his palms to the sky:

"Zeus, Father, Lord of Ida,
Greatest and most glorious;

Helios, who sees all and hears all;
Rivers and Earth, and Powers below
Who punish perjurers after death,
Witness and protect these sacred Oaths:                    300
If Paris Alexander kills Menelaus,
Helen and all her goods are his,
And we will sail away in our ships.
But if Menelaus kills Paris,
The Trojans will surrender Helen
With all her goods and pay the Argives
A fit penalty for generations to come.
If Priam and Priam's sons refuse,
Upon Paris' death, this penalty to me,
I swear to wage this war to its end."                    310

He spoke, then slashed the rams' throats
And put the gasping animals on the ground,
Their proud temper undone by whetted bronze.

Then they all filled their cups
With wine from the bowl and poured libations
To the gods eternal and prayed,
Greek and Trojan alike, in words like these:

"Zeus almighty and most glorious
And all you other immortal gods,
Whoever breaks this oath and truce,                    320
May their brains spill to the ground
Like this wine, theirs and their children's,
And may other men master their wives."

But Zeus would not fulfill their prayers.

Then Priam spoke his mind:

"Hear me, Trojans and Achaean soldiers:
I am going back now to windswept Ilion
Since I cannot bear to see with my own eyes
My dear son fighting with Menelaus,
Who is dear to Ares. Zeus and the other immortals                    330

Doubtless know whose death is destined."

And this man who was a god's equal
Loaded the rams onto his chariot
For interment in Trojan soil, mounted,
And took the reins. Antenor stood behind him
And together they drove back to Ilion.

Priam's son Hector and brilliant Odysseus
First measured off an arena and then
Shook lots in a bronze helmet to decide
Which of the two would cast his spear first.               340
You could see hands lifted to heaven
On both sides and hear whispered prayers:

"Death, Lord Zeus,
For whichever of the two
Started this business,
But grant us your peace."

Great Hector shook the helmet, sunlight
Glancing off his own as he looked away,
And out jumped Paris' lot.

                         The armies                        350
Sat down, rank after rank, tooled weapons
And high-stepping horses idle by each man.

The heroes armed.

Paris, silken-haired Helen's present husband,
Bound greaves on his shins with silver clasps,
Put on his brother Lycaon's breastplate,
Which fit him well, slung around his shoulders
A bronze sword inlaid with silver
And a large, heavy shield. On his head he placed
A crested helmet, and the horsehair plume                  360
Nodded menacingly.

Likewise Menelaus' gear.

They put their armor on in the ranks
And then stepped out into no-man's-land,
A cold light in their eyes.

Veterans on both sides, horse-breaking Trojans
And bronze-kneed Greeks, just sat and stared.

They stood close, closer, in the measured arena,
Shaking their spears, half-mad with jealousy.
And then Paris threw. A long shadow trailed his spear        370
As it moved through the air, and it hit the circle
Of Menelaus' shield, but the spearpoint crumpled
Against its tough metal skin. It was Menelaus' turn now,
And as he rose in his bronze he prayed to Zeus:

"Lord Zeus, make Paris pay for the evil he's done to me,
Smite him down with my hands so that men for all time
Will fear to transgress against a host's offered friendship."

With this prayer behind it Menelaus' spear
Carried through Paris' polished shield
And bored into the intricate breastplate,        380
The point shearing his shirt and nicking his ribs
As Paris twisted aside from black fatality.
Menelaus drew his silver-hammered sword
And came down with it hard on the crest
Of Paris' helmet, but the blade shattered
Into three or four pieces and fell from his hands.
Menelaus groaned and looked up to the sky:

"Father Zeus, no god curses us more than you.
I thought Paris was going to pay for his crimes,
And now my sword has broken in my hands,        390
And my spear's thrown away. I missed the bastard!"

As Menelaus spoke he lunged forward
And twisted his fingers into the thick horsehair

On Paris' helmet, pivoted on his heel,
And started dragging him back to the Greeks.
The tooled-leather chinstrap of Paris' helmet
Was cutting into his neck's tender skin,
And Menelaus would have dragged him
All the way back and won no end of glory.
But Aphrodite, Zeus' daughter, had all this                    400
In sharp focus and snapped the oxhide chinstrap,
Leaving Menelaus clenching an empty helmet,
Which the hero, spinning like a discus thrower,
Heaved into the hands of the Greek spectators.
Then he went back for the kill.

                    But Aphrodite
Whisked Paris away with the sleight of a goddess,
Enveloping him in mist, and lofted him into
The incensed air of his vaulted bedroom.
Then she went for Helen, and found her                         410
In a crowd of Trojan women high on the tower.

A withered hand tugged at Helen's fragrant robe.

The goddess was now the phantom of an old woman
Who had spun wool for Helen back in Lacedaemon,
Beautiful wool, and Helen loved her dearly.
In this crone's guise Aphrodite spoke to Helen:

"Over here. Paris wants you to come home.
He's propped up on pillows in your bedroom,
So silky and beautiful you'd never think
He'd just come from combat, but was going to a dance,          420
Or coming from a dance and had just now sat down."

This wrung Helen's heart. She knew
It was the goddess—the beautiful neck,
The irresistible line of her breasts,
The iridescent eyes. She was in awe
For a moment, and then spoke to her:

"You eerie thing, why do you love
Lying to me like this? Where are you taking me now?

Phrygia? Beautiful Maeonia? Another city
Where you have some other boyfriend for me?                    430
Or is it because Menelaus, having just beaten Paris,
Wants to take his hateful wife back to his house
That you stand here now with treachery in your heart?
Go sit by Paris yourself! Descend from the gods' high road,
Allow your precious feet not to tread on Olympus,
Go fret over him constantly, protect him.
Maybe someday he'll make you his wife—or even his slave.
I'm not going back there. It would be treason
To share his bed. The Trojan women
Would hold me at fault. I have enough pain as it is."          440

And Aphrodite, angry with her, said:

"Don't vex me, bitch, or I may let go of you
And hate you as extravagantly as I love you now.
I can make you repulsive to both sides, you know,
Trojans and Greeks, and then where will you be?"

Helen was afraid, and this child of Zeus
Pulled her silvery-white linens around her
And walked silently through the Trojan women,
Eluding them completely. The goddess went ahead
And led her to Paris' beautiful house. The servants        450
Suddenly all found something to do.
Helen moved like daylight to the vaulted bedroom,
Where Aphrodite, smiling, placed a chair for her
Opposite Paris. Helen, daughter of Zeus,
Sat down and, averting her eyes, said reproachfully:

"Back from the war? You should have died out there,
Beaten by a real hero, my former husband.
You used to boast you were better than Menelaus,
When it came to spear work and hand-to-hand combat.
Why don't you go challenge him to fight again,             460
Right now? I wouldn't recommend it, though,
A fair fight between you and Ares' redhead darling.
You'd go down in no time under his spear."

Paris answered her:

"Don't insult me, Helen.
Menelaus beat me this time—with Athena's help.
Next time I'll beat him. We have gods on our side too.
Enough of this.
          Let's go to bed now and make love.
I've never wanted you so much,            470
Not even when I first took you away
From Lacedaemon in my sailing ship
And made love to you on the island of Cranae.
I want you even more now than I wanted you then."

He walked to the bed, and Helen followed.

While the two of them slept in their bed,
Menelaus prowled the ranks looking for Paris.
The Trojan troops, as much as they would have liked to,
Could not produce him. To a man,
They hated Paris as they hated death itself.        480
So Agamemenon, as commander-in-chief, proclaimed:

"Hear me, Trojans, allied troops, and Dardanians:
The victory clearly belongs to Menelaus.
Surrender therefore Argive Helen
And all the possessions that come with her.
We will further assess a suitable penalty,
A tribute to be paid for generations to come."

Thus Agamemnon. And the Greeks cheered.

# ILIAD 4

The gods were seated with Zeus
On his golden terrace, and Hebe
Was pouring them nectar. They toasted
Each other with golden cups
As they looked out at Troy.
                    Zeus all at once
Started to provoke Hera with taunts:

"Well, Menelaus has a pair of goddesses
To help him, Hera of Argos
And Athena the Defender,                                    10
But they prefer to sit on the sidelines
Enjoying themselves. Aphrodite, now,
Smiling as always, stays with her hero
And manages to stave off his doom.
Did you see how she saved him just now
When it looked like he was about to die!
Still, Menelaus, Ares' favorite, clearly won.
But we should decide all this now.
Should we let war rage again
Or establish peace between the two sides?        20
If somehow we all could agree to do this
Priam's city might still be a place to live,
And Menelaus could take Argive Helen home."

He had no sooner finished
Than Athena and Hera were whispering
To each other with their heads together,
Plotting trouble for the Trojans.
                                    Athena
Didn't say a word, although she was furious
With her father.                                                    30
                        Hera, however,
Couldn't contain her anger, and said:

"Awesome son of Cronus! What a thing to say!
How dare you undo all my hard work.
The sweat I sweated driving my poor team
To raise an army against Priam and his sons!
Do it. But don't expect us all to approve."

Zeus brooded like a thunderhead, and answered:

"I don't understand you, woman. What have
Priam and his children done to you                                 40
That you are so fixed on demolishing
Ilion's stronghold down to its last well-laid brick?
Do you think if you were to enter its gates,
Get inside its long walls, and chew up Priam
And Priam's children raw, and the rest of the Trojans,
You might find some relief from this livid hate?
Do as you please. I don't want this quarrel
To become a source of strife between us.
But I'll tell you this, and you take it to heart.
The next time I have a passion to smash a city                     50
And I choose one with men dear to you in it,
Don't try to curb my anger. Just let me do it.
I've given in to you, though unwilling at heart.
For of all the cities under the sun and stars,
Of all the cities on earth that men inhabit,
Sacred Ilion is the dearest to my soul,
And Priam and the people of ashen-spear Priam.
My altar there has never lacked libations
Or the steamy savor that is our due worship."

And Hera, the queen, her eyes big as an ox's:                    *60*

"There are three cities especially dear to me:
Argos, Sparta, and broad Mycenae.
Waste these if they ever annoy you.
I won't stand in the way or take it too hard.
Even if I begrudged you their destruction,
What could I do against your superior strength?
Still, it's not right to cancel all my hard work.
I too am a god, from the same stock as you,
The eldest daughter of devious Cronus,
And honored both by position of birth                            *70*
And as the wife of the lord of all the immortals.
Let's call this a draw and yield to each other,
I to you, and you to me, and the other gods
Will all fall in line. Quickly now,
Dispatch Athena into the war zone
To maneuver the Trojans to break the truce
And do some damage to the exultant Greeks."

Zeus had no wish to argue this,
And he winged these words to Pallas Athena:

"Go down instantly to the battlefield.                           *80*
Get the Trojans to break the truce
And do some damage to the exultant Greeks."

Athena had been longing for action.
She flashed down from the peaks of Olympus

> *Like a star that the son of devious Cronus*
> *Sends as a portent to sailors, or to an army*
> *Camped on a wide plain, a brilliant meteor*
> *That sheds sparks all along its shining furrow.*

This was Pallas Athena rocketing down
Into no-man's-land. They were frozen with awe,           *90*
Horse-breaking Trojans and bronze-kneed Greeks,
Soldiers glancing at each other, saying things like:

"We'll be fighting again soon."

                                    "This could mean peace."

"It means war, if Zeus wants to bring it."

While they exchanged words to this effect,
Athena blended into the crowd, disguised
As a Trojan, Antenor's son Laodocus,
A good man with a spear, and went in search
Of Pandarus and found that son of Lycaon,                          100
Strong and not a blemish on him, standing
With rank on rank of tough, shield-bearing troops
Around him, his men from the banks of Aesepus.
Athena stood next to him and her words flew fast:

"If you listened to me, wise son of Lycaon,
You would take a shot at Menelaus
And win glory and gratitude from the Trojans,
Especially from prince Alexander.
He would give you splendid gifts
If he saw Menelaus, Atreus' warrior son,                           110
Felled by your arrow and laid on the pyre.
Come on, one swift arrow aimed at Menelaus,
And vow to Apollo, the Wolf-born Archer,
That you will offer a hundred firstling lambs
When you come home to your city, sacred Zeleia."

Athena spoke and convinced the fool.
He took out his polished bow, made of the horns
Of a wild ibex that he himself had killed
As it came from behind a rock. Waiting for it,
He shot it in the chest, and it fell back in a cleft.              120
The horns measured sixteen palms from the head,
And the worker in horn fitted them together,
Smoothed it all and tipped it with gold.
This was the bow he bent, bracing it
Carefully on the ground while his men concealed him
With shields, so the Greeks couldn't react
Before Menelaus was hit. He took the lid

From the quiver and drew out a feathered arrow,
Barbed with black pain, that had never been shot.
He fit the bitter arrow quickly to the string                    130
And vowed to Apollo, the Wolf-born Archer,
He would offer a hundred firstling lambs
When he came home to his city, sacred Zeleia.
He drew back the notched arrow until the string
Reached his nipple and the iron arrowhead the bow,
Which bent until it arched into a circle,
Then snapped back twanging, and the string hummed
As the arrow needled over the crowded plain.

But the gods were watching you, Menelaus,
Yes, and especially Athena, who stretched out            140
Her immortal hand and whisked the arrow away
From your bare flesh as lightly as a mother
Sweeps a fly from her sleeping child.
The goddess redirected the arrow
To the golden clasps of your belt
Where the corselet had an extra fold.
The bitter arrow hit the buckled belt
And drove right through its rich design
And pierced the filigreed corselet
And penetrated even the kilt-piece beneath            150
That he wore as proof against javelins.
The arrow's tip just grazed the human skin,
And dark blood started to flow from the wound.

   *In Maeonia and Caria women stain ivory*
   *With scarlet, to be cheek pieces for horses.*
   *Such a piece will lie in a treasure chamber,*
   *And though many horsemen pray to use it*
   *As an ornament for the horse and glory*
   *For the driver, it lies there as a king's prize.*

That, Menelaus, was how your thighs were stained            160
With blood, and your fine shins and ankles beneath.

The warlord Agamemnon went numb
When he saw black blood flowing from the wound,

As did Menelaus himself, whom Ares loved.
But when he saw that the ferrule and barbs
Had not gone in, he breathed easier and revived.
Agamemnon, though, was still groaning deeply,
Holding Menelaus' hand, and his comrades
Added their groans. Agamemnon spoke for them all:

"Dear brother, my oath was your death,                      170
Setting you up to fight the Trojans for us,
And now they've trampled their oath and hit you.
But oaths are not empty: we pledged lambs' blood,
Poured strong wine, and clasped our right hands.
If the Olympian does not act on this immediately
He will in good time, and they will pay heavily
With their heads, their wives, and their children.
Deep down inside I know this for sure:
There will come a day when holy Troy will perish,
And Priam and the people under Priam's ashen spear.      180
Zeus himself, throned in heaven on high,
Will shake his dark aegis over them all
In his wrath for this treachery. This shall be done.
But dreadful grief will be mine if you die,
Menelaus, and meet your destiny now.
I will return to Argos in utter disgrace,
For the Greeks will turn their minds homeward now,
And we will leave Priam and the Trojans to boast
They have Argive Helen. And your bones will rot
As you lie in Trojan soil, your work unfinished.         190
And some arrogant Trojan will say as he leaps
Onto the barrow of glorious Menelaus:
'So much for the wrath of Agamemnon,
Who led the Greek army here for nothing
And has now gone home to his native land
With empty ships, and without good Menelaus.'
On that day may the earth gape open for me."

And Menelaus, cheering him up:

"It's all right. Don't frighten the others.
The arrow didn't hit a fatal spot. My belt                200

Stopped it before it got in very far, that
And the banded kilt-piece the bronzesmiths made."

And lord Agamemnon's response:

"May it be so, dear Menelaus.
But our physician will palpate the wound
And apply medications to stop the pain."

And he said to Talthybius, the godlike herald:

"Talthybius, call Machaon here on the double,
Asclepius' son, our faultless physician,
To see Menelaus. Someone has shot him,                    210
Someone really good with a bow, a Trojan
Or Lycian, to his glory and our grief."

Following his orders, the herald
Went through the welter of Greek bronze,
Looking for Machaon, and spotted him
Standing in the midst of his men, tough
Shield-bearing troops from Tricca's pastures.
He came up to him and spoke winged words:

"Son of Asclepius, lord Agamemnon calls you
To see Menelaus. Someone has shot him,                    220
Someone really good with a bow, a Trojan
Or Lycian, to his glory and our grief."

Machaon's heart was pounding as he made his way
Across the crowded sand and through the troops
Until he came to where Menelaus lay wounded,
All the army's best gathered around him
In a circle, into which he stepped like a god
And quickly drew the arrow from the clasped belt.
As it came out the barbs were broken backward.
Then he undid the metallic belt and, beneath it,          230
The band with the beaten bronze kilt-piece.
When he saw the wound the arrow had made
He sucked out the blood and smeared on

Soothing ointments Chiron had given his father.

   While they were attending to Menelaus,
The Trojans came on under their shields,
As the Greeks strapped on their gear,
And reminded themselves of the joys of war.

Agamemnon swung into action.
You could not have detected in him then                    240
Any tendency toward sloth or cowardice.
He left his bronze-filigreed chariot
With his squire, Eurymedon, who held
The snorting horses off to the side,
And charged him to have them ready
Should he become fatigued. Then he set out,
On foot, to tour the ranks of his army.
He had two set speeches. When he saw men
Eager to fight, he used encouraging words:

"Soldiers of Greece, keep up your fighting spirit!          250
Father Zeus will not aid Trojan perjury.
Those who violated their sacred oaths
Will have vultures feeding on their pudgy flesh,
And their wives and children will be our cargo
After we have taken their city's high rock."

But when he saw men shirking the rigors of war,
He scalded their ears with words like these:

"You pansy archers, you're a disgrace to Greece!
Standing here like a bunch of knock-kneed fawns
Worn out from running across a wide field,                  260
Gaping stupidly without an ounce of strength left.
Are you waiting for the Trojans to come over here
Where your pretty boats are lined up on the shore
So you can see if Zeus will lend you a hand?"

Thus Agamemnon, ranging through the troops,
And in his tour he came to where the Cretans
Were arming themselves around their commander,

Idomeneus, a man with a razor-sharp mind
And the imposing presence of a wild boar,
As he stood in the front ranks, while Meriones          270
Was busy marshalling the lines in the rear.
The warlord Agamemnon liked what he saw
And had some cordial words for Idomeneus:

"Idomeneus, I hold you in the highest regard,
Both in war and in every other activity,
Certainly in the feast, when the Argive lords
Mix wine in the bowl at the council of elders.
Even if every flowing-haired Greek chieftain
Drinks a fixed measure, your cup stays full,
And you drink, as I do, to your heart's content.       280
To battle then, and live up to your old boasts!"

And Idomeneus, the Cretan commander:

"Son of Atreus, you can count on me
To live up to my original pledge.
But rouse the other flowing-haired Greeks
So we can get into battle. The Trojans
Have broken their oath. They will suffer and die
For violating their sacred word."

Agamemnon smiled and moved on,
Coming next to the two captains                         290
Who shared the name Ajax
As they were strapping on their helmets.
Behind them a cloud of infantry loomed.

*A goatherd standing on a rocky lookout*
*Sees a cloud moving in over the purple sea.*
*As a westerly gale sweeps it closer to land*
*It looks blacker than pitch. The sea ruffles*
*Beneath it, the air suddenly turns cold,*
*And the goatherd drives his flock to a cave.*

So the dark battalions behind the two Ajaxes,          300
Squall lines of young men nurtured under the sky,

Bristling with shields and spears.
                                    Agamemnon
Was glad to see them, and his words flew out:

"Ajax, both of you, Achaean commanders,
I would be out of line if I issued you orders.
You push your men to fight hard on your own.
By Father Zeus, by Athena and Apollo,
If all of my men had your kind of heart,
King Priam's city would soon bow her head,                      310
Taken and ravaged under our hands."

He spoke and moved on to the next contingent.
There he found Nestor, the clear-toned orator,
Urging his Pylians on to battle
And arraying them around his captains:
Great Pelagon, Alastor, Chromius,
Haemon, and Bias, shepherd of his people.
Nestor positioned the chariots in front
And massed the best foot soldiers at the rear.
Within this double wall he stationed the riffraff,             320
So that willing or not they would be forced to fight.
Nestor briefed his charioteers first,
Reminding them to control their horses
And not drive recklessly into the mêlée:

"Now don't get overconfident, any of you,
Or be too eager to fight the Trojans alone,
In front of the rest. But no falling back either.
Either course will weaken the line.
When you make contact with an enemy chariot,
Stay in your own and thrust with your spear.                   330
These are battle-proven, time-tested tactics
Used by our ancestors to capture walled towns."

The old man had years of experience in battle.
The warlord Agamemnon was glad to see him
And addressed him with winged words:

"Nestor, old sir! If only your knees

Were as strong as your spirit, but old age
Has worn you down. I'd rather have
Someone else old, and you among the young."

And Nestor, the Gerenian horseman, answered:                340

"Son of Atreus, I wish so myself! To be
As I was when I killed Ereuthalion!
But the gods do not give us all things at once.
I was young then, and now I am old.
Even so, I will be with the charioteers
And urge them on with counsel and words,
As is an elder's privilege. Spearwork
Is for the young men, who trust their strength."

And Agamemnon moved on, glad in his heart.
He found Menestheus next, Peteus' son, standing          350
With his Athenians, masters of the war cry,
And farther up the line crafty Odysseus
With his tough Cephallenians. These troops
Had not yet heard a signal—since the armies
On both sides were just now starting to move—
And were waiting for other Greek battalions
To advance and begin the attack on the Trojans.
When the warlord Agamemnon saw them,
He sent a few barbed words winging their way:

"Son of Peteus—a king nurtured by Zeus—                   360
And you, with all your famous dirty tricks,
Why are you lagging back here, waiting for others?
You two should be taking your stand up front
And throwing yourselves into the heat of battle.
Both of you are first in line when you hear
I am giving a feast for the council of elders.
You like to eat roast meat well enough then
And drink cups of honeyed wine all night,
But now you'd be glad to see ten Greek battalions
Carving up the enemy ahead of you with bronze."          370

Odysseus scowled darkly as he answered:

"What kind of talk is that, Agamemnon?
How can you say we are slack in battle
Whenever the Greeks engage the Trojans?
You will have a chance to see, if you really care,
How Telemachus' father mixes it up
With the horse-whipping Trojans.
What you're saying now is a lot of hot air."

Agamemnon could see he was angry,
And, with a smile, he took back his words:                    380

"Son of Laertes in the line of Zeus,
Odysseus, the master tactician,
I don't mean to give you a hard time.
You and I understand each other.
Go now. We will make it up later.
If there have been any hard words here
May the gods blow them away on the winds."

Leaving them there he went on
And found Diomedes, son of Tydeus,
Standing by his horses and chariot,                          390
With Sthenelus, Capaneus' son, at his side.
When the warlord Agamemnon saw them,
He sent a few barbed words winging their way:

"What's this, the son of the hero Tydeus
Squinting down the lanes of battle from the rear?
It wasn't like Tydeus to cower like this.
He fought the enemy out front with his friends,
As those who saw him in action say. I never
Saw him myself, but they say he was the best.
He came to Mycenae once, not as an enemy                     400
But as a guest, when he and Polyneices
Were taking the field against Thebes' sacred walls.
They needed allies, and the Mycenaeans
Were ready to accede to their request,
But Zeus changed their minds with unlucky omens.
So they left and came in their journey
To the Asopus' deep reeds and grassy banks,

And the Achaeans sent Tydeus out again
On another mission, north to Thebes.
So he went, and found a crowd of Cadmeians                        410
At a feast in mighty Eteocles' house.
Alone as he was, and a stranger there,
The horseman Tydeus was not afraid.
He challenged them all to athletic contests
And easily won every single event,
So much help did Athena give him.
The Cadmeians were angry, and when he left
They laid an ambush along his route back,
Fifty young men under two commanders,
Maeon, son of Haemon, a match for the gods,                      420
And Autophonus' son, staunch Polyphontes.
But Tydeus brought them to an ugly end,
Killing all but one. Maeon alone
He allowed to return, persuaded by portents.
That's what Tydeus the Aetolian was like,
But he had a son who cannot fight so well,
Though he speaks better in council."

He spoke, and Diomedes said nothing at all,
A mark of respect for the royal reproach.
But Capaneus' son, Sthenelus, responded:                         430

"Son of Atreus, don't lie when you know
How to speak the plain truth. We are proud
That we are better than our fathers. We took
Thebes with its seven gates, a lesser army
Against a stronger wall, trusting in the gods.
But our fathers perished by their own recklessness.
So don't put them on a level with us."

Diomedes frowned at this and said:

"Take it easy there, and listen to me.
I don't hold anything against Agamemnon                           440
For getting the troops into gear. After all,
He has more at stake here, greater glory
If the Greeks win and capture Ilion,

And greater grief if the Greeks are defeated.
Let's you and I just keep our minds on fighting."

And he jumped down from his chariot
In full metal. The clang of bronze on his chest
As he moved out would have unnerved anyone.

*A swollen wave pushed by the West Wind*
*Moves closer and closer to a thundering beach.*          450
*It crests in deep water and then breaks*
*Onto the shore with a huge roar and curls over*
*And around the jutting rocks in a spray of brine.*

So too wave after wave of Greek battalions
Moving into combat.
                    The captains
Issued commands; the rest marched on
In such an eerie silence you would have said
That not a soldier in the army had a voice,
But in fact the silence was terror                        460
Of their commanders, and only the mute glow
From their detailed weaponry signalled their advance.

Not so with the Trojan army.

*More ewes than anyone could ever count*
*Are penned in the court of a man of means,*
*Waiting, waiting to give their white milk*
*And bleating incessantly when they hear the lambs.*

Thus the clamor from the immense Trojan muster,
Not one voice, one language,
But a cacophony of tongues from different lands.          470

Behind them, Ares, as behind the Greeks
The goddess Athena with sea-grey eyes,
And on both sides Terror and Panic
And Ares' murderous sister, Eris,
Small when her crest first appears
But so ravenous and relentless in her ways

That she soon thrusts her head into the sky
Even while she keeps her feet on the earth.
This horror now infused equal parts of strife
Into both armies as she patrolled their ranks,     *480*
Swelling the volume of human suffering.

When the two sides closed with each other
They slammed together shields and spears,
Rawhide ovals pressed close, bronze thoraxes
Grinding against each other amid the groans
And exultations of men being slain
And of those slaying, as the earth ran with blood.

*Swollen winter torrents flow together*
*Where two valleys meet. The heavy water*
*From both streams joins in a gorge,*     *490*
*And far off in the mountains*
*A shepherd hears a single, distant roar.*

Equally indistinguishable the shrieking
Of these warriors laboring in union.

Antilochus drew first blood, killing
Echepolus, one of Troy's best.
The quick thrust of Antilochus' spear
Glanced off the rim of his plumed helmet,
But the bronze point pegged his forehead
And bored through the bone. Darkness     *500*
Enveloped him as he fell like a wall.
As he went down, Elephenor,
The Abantes' captain, grabbed him
By the feet and tried to drag him
Quickly out of range to strip the armor.
This effort was short-lived. As Elephenor
Stooped to haul the corpse, Agenor saw him,
And where his shield left his left side exposed
Agenor thrust, crumpling him with his spear.
The life drained out of him, and over his body     *510*
The fighting intensified, Greeks and Trojans
Battering each other like leaping wolves.

One early victim was Anthemion's son,
Simoeisius, a blossoming lad
Whom Telamonian Ajax marked and hit.
His mother bore him on the Simois' banks
On her way down from the slopes of Ida
Where she had gone to see her family's flocks.
So his parents called him Simoeisius,
But he died before he could pay them back                   520
For rearing him. As he advanced
In the Trojan front lines, the bronze point
Of Ajax's spear pierced his right nipple
And ripped through his shoulder. He fell
Down to the ground and lay in the dust.

> *A poplar that has grown up in rich bottom soil,*
> *With a smooth trunk branching out at top,*
> *Catches the eye of a wainwright, who wants*
> *To curve it into a pole for a fine chariot.*
> *He cuts it with a few flashing strokes of his axe,*     530
> *And now it lies drying by the river bank.*

When Ajax had dispatched him, Antiphus,
One of Priam's sons, gleaming in his corselet,
Threw his javelin at him through the crowd,
Missing Ajax but hitting a man named Leucas,
One of Odysseus' companions, in the groin,
As he was hauling the body off to one side.
The corpse fell from his hands and he slumped over it.
Odysseus took his death hard. He strode forward
Through the front ranks glowing in his bronze              540
And, sweeping the enemy lines with his eyes,
Cast his javelin. The Trojans fell back
As the javelin homed in on Democoön,
Priam's bastard son from his horse farm in Abydos.
With the weight of Odysseus' anger behind it
The spearpoint entered one temple and came out
Through the other. Darkness enveloped
Democoön's eyes. He fell with a thud,
And his armor clattered on his back.
The Trojan front lines, and Hector with them,             550

Gave ground. The Greeks cheered, dragged off
The bodies, and charged far ahead.
　　　　　　　　　　　　　　Apollo,
Looking down at all this from Pergamum,
Was indignant, and yelled to the Trojans:

"Get back into the fight! Greek skin
Is not stone or iron. It will not deflect bronze.
Nor is Achilles, son of Thetis, in combat,
But nurses his rage in the beachhead camp."

Thus the dread god spoke from the city.　　　　　　　560
　　　　　　　　　　　　But the Greeks
Were urged on by Zeus' daughter
Wherever she saw them faltering.

Diores, though, was skewered by Fate.
Peirus, the Thracian leader, had caught him
Just above the ankle with a jagged stone
That crushed both tendons and bones.
He fell backward into the dust, hands stretched
Toward his friends, gasping out his life.
Peirus ran up and finished him off　　　　　　　570
With a slicing spear thrust near his navel.
His guts spilled out, and everything went black.
As Peirus jumped back, Thoas the Aetolian
Hit him in the chest above the nipple.
The bronze caught in his lung. Thoas closed,
Pulled the spear out, drew his sword
And slashed his belly open. This finished him,
But Thoas did not get to strip off Peirus' armor
Because his men, top-knotted Thracians
With long spears in hand, drove him off,　　　　　　580
Big as he was, and sent him reeling.

And so the two lay side by side in the dust,
The Thracian leader stretched out by the Epeian,
And around them many others were killed.

No one could trust his immunity any longer,

Not even those who had danced their way through
Unscathed until now, led by the hand by Pallas Athena
Through the hail of whetted bronze instruments.
This was a day many Greeks and Trojans
Paired off with each other to lie in the dust.                        590

# ILIAD 5

Pallas Athena now gave to Diomedes,
Tydeus' son, the strength and courage
That would make him shine
Among the Greeks and win him glory.
Starlight flowed from his helmet and shield,
As if Sirius had just risen from the sea
Before dawn in autumn, and that brightest of stars
Was blazing from his torso and face
Instead of from the sky.
                              Athena aimed him                    10
To where the battle was thickest.

There was a Trojan named Dares,
A rich man without a blemish on him
And a priest of Hephaestus. He had two sons,
Phegeus and Idaeus, trained warriors.
These two now separated themselves
From the crowd and went for Diomedes,
They in their chariot, he on foot.
When they closed, Phegeus threw.
His spear sailed high, passing well over               20
The left shoulder of Diomedes,
Who kept on coming, launching a shot
That hit Phegeus' chest between his nipples
And knocked him from his rig. Idaeus
Jumped for it, abandoning his chariot

And his slain brother, whose prostrate corpse
He did not have the courage to defend.
He himself would not have escaped black death
If Hephaestus had not got him out of there,
Wrapping him in night, so that the old man, 30
His priest, would not be utterly bereaved.
Diomedes did get the horses though,
And had his men drive them back to the ships.
When the Trojans saw Dares' two sons,
One in flight, the other dead by his chariot,
Their hearts shrivelled. Athena's cold grey eyes
Bored in on Ares. She took his hand and said:

"Ares, you bloodthirsty marauder,
Why don't we let the Greeks and Trojans fight,
And see to which side Father Zeus gives glory. 40
We'd both best withdraw, and avoid his anger."

And with that she led Ares away from the battle
And made him sit on the Scamander's sandy banks,
While the Greeks pushed the Trojans back. Each leader
Took out his man. First, the warlord Agamemnon
Knocked Odius, the Halizones' commander,
Out of his chariot as he led the retreat,
Planting a spear between his shoulder blades
And driving it out through his chest. He fell
With a thud, and his armor clanged on his body. 50

Idomeneus killed Phaestus, the Maeonian
Who had come from Tarne's black soil,
Threading his spear through his right shoulder
As he tried to mount his chariot but instead
Fell back from it into the loathsome dark.
Idomeneus' squires stripped off his armor.

Menelaus killed Scamandrius.
This man had been taught to hunt
By Artemis herself, and could shoot
Any animal the mountain forest nourished. 60
But neither the goddess nor all his old skill

In archery could help him now. Menelaus
Planted a spear between his shoulder blades
And drove it out through his chest. He fell
With a thud, and his armor clanged on his body.

Meriones killed Phereclus, whose father
Was Tecton and grandfather Harmon
And who was himself a skilled craftsman,
For Pallas Athena loved him prodigiously.
He could build all sorts of intricate things,                    70
And had built for Paris the doomed hulls
That first spelled evil for Troy, and for himself,
Since he had no inkling of the gods' oracles.
Meriones ran him down from behind
And hit him in the right buttock. The spearpoint
Slid beneath the bone clear through the bladder.
He fell to his knees, and groaned as death took him.

Meges took out Pedaeus, Antenor's son.
Though he was a bastard, Theano raised him
As one of her own, to please her husband.                        80
Now Meges got close enough to him
To send his spear through the tendon
At the back of his neck and on into his mouth,
Cutting away the tongue at its root. He fell
Into the dust, his teeth clenched on cold bronze.

Eurypylus got Hypsenor, son of Dolopion
And honored priest of the River Scamander.
Euaemon's glorious son Eurypylus
Caught up with him as he sprinted away
And, without breaking stride, slashed                            90
At the man's shoulder with his sword
And lopped off his arm, which fell
In a bloody mass to the ground. Death
Covered his eyes with a purple haze.

This was their labor in the crush of battle.
As for Diomedes, you could not tell
Which side he belonged to, Greek or Trojan,

As he boiled across the plain.

> *A winter torrent*
> *Will sweep away the thickset riprap*                                    100
> *Meant to contain it, and flood over also*
> *The vineyard walls, when the rain of Zeus*
> *Makes its swollen waters suddenly rise*
> *And obliterate many fine human works.*

So too before Tydeus' son were driven
Thick Trojan battalions. Many as they were,
They could not withstand this single human tide.

When Pandarus saw him storming across the plain
And driving entire battalions before him,
He bent his curved bow and, taking aim at Diomedes,                   110
Hit him on the fly in his right shoulder,
The arrow piercing the corselet plate
And spattering it with blood as it punched through.
And Pandarus whooped:

"Got him! Take heart, Trojan horsemen,
The best of the Achaeans is hit! I don't think
He will hold up long under that stiff shaft
If Apollo in truth sent me forth from Lycia."

Half prayer, half boast. But the arrow didn't kill him.
Diomedes took cover next to his horses and car                        120
And, still standing, said to Sthenelus, his driver:

"Son of Capaneus, get down from the car
And pull this arrow out of my shoulder."

Sthenelus vaulted down to the ground,
Steadied himself, and drew the arrow
Clean through his shoulder and out the other side.
Blood spurted through the linked tunic,
And Diomedes, good at the war shout, prayed:

"Hear me, daughter of Zeus! If ever
You stood by my father's side, a friend                    *130*
In the heat of battle, stand by me now,
Goddess Athena. Deliver unto me
And place within the range of my spear
The man who hit me before I saw him
And boasted I would not see for long
The brilliant light of Helios the Sun."

Pallas Athena heard Diomedes' prayer.
She made his body lithe and light,
Then feathered these words into his ear:

"Go after the Trojans for all you're worth,             *140*
Diomedes. I have put into your heart
Your father's heroic temper, the fearless
Fighting spirit of Tydeus the horseman,
Tydeus the Shield. And I have removed
The mist that has clouded your eyes
So that now you can tell god from man.
Do not fight with any immortal
Who might come and challenge you,
Except Aphrodite, daughter of Zeus.
If she comes you may wound her with bronze."           *150*

With these words the grey-eyed one was gone,
And Diomedes returned to the front.
He had been eager before to fight the Trojans
But now his fury was tripled.

*A shepherd wounds a lion as he leaps a pen's wall.*
*But far from being weakened, the lion*
*Gains in strength, and the unprotected flock*
*Is little more than a pile of bloody fleece*
*Before the angered lion leaps out again.*

So too Diomedes among the Trojans,                     *160*
Killing next Astynous and Hypeiron,

One with a spearcast above his nipple,
The other with a swordstroke to the collar-bone,
Shearing off the entire shoulder
From the neck and back. He let them lie
And went after Abas and Polyidus,
Sons of old Eurydamas, who read dreams,
But read no dreams for them when they left home.
Diomedes cut them down and moved on.
There were two more brothers, Xanthus and Thoön,            170
Sons of Phaenops, who loved them well.
He was worn out with old age and its miseries
And had no other son to be his heir.
Diomedes killed them too, taking their lives
And leaving for the father sorrow and grief.
They would not live to be welcomed home,
And others would divide their inheritance.

His next victims were two sons of Priam,
Echemmon and Chromius, in one chariot.
Diomedes jumped on them                                     180

                    *as a lion*
      *Leaps on a heifer grazing peacefully*
      *In a woodland pasture, and breaks her neck.*

It was a brutal dismount the son of Tydeus
Forced them to make. He then stripped their armor,
And his men drove their horses back to the ships.

   Aeneas saw him wrecking the Trojan ranks
And made his way through the busy spears
Searching for Pandarus. When he found him,
Looking like the match for a god that he was,               190
He went up to him and had this to say:

"Pandarus, where are your arrows and bow,
And your fame? No one here or in all Lycia
Can compete with you or claim to be better.
Say a prayer to Zeus and take a shot at this man—

Whoever he is—who is beating the daylights
Out of the Trojans, some of our best too.
It could be he's a god, angry with the Trojans
Over some sacrifice. That would be tough."

Lycaon's splendid son came back with this:                    *200*

"Aeneas, he looks like Diomedes to me,
His shield, his grooved helmet, his horses.
I'm not at all sure that he's not a god,
But if he is who I think he is, Tydeus' son,
He's not fighting like this without some god
Standing at his side and cloaked in mist.
I swear one of the immortals turned aside
An arrow I already shot at him
Just as it struck. It wound up hitting him
In the right shoulder, clean through his breastplate.    *210*
I thought I had sent him down to Hades,
But I didn't get him. *Some* god is sure angry.
Anyway, I don't have a chariot now,
Or horses to pull it—not that there aren't eleven
Beautiful new chariots back in Lycaon's palace,
Covered with cloths, and a yoke of horses
Beside each one eating white barley and spelt.
Yes, and Lycaon, the old spearman,
Told me as I left to go to war mounted,
Advice I should have taken but didn't,                        *220*
Sparing the horses because I was afraid
That in an army this big they would lack feed,
And they had been used to eating all they wanted.
So I left them, and came to Ilion on foot,
Trusting my bow, for all the good it has done.
I've taken shots at two of their best,
Diomedes and Menelaus, and hit them both,
Drew blood for sure, and only made them madder.
Curse the day I took my bow from its peg
And led my Trojan troops to lovely Ilion                      *230*
As a favor to Hector. If I ever return
And see my land, my wife, and my high-roofed home,

May my throat be cut by a thief in the night
If I fail to smash my bow in pieces
And throw it in the fire. It's been a piece of junk."

And Aeneas, the Trojan commander, replied:

"Don't talk like that. Things won't get any better
Until you and I take a chariot
And face him in combat. Come on, get in mine,
And you'll see what the horses of Tros can do.                    240
They know how to eat up the plain, and how to
Cut and turn, in pursuit or flight,
And they will get us back to the city in safety
If Zeus gives Diomedes the glory again.
Get in and take the lash and the reins,
And I'll dismount to fight; or you
Take him on, and leave the horses to me."

Lycaon's splendid son came back with this:

"Keep the reins, Aeneas, and drive your own horses.
They will pull better for a driver they know              250
In case we have to run from the son of Tydeus.
I wouldn't want them to be spooked, and shy
From pulling us out because they miss your voice—
Not with Diomedes all over us. He'd kill us both
And make off with your horses. No, you drive them,
And I'll meet his charge with my spear."

So they mounted the chariot and drove off
Full speed ahead toward the son of Tydeus.

Sthenelus saw them coming and said to Diomedes:

"Here comes a duo now with muscle to spare              260
And hot to fight you. One is good with a bow,
Pandarus, who boasts he is Lycaon's son.
The other is Aeneas, who says his mother
Is Aphrodite, and Anchises his father.
Let's retreat in the chariot. Calm down

And get out of action or you'll get yourself killed."

Diomedes looked him up and down and said:

"Don't talk to me about retreating, Sthenelus.
It's not in me to dodge a fight. Besides,
I still have my strength. I'm not even going                    270
To get in the chariot, much less retreat in it.
I'll take them on just like this. Pallas Athena
Won't *let* me back down. As for these two,
Their horses won't be carrying them both away,
Even if one of them manages to escape.
And one thing more. Athena has many plans,
But if she does give me the glory here
And I kill them both, hold our horses
On this spot, tying the reins to the chariot rail,
And rush Aeneas' horses. Drive them back                       280
Away from the Trojans and to the Greek lines.
These horses come from the stock that Zeus
Gave to Tros as payment for his son Ganymede.
The finest horses under the sun. Anchises
Stole some of the breed from Laomedon
By secretly putting his mares to them,
And so got six colts born in his own palace.
Four he kept for himself and reared at the stall,
And two he gave to Aeneas, superb warhorses.
If we could take these, it'd be a real coup."                  290

Thus Diomedes and his driver.
                              Their two opponents
Drove their thoroughbreds hard
And quickly closed the gap, and Pandarus,
Lycaon's splendid son, called out:

"You're tough, Diomedes, a real pedigreed hero.
So I only stung you with that arrow?
Well, let's see what I can do with a spear."

The shaft cast a long shadow as it left his hand
And hit Diomedes' shield. The bronze apex                      300

Sheared through and stopped
Just short of his breastplate.
Pandarus, thinking he had hit him, whooped again:

"Got you right through the belly, didn't I?
You're done for, and you've handed me the glory."

Diomedes answered him levelly:

"You didn't even come close, but I swear
One of you two goes down now
And gluts Ares with his blood."

His javelin followed his voice, and Athena                        *310*
Guided it to where the nose joins the eye-socket.
The bronze crunched through the pearly teeth
And sheared the tongue at its root, exiting
At the base of the chin.
                          Pandarus fell from the car,
His armor scattering the hard light
As it clattered on his fallen body.
His horses shied—
          Quick movement of hooves—
As his soul seeped out into the sand.                              *320*

Aeneas vaulted down with his shield and spear,
Afraid that the Greeks might drag the body away.
He straddled it like a lion sure of its strength,
Spear straight out, crouched behind his shield's disk,
Only too glad to kill whoever stood up to him,
His mouth open in a battle-howl.
                          But Tydeus' son
Levered up in one hand a slab of stone
Much too large for two men to lift—
As men are now—lifted it and smashed it                           *330*
Into Aeneas' hip, where the thigh-bone turns
In the socket that medics call the cup.
The rough stone shattered this joint and severed
Both tendons, ripping open the skin. The hero
Sank to his knees, clenching the dirt with one hand,

While midnight settled upon both his eyes.

That would have been the end of Aeneas,
But his mother Aphrodite, Zeus' daughter
(Who bore Aeneas to Anchises the oxherd),
Had all this in sharp focus. Her milk-white arms                340
Circled around him and she enfolded him
In her radiant robe to prevent the Greeks
From killing him with a spear to the chest.

As she was carrying him out of the battle,
Sthenelus remembered the instructions
Diomedes had given him. He held his own horses
Away from the boiling dust, tying the reins
To the chariot rail, and, on foot, stampeded
Aeneas' beautiful horses toward the Greek lines,
Giving them to Deipylus, the boyhood friend                    350
He valued most and whose mind was like his,
To drive back to the ships. Then he mounted
His own chariot, took the glossy reins in hand,
And drove his heavy-hooved horses off to find
Tydeus' son, who was himself in armed pursuit
Of Aphrodite. Diomedes knew
This was a weakling goddess, not one of those
Who control human warfare—no Athena,
No Enyo here, who demolishes cities—
And when he caught up to her in the mêlée                      360
He pounced at her with his spear and, thrusting,
Nicked her on her delicate wrist, the blade
Piercing her skin through the ambrosial robe
That the Graces themselves had made for her.
The cut was just above the palm, and the goddess'
Immortal blood oozed out, or rather
The ichor that flows in the blessed gods' veins,
Who, eating no bread and drinking no wine,
Are bloodless and therefore deathless as well.
The goddess shrieked and let her son fall,                     370
And Phoebus Apollo gathered him up
In an indigo cloud to keep the Greeks
From killing him with a spear to the chest.

And Diomedes, yelling above the battle noise:

"Get out of the war, daughter of Zeus!
Don't you have enough to do distracting
Weak women? Keep meddling in war and
You'll learn to shiver when it's even mentioned."

The goddess, in extreme distress now,
Went off in a daze. Wind-footed Iris                    380
Took her and led her through the throng,
Throbbing with pain, her pale skin bruised.
After a while she found Ares, sitting
On the left of the battle, his spear propped
Against a bank of mist, his horses standing by.
Aphrodite fell to her knees and begged
Her brother for his gold-frontleted horses:

"Brother dear, lend me your horses
And help me get to Olympus. I'm hurt,
Wounded by a mortal, Diomedes,                          390
Who would fight even Father Zeus."

Ares gave her the gold-frontleted horses.
She mounted the chariot gingerly,
And Iris stepped in and took the reins.
She cracked the whip and the team flew off
And came in no time to steep Olympus,
The gods' homestead.
                        Iris, a blur of windy light,
Halted the team, unyoked them,
And cast before them their ambrosial fodder.            400

Aphrodite went in to her mother,
Dione, and fell in her lap.
                        And Dione,
Cradling her daughter in her arms,
And stroking her with her hand, said:

"Oh my poor baby, who did this to you?
To treat you like this! What did you do?"

And Aphrodite, the goddess who loved to smile:

"Tydeus' son wounded me, that bully
Diomedes, because I was carrying my son           410
Out of range, Aeneas, who is my dearest.
The war has gone far beyond Trojans and Greeks.
The Greeks are fighting the immortal gods."

Dione answered in her lustrous voice:

"You must bear it, my child. I know it hurts.
Many of us Olympians have suffered harm
From men, giving tit for tat to each other.
Ares did, when Otus and Ephialtes,
Those bullies, sons of Aloeus, kept him tied him up
In a bronze jar for thirteen months.                  420
They would have destroyed the God of War
If their stepmother, beautiful Eëriboea,
Hadn't told Hermes. He got Ares out,
But the painful bonds had about done him in.
Hera suffered too, when Heracles shot her
Right in the breast with a triple-pronged arrow,
And there was no helping the pain she had then.
Hades too, formidable as he is, had to endure
An arrow the same man shot him with
Among the dead in Pylos, making him suffer.          430
He went to the house of Zeus on Olympus
In agony, pierced with pain. The arrow
Had driven right through his shoulder.
Paieon rubbed on an anodyne
And healed him, Hades being no mortal.
Heracles was simply outrageous and reckless
To provoke the Olympian gods with arrows.
And now Athena has set this man upon you,
This fool Diomedes, who doesn't understand
That a man who fights with gods doesn't last long,   440
His children don't sit on his lap calling him 'Papa'
To welcome him home from the horrors of war.
So as strong as he is, he had better watch out
Or someone braver than you might fight him,

And Aegialeia, Adrastus' heroic daughter,
The wife of Diomedes, tamer of horses,
Will wake her family from sleep with lamenting
Her wedded husband, the best of the Achaeans."

And with both her hands she wiped off the ichor.
The wrist was healed, and the pain subsided.                    450

Athena and Hera were looking on
And making snide remarks to provoke Zeus.
The grey-eyed goddess opened with this:

"You won't get angry if I say something,
Will you, Father Zeus? The truth is this:
Aphrodite has been urging some Greek lady
To traipse after her beloved Trojans,
And while she was stroking this gowned beauty
She scratched her frail little hand on a golden brooch."

The Father of Gods and Men smiled                              460
And calling Aphrodite said to her:

"Dear child, war isn't your specialty, you know.
You just take care of the pleasures of love
And leave the fighting to Ares and Athena."

While these gods were talking to each other,
Diomedes leapt upon Aeneas, even though
He knew Apollo's hands were there above him.
Great as Apollo was, Diomedes meant
To kill the Trojan and strip off his armor.
Three times he leapt in homicidal frenzy,                      470
Three times Apollo flicked his lacquered shield,
But when he charged a fourth, last time,
He heard a voice that seemed to come
From everywhere at once, and knew it was
Apollo's voice, saying to him:

"Think it over, son of Tydeus, and get back.
Don't set your sights on the gods. Gods are

To humans what humans are to crawling bugs."

Even at this, Diomedes only backed up a little,
Just out of range of the wrathful god.     *480*

And Apollo took Aeneas from the swarm
Up to his temple on sacred Pergamum.
There Leto and arrowy Artemis healed him
In the great sanctuary, and made him glorious.
And silver-bowed Apollo made a phantom
To look like Aeneas, armor and all,
And over this wraith the Greeks and Trojans
Battered each other with their rawhide shields
Until the edges were tattered into leather fringe.
Apollo then called out to the God of War:     *490*

"Ares, you bloodthirsty marauder,
Would you be so kind as to take this Diomedes
Out of action, before he goes up against Zeus?
He's already wounded Cypris on the wrist,
And came after me like a raging demon."

Apollo then sat down on Pergamum's height,
While Ares went to spur on the Trojans,
Disguised as Acamas, the Thracian commander.
He called out to the well-born sons of Priam:

"You sons of Priam, a king bred by Zeus,     *500*
How long will you allow your men to be killed
By the Achaean forces? Perhaps until
They are fighting right in front of our gates?
Aeneas is down, son of noble Anchises,
A man whom we honored as much as Hector.
Let's save our comrade from the boiling dust."

This caught their attention. And Sarpedon
Added his voice, scolding Hector sternly:

"Where has your will to fight gone, Hector?
You used to say you could hold the city     *510*

Without any allies, just yourself
Backed by your brothers and sisters' husbands.
I don't see a single one of them now
Who's not cringing like a dog before a lion.
The only ones fighting are us, the allies.
I'm only an ally myself, from a long way off.
It's a long way to Lycia, by eddying Xanthus,
Where I left my dear wife and baby boy,
And all my property and envied wealth.
And yet I press my Lycians into battle                    520
And take on my man, with nothing of mine here
For the Achaeans to take or drive away.
But you can't even be troubled to urge your men
To take a stand and defend their own wives.
Watch out you're not caught like flies in a web,
An easy prey for your enemies,
Who will waste your populous city.
You should be worrying about this day and night
And begging the captains of your gallant allies
To hold their ground—or take the heat yourself."        530

Sarpedon's speech cut Hector to the quick.
He leapt to the ground with all his gear
And, brandishing a pair of sharp spears,
Roamed the ranks, urging everyone to fight.
The noise intensified, and with a roar
The Trojans whirled to face the Achaeans,
Who remained in tight formation and did not flinch.

*Wind carries chaff over the holy threshing floors*
*When men are winnowing, and Demeter herself,*
*Blonde in the blowing wind, separates*                  540
*The grain from the chaff, and the piles of chaff*
*That accumulate grow whiter and whiter.*

So too the Greeks under the cloud of white dust
Their horses' hooves kicked up from the plain
As the chariots wheeled into action again
And men locked up in hand-to-hand combat.

The bronze sky paled. Ares, who was everywhere
At once now, covered the battle with night
To help the Trojans, honoring the request
Of sungold Apollo, who had asked him to rouse          550
The Trojans' spirit when he saw that Athena,
Who supported the Greeks, had gone off.
Apollo chose this moment to send forth Aeneas
From his rich sanctuary, infused with strength.
Aeneas took his place in the ranks. The men
Were glad to see him come back to join them,
Alive and well and in good fighting form.
But they did not have time to question him,
Busy as they were with what Apollo was doing
With the help of Ares and ravenous Strife.          560

The Greeks were rallied by the two Ajaxes
Along with Odysseus and Diomedes—
Not that they quailed before the Trojan attack.

> *In still weather, when the winds that usually*
> *Scatter the shadowy clouds are asleep,*
> *Huge banks of mist lie absolutely steady*
> *Where Zeus has set them on the mountain tops.*

The Greeks met the Trojans without a tremor.

Agamemnon ranged among them, commanding:

"Be men, my friends. Fight with valor          570
And with a sense of shame before your comrades.
You're less likely to be killed with a sense of shame.
Running away never won glory or a fight."

And with a quick throw of his spear he hit
One of Aeneas' men, Deicoön,
Son of Pergasus, whom the Trojans respected
As much as Priam's sons, quick as he was
To fight in the front lines. Agamemnon's spear
Hit his shield, which did not stop the bronze point

From penetrating all the way through                590
And into his belly, below his belt. He fell
With a thud, and his armor clanged.

Then Aeneas killed two of Greece's best,
Crethon and Orsilochus, the sons of Diocles,
A man of substance who lived in Pherae
And was descended from the river Alpheus,
Whose broad stream flows through the Pylians' land,
And who begot Ortilochus to rule over many.
This Ortilochus was the father of Diocles,
Who had twin sons, Crethon and Orsilochus,           590
Highly trained warriors. They had just reached
Manhood when they went with the Argives
On the black ships to Ilion, famed for its horses,
To win recompense for the sons of Atreus,
But death enfolded them both in that land.

> *Two cubs a mother lion has reared in the mountains,*
> *Where the woods are thick, will begin snatching*
> *Cattle and sheep from human settlements*
> *And continue ravaging the flocks for years*
> *Until humans finally hunt them down.*            600

So these two brothers, beaten to the ground
By Aeneas.
               They fell like tall fir trees,
And as they fell Menelaus pitied them.
He strode through the foremost fighters
Gleaming in his bronze and shaking two spears,
Spurred on by Ares, whose intention was
That Menelaus go down at Aeneas' hands.
But Antilochus, Nestor's son, saw him
And strode through the front lines, afraid          610
That if anything happened to Menelaus
The Greeks would be robbed of all their hard work.
The two had just squared off, their spears
Pointed directly at each other, when Antilochus
Took his place right next to Menelaus.
Aeneas, quick as he was in battle,

Did not stay around when he saw the two of them
Standing their ground together. They pulled
The dead brothers back to the Achaean lines
And put them in their comrades' arms,                         620
Then returned to fight in the foremost ranks.

Working as a team, they killed Pylaemenes,
The great Paphlagonian commander,
And Mydon his charioteer. Menelaus
Put his spear through Pylaemenes' collarbone
As he stood stock-still. His squire Mydon
Was trying to turn the horses when Antilochus
Hit him with a stone on the elbow. The reins,
White with ivory, fell from his hands to the ground,
And Antilochus jumped him, driving his sword               630
Through his temple. He gasped and pitched forward,
Landing headfirst in the soft, deep sand,
Where he stuck up to his shoulders, feet upright,
And held that position for some time, until
His horses knocked him over with their hooves.
Antilochus drove them back toward the camp.

Hector saw all this from across the ranks
And charged them with a shout. Trojans
Poured after him in force, led by Ares
And Enyo in her power, who held in her hands            640
The deafening, shameless horror of War.
Ares cradled an enormous spear in his hands
And fell in with Hector, moving ahead of him
Or a pace or two behind. Diomedes
Stopped dead in his tracks when he saw him.

> *A man crossing the great plains comes to a river*
> *And is so startled when he sees the water*
> *Churning to the sea that he takes a step backward.*

So Diomedes gave ground, and said to his men:

"Well, my friends, we always thought Hector              650
Was a good man with a spear, a real fighter.

It turns out a god is always at his side,
Ares right now, disguised as a mortal.
Keep your face toward the enemy and back up
Steadily. Don't be too eager to fight with gods."

Thus Diomedes, and the Trojans closed in.
Hector killed two men, good fighters,
Menesthes and Anchialus, riding together.
As they fell, big Ajax pitied them
And came to stand close by. He threw                    660
His shining spear and hit Amphius,
Son of Selagus, a man from Paesus
Who had rich farms there, but Fate led him
To come to the aid of Priam and his sons.
Ajax's tree of a spear hit him in the belly,
Going right through the belt. He fell heavily,
And Ajax rushed up to strip his armor
But was met with a hail of Trojan missiles
Gleaming in the air, many of which
He collected on his shield. Still, big Ajax           670
Planted his heel upon the corpse and pulled out
His bronze spear. He was not able, though,
To get the armor unstrapped, pressed as he was
By the spears, and fearing a pincer movement
By the numerous and now confident Trojans.
Big as Ajax was, they pushed him back,
And he staggered as he gave ground.

While these struggles were going on,
Fate aroused Tlepolemus,
A son of Heracles, tall and handsome,                  680
To go up against godlike Sarpedon.
When these two were in range of each other,
Son and grandson of Zeus in the clouds,
It was Tlepolemus who was first to speak:

"Well, well, Sarpedon the Lycian.
What are you doing skulking around here?
You wouldn't know what to do in a fight.
They lie when they say you're a son of Zeus.

You don't even come close to the heroes
Who were born from Zeus in the old days—                    *690*
Like my father, lion-hearted Heracles,
Who came here once for Laomedon's mares
With only six ships and a few men
But sacked Troy and emptied her streets.
You have a coward's heart, and your race is dying.
Your coming from Lycia is not going to help
The men of Troy. I don't care how strong you are,
You're going through Hades' gates, beaten by me."

And Sarpedon, the Lycian commander:

"Tlepolemus, your father sacked Ilion                       *700*
Because Laomedon was foolish enough
To deride the man who had helped him
And withhold the horses he had come so far to get.
As for you, I'm going to work out
A bloody death for you. You're going to give
Glory to me, and your soul to Hades."

Sarpedon spoke, and Tlepolemus lifted
His ash-wood spear. They both cast at once,
And the spears crossed in flight. Sarpedon's
Hit Tlepolemus full in the neck. The point          *710*
Passed completely, and painfully, through,
And ebony night enfolded his eyes.
Tlepolemus' spear hit Sarpedon's left thigh.
The point slashed through with a vengeance
And grazed the bone, but his father saved him, for now.

Sarpedon's men carried him out of battle,
The long spear trailing heavily. In their haste,
No one noticed it or thought to draw it out,
Which would have allowed him to use his legs.
It was difficult work tending him at all.                    *720*

On the other side, the Greeks bore Tlepolemus
Away from the fighting.
                         Odysseus

Saw all this and longed for action.
He debated inwardly whether he should
Pursue the son of thundering Zeus
Or take instead many Lycian lives.
It was not Odysseus' fate to kill Sarpedon,
So Athena focussed his mind on the Lycians.
He killed Coeranus, Alastor, and Chromius,                    730
Alcandrus, Halius, Noemon, and Prytanis,
And he would have killed more, but Hector
Was quick to see what was going on,
And strode through the foremost fighters,
Helmet shining above his flaming bronze,
Bringing terror to the Greeks and joy
To Sarpedon, who groaned as he spoke:

"Son of Priam, don't let me lie here
As prey for the Greeks. Help me.
If I must die, let me die in your city,                        740
Since I will never return to my own land
To make glad my wife and infant son."

Hector did not waste any time answering
But sprinted past, helmet glancing in light,
In his passion to drive the Argives back
And kill as many of them as he could.

And godlike Sarpedon was made to sit
Beneath the beautiful oak sacred to Zeus,
And Pelagon, his comrade, pulled the spear
Out of his thigh. His spirit left him,                        750
And a mist poured down over his eyes.
Then the North Wind blew upon him, and he
Breathed again, though he had gasped out his soul.

Under pressure from Ares and Hector,
The Greeks neither turned and made for their ships,
Nor held their own in the fight, but eased themselves
Backward, now that they knew the Trojans had Ares.

The killing began with certain Greeks
Distinguished as Hector's and Ares' victims:
Godlike Teuthras; Orestes, a horsedriver;                     *760*
Oenomaus and Trechus, Aetolian spearmen;
Helenus, son of Oenops; and Oresbius,
A prosperous Boeotian with a gilded corselet.

The havoc continued, and when Hera noticed
That the Greeks were being crushed in battle,
Her words flew fast to Pallas Athena:

"This is a disaster, daughter of Zeus.
Our word to Menelaus that he would go home
With Troy demolished will come to nothing
If we allow Ares to rage on like this.                        *770*
Come. It's time we remembered how to fight."

Athena, the grey-eyed goddess, agreed.
And Hera, queen of heaven, daughter of Cronus,
Got busy harnessing the horses, gold-frontleted,
While Hebe slid the bronze, eight-spoked wheels
Onto the car's iron axle, wheels with pure gold rims
Fitted with bronze tires, a stunning sight,
And the hubs spinning on both sides were silver.
The car's body was made of gold and silver straps
Stretched tight, and had a double railing.                    *780*
From it projected a silver pole, and at its end
Hebe bound the golden yoke, and on that she hung
The golden harness. Hera led the quick-hooved horses
Beneath the yoke, her heart pounding for war.

Athena, meanwhile, Zeus' favorite daughter,
Let her supple robe slip down to her father's floor,
This embroidered garment her own handiwork.
She put on one of cloudy Zeus' tunics
And strapped on her armor. Around her shoulders
She flung the tasseled aegis, bordered with Rout             *790*
And inset with the blood-chilling horrors of War,

In the center of which was a Gorgon's head,
The dread insignia of Zeus Aegis-Holder.
On her head she put a gold helmet, knobbed and horned,
And embossed with a hundred cities' soldiery.
She stepped into the blazing chariot cradling a spear
Long and thick enough for heaven's daughter
To level battalions of heroes in her wrath.

Hera quickly flicked the horses with the lash,
And the automatic gates of heaven                                    800
Groaned open, as willed by the Hours,
Who control access to Olympus and heaven,
Opening and shutting the dense cloudbanks.
Through this gate they drove the patient horses
And found Zeus sitting apart from the other gods
On the highest peak of ridged Olympus.
White-armed Hera reined in the horses there
And put her questions to the Most High:

"Father Zeus, doesn't Ares infuriate you
With his reckless destruction of so many Greeks,                     810
Much to my sorrow, while Cypris and Apollo,
Smug at their success, are lounging around
With this mindless bully who knows no law?
Father Zeus, will you be angry with me
If I knock Ares silly and out of the battle?"

And Zeus, clouds scudding around him:

"Better to put Athena onto him;
She's always been the best at giving him grief."

White-armed Hera did not disobey.
She lashed the horses and they flew with a will                      820
Between the starry heavens and earth.
One bound of the gods' horses
Takes them as far into the misty distance
As a lookout can see over the wine-blue Aegean.

When they came to Troy and to the confluence
Of the Scamander and Simois rivers,
The white-armed goddess reined in the horses,
Unyoked them, and shed a thick mist around them.
Simois made ambrosia sprout up for them.

The two goddesses, though passionate to come                    *830*
To the aid of the Greeks, stepped forward
As quietly as doves. They were soon in the thick of things
Where the army's elite, drawn to Diomedes' strength,
Clustered around him like huge animals, lions
Or razorback hogs that can rip a man apart.
Hera took her stance there and transformed herself
To look like Stentor, whose bronze voice sounds as loud
As fifty voices combined. And she yelled:

"For shame, Greeks! You're all show and no fight.
When godlike Achilles used to enter battle                      *840*
The Trojans wouldn't so much as leave their gates
Out of fear for what his spear could do.
Now they have us backed up against our ships."

This got their fighting spirit up. Meanwhile,
Grey-eyed Athena flashed to Diomedes' side.
She found that prince beside his horses and car,
Cooling the wound from Pandarus' arrow.
The sweat where his broad shield strap rubbed
Was bothering him, and his arm was sore.
He was lifting the strap and wiping off                         *850*
The dark, clotted blood when the goddess,
Casually grasping the horses' yoke, said to him:

"You're not very much like your father, you know.
Tydeus had a small build, but he was a fighter—
Even when I wouldn't allow him to fight
Or show his stuff. Like the time he came to Thebes
As a solo envoy to all those Cadmeians.
I ordered him to keep his peace at the banquet,

But he had a lot of heart, as he always had,
And challenged the Cadmeian youths and beat them all,     860
Effortlessly. Of course I was there beside him.
But you, I stand by you, I protect you,
I tell you not to worry, to fight the Trojans,
And here you are, either bone-tired
Or paralyzed with fear. No, you're no son
Of Tydeus or grandson of sharp old Oeneus."

And Diomedes, as tough as they come, answered:

"I know it's you, goddess, daughter of Zeus,
And so I will answer you frankly. No, I'm not
Paralyzed by fear, and I'm not slacking off.     870
But I am following the orders you gave me
When you told me not to fight face to face
With any of the gods except Aphrodite.
If she came, you said I could wound her with bronze.
That's why I've withdrawn and given orders
For all of the troops to fall back to this spot.
I know that Ares is controlling the battle."

And Athena, whose eyes were as grey as owls:

"Diomedes, son of Tydeus, I do love you.
You don't have to fear Ares or any other     880
Of the immortals. Look who is here beside you.
Drive your horses directly at Ares
And when you're in range, strike.
Don't be in awe of Ares. He's nothing but
A shifty lout. He promised Hera and me
He would fight against Troy and help the Greeks.
Now he's turned Trojan and abandoned us."

With that, she pulled Sthenelus back and pushed him
Off the chariot. Sthenelus went flying,
And Athena got in next to Diomedes,     890
Who seemed to glow beside the eager goddess,
And the solid-oak axle groaned under the load
Of an awesome deity and a hero at his best.

Pallas Athena handled the reins and whip
And drove the horses directly at Ares,
Who at that moment was stripping the armor
From a warrior named Periphas, a huge man,
Aetolia's finest and his father's glory.
Ares was busy removing the dead man's armor
And getting smeared with blood. Athena                              900
Put on Hades' helmet so Ares couldn't see her.
But Ares did see Diomedes, and when he did,
He dropped Periphas to lie in his own gore
And headed straight for the hero.
As soon as they were in range of each other
Ares leaned out over his horses' backs
And thrust, frantic for a kill. Athena's hand
Deflected the spear in mid-air and sent it
Sailing harmlessly over Diomedes' chariot,
And when Diomedes thrust next,                                      910
She drove his spear home to the pit
Of Ares' belly, where the kilt-piece covered it.
The spearhead sliced right through to the flesh,
And when Diomedes pulled it out,
Ares yelled, so loud you would have thought
Ten thousand warriors had shouted at once,
And the sound reverberated in the guts of Greeks and Trojans,
As if Diomedes had struck not a god in armor
But a bronze gong nine miles high.

> *After a period of heat, when the low clouds*                    920
> *Are massed like wool, you will sometimes see*
> *A darker clot of air whirling off*
> *On its way to becoming a tornado—*

That is how Ares appeared to Diomedes,
Moving off through the clouds and up the big sky.

He quickly scaled the heights of Olympus,
Sat down sulking beside Cronion Zeus,
Showed him the immortal blood oozing
From his wound, and whined these winged words:

"Father Zeus, doesn't it infuriate you                               930
To see this violence? We gods
Get the worst of it from each other
Whenever we try to help out men.
Why did you have to give birth to that madwoman,
Your marauding daughter who is always
Breaking the rules? All the rest of us gods,
Every one on Olympus, listen to you.
But she can say or do whatever she wants.
You even urge her on, your grey-eyed girl.
Just now she's been egging on Diomedes                               940
To rampage against the immortal gods.
He wounded Cypris first, got her on the wrist,
Then charged at me like an avenging spirit.
My fast footwork saved me, or I would be
Lying in a heap of gruesome corpses,
Or barely alive from taking hits from his spear."

And Zeus, from under thunderhead brows:

"Shifty lout. Don't sit here by me and whine.
You're the most loathsome god on Olympus.
You actually like fighting and war.                                  950
You take after your hardheaded mother,
Hera. I can barely control her either.
One way or another, she got you into this.
Be that as it may, I cannot tolerate your being in pain.
Your mother did, after all, bear you to me.
But if you were born to any other god,
You'd be long buried in hell below the Titans."

And he called Paieon to doctor his wound.
Paieon rubbed on an anodyne to kill the pain.
And then,                                                            960

    *As quickly as white milk*
    *Thickened with fig juice*
    *Curdles when stirred,*

Paieon healed impetuous Ares.
And Hebe bathed him and dressed him handsomely,
And he sat beside Zeus exulting in glory.

Then back to the palace of great Zeus
Came Argive Hera and Athena the Protector,
Having stopped brutal Ares from butchering men.

# ILIAD 6

The battle was left to rage on the level expanse
Between Troy's two rivers. Bronze spearheads
Drove past each other as the Greek and Trojan armies
Spread like a hemorrhage across the plain.

Telamonian Ajax, the Achaean wall,
Was the first Greek to break the Trojan line
And give his comrades some daylight.
He killed Thrace's best, Acamas,
Son of Eussorus, smashing through the horn
Of his plumed helmet with his spear                        10
And driving through until the bronze tip
Pierced the forehead's bone. Acamas' eyes went dark.

Diomedes followed up by killing Axylus,
Teuthras' son, a most hospitable man.
His comfortable home was on the road to Arisbe,
And he entertained all travellers, but not one
Came by to meet the enemy before him
And save him from death. Diomedes killed
Not only Axylus but Calesius, his driver,
Two men who would now be covered by earth.              20

Then Euryalus killed Opheltius and Dresus
And went on after Aesepus and Pedasus,
Twins whom the naiad Abarbarea

112

Bore to Bucolion, Laomedon's eldest
Though bastard son. He was with his sheep
When he made love to the nymph. She conceived,
And bore him the twins whom Euryalus
Now undid. He left their bright bodies naked.

Then Polypoetes killed Astyalus;
Odysseus got Pidytes with his spear;                    30
And Teucer took out Aretaon, a good man.
Nestor's son Antilochus killed Ablerus;
The warlord Agamemnon killed Elatus,
Who lived in steep Pedasus on the Satnioeis;
Leitus killed Phylacus as he fled;
And Eurypylus unmanned Melanthius.

But Menelaus took Adrastus alive.
Adrastus' terrified horses became entangled
In a tamarisk as they galloped across the plain,
And, breaking the pole near the car's rim,                    40
Bolted toward the city with the others.
Their master rolled from the car by the wheel
And fell face-first into the dust. Menelaus
Came up to him with his long-shadowed spear,
And Adrastus clasped his knees and prayed:

"Take me alive, son of Atreus, and accept
A worthy ransom from the treasure stored
In my father's palace, bronze, gold, wrought iron.
My father would lavish it all on you if he heard
I was still alive among the Achaean ships."                    50

The speech had its intended effect.
Menelaus was about to hand him over
To be led back to the ships, but Agamemnon
Came running over to call him on it:

"Going soft, Menelaus? What does this man
Mean to you? Have the Trojans ever shown you
Any hospitality? Not one of them
Escapes sheer death at our hands, not even

The boy who is still in his mother's womb.
Every Trojan dies, unmourned and unmarked."                    60

And so the hero changed his brother's mind
By reminding him of the ways of conduct and fate.
Menelaus shoved Adrastus aside,
And Agamemnon stabbed him in the flank.
He fell backward, and the son of Atreus
Braced his heel on his chest and pulled out the spear.

Then Nestor shouted and called to the Greeks:

"Soldiers of Greece, no lagging behind
To strip off armor from the enemy corpses
To see who comes back to the ships with the most.          70
Now we kill men! You will have plenty of time later
To despoil the Trojan dead on the plain."

Nestor's speech worked them up to a frenzy,
And the Trojans would have been beaten
Back to Ilion by superior force
Had not Helenus, Priam's son
And Troy's prophet, approached Aeneas and Hector:

"Aeneas and Hector, the Trojans and Lycians
Are counting on you. You two are the leaders
In every initiative in council and battle—                  80
So make a stand here. Go through the ranks
And keep our men back from the gates,
Before they run through them and fall
Into their women's arms, making our enemies laugh.
Once you have bolstered our troops' morale,
We will stand our ground and fight the Danaans,
Tired as we are. We have our backs to the wall.
Hector, go into the city and find our mother.
Tell her to take a company of old women
To the temple of Athena on the acropolis                    90
With the largest and loveliest robe in her house,
The one that is dearest of all to her,
And place it on the knees of braided Athena,

And promise twelve heifers to her in her temple,
Unblemished yearlings, if she will pity
The town of Troy, its wives and its children,
And if she will keep from holy Ilion
Wild Diomedes, who is raging with his spear.
I think he's the strongest of all the Achaeans.
We never even feared Achilles like this,                    100
And they say he is half-divine. But this man
Won't stop at anything. No one can match him."

Hector took his brother's advice.
He jumped down from his chariot with his gear
And toured the ranks, a spear in each hand.
He urged them on, and with a trembling roar
The Trojans turned to face the Achaeans.
The Greeks pulled back. It looked to them
As if some god had come from the starry sky
To help the Trojans. It had been a sudden rally.                    110
Hector shouted and called to the Trojans:

"Soldiers of Troy, and illustrious allies,
Remember to fight like the men that you are,
While I go to the city and ask the elders
Who sit in council, and our wives, to pray
To the gods and promise bulls by the hundred."

And Hector left, helmet collecting light
Above the black-hide shield whose rim tapped
His ankles and neck with each step he took.

Then Glaucus, son of Hippolochus,                    120
Met Diomedes in no-man's-land.
Both were eager to fight, but first Tydeus' son
Made his voice heard above the battle noise:

"And which mortal hero are you? I've never seen you
Out here before on the fields of glory,
And now here you are ahead of everyone,
Ready to face my spear. Pretty bold.
I feel sorry for your parents. Of course,

You may be an immortal, down from heaven.
Far be it from me to fight an immortal god.                          130
Not even mighty Lycurgus lived long
After he tangled with the immortals,
Driving the nurses of Dionysus
Down over the Mountain of Nysa
And making them drop their wands
As he beat them with an ox-goad. Dionysus
Was terrified and plunged into the sea,
Where Thetis received him into her bosom,
Trembling with fear at the human's threats.
Then the gods, who live easy, grew angry                             140
With Lycurgus, and the Son of Cronus
Made him go blind, and he did not live long,
Hated as he was by the immortal gods.
No, I wouldn't want to fight an immortal.
But if you are human, and shed blood,
Step right up for a quick end to your life."

And Glaucus, Hippolochus' son:

"Great son of Tydeus, why ask about my lineage?
Human generations are like leaves in their seasons.
The wind blows them to the ground, but the tree                     150
Sprouts new ones when spring comes again.
Men too. Their generations come and go.
But if you really do want to hear my story,
You're welcome to listen. Many men know it.
  Ephyra, in the heart of Argive horse country,
Was home to Sisyphus, the shrewdest man alive,
Sisyphus son of Aeolus. He had a son, Glaucus,
Who was the father of faultless Bellerophon,
A man of grace and courage by gift of the gods.
But Proetus, whom Zeus had made king of Argos,                      160
Came to hate Bellerophon
And drove him out. It happened this way.
Proetus' wife, the beautiful Anteia,
Was madly in love with Bellerophon
And wanted to have him in her bed.
But she couldn't persuade him, not at all,

Because he was so virtuous and wise.
So she made up lies and spoke to the king:
'Either die yourself, Proetus, or kill Bellerophon.
He wanted to sleep with me against my will.'                    170
The king was furious when he heard her say this.
He did not kill him—he had scruples about that—
But he sent him to Lycia with a folding tablet
On which he had scratched many evil signs,
And told him to give it to Anteia's father,
To get him killed. So off he went to Lycia,
With an immortal escort, and when he reached
The river Xanthus, the king there welcomed him
And honored him with entertainment
For nine solid days, killing an ox each day.                    180
But when the tenth dawn spread her rosy light,
He questioned him and asked to see the tokens
He brought from Proetus, his daughter's husband.
And when he saw the evil tokens from Proetus,
He ordered him, first, to kill the Chimaera,
A raging monster, divine, inhuman—
A lion in the front, a serpent in the rear,
In the middle a goat—and breathing fire.
Bellerophon killed her, trusting signs from the gods.
Next he had to fight the glorious Solymi,                    190
The hardest battle, he said, he ever fought,
And, third, the Amazons, women the peers of men.
As he journeyed back the king wove another wile.
He chose the best men in all wide Lycia
And laid an ambush. Not one returned home;
Blameless Bellerophon killed them all.
When the king realized his guest had divine blood,
He kept him there and gave him his daughter
And half of all his royal honor. Moreover,
The Lycians cut out for him a superb                    200
Tract of land, plow-land and orchard.
His wife, the princess, bore him three children,
Isander, Hippolochus, and Laodameia.
Zeus in his wisdom slept with Laodameia,
And she bore him the godlike warrior Sarpedon.
But even Bellerophon lost the gods' favor

And went wandering alone over the Aleian plain.
His son Isander was slain by Ares
As he fought against the glorious Solymi,
And his daughter was killed by Artemis                                210
Of the golden reins. But Hippolochus
Bore me, and I am proud he is my father.
He sent me to Troy with strict instructions
To be the best ever, better than all the rest,
And not to bring shame on the race of my fathers,
The noblest men in Ephyra and Lycia.
This, I am proud to say, is my lineage."

Diomedes grinned when he heard all this.
He planted his spear in the bounteous earth
And spoke gently to the Lycian prince:                                220

"We have old ties of hospitality!
My grandfather Oeneus long ago
Entertained Bellerophon in his halls
For twenty days, and they gave each other
Gifts of friendship. Oeneus gave
A belt bright with scarlet, and Bellerophon
A golden cup, which I left at home.
I don't remember my father Tydeus,
Since I was very small when he left for Thebes
In the war that killed so many Achaeans.                              230
But that makes me your friend and you my guest
If ever you come to Argos, as you are my friend
And I your guest whenever I travel to Lycia.
So we can't cross spears with each other
Even in the thick of battle. There are enough
Trojans and allies for me to kill, whomever
A god gives me and I can run down myself.
And enough Greeks for you to kill as you can.
And let's exchange armor, so everyone will know
That we are friends from our fathers' days."                         240

With this said, they vaulted from their chariots,
Clasped hands, and pledged their friendship.
But Zeus took away Glaucus' good sense,

For he exchanged his golden armor for bronze,
The worth of one hundred oxen for nine.

When Hector reached the oak tree by the Western Gate,
Trojan wives and daughters ran up to him,
Asking about their children, their brothers,
Their kinsmen, their husbands. He told them all,
Each woman in turn, to pray to the gods.                    250
Sorrow clung to their heads like mist.

Then he came to Priam's palace, a beautiful
Building made of polished stone with a central courtyard
Flanked by porticoes, upon which opened fifty
Adjoining rooms, where Priam's sons
Slept with their wives. Across the court
A suite of twelve more bedrooms housed
His modest daughters and their husbands.
It was here that Hector's mother met him,
A gracious woman, with Laodice,                             260
Her most beautiful daughter, in tow.
Hecuba took his hand in hers and said:

"Hector, my son, why have you left the war
And come here? Are those abominable Greeks
Wearing you down in the fighting outside,
And does your heart lead you to our acropolis
To stretch your hands upward to Zeus?
But stay here while I get you
Some honey-sweet wine, so you can pour a libation
To Father Zeus first and the other immortals,             270
Then enjoy some yourself, if you will drink.
Wine greatly bolsters a weary man's spirits,
And you are weary from defending your kinsmen."

Sunlight shimmered on great Hector's helmet.

"Mother, don't offer me any wine.
It would drain the power out of my limbs.
I have too much reverence to pour a libation
With unwashed hands to Zeus almighty,

Or to pray to Cronion in the black cloudbanks
Spattered with blood and the filth of battle.                    280
But you must go to the War Goddess's temple
To make sacrifice with a band of old women.
Choose the largest and loveliest robe in the house,
The one that is dearest of all to you,
And place it on the knees of braided Athena.
And promise twelve heifers to her in her temple,
Unblemished yearlings, if she will pity
The town of Troy, its wives, and its children,
And if she will keep from holy Ilion
Wild Diomedes, who's raging with his spear.                    290
Go then to the temple of Athena the War Goddess,
And I will go over to summon Paris,
If he will listen to what I have to say.
I wish the earth would gape open beneath him.
Olympian Zeus has bred him as a curse
To Troy, to Priam, and all Priam's children.
If I could see him dead and gone to Hades,
I think my heart might be eased of its sorrow."

Thus Hector. Hecuba went to the great hall
And called to her handmaidens, and they                    300
Gathered together the city's old women.
She went herself to a fragrant storeroom
Which held her robes, the exquisite work
Of Sidonian women whom godlike Paris
Brought from Phoenicia when he sailed the sea
On the voyage he made for high-born Helen.
Hecuba chose the robe that lay at the bottom,
The most beautiful of all, woven of starlight,
And bore it away as a gift for Athena.
A stream of old women followed behind.                    310

They came to the temple of Pallas Athena
On the city's high rock, and the doors were opened
By fair-cheeked Theano, daughter of Cisseus
And wife of Antenor, breaker of horses.

The Trojans had made her Athena's priestess.
With ritual cries they all lifted their hands
To Pallas Athena. Theano took the robe
And laid it on the knees of the rich-haired goddess,
Then prayed in supplication to Zeus' daughter:

"Lady Athena who defends our city,                          320
Brightest of goddesses, hear our prayer.
Break now the spear of Diomedes
And grant that he fall before the Western Gate,
That we may now offer twelve heifers in this temple,
Unblemished yearlings. Only do thou pity
The town of Troy, its wives and its children."

But Pallas Athena denied her prayer.

While they prayed to great Zeus' daughter,
Hector came to Paris' beautiful house,
Which he had built himself with the aid                          330
Of the best craftsmen in all wide Troy:
Sleeping quarters, a hall, and a central courtyard
Near to Priam's and Hector's on the city's high rock.
Hector entered, Zeus' light upon him,
A spear sixteen feet long cradled in his hand,
The bronze point gleaming, and the ferrule gold.
He found Paris in the bedroom, busy with his weapons,
Fondling his curved bow, his fine shield, and breastplate.
Helen of Argos sat with her household women
Directing their exquisite handicraft.                          340

Hector meant to shame Paris and provoke him:

"This is a fine time to be nursing your anger,
You idiot! We're dying out there defending the walls.
It's because of you the city is in this hellish war.
If you saw someone else holding back from combat
You'd pick a fight with him yourself. Now get up
Before the whole city goes up in flames!"

And Paris, handsome as a god:

"That's no more than just, Hector,
But listen now to what I have to say.                    350
It's not out of anger or spite toward the Trojans
I've been here in my room. I only wanted
To recover from my pain. My wife was just now
Encouraging me to get up and fight,
And that seems the better thing to do.
Victory takes turns with men. Wait for me
While I put on my armor, or go on ahead—
I'm pretty sure I'll catch up with you."

To which Hector said nothing.

But Helen said to him softly:                           360

                    "Brother-in-law
Of a scheming, cold-blooded bitch,
I wish that on the day my mother bore me
A windstorm had swept me away to a mountain
Or into the waves of the restless sea,
Swept me away before all this could happen.
But since the gods have ordained these evils,
Why couldn't I be the wife of a better man,
One sensitive at least to repeated reproaches?
Paris has never had an ounce of good sense          370
And never will. He'll pay for it someday.
But come inside and sit down on this chair,
Dear brother-in-law. You bear such a burden
For my wanton ways and Paris' witlessness.
Zeus has placed this evil fate on us so that
In time to come poets will sing of us."

And Hector, in his burnished helmet:

"Don't ask me to sit, Helen, even though
You love me. You will never persuade me.
My heart is out there with our fighting men.          380
They already feel my absence from battle.

Just get Paris moving, and have him hurry
So he can catch up with me while I'm still
Inside the city. I'm going to my house now
To see my family, my wife and my boy. I don't know
Whether I'll ever be back to see them again, or if
The gods will destroy me at the hands of the Greeks."

And Hector turned and left. He came to his house
But did not find white-armed Andromache there.
She had taken the child and a robed attendant        390
And stood on the tower, lamenting and weeping—
His blameless wife. When Hector didn't find her inside,
He paused on his way out and called to the servants:

"Can any of you women tell me exactly
Where Andromache went when she left the house?
To one of my sisters or one of my brothers' wives?
Or to the temple of Athena along with the other
Trojan women to beseech the dread goddess?"

The spry old housekeeper answered him:

"Hector, if you want the exact truth, she didn't go      400
To any of your sisters, or any of your brothers' wives,
Or to the temple of Athena along with the other
Trojan women to beseech the dread goddess.
She went to Ilion's great tower, because she heard
The Trojans were pressed and the Greeks were strong.
She ran off to the wall like a madwoman,
And the nurse went with her, carrying the child."

Thus the housekeeper, but Hector was gone,
Retracing his steps through the stone and tile streets
Of the great city, until he came to the Western Gate.   410
He was passing through it out onto the plain
When his wife came running up to meet him,
His beautiful wife, Andromache,
A gracious woman, daughter of great Eëtion,
Eëtion, who lived in the forests of Plakos
And ruled the Cilicians from Thebes-under-Plakos—

His daughter was wed to bronze-helmeted Hector.
She came up to him now, and the nurse with her
Held to her bosom their baby boy,
Hector's beloved son, beautiful as starlight,                    420
Whom Hector had named Scamandrius
But everyone else called Astyanax, Lord of the City,
For Hector alone could save Ilion now.
He looked at his son and smiled in silence.
Andromache stood close to him, shedding tears,
Clinging to his arm as she spoke these words:

"Possessed is what you are, Hector. Your courage
Is going to kill you, and you have no feeling left
For your little boy or for me, the luckless woman
Who will soon be your widow. It won't be long          430
Before the whole Greek army swarms and kills you.
And when they do, it will be better for me
To sink into the earth. When I lose you, Hector,
There will be nothing left, no one to turn to,
Only pain. My father and mother are dead.
Achilles killed my father when he destroyed
Our city, Thebes with its high gates,
But had too much respect to despoil his body.
He burned it instead with all his armor
And heaped up a barrow. And the spirit women           440
Came down from the mountain, daughters
Of the storm god, and planted elm trees around it.
I had seven brothers once in that great house.
All seven went down to Hades on a single day,
Cut down by Achilles in one blinding sprint
Through their shambling cattle and silver sheep.
Mother, who was queen in the forests of Plakos,
He took back as prisoner, with all her possessions,
Then released her for a fortune in ransom.
She died in our house, shot by Artemis' arrows.        450
Hector, you are my father, you are my mother,
You are my brother and my blossoming husband.
But show some pity and stay here by the tower,
Don't make your child an orphan, your wife a widow.
Station your men here by the fig tree, where the city

Is weakest because the wall can be scaled.
Three times their elite have tried an attack here
Rallying around Ajax or glorious Idomeneus
Or Atreus' sons or mighty Diomedes,
Whether someone in on the prophecy told them                460
Or they are driven here by something in their heart."

And great Hector, helmet shining, answered her:

"Yes, Andromache, I worry about all this myself,
But my shame before the Trojans and their wives,
With their long robes trailing, would be too terrible
If I hung back from battle like a coward.
And my heart won't let me. I have learned to be
One of the best, to fight in Troy's first ranks,
Defending my father's honor and my own.
Deep in my heart I know too well                            470
There will come a day when holy Ilion will perish,
And Priam and the people under Priam's ash spear.
But the pain I will feel for the Trojans then,
For Hecuba herself and for Priam king,
For my many fine brothers who will have by then
Fallen in the dust behind enemy lines—
All that pain is nothing to what I will feel
For you, when some bronze-armored Greek
Leads you away in tears, on your first day of slavery.
And you will work some other woman's loom                   480
In Argos or carry water from a Spartan spring,
All against your will, under great duress.
And someone, seeing you crying, will say,
'That is the wife of Hector, the best of all
The Trojans when they fought around Ilion.'
Someday someone will say that, renewing your pain
At having lost such a man to fight off the day
Of your enslavement. But may I be dead
And the earth heaped up above me
Before I hear your cry as you are dragged away."            490

With these words, resplendent Hector
Reached for his child, who shrank back screaming

Into his nurse's bosom, terrified of his father's
Bronze-encased face and the horsehair plume
He saw nodding down from the helmet's crest.
This forced a laugh from his father and mother,
And Hector removed the helmet from his head
And set it on the ground all shimmering with light.
Then he kissed his dear son and swung him up gently
And said a prayer to Zeus and the other immortals:            500

"Zeus and all gods: grant that this my son
Become, as I am, foremost among Trojans,
Brave and strong, and ruling Ilion with might.
And may men say he is far better than his father
When he returns from war, bearing bloody spoils,
Having killed his man. And may his mother rejoice."

And he put his son in the arms of his wife,
And she enfolded him in her fragrant bosom
Laughing through her tears. Hector pitied her
And stroked her with his hand and said to her:               510

"You worry too much about me, Andromache.
No one is going to send me to Hades before my time,
And no man has ever escaped his fate, rich or poor,
Coward or hero, once born into this world.
Go back to the house now and take care of your work,
The loom and the shuttle, and tell the servants
To get on with their jobs. War is the work of men,
Of all the Trojan men, and mine especially."

With these words, Hector picked up
His plumed helmet, and his wife went back home,             520
Turning around often, her cheeks flowered with tears.
When she came to the house of man-slaying Hector,
She found a throng of servants inside,
And raised among these women the ritual lament.
And so they mourned for Hector in his house
Although he was still alive, for they did not think
He would ever again come back from the war,
Or escape the murderous hands of the Greeks.

Paris meanwhile
Did not dally long in his high halls.                               530
He put on his magnificent bronze-inlaid gear
And sprinted with assurance out through the city.

*Picture a horse that has fed on barley in his stall*
*Breaking his halter and galloping across the plain,*
*Making for his accustomed swim in the river,*
*A glorious animal, head held high, mane streaming*
*Like wind on his shoulders. Sure of his splendor*
*He prances by the horse-runs and the mares in pasture.*

That was how Paris, son of Priam, came down
From the high rock of Pergamum,                                    540
Gleaming like amber and laughing in his armor,
And his feet were fast.
                    He caught up quickly
With Hector just as he turned from the spot
Where he'd talked with his wife, and called out:

"Well, dear brother, have I delayed you too much?
Am I not here in time, just as you asked?"

Hector turned, his helmet flashing light:

"I don't understand you, Paris.
No one could slight your work in battle.                           550
You're a strong fighter, but you slack off—
You don't have the will. It breaks my heart
To hear what the Trojans say about you.
It's on your account they have all this trouble.
Come on, let's go. We can settle this later,
If Zeus ever allows us to offer in our halls
The wine bowl of freedom to the gods above,
After we drive these bronze-kneed Greeks from Troy."

# ILIAD 7

Hector rushed through the gates,
And his brother Paris came with him,
Their hearts eager for battle.

*Zeus sometimes gives a tailwind to sailors*
*At just the moment their arms and legs*
*Can push no more their polished firwood oars.*

So these two appeared to the Trojans.

Each took out his man, Paris killing
Menesthius, son of ox-eyed Phylomedousa
And Areithous, whose iron mace ruled Arne.                    10
Hector's spearblade sliced Eioneus' neck
Beneath his bronze helmet; his limbs went limp.
Elsewhere in the crush of battle, Glaucus,
Son of Hippolochus and Lycian commander,
Hit Iphinous on the shoulder with his spear
As he clambered up behind his racing mares.
He fell from his chariot and his limbs went slack.

Athena's grey eyes had all this in focus,
And when she saw the Greeks being beaten
She swooped down from the peaks of Olympus            20
To sacred Ilion. Apollo,
Who wanted victory for the Trojans,

128                                                    [1–21]

Saw her coming as he watched from his lookout
On Pergamum, and he rose up to meet her.

They met by the ancient oak tree.
Lord Apollo, Zeus' son, spoke first:

"Daughter of great Zeus, why have you come
Again from Olympus? What mission are you on now?
Is it to turn the tide of battle for the Greeks
Since you have no pity for the Trojans' losses?                    30
I have a better idea. Let's halt the bloodshed
For today. They can fight later
With Ilion on the line, since you deathless ones
Have your hearts set on destroying this city."

And the grey-eyed goddess Athena replied:

"So be it, Apollo. This is just what I had in mind
In coming from Olympus to the Trojans and Greeks.
But how do you intend to stop them from fighting?"

Lord Apollo, son of Zeus, replied:

"We could rouse the hard spirit of Hector                          40
And have him challenge one of the Greeks
To fight against him, man to man.
The Greeks would be indignant and rouse someone
To battle Hector in single combat."

Grey-eyed Athena agreed to his plan.

And Helenus, Troy's seer and Priam's son,
Understood in his heart what these gods
Had agreed to. He went up to Hector
And spoke to him in convincing tones:

"Hector, son of Priam, Zeus' equal in wisdom,                      50
Will you listen to me? I am your brother.
Have all the Greeks and Trojans sit down.
Challenge the best of the Greeks to fight you

Man to man in single combat.
It is not your fate to meet your end now.
Thus I have heard from the gods eternal."

Thus Helenus, and Hector was persuaded.
He went out in front along the Trojan ranks
Holding a spear broadside, and they all sat down.
Agamemnon had his Greeks sit down,                    60
And Athena and silver-bowed Apollo
Sat like vultures in Zeus' tall oak
Enjoying the warriors, who sat rank on rank,
Bristling with shields, helmets, and spears.

   *As a fresh blast of the West Wind ripples*
   *The sea, and the sea blackens beneath it,*

So sat the ranks of Trojans and Greeks
Across the plain.
                        And Hector spoke to them:

"Hear me out, Trojans, and Achaean warriors,           70
Until I have spoken what my heart commands.
Zeus on high has made our oaths nothing.
Hostile to both sides, he means for us to fight
Until you either take the towers of Troy
Or are beaten down beside your seafaring ships.
There are among you the best of all Greece.
If any of you have the will to fight me,
None other than Hector, come forward now.
I declare these terms, with Zeus as my witness:
If your champion cuts me down with bronze,             80
He can strip my armor and take it back to your ships.
My body, though, he will return to my home
To be burned in honor by Trojans and their wives.
If I kill him, if Apollo gives me that glory,
I will take his armor to holy Ilion
And hang it in the temple of the Archer God.
The corpse I will send back to your hollow ships
So you long-haired Achaeans can give it burial
And heap up a tomb by the broad Hellespont.

So someone in generations yet to come                    *90*
Will say as he sails by on the darkening sea,
'That is the tomb of a man long dead,
Killed in his prime by glorious Hector.'
Someone will say that, and my fame will not die."

So he spoke, and they were all hushed and silent,
Ashamed to refuse and afraid to accept.
Finally, Menelaus stood up. He was groaning inwardly
But spoke to them in contemptuous tones:

"It seems we're good at threatening the Trojans,
But when it comes down to it we're women, not men!    *100*
This day will go down in infamy
If no Danaan meets Hector's challenge now.
May you all turn to mud, sitting here
Without any guts and no call to glory!
I'll put on armor myself. Win or lose,
It's all in the hands of the immortal gods."

And with that he put on his armor,
And yes, Menelaus, your life would have
Flickered out then in Hector's palms,
Because he was far stronger, had not                      *110*
The Achaean commanders run up and grabbed you,
Agamemnon too, the great warlord,
Holding you back with his right hand, saying:

"Have you lost your royal mind, Menelaus?
There's no call for you to behave like this.
Get hold of yourself. You don't volunteer
In the spirit of rivalry to fight someone
You're no match for. This is Priam's son Hector
We're talking about. Everyone fears him.
Even Achilles tightens up at the thought                  *120*
Of facing him in battle, and he's far better than you.
Just sit down here with your troops now.
The Achaeans will come up with another champion,
And even if he's a fearless glutton for combat
He'll be glad to bend his knees and rest

If he ever gets out of this one alive."

Agamemnon said all the right things
And changed his brother's mind. Relieved,
Menelaus' aides took off his armor.
Then Nestor stood up and spoke:                    130

"It's a sad day for Greece, a sad day.
Old Peleus the charioteer would groan,
The Myrmidons' great counsellor and king
Who questioned me once in his house
And revelled in all our heroic lineages.
If he were to hear of all these men cowering
Before Hector, he would lift his hands
To the immortal gods and pray for his soul
To leave his body and sink into Hades.
O Father Zeus and Athena and Apollo,              140
If only I were young again, as in the days
The Pylians and spear-mad Arcadians
Gathered near the rushing Celadon and fought
Under Pheia's walls by the streams of Iardanus.
On their side Ereuthalion, a man like a god,
Stood forth as champion, wearing the armor
Of King Areithous, the mace-man,
As men and satin-waisted women called him,
Because he fought with neither bow nor spear
But broke battalions with his iron mace.           150
Well, Lycurgus killed him, by guile, not strength,
In a narrow pass where his mace of iron
Did him no good. Before he could react
Lycurgus skewered him with his spear.
Down he went, and Lycurgus stripped from him
The armor he had gotten from bronze Ares,
And he wore that armor whenever he went to war.
And when Lycurgus was an old man in his halls
He gave it to Ereuthalion, who had been his squire.
Wearing that armor he challenged all our best.     160
They all trembled with fear. No one dared
But me—my heart pumped me up for battle
Although I was the youngest of them all.

And so we fought, and Athena gave me glory.
That was the tallest and strongest man I've ever killed,
An enormous hulk sprawled out on the ground.
If I were as young now and my strength still firm,
Helmeted Hector would have a fight on his hands.
But now here you are, the best of the Achaeans,
And not one is ready to face off with this Trojan."          170

The old man scolded them, and nine stood up.

First up was the warlord Agamemnon,
Followed by Tydeus' son Diomedes
And the two Ajaxes, clothed in fury.
Next were Idomeneus and his companion
Meriones, who weighed in like Ares,
And Eurypylus, Euaemon's fine son,
And up rose Thoas, and brilliant Odysseus—

All of them willing to do battle with Hector.

Then the horseman Nestor spoke out again:          180

"Now cast lots to see who will be chosen.
Whoever it is will enrich the Achaeans
And enrich his own heart, if he gets out alive
From the grim business of bloody combat."

He spoke, and each man marked his lot
And cast it into Agamemnon's helmet.
Hands lifted to the gods, the troops said their prayers.
Someone would say with a glance at the sky:

"Let it be Ajax, Father Zeus, or Diomedes,
Or the king of golden Mycenae himself."          190

Nestor shook the helmet, and out jumped the lot
Of the man they all wanted. It was Ajax's.
A herald took it down the line from left to right
And showed it to each of the Achaean elite.
They all disclaimed it until he came to Ajax,

Who held out his hand. The herald gave him the lot.
When Ajax saw it was his, he smiled inwardly
And threw it on the ground by his foot and said:

"My friends, the lot is mine, and I'm glad of it,
Because I think I'm going to beat Hector.                    *200*
But listen. While I am putting on my battle gear,
Pray to Lord Zeus, the son of Cronus,
Silently to yourselves, so the Trojans won't hear—
Or pray openly, since there is no one we fear.
No one can drive me off against my will
By force or skill. I was born and bred
In Salamis, and I know I am no fool."

Thus Ajax. You could hear the Greeks
Saying their prayers to Lord Zeus,
Eyes lifted up to broad, flat sky:                    *210*

"Father Zeus on Ida above,
Grant the splendor of victory to Ajax,
But if you love Hector and care for him too,
Vouchsafe to both equal power and glory."

While they prayed, Ajax was clapping on
Gleaming bronze armor, and when every inch
Of his skin was covered he hustled forward
Like the giant God of War himself
When he enters a soul-devouring battle
That men have joined but Zeus has ordained.                    *220*
Ajax was that big, a human barricade, a Greek wall,
The gristle that was his face arranged in a smile,
And with every huge stride the long shadow
Of his spear sagged and quivered. The Greeks
Liked what they saw, but the Trojans trembled,
And Hector felt his heart pounding in his chest.
It was impossible for him, though, to melt back
Into the ranks: he had issued the challenge.
Ajax kept coming, holding a shield that was like
A city tower, seven folds of oxhide                    *230*
Mastered with bronze, the work of Tychius,

Whose shop was in Hyle, the best leather worker
On earth, who had made this shimmering shield
From seven tough hides and an eighth layer of bronze.
Telamonian Ajax held it in front of his chest now
And put his face in Hector's as he said:

"Take a good look, Hector. This is what
The heroes are like in the Greek army
Even when Achilles isn't here smashing skulls.
He's back there with the ships now,                          240
Nursing his grudge against Agamemnon,
But we still have a few good men to fight you.
More than a few. It's your move."

Hector's helmet gathered the fading light:

"Telamonian Ajax. Zeus-born. The Captain.
Don't try to unnerve me, as if I were
Some kid, or a woman who wouldn't know
One end of a spear from another.
I've been in a few battles and killed a few men,
And I know a few moves. I can go with this shield           250
To the right or the left, dodge through charging horses,
Or fight hand to hand with fancy footwork.
But I'm not going to try anything fancy on you.
I'm going to hit you straight on, if my aim is good."

The taunts were over. Hector carefully
Balanced his spear, and when he threw it
Its long shadow swept over the earth
And it bored through the bronze skin
Of Ajax's shield and through six oxhide layers,
But the seventh layer of leather stopped it.                260
It was Ajax's turn now. His long-shadowed spear
Crashed through the round of Hector's shield
And ripped into the intricate breastplate,
The point shearing his shirt and nicking his ribs
As Hector twisted aside from black fatality.
They wrenched their spears back out
And went at each other again,

*like lions*
*After raw meat, or wild boars in rut.*

                             Hector        270
Stabbed his spear dead center into Ajax's shield
But the bronze point crumpled on its surface,
And Ajax was upon him, thrusting his spear hard
Through Hector's shield. The force of the blow
Stunned him, and the point grazed his neck,
Drawing dark blood. This didn't stop Hector.
He gave ground and picked up a stone, gripping it
In one hand, a huge black slab lying in the plain,
And heaved it onto Ajax's massive shield,
Hitting it on the boss. The bronze rang like a gong.    280
Ajax in turn picked up a much bigger rock,
The size of a millstone, and, whirling around,
Put his enormous strength into the throw,
Crushing Hector's shield and buckling his knees.
He lay curled on his back under his shield,
But Apollo quickly put him on his feet again.
And they would have gone at each other with swords
Had not the heralds, Zeus' messengers and men's,
Come forward from both sides—
Talthybius and Idaeus, prudent men both.    290
They held their staffs between the two combatants,
And Idaeus made this formal pronouncement:

"Fight no more, dear sons, nor battle more.
Zeus beyond the clouds loves you both,
And you are both spearmen, as we all know.
Now it is night, and it is good to yield to night."

Telamonian Ajax said in response:

"Have Hector speak these words, Idaeus.
He was the one who challenged our best to fight.
It's his call. I'll go along with what he says."    300

And great Hector, helmeted in gold, replied:

"Ajax, since a god has given you size and strength
And wisdom too, and you are the best of the Achaeans
With a spear, let us call a truce to our hostilities
For today. Another time we will fight again
Until Zeus grants one of us the victory.
Now it is night, and it is good to yield to night,
You to make glad the Greeks beside your ships,
And especially the kinfolk and friends you have;
Myself to make glad throughout Priam's city                    310
The Trojans and their wives in long trailing robes
Who will for my sake throng Ilion's shrines.
But now we should exchange glorious gifts,
So that the Greeks and Trojans will say of us,
'They fought each other in soul-devouring strife,
But agreed to part in the spirit of friendship.'"

And he gave him his silver-studded sword
Along with its scabbard and tooled belt.
Ajax gave him his own belt, bright with scarlet.
Then they parted. Ajax went to the Greeks,                     320
Hector to the Trojans, who were glad to see him
Coming back to join them, having escaped
With his life from the grim hands of Ajax.
They led him back to the city, scarcely believing
He was really safe. On their side, the Greeks
Led Ajax to Agamemnon, glad he had won.

When they were in Agamemnon's quarters
The warlord sacrificed an ox for them,
A bull of five years, to almighty Cronion.
They flayed and dressed it, jointed the limbs              330
And sliced them skillfully, skewered the pieces,
Roasted them carefully, and drew them off the spits.
When they were done and the feast was ready,
Feast they did, and no one lacked an equal share.
The long chine was given in honor to Ajax
By the commander-in-chief, Lord Agamemnon.
When they had enough of food and drink,
The first to spin out his plan was Nestor,

Whose advice had always seemed best before.
He was full of good will in the speech he made:            *340*

"Son of Atreus and Greek leaders all,
Many of our flowing-haired boys are dead,
Their blood spilled by Ares near the Scamander,
Their souls bound for Hades. And so there is need
For the army to pause from combat, and at dawn
Collect the corpses and wheel them back here
By ox and mule cart. We will burn them
Near the ships, so that when we return to our land
We may bear their bones home to their children.
Near the pyre we will heap a common barrow            *350*
Out into the plain, and up against it we will build
A high wall, working fast, a defense for our ships
And for ourselves, and set in it close-fitting gates,
So there will be a way to drive chariots through.
Just outside the wall we will dig a deep trench
As a hazard for enemy troops and horses,
Should the proud Trojans ever press us hard."

Thus Nestor, and all the kings assented.

Meanwhile, on the acropolis of Troy,
An unruly assembly mobbed Priam's doors.            *360*
Wise Antenor led off with this speech:

"Hear me, Trojans and Dardanian allies,
That I might speak my heart. All right, then.
Let us give Helen of Argos to Atreus' sons,
Her and her possessions, for them to take away.
We are fighting in false faith and can have
No profit from it. This is our only hope."

He had his say and sat down. Then up stood
Rich-haired Helen's husband, godlike Paris,
Who answered him with these winged words:            *370*

"I don't like what you are saying, Antenor.
You know how to speak better than this.

But if you really mean what you are saying,
Then the gods must have destroyed your wits.
This is what I have to say to the Trojans,
And I'll say it straight out: I won't give her back.
But the treasure I brought with her from Argos
I will give back, and add some of my own."

He had his say and sat down. Then up rose
Dardanian Priam, peer of the gods in counsel,                    *380*
Full of good will in the speech that he made:

"Hear me, Trojans and Dardanian allies,
That I might speak my heart. For the present,
Take your dinner throughout the city as usual,
And each man of you be alert and on watch.
At dawn Idaeus will go to the Greek ships
To tell Atreus' sons, Menelaus and Agamemnon,
The word of Alexander, who is the cause of this war,
And to propose an armistice to burn the dead.
Later we will fight again, until the deity                       *390*
Decides between us and bestows the victory."

He spoke, they listened, and they did as he said.
The army took their supper by platoons.
At dawn Idaeus went down to the ships
And found the Greek warlords assembled
Beside the stern of Agamemnon's vessel.
The wind from the Aegean carried his voice:

"Son of Atreus, and Achaean princes all:
Priam and the other lords of Troy bid me
Tell you—and may it be sweet to your ears—                       *400*
The word of Alexander, the cause of our strife.
All of the treasure he brought back to Troy
In his ship's hold—would he had died beforehand—
He will give back, and add some of his own.
But the former wife of renowned Menelaus
He will not give back, though the Trojans bid him,
As they bid me also, propose, if you are willing,
An armistice until we can burn the dead.

Later we will fight again, until the deity
Decides between us and bestows the victory." 410

He spoke, and they were all hushed in silence
Until Diomedes' martial voice boomed out:

"Accept nothing from Alexander,
Not even Helen! Even a fool can see
The noose is tightening around the Trojans."

The Greeks cheered when they heard this,
Delighted with Diomedes' blunt reply,
And Lord Agamemnon addressed Idaeus:

"Idaeus, you yourself hear the Greeks' answer,
And it is my pleasure too. As for burning 420
The corpses, I do not begrudge it at all.
One does not stint the dead, or deny to them
The swift consolation of fire. May Zeus,
Hera's thundering consort, witness our oaths."

And he lifted up his staff to the gods.

Idaeus went back to sacred Ilion, where
Trojans and Dardanians sat in assembly
Awaiting his return. He stood in their midst
And delivered his message, and they set to work
To bring in the dead and gather wood. 430
Likewise the Greeks, hurrying from their ships
Brought in their dead and gathered wood.

The sun's light lay new on the fields
As it rose from deep, soft waters of Ocean
And climbed the sky.

The armies met on the plain.
It was difficult to recognize each of the dead,
But they washed the clotted blood with water,
And, shedding hot tears, lifted them onto carts.
Great Priam would not allow his people 440

To wail aloud, so in silence they heaped
The corpses on the pyre, grieving at heart,
And when they had burned them they returned
To sacred Ilion. And the Greeks, too, heaped
The corpses on their pyre, grief in their hearts,
And having burned them, returned to the ships.

It was twilight before the following dawn
When chosen Greek troops gathered at the pyre.
Working fast, they heaped around it
A common barrow extending out on the plain,          450
And up against it they built a high wall
To protect their camp, complete with tight gates
So there would be a way to drive chariots through.
Just outside the wall they dug a trench,
Deep and wide, and in it planted stakes.

   As the Greeks toiled, their hair flowing
Around their shoulders and bronze chests,
The gods, seated around lightning Zeus,
Marvelled at their work. Poseidon,
Lord of the islands, was first to speak:               460

"Father Zeus, is there now any mortal
In all the wide world who will tell the gods
What he intends? Do you see that the Greeks
Have built a wall and trench around their ships
Without offering us bulls by the hundred?
Fame of this will reach as far as Dawn spreads light,
And men will forget the wall that Apollo and I
Built with toil for the hero Laomedon."

This provoked a troubled, gloomy response:

"What a thing for you to say, you, the Temblor.        470
Some lesser god might fear this ploy,
But not you, whose fame will reach
As far as Dawn spreads light. Choose your time.
When the Greeks have left with their ships for home,
Smash the wall to bits and sweep it out to sea,

And cover the great beach again with sand,
So that the Achaeans' wall becomes a dwindling thought."

As they spoke to each other in this way
The sun went down, and the Greeks' work was done.
They slaughtered oxen and took their supper                        *480*
Outside their huts. Wine-ships from Lemnos
Had just sailed in, sent by Jason's son, Euneus,
The son Hypsipyle bore to the great adventurer.
Euneus had shipped for the sons of Atreus,
Agamemnon and Menelaus, a special consignment,
A thousand liters of sweet red. The other Greeks
Went on board to barter for their wine,
Some with bronze, others with iron, hides,
Cattle, or slaves. They made a rich feast.

All night long the Greeks feasted, and the Trojans            *490*
Feasted with their allies throughout the city.
And all night long Zeus the Counsellor
Devised evil for them, thundering terribly.
Pale fear seized them, and no man dared drink
Before spilling wine to Cronus' mighty son.
Sleep was welcome when it finally came.

# ILIAD 8

Dawn.
Saffron light over all the earth.

Zeus, who plays in thunder, had the gods
Assembled on the utmost peak
Of the rugged Olympic massif,
And now enjoyed their undivided attention:

"Listen to me, divine ones,
So I can tell you what I want.
What I don't want is any god—male or female—
Attempting to brook my word. You are all                    10
To assent, so we can get this over with.
If I catch any one of you with a private plan
To assist either the Greeks or Trojans,
He—or she—will return to Olympus
A crippled wreck—unless of course I hurl
Him—or her—into moldy Tartarus,
Down into the deepest underground abyss,
Iron-gated and bronze-stooped,
As far beneath Hades as the sky is above earth.
Then you will know who is supreme around here.           20
Or would you like to find out now?
Come on. Hang a gold cable down from the sky.
All you gods and goddesses holding the end
Couldn't drag down from sky to earth

Zeus the Master, no matter how hard you tried.
But if I wanted to I could haul up all of you,
With the earth itself and the very sea,
Then loop the cable around a spur of Olympus,
And the totality would hang suspended in space.
That's how superior I am to gods and men."                    30

They were stunned to silence, aghast
At his words. It had been a masterful speech.
Finally, grey-eyed Athena spoke up:

"Well, our Father who art the highest,
We know very well your might is unyielding.
Still, we have pity for the Danaan spearmen
Who are now destined to die an ugly death.
We will withdraw from the war if you
Command it. But we will still advise the Greeks,
So they won't all be casualties of your wrath."            40

And Zeus, smiling at her, answered:

"There, there, daughter. My heart really
Isn't in it. I want to be gentle to you, child."

With that, he harnessed his horses,
Bronze-hooved, gold-maned, and swift,
And clothed himself in gold, and gripped
His golden whip, and stepped onto his chariot,
And with a touch of his lash they were off,
Flying between earth and the starry universe.
He came to Ida, with its springs and wild beasts,            50
A mountain mother, and to Gargaros there,
Where his precinct and smoking altar stood.
There Zeus reined in his horses, unhitched them
From the car, and shed upon them a heavy mist.
Then he sat among the peaks exulting in glory
With the city of Troy and the Greek ships in view.

The Greeks were taking a hurried meal
In their huts, and then armed themselves quickly.

Likewise the Trojans throughout the city,
A smaller army but much more desperate        *60*
To engage the enemy: they were fighting
For their children and for their wives.
All the gates were opened, and the troops
Poured through them, on foot and in war cars.
When the two sides closed with each other
They slammed together shields and spears—
Rawhide ovals pressed close, bronze thoraxes
Grinding against each other, and the groans
Of men being slain and the cries of those slaying
Hung in the air as the earth ran with blood.        *70*

As long as the holy light climbed toward noon
Soldiers on both sides were hit and fell.
But when the sun straddled heaven's meridian,
The Father stretched out his golden scales.
On them he placed two dooms of agonizing death,
One for the Trojans, one for the Greeks.
He held the scales in the middle, and down sank
The Greek day of doom, down to the fertile earth,
While the Trojans' soared up to the sky's expanse.
Then Zeus thundered from Ida, and sent a blazing flash        *80*
Into the Greek army. The soldiers gaped
In wonder, and their blood turned milky with fear.

Idomeneus lost his nerve and ran,
Followed by Agamemnon and both Ajaxes.
Nestor was the only Greek commander left,
Not that he wanted to stay, but Paris,
Helen's fair-haired lord, had hit his trace horse
With an arrow to the forelock, and the animal
Reared in pain, pawing the air frantically
And throwing the other horses into confusion        *90*
As it writhed against the bronze point in its brain.
The old man was cutting the traces with his sword
When the horses of an enemy chariot
Loomed ahead, Hector's horses, and yes,
Hector himself at the reins. Nestor's death
Would have been assured, had not Diomedes

Had all this in sharp focus. His soldier's yell
Boomed across the plain to Odysseus:

"Son of Laertes, Odysseus, the clever Ithacan—
Watch out you don't catch an arrow in your back,                100
Retreating like some gutless wonder. Come on,
Let's save the old man from this maniac."

Odysseus didn't hear, or pretended not to.
He went right past toward the Achaean ships.
No matter. Alone as he was, Diomedes
Shouldered his way over to Nestor's horses
And taking his stand said to the old man:

"Here you are, old and broken down,
With all these young bruisers at your throat.
Your driver isn't much help either, is he?                      110
Here, get up into my chariot
And see what the horses of Tros can do.
They know how to eat up the plain, and how to
Cut and turn, in pursuit or in flight.
I got them from Aeneas, a pair of real terrors.
Our men can mind your horses. As for you and me,
Let's drive this team straight at the Trojans
So that Hector too can feel my spear's bite."

That was enough for the old Gerenian horseman.
Sthenelus and Eurymedon tended his mares,                       120
And Nestor got in with Diomedes,
Taking the silky reins and touching the horses
With the lash. They closed ground quickly,
And Diomedes threw as Hector came at them,
Missing his target but hitting Hector's driver,
Eniopoeus, square in the chest as he held the reins.
He fell from the chariot, the horses swerved,
And Eniopoeus' soul crawled off in the dust.
Hector took his death hard, but let him lie there
As he went off to find another charioteer,                      130
And soon found one, Archeptolemus,
Iphitus' son. Hector had him mount

Behind the horses, and put the reins in his hands.

Things would have gone badly for the Trojans then,
And they would have been penned in Ilion like lambs,
Had Father Zeus not had all this in sharp focus.
He thundered terribly and threw a white lightning-bolt
That landed in front of Diomedes' horses
And shot up in a flame of burning sulfur.
The horses shied and backed into the car.                    140
The reins slipped out of Nestor's hands,
And with fear in his heart he said to Diomedes:

"Son of Tydeus, turn your horses around.
Zeus has given this man the glory today.
Another day he may give it to us,
But no one can change the purpose of Zeus."

And Diomedes, good at the war cry:

"Yes, old sir, everything you say is right,
But it cuts deep that Hector will someday crow,
'I made Tydeus' son turn tail and run.'                      150
When he makes that boast to the men of Troy,
I'd just as soon fall through a crack in the earth."

And Nestor, the Gerenian horseman:

"What a thing for wise Tydeus' son to say.
Hector may call you a coward and weakling,
But the Trojans will not agree with him,
Nor will the Dardanians, nor will the widows
Of all those men you laid low in the dust."

And he wheeled the horses around and fled,
Back through the tumult, with howling Trojans                160
Raining barbed missiles on them from behind
And Hector's taunting voice in their ears:

"Son of Tydeus, the Greeks used to honor you
With the best seat, full cups, and red meat.

No more! It turns out you're no better than
A woman, a rag doll. Get out of here.
Did you think I would just stand by and watch
While you climbed our walls and carried our women
Off in your ships? I'll send you to hell first."

Diomedes was tempted to wheel around                170
And deal with Hector face to face.
Three times he wavered and was about to turn,
And every time Zeus thundered from Ida,
Signalling that it was the Trojans' turn to win.

Hector shouted to his troops:

"Trojans, Lycians, Dardanian soldiers,
Remember to fight like the men that you are.
Zeus I know has decreed glory for me
And victory—and for the Danaans defeat.
Look at this puny wall they've put up.               180
It will never withstand the force of our attack,
And our horses will easily jump this ditch.
Once I get to their ships, get me some fire
So I can burn the fleet and kill dazed Greeks in the smoke."

Then he called to his horses:

"Xanthus and Podargus, Aethon and Lampus,
Pay me back now for all the tender care
Andromache daughter of Eëtion showed you,
Setting out for you sweet mash with wine
Before serving a meal to me, her husband.            190
Now pour on the speed, so we can capture
The world-renowned shield of Nestor,
Solid gold from the rods to the core,
And Diomedes' corselet, forged by Hephaestus.
If we could take both of these, we could expect
The Greeks to sail away this very night."

Thus Hector's vaunts, and Hera shook with rage
As she sat on her throne, making Olympus tremble.

She turned to the great god Poseidon and said:

"Ah, Earthshaker, you have all that power,                              *200*
But no pity in your heart for the Danaans dying.
And yet they honor you with many lovely gifts
At Helice and Aegae, and up until now
You wanted victory for them. If we had the will—
All of us who favor the Greeks, to drive
The Trojans back and hold Zeus in check—
He would sit alone and frustrated up there on Ida."

And the Earthshaker's troubled, gloomy response:

"That's reckless talk, Hera. Far be it from me
To endorse a fight between Cronion Zeus                                *210*
And all the rest of us. He is stronger by far."

While they talked to each other this way,
The space between the trenched wall and the ships
Was crammed with horses and men with shields,
Corralled there by Hector, son of Priam
And peer of swift Ares, Zeus' glory upon him.
And he would have set fire to the upswept hulls
Had not Hera put it in Agamemnon's mind
To make a last-ditch effort to rouse the Greeks.
He went through the Achaean ships and huts                             *220*
Clutching his great purple cloak, and took his stand
On the huge black hull of Odysseus' ship,
From which a shout would reach either end of camp,
To Telamonian Ajax's quarters at one end
And Achilles' at the other, for these two heroes
Had drawn up their ships at the extremities,
Trusting their manhood and the strength of their hands.

Agamemnon's voice reached every Greek ear:

"For shame, Argives!
You're nothing but poor excuses for soldiers!                          *230*
What happened to all our boasts, all the big talk
That we were the best? Remember Lemnos?

All the beef and wine you ate there? Remember saying
That each of you could take on a hundred Trojans,
Two hundred? Well now we can't match even one,
This Hector, who is about to burn our ships.
   Father Zeus,
Has there ever been another mighty king
Whom you have blinded with blindness like this,
Robbed him of glory, as you have robbed me?                    240
And yet I never sailed past any altar of yours,
I swear, on this misbegotten voyage here
Without offering oxen at every single one
In my zeal to make rubble of the walls of Troy.
At least, Zeus, grant me this prayer:
Let my people escape. Don't let the Trojans
Annihilate the Achaeans like this."

Zeus pitied his tears, and with a nod
Agreed that his people would not be destroyed.
He sent an eagle, the surest omen on wings,                    250
Holding in his talons a fawn, which he dropped
Beside the altar where the Achaeans
Sacrificed to oracular Zeus.
When they saw that the bird had come from him,
The Greeks smiled, and counterattacked.

Of all the Danaans, not one could claim
To cross the trench and engage the enemy
Before Diomedes. The armored Trojan he killed
Was named Agelaus, Phradmon's son.
He was in the act of wheeling his horses around              260
When Diomedes planted a spear in his back
With enough force to drive it out through his chest.
He fell from his car with a clang of metal.
Next out were the two sons of Atreus,
Followed by both Ajaxes, clothed in fury.
Then came Idomeneus and his companion
Meriones, who weighed in like Ares,
And Eurypylus, Euaemon's fine son.
Ninth was Teucer, stretching his bow

As he took his stand behind Ajax's shield.                    270
Big Ajax would move his shield aside
And Teucer would spot his target and shoot.
His victim would drop in his tracks, and Teucer
Would run back to Ajax like a child to its mother
And take cover again behind his shining shield.
Teucer could do no wrong. In short order he killed
Orsilochus, Ormenus, and Ophelestes,
Daetor, Chromius, and godlike Lycophontes,
Polyaemon's son Amopaon, and Melanippus.
When he had brought these down, one after another,        280
His great bow devastating the Trojan ranks,
Agamemnon took notice and came by to say:

"Teucer, my man, son of Telamon,
Keep shooting like this and you will save the day
For the Greeks, and be the light of Telamon's life,
Who raised and cherished you in his own house
Though you were a bastard. Today you can
Bring glory to him, far away as he is.
And I give you my solemn word of honor:
If Zeus Aegis-Holder and Athena allow me                   290
To strip Troy down to its stone foundations,
I will place in your hand special reward,
Second only to mine—a cauldron, or a chariot and team,
Or a woman who will go to your bed."

And Teucer, who was beyond reproach:

"Most glorious son of Atreus, why urge me on
When I'm at my top speed? I haven't let up
Since we started to push them back to the city.
I just pick my spots and shoot Trojans dead.
Eight long-tipped arrows I've let fly now,                 300
And all of them are stuck in some hero's flesh.
There's only this one mad dog I can't hit."

And he let another arrow jump from the string
Straight for Hector. He longed to hit him,

But the arrow missed, finding instead
The chest of Gorgythion, a son of Priam
By a woman from Aesyme he had taken as wife,
Castianeira, beautiful as a goddess.
His head sagged to one side—

                          *like a poppy*                    310
  *In a garden, heavy with seeds and spring rain,*

Gorgythion's head, weighted with his helmet.

Teucer let another arrow jump from the string
Straight for Hector. He longed to hit him,
But missed again. This time Apollo
Made the arrow swerve, and this time it hit
Archeptolemus, Hector's charioteer,
Square in the chest as he hurled himself on.
He fell from the chariot, the horses shied,
And Archeptolemus' life drained away in the dust.          320
Hector flushed with grief for his fallen driver
But let him lie there, and ordered Cebriones,
Who was his own brother, and close at hand,
To take the reins. Cebriones did so,
And Hector vaulted down from his chariot
With a bloodcurdling scream. Scooping up a stone
In one hand he made straight for Teucer,
Who had drawn an arrow from his quiver,
Notched it on the string, and was pulling it back.
He was taking dead aim at Hector in his shining helmet,    330
When the stone caught him just where the collarbone
Divides the neck from the chest, a vulnerable spot.
The jagged rock broke the string, his hand went numb;
He staggered, fell to his knees, and dropped the bow.
When Ajax saw his brother go down
He straddled him and sheltered him with his shield
Until two of his men, Mecistius and Alastor,
Bore him, groaning heavily, back to the ships.

Then once again the Olympian lifted
The Trojans' spirits, and they pushed the Greeks            340

Straight toward their deep ditch
With Hector out front, thoroughly enjoying himself.

*A hound goes after a wild hog or a lion*
*Nipping at its buttocks from behind,*
*Sure of its own speed but always watching*
*For its prey to whirl around.*

Thus Hector pressed the long-haired Greeks,
Picking off the hindmost one by one.

They were in full retreat until they passed
The palisade and ditch. By then many had fallen.      350
When they reached their ships they halted
And called out to each other, and to every god
They could think of, lifting their arms high,
Palms flat to heaven, while Hector wheeled
His glossy horses right and left, staring toward the Greeks
With eyes like a Gorgon's, or like butchering Ares'.

Watching all this, Hera was moved to pity
And said to Athena in a flurry of words:

"Don't the two of us care any more that the Greeks
Are being beaten? This may be the end.      360
One single man, Priam's son Hector,
Is pushing them all to the brink of doom.
His rampage is no longer bearable.
Just look at how much harm he has done!"

And the grey-eyed goddess said to her:

"I would love to have this man snuffed out,
Killed by the Argives in his own native land.
But my father is on a rampage himself now,
And constantly thwarts all my best efforts.
He has conveniently forgotten how many times      370
I rescued his son Heracles when he was struggling
With Eurystheus' labors. He would cry to heaven
And Zeus would dispatch me to save his neck.

Had I been sharp enough to know all this
When he was sent to Hades to fetch the hellhound,
He never would have made it back up from Styx.
At any rate, Zeus hates me now and has executed
The plan Thetis sold him on when she kissed his knees
And grabbed his beard, begging him to honor
Her son Achilles, sacker of cities.                    380
Well, one day he'll call me his grey-eyed girl again.
But for now, you get our horses ready
While I go to the house of Zeus Aegis-Holder
And put on my war gear. I want to see
The expression on Hector's helmeted face
When we two appear in the lanes of battle.
Many a Trojan will glut the dogs and birds
With their soft flesh after they fall by the ships."

Hera, the white-armed goddess, agreed,
And the queen of heaven, daughter of Cronus,                    390
Hastened to harness the gold-frontleted horses.
Athena, meanwhile, Zeus' favorite daughter,
Let her supple robe slip down to her father's floor,
This embroidered garment her own handiwork.
She put on one of cloudy Zeus' tunics,
Strapped on her battle gear, and then stepped
Into the blazing chariot cradling a spear
Long and thick enough for heaven's daughter
To level battalions of men in her wrath.

Hera quickly flicked the horses with the lash,                    400
And the automatic gates of heaven
Groaned open, as willed by the Hours,
Who control access to Olympus and heaven,
Opening and shutting the dense cloudbanks.
Through this gate they drove the patient horses.

Zeus saw them from Ida and seethed with anger.
He sent golden-winged Iris to bear this message:

"Go, swift Iris. Turn them back,
And don't let them come face to face with me.

It would not be pretty if we had to fight.                    *410*
This is my solemn word on the subject:
I will maim their horses, throw them
From the chariot, and smash it to bits.
Not in ten circling years will they be healed
Of the wounds the thunderbolt will inflict.
The grey-eyed one must learn what it means
To fight with her father. As for Hera,
I am not so angry with her, since she
Always opposes whatever I say."

He spoke, and Iris stormed from Ida's peaks          *420*
To the Olympic range, and caught them
Just at the gates and repeated Zeus' words:

"Where are you two off to in such a hurry?
Zeus will not allow you to help the Greeks.
This is his solemn word on the subject:
He will maim your horses, throw you
From the chariot, and smash it to bits.
Not in ten circling years will you be healed
Of the wounds the thunderbolt will inflict.
That's so you, grey eyes, will see                    *430*
What it means to fight with your father.
Hera he's not so upset with, since she
Always opposes whatever he says.
But you are awesome indeed, and a fearless bitch,
If you dare lift your spear against Zeus."

Iris spoke and was gone in a blur of wind.
Hera turned to Athena and said:

"Daughter of the Aegis-Holder, I can no longer
Countenance our fighting with Zeus
For the sake of mere mortals. Let one fall          *440*
And another live, as chance may have it.
And let Zeus judge by his own lights
Between Trojans and Greeks, as is only proper."

With that she turned her hooved horses around.

The Hours unyoked them for the goddesses,
And tethered them at their ambrosial stalls,
And leaned the chariot on the shining gateway.
They went inside and sat on golden thrones
With the other immortals, and nursed their grief.

Zeus wheeled his chariot from Ida                                   450
To Olympus, where the gods sat assembled.
No one less than Poseidon unyoked his team,
Set the car on its stand, and draped it with a cloth
While Zeus rumbled onto his golden throne
And mighty Olympus trembled under his feet.
Only Hera and Athena sat apart from Zeus
And failed to address him or ask him a question.
He knew what was wrong and said:

"Why are you two so upset, Athena and Hera?
It's not battle fatigue. You two never get tired             460
Of pulverizing Trojans, your mortal enemies.
It all comes down to this: these two hands are more powerful
Than all the gods on Olympus combined.
As for you two, your shining limbs trembled
Before you got close enough to see the front lines.
And it's just as well, because one thing is certain:
Once you had been struck by my thunderbolt
You would never have made it back to Olympus."

The two goddesses murmured to each other,
Huddling close and still scheming against Troy.              470
Athena kept silent and said nothing out loud,
Although she was furious at her father Zeus.
Hera, however, could not contain her anger:

"The awesome son of Cronus has spoken again!
We're all too familiar with your irresistible strength,
But we still feel pity for the Danaan spearmen
Who are now destined to die an ugly death.
Fine! We will withdraw from the war,
If you command it. But we will still advise the Greeks,
So they won't all be casualties of your wrath."              480

And Zeus, clouds gathering around him:

"At dawn you will see Cronus' almighty son,
If you wish, my ox-eyed lady Hera,
Making casualties of much of the Greek army.
Hector will not be absent from the war
Until Achilles has risen up from beside his ship
On the day when the fighting for Patroclus' dead body
Reaches its fever pitch by the ships' sterns.
That is divinely decreed.
                              Your wrath is nothing to me,          490
Not even if you go to the deepest foundations
Of Earth and Sea, where Cronus and Iapetus
Dwell out of the light of Hyperion the Sun,
Cooled by no winds, in the trench of Tartarus—
Not even then will I care that you are angry,
Because there is nothing more shameless than you."

He spoke, and white-armed Hera said nothing.

The sunlight fell into the Ocean, drawing
Black night over earth's fields, a sunset
The Trojans resented, but to the Greeks                             500
Welcome, thrice-prayed-for ebony night.

   Hector made camp, leading the Trojans
Along the river some distance from the ships
To an open space that was clear of the dead.
They stepped to the ground from their chariots
To hear Hector speak. In his hand was a spear
Sixteen feet long, bronze point gleaming, the ferrule gold.
Leaning on this spear, he addressed the troops:

"Hear me, Trojans, Dardanians, and allies.
I had thought to destroy the Greeks and their ships              510
And be back by now to windy Ilion.
But darkness intervened. This more than anything
Has saved them and their fleet parked on our beach.
So for now, let us yield to black night
And prepare our supper. Unyoke your horses

And feed them. Bring cattle and sheep from the city,
And get bread and mellow wine from your houses.
And gather tons of firewood, so that all night long
Until early dawn we can burn fires enough
To light up the sky, in case the long-haired Greeks          520
Have any idea of sailing off by night.
We'll not let them board their ships at ease
Or without a fight. Let them each have a wound
From an arrow or spear to brood over at home,
A going-away present as they jump on their ships,
And a lesson to others not to make war on Troy.
Heralds should proclaim throughout the city
That boys and greybeards bivouac tonight
All around the city on our god-built walls.
As for the women, each of them should light          530
A fire in her house. The city needs to guard
Against a sneak attack while the army is away.
Enough for now. This is sound strategy.
In the morning I will address the troops again.
I hope and pray to Zeus and all gods
To drive off this visitation of foreign dogs
The fates have brought us in the black ships.
For tonight, we will take care of ourselves.
At the crack of dawn we arm ourselves
And hit the Greeks hard in their beachhead camp.          540
I will find out whether the great Diomedes
Will drive me back from the ships to our wall,
Or whether I will walk off with his bloody gear.
And tomorrow he will know what he is made of,
And whether he can stand up to my spear.
My hunch is that he will find himself lying wounded
In the front lines, with his friends all around him,
At sunup tomorrow. I wish I were as sure
Of immortality and eternal youth
And honor like Apollo's and Pallas Athena's          550
As I am that this is a black day for the Greeks."

Thus Hector, and the Trojans cheered.
They unyoked their sweating horses
And tethered them with thongs to their chariots.

They brought cattle and sheep from the city,
Got bread and mellow wine from their houses,
And gathered firewood. They offered
Bulls by the hundred to the immortal gods,
And onshore winds carried the smoky savor
Up to the sky. But the blessed ones disdained                    560
To partake. They abhorred holy Ilion,
And Priam, and the people under Priam's ash spear.

But the Trojans had great notions that night,
Sitting on the bridge of war by their watchfires.

> *Stars: crowds of them in the sky, sharp*
> *In the moonglow when the wind falls*
> *And all the cliffs and hills and peaks*
> *Stand out and the air shears down*
> *From heaven, and all the stars are visible*
> *And the watching shepherd smiles.*                            570

So the bonfires between the Greek ships
And the banks of the Xanthus, burning
On the plain before Ilion.
                            And fifty men
Warmed their hands by the flames of each fire.

And the horses champed white barley,
Standing by their chariots, waiting for Dawn
To take her seat on brocaded cushions.

# ILIAD 9

So the Trojans kept watch. But Panic,
Fear's sister, had wrapped her icy fingers
Around the Greeks, and all their best
Were stricken with unendurable grief.

*When two winds rise on the swarming deep,*
*Boreas and Zephyr, blowing from Thrace*
*In a sudden squall, the startled black waves*
*Will crest and tangle the surf with seaweed.*

The Greeks felt like that, pummeled and torn.

Agamemnon's heart was bruised with pain          10
As he went around to the clear-toned criers
Ordering them to call each man to assembly,
But not to shout. He pitched in himself.
It was a dispirited assembly. Agamemnon
Stood up, weeping, his face like a sheer cliff
With dark springwater washing down the stone.
Groaning heavily he addressed the troops:

"Friends, Argive commanders and counsellors:
Great Zeus, son of Cronus,
Is a hard god, friends. He's kept me in the dark          20
After all his promises, all his nods my way
That I'd raze Ilion's walls before sailing home.

160

It was all a lie, and I see now that his orders
Are for me to return to Argos in disgrace,
And this after all the armies I've destroyed.
I have no doubt that this is the high will
Of the god who has toppled so many cities
And will in the future, all glory to his power.
So this is my command for the entire army:
Clear out with our ships and head for home.                    30
There's no hope we will take Troy's tall town."

He spoke, and they were all stunned to silence,
The silence of an army too grieved to speak,
Until at last Diomedes' voice boomed out:

"I'm going to oppose you if you talk foolishness—
As is my right in assembly, lord. Keep your temper.
First of all, you insulted me, saying in public
I was unwarlike and weak. Every Greek here,
Young and old alike, knows all about this.
The son of crooked Cronus split the difference                 40
When he gave you gifts. He gave you a scepter
And honor with it, but he didn't give you
Strength to stand in battle, which is real power.
Are you out of your mind? Do you really think
The sons of the Achaeans are unwarlike and weak?
If you yourself are anxious to go home,
Then go. You know the way. Your ships are here
Right by the sea, and a whole fleet will follow you
Back to Mycenae. But many a long-haired Achaean
Will stay, too, until we conquer Troy. And if they won't—       50
Well, let them all sail back to their own native land.
The two of us, Sthenelus and I, will fight on
Until we take Ilion. We came here with Zeus."

He spoke, and all the Greeks cheered
The speech of Diomedes, breaker of horses.
Then up stood Nestor, the old charioteer:

"Son of Tydeus, you are our mainstay in battle
And the best of your age in council as well.

No Greek will find fault with your speech
Or contradict it. But it is not the whole story.                    60
You are still young. You might be my son,
My youngest. Yet you have given prudent advice
To the Argive kings, since you have spoken aright.
But I, who am privileged to be your senior,
Will speak to all points. Nor will anyone
Scorn my words, not even King Agamemnon.
Only outlaws and exiles favor civil strife.
For the present, however, let us yield to night
And have our dinner. Guards should be posted
Outside the wall along the trench. I leave                          70
This assignment to the younger men. But you,
Son of Atreus, take charge. You are King.
Serve the elders a feast. It is not unseemly.
Your huts are filled with wine which our ships
Transport daily over the sea from Thrace.
You have the means to entertain us and the men.
Then choose the best counsel your assembled guests
Can offer. The Achaeans are in great need
Of good counsel. The enemies' campfires
Are close to our ships. Can this gladden any heart?                 80
This night will either destroy the army or save it."

They all heard him out and did as he said.
The guard details got their gear and filed out
On the double under their commanders:
Thrasymedes, Nestor's son; Ascalaphus
And Ialmenus, sons of Ares; Meriones,
Aphareus, and Diphyrus; and Creion,
The son of Lycomedes. Each of these seven
Had a hundred men under his command.
Spears in hand, they took up their positions                       90
In a long line between the wall and the trench,
Where they lit fires and prepared their supper.

Agamemnon meanwhile gathered the elders
Into his hut and served them a hearty meal.
They helped themselves to the dishes before them,
And when they had enough of food and drink,

The first to spin out his plan for them was Nestor,
Whose advice had always seemed best before,
And who spoke with their best interests at heart:

"Son of Atreus, most glorious lord,                        100
I begin and end with you, since you are
King of a great people, with authority
To rule and right of judgment from Zeus.
It is yours to speak as well as to listen,
And to stand behind others whenever they speak
To our good. The final word is yours.
But I will speak as seems best to me.
No one will have a better idea
Than I have now, nor has anyone ever,
From the time, divine prince, you wrested away          110
The girl Briseis from Achilles' shelter,
Defying his anger and my opposition.
I tried to dissuade you, but you gave in
To your pride and dishonored a great man
Whom the immortals esteem. You took his prize
And keep it still. But it is not too late. Even now
We must think of how to win him back
With appeasing gifts and soothing words."

And the warlord Agamemnon responded:

"Yes, old man, you were right on the mark                 120
When you said I was mad. I will not deny it.
Zeus' favor multiplies a man's worth,
As it has here, and the army has suffered for it.
But since I did succumb to a fit of madness,
I want to make substantial amends.
I hereby announce my reparations:
Seven unfired tripods, ten gold bars,
Twenty burnished cauldrons, a dozen horses—
Solid, prizewinning racehorses
Who have won me a small fortune—                         130
And seven women who do impeccable work,
Surpassingly beautiful women from Lesbos
I chose for myself when Achilles captured the town.

And with them will be the woman I took,
Briseus' daughter, and I will solemnly swear
I never went to her bed and lay with her
Or did what is natural between women and men.
All this he may have at once. And if it happens
That the gods allow us to sack Priam's city,
He may when the Greeks are dividing the spoils           140
Load a ship to the brim with gold and bronze,
And choose for himself the twenty Trojan women
Who are next in beauty to Argive Helen.
And if we return to the rich land of Argos,
He will marry my daughter, and I will honor him
As I do Orestes, who is being reared in luxury.
I have three daughters in my fortress palace,
Chrysothemis, Laodice, and Iphianassa.
He may lead whichever he likes as his bride
Back to Peleus' house, without paying anything,           150
And I will give her a dowry richer than any
A father has ever given his daughter.
And I will give him seven populous cities,
Cardamyle, Enope, grassy Hire,
Sacred Pherae, Antheia with its meadowlands,
Beautiful Aepeia, and Pedasus, wine country.
They are all near the sea, on sandy Pylos' frontier,
And cattlemen live there, rich in herds and flocks,
Who will pay him tribute as if he were a god
And fulfill the shining decrees of his scepter.           160
I will do all this if he will give up his grudge.
And he should. Only Hades cannot be appeased,
Which is why of all gods mortals hate him most.
And he should submit to me, inasmuch as I
Am more of a king and can claim to be elder."

And then spoke Nestor, the Gerenian rider:

"Son of Atreus, most glorious Agamemnon,
Your gifts for Achilles are beyond reproach.
But come, we must dispatch envoys
As soon as possible to Achilles' tent,                    170

And I see before me who should volunteer.
Phoenix, dear to Zeus, should lead the way,
Followed by Ajax and brilliant Odysseus.
Odius and Eurybates can attend them as heralds.
Now bring water for our hands and observe silence,
That we may beseech Zeus to have mercy on us."

Nestor spoke, and his speech pleased them all.
Heralds poured water over their hands,
And then youths filled bowls to the brim with drink
And served it all around, first tipping the cups.          180
Having made their libations and drunk their fill,
They went out in a body from Agamemnon's hut.
Gerenian Nestor filled their ears with advice,
Glancing at each, but especially at Odysseus,
On how to persuade Peleus' peerless son.

They went in tandem along the seething shore,
Praying over and over to the god in the surf
For an easy time in convincing Achilles.
They came to the Myrmidons' ships and huts
And found him plucking clear notes on a lyre—            190
A beautiful instrument with a silver bridge
He had taken when he ransacked Eëtion's town—
Accompanying himself as he sang the glories
Of heroes in war. He was alone with Patroclus,
Who sat in silence waiting for him to finish.
His visitors came forward, Odysseus first,
And stood before him. Surprised, Achilles
Rose from his chair still holding his lyre.
Patroclus, when he saw them, also rose,
And Achilles, swift and sure, received them:             200

"Welcome. Things must be bad to bring you here,
The Greeks I love best, even in my rage."

With these words Achilles led them in
And had them sit on couches and rugs
Dyed purple, and he called to Patroclus:

"A larger bowl, son of Menoetius,
And stronger wine, and cups all around.
My dearest friends are beneath my roof."

Patroclus obliged his beloved companion.
Then he cast a carving block down in the firelight                    210
And set on it a sheep's back and a goat's,
And a hog chine too, marbled with fat.
Automedon held the meat while Achilles
Carved it carefully and spitted the pieces.
Patroclus, godlike in the fire's glare,
Fed the blaze. When the flames died down
He laid the spits over the scattered embers,
Resting them on stones, and sprinkled the morsels
With holy salt. When the meat was roasted
He laid it on platters and set out bread                    220
In exquisite baskets. Achilles served the meat,
Then sat down by the wall opposite Odysseus
And asked Patroclus to offer sacrifice.
After he threw the offerings in the fire,
They helped themselves to the meal before them,
And when they had enough of food and drink,
Ajax nodded to Phoenix. Odysseus saw this,
And filling a cup he lifted it to Achilles:

"To your health, Achilles, for a generous feast.
There is no shortage in Agamemnon's hut,                    230
Or now here in yours, of satisfying food.
But the pleasures of the table are not on our minds.
We fear the worst. It is doubtful
That we can save the ships without your strength.
The Trojans and their allies are encamped
Close to the wall that surrounds our black ships
And are betting that we can't keep them
From breaking through. They may be right.
Zeus has been encouraging them with signs,
Lightning on the right. Hector trusts this—                    240
And his own strength—and has been raging
Recklessly, like a man possessed.
He is praying for dawn to come early

So he can fulfill his threat to lop the horns
From the ships' sterns, burn the hulls to ash,
And slaughter the Achaeans dazed in the smoke.
This is my great fear, that the gods make good
Hector's threats, dooming us to die in Troy
Far from the fields of home. Up with you, then,
If you intend at all, even at this late hour,                    250
To save our army from these howling Trojans.
Think of yourself, of the regret you will feel
For harm that will prove irreparable.
This is the last chance to save your countrymen.
Is it not true, my friend, that your father Peleus
Told you as he sent you off with Agamemnon:
'My son, as for strength, Hera and Athena
Will bless you if they wish, but it is up to you
To control your proud spirit. A friendly heart
Is far better. Steer clear of scheming strife,                  260
So that Greeks young and old will honor you.'
You have forgotten what the old man said,
But you can still let go of your anger, right now.
Agamemnon is offering you worthy gifts
If you will give up your grudge. Hear me
While I list the gifts he proposed in his hut:
Seven unfired tripods, ten gold bars,
Twenty burnished cauldrons, a dozen horses—
Solid, prizewinning racehorses
Who have won him a small fortune—                               270
And seven women who do impeccable work,
Surpassingly beautiful women from Lesbos
He chose for himself when you captured the town.
And with them will be the woman he took from you,
Briseus' daughter, and he will solemnly swear
He never went to her bed and lay with her
Or did what is natural between women and men.
All this you may have at once. And if it happens
That the gods allow us to sack Priam's city,
You may when the Greeks are dividing the spoils               280
Load a ship to the brim with gold and bronze,
And choose for yourself the twenty Trojan women
Who are next in beauty to Argive Helen.

And if we return to the rich land of Argos,
You would marry his daughter, and he would honor you
As he does Orestes, who is being reared in luxury.
He has three daughters in his fortress palace,
Chrysothemis, Laodice, and Iphianassa.
You may lead whichever you like as your bride
Back to Peleus' house, without paying anything,                    290
And he would give her a dowry richer than any
A father has ever given his daughter.
And he will give you seven populous cities,
Cardamyle, Enope, grassy Hire,
Sacred Pherae, Antheia with its meadowlands,
Beautiful Aepeia, and Pedasus, wine country.
They are all near the sea, on sandy Pylos' frontier,
And cattlemen live there, rich in herds and flocks,
Who will pay you tribute as if you were a god
And fulfill the shining decrees of your scepter.                    300
All this he will do if you give up your grudge.
But if Agamemnon is too hateful to you,
Himself and his gifts, think of all the others
Suffering up and down the line, and of the glory
You will win from them. They will honor you
Like a god.
                    And don't forget Hector.
You just might get him now. He's coming in close,
Deluded into thinking that he has no match
In the Greek army that has landed on his beach."                    310

And Achilles, strong, swift, and godlike:

"Son of Laertes in the line of Zeus,
Odysseus the strategist—I can see
That I have no choice but to speak my mind
And tell you exactly how things are going to be.
Either that or sit through endless sessions
Of people whining at me. I hate like hell
The man who says one thing and thinks another.
So this is how I see it.
I cannot imagine Agamemnon,                                         320
Or any other Greek, persuading me,

Not after the thanks I got for fighting this war,
Going up against the enemy day after day.
It doesn't matter if you stay in camp or fight—
In the end, everybody comes out the same.
Coward and hero get the same reward:
You die whether you slack off or work.
And what do I have for all my suffering,
Constantly putting my life on the line?
Like a bird who feeds her chicks                              *330*
Whatever she finds, and goes without herself,
That's what I've been like, lying awake
Through sleepless nights, in battle for days
Soaked in blood, fighting men for their wives.
I've raided twelve cities with our ships
And eleven on foot in the fertile Troad,
Looted them all, brought back heirlooms
By the ton, and handed it all over
To Atreus' son, who hung back in camp
Raking it in and distributing damn little.                   *340*
What the others did get they at least got to keep.
They all have their prizes, everyone but me—
I'm the only Greek from whom he took something back.
He should be happy with the woman he has.
Why do the Greeks have to fight the Trojans?
Why did Agamemnon lead the army to Troy
If not for the sake of fair-haired Helen?
Do you have to be descended from Atreus
To love your mate? Every decent, sane man
Loves his woman and cares for her, as I did,                 *350*
Loved her from my heart. It doesn't matter
That I won her with my spear. He took her,
Took her right out of my hands, cheated me,
And now he thinks he's going to win me back?
He can forget it. I know how things stand.
It's up to you, Odysseus, and the other kings
To find a way to keep the fire from the ships.
He's been pretty busy without me, hasn't he,
Building a wall, digging a moat around it,
Pounding in stakes for a palisade.                           *360*
None of that stuff will hold Hector back.

When I used to fight for the Greeks,
Hector wouldn't come out farther from his wall
Than the oak tree by the Western Gate.
He waited for me there once, and barely escaped.
Now that I don't want to fight him anymore,
I will sacrifice to Zeus and all gods tomorrow,
Load my ships, and launch them on the sea.
Take a look if you want, if you give a damn,
And you'll see my fleet on the Hellespont                    370
In the early light, my men rowing hard.
With good weather from the sea god,
I'll reach Phthia after a three-day sail.
I left a lot behind when I hauled myself here,
And I'll bring back more, gold and bronze,
Silken-waisted women, grey iron—
Everything except the prize of honor
The warlord Agamemnon gave me
And in his insulting arrogance took back.
So report back to him everything I say,                      380
And report it publicly—get the Greeks angry,
In case the shameless bastard still thinks
He can steal us blind. He doesn't dare
Show his dogface here. Fine. I don't want
To have anything to do with him either.
He cheated me, wronged me. Never again.
He's had it. He can go to hell in peace,
The half-wit that Zeus has made him.
His gifts? His gifts mean nothing to me.
Not even if he offered me ten or twenty times              390
His present gross worth and added to it
All the trade Orchomenus does in a year,
All the wealth laid up in Egyptian Thebes,
The wealthiest city in all the world,
Where they drive two hundred teams of horses
Out through each of its hundred gates.
Not even if Agamemnon gave me gifts
As numberless as grains of sand or dust,
Would he persuade me or touch my heart—
Not until he's paid in full for all my grief.               400
His daughter? I would not marry

The daughter of Agamemnon son of Atreus
If she were as lovely as golden Aphrodite
Or could weave like owl-eyed Athena.
Let him choose some other Achaean
More to his lordly taste. If the gods
Preserve me and I get home safe
Peleus will find me a wife himself.
There are many Greek girls in Hellas and Phthia,
Daughters of chieftains who rule the cities.                     410
I can have my pick of any of them.
I've always wanted to take a wife there,
A woman to have and to hold, someone with whom
I can enjoy all the goods old Peleus has won.
Nothing is worth my life, not all the riches
They say Troy held before the Greeks came,
Not all the wealth in Phoebus Apollo's
Marble shrine up in craggy Pytho.
Cattle and flocks are there for the taking;
You can always get tripods and chestnut horses.                  420
But a man's life cannot be won back
Once his breath has passed beyond his clenched teeth.
My mother Thetis, a moving silver grace,
Tells me two fates sweep me on to my death.
If I stay here and fight, I'll never return home,
But my glory will be undying forever.
If I return home to my dear fatherland
My glory is lost but my life will be long,
And death that ends all will not catch me soon.
As for the rest of you, I would advise you too              430
To sail back home, since there's no chance now
Of storming Ilion's height. Zeus has stretched
His hand above her, making her people bold.
What's left for you now is to go back to the council
And announce my message. It's up to them
To come up with another plan to save the ships
And the army with them, since this one,
Based on appeasing my anger, won't work.
Phoenix can spend the night here. Tomorrow
He sails with me on our voyage home,                        440
If he wants to, that is. I won't force him to come."

He spoke, and they were hushed in silence,
Shocked by his speech and his stark refusal.
Finally the old horseman Phoenix spoke,
Bursting into tears. He felt the ships were lost.

"If you have set your mind on going home,
Achilles, and will do nothing to save the ships
From being burnt, if your heart is that angry,
How could I stay here without you, my boy,
All by myself? Peleus sent me with you                          450
On that day you left Phthia to go to Agamemnon,
A child still, knowing nothing of warfare
Or assemblies where men distinguish themselves.
He sent me to you to teach you this—
To be a speaker of words and a doer of deeds.
I could not bear to be left behind now
Apart from you, child, not even if a god
Promised to smooth my wrinkles and make me
As young and strong as I was when I first left
The land of Hellas and its beautiful women.                     460
I was running away from a quarrel with Amyntor,
My father, who was angry with me
Over his concubine, a fair-haired woman
Whom he loved as much as he scorned his wife,
My mother. She implored me constantly
To make love to his concubine so that this woman
Would learn to hate the old man. I did as she asked.
My father found out and cursed me roundly,
Calling on the Furies to ensure that never
Would a child of mine sit on his knees.                         470
The gods answered his prayers, Underworld Zeus
And dread Persephone. I decided to kill him
With a sharp sword, but some god calmed me down—
Putting in my mind what people would say,
The names they would call me—so that in fact
I would not be known as a parricide.
From then on I could not bear to linger
In my father's house, although my friends
And my family tried to get me to stay,
Entreating me, slaughtering sheep and cattle,                   480

Roasting whole pigs on spits, and drinking
Jar after jar of the old man's wine.
For nine solid days they kept watch on me,
Working in shifts, staying up all night.
The fires stayed lit, one under the portico
Of the main courtyard, one on the porch
In front of my bedroom door. On the tenth night,
When it got dark, I broke through the latches
And vaulted over the courtyard fence,
Eluding the watchmen and servant women.                    490
I was on the run through wide Hellas
And made it to Phthia's black soil, her flocks,
And to Lord Peleus. He welcomed me kindly
And loved me as a father loves his only son,
A grown son who will inherit great wealth.
He made me rich and settled me on the border,
Where I lived as king of the Dolopians.
I made you what you are, my godlike Achilles,
And loved you from my heart. You wouldn't eat,
Whether it was at a feast or a meal in the house,        500
Unless I set you on my lap and cut your food up
And fed it to you and held the wine to your lips.
Many a time you wet the tunic on my chest,
Burping up wine when you were colicky.
I went through a lot for you, because I knew
The gods would never let me have a child
Of my own. No, I tried to make you my child,
Achilles, so you would save me from ruin.
But you have to master your proud spirit.
It's not right for you to have a pitiless heart.          510
Even the gods can bend. Superior as they are
In honor, power, and every excellence,
They can be turned aside from wrath
When humans who have transgressed
Supplicate them with incense and prayers,
With libations and savor of sacrifice.
Yes, for Prayers are daughters of great Zeus.
Lame and wrinkled and with eyes averted,
They are careful to follow in Folly's footste
But Folly is strong and fleet, and outruns th

Beating them everywhere and plaguing humans,
Who are cured by the Prayers when they come behind.
Revere the daughters of Zeus when they come,
And they will bless you and hear your cry.
Reject them and refuse them stubbornly,
And they will ask Zeus, Cronus' son, to have
Folly plague you, so you will pay in pain.
No, Achilles, grant these daughters of Zeus
The respect that bends all upright men's minds.
If the son of Atreus were not offering gifts                            530
And promising more, if he were still raging mad,
I would not ask you to shrug off your grudge
And help the Greeks, no matter how sore their need.
But he is offering gifts and promising more,
And he has sent to you a delegation
Of the best men in the army, your dearest friends.
Don't scorn their words or their mission here.
    No one could blame you for being angry before.
We all know stories about heroes of old,
How they were furiously angry, but later on                             540
Were won over with gifts or appeased with words.
I remember a very old story like this, and since
We are all friends here, I will tell it to you now.
    The Curetes were fighting the Aetolians
In a bloody war around Calydon town.
The Aetolians were defending their city
And the Curetes meant to burn it down.
This was all because gold-throned Artemis
Had cursed the Curetes, angry that Oeneus
Had not offered her his orchard's first fruits.                         550
The other gods feasted on bulls by the hundred,
But Oeneus forgot somehow or other
Only the sacrifice to great Zeus' daughter.
So the Archer Goddess, angry at heart,
Roused a savage boar, with gleaming white tusks,
And sent him to destroy Oeneus' orchard.
The boar did a good job, uprooting trees
    nd littering the ground with apples and blossoms.
      t Oeneus' son, Meleager, killed it
       r getting up a party of hunters and hounds                       560

From many towns: it took more than a few men
To kill this huge boar, and not before
It set many a hunter on the funeral pyre.
But the goddess caused a bitter argument
About the boar's head and shaggy hide
Between the Curetes and Aetolians.
They went to war. While Meleager still fought
The Curetes had the worst of it
And could not remain outside Calydon's wall.
But when wrath swelled Meleager's heart,                    570
As it swells even the hearts of the wise,
And his anger rose against Althaea his mother,
He lay in bed with his wife, Cleopatra,
Child of Marpessa and the warrior Idas.
Idas once took up his bow against Apollo
To win lissome Marpessa. Her parents
Called the girl Halcyone back then
Because her mother wept like a halcyon,
The bird of sorrows, because the Archer God,
Phoebus Apollo, had stolen her daughter.                    580
Meleager nursed his anger at Cleopatra's side,
Furious because his mother had cursed him,
Cursed him to the gods for murdering his uncle,
Her brother, that is, and she beat the earth,
The nurturing earth, with her hands, and called
Upon Hades and Persephone the dread,
As she knelt and wet her bosom with tears,
To bring death to her son. And the Fury
Who walks in darkness heard her
From the pit of Erebus, and her heart was iron.             590
Soon the enemy was heard at the walls again,
Battering the gates. The Aetolian elders
Sent the city's high priests to pray to Meleager
To come out and defend them, offering him
Fifty acres of Calydon's richest land
Wherever he chose, half in vineyard,
Half in clear plowland, to be cut from the plain.
And the old horseman Oeneus shook his doors,
Standing on the threshold of his gabled room,
And recited a litany of prayers to his son,                 600

As did his sisters and his queenly mother.
He refused them all, and refused his friends,
His very best friends and boon companions.
No one could move his heart or persuade him
Until the Curetes, having scaled the walls
Were burning the city and beating down
His bedroom door. Then his wife wailed
And listed for him all the woes that befall
A captured people—the men killed,
The town itself burnt, the women and children          610
Led into slavery. This roused his spirit.
He clapped on armor and went out to fight.
And so he saved the Aetolians from doom
Of his own accord, and they paid him none
Of those lovely gifts, savior or not.
  Don't be like that. Don't think that way,
And don't let your spirit turn that way.
The ships will be harder to save when they're burning.
Come while there are gifts, while the Achaeans
Will still honor you as if you were a god.          620
But if you go into battle without any gifts,
Your honor will be less, save us or not."

And strong, swift-footed Achilles anwered:

"I don't need that kind of honor, Phoenix.
My honor comes from Zeus, and I will have it
Among these beaked ships as long as my breath
Still remains and my knees still move.
Now listen to this. You're listening? Good.
Don't try to confuse me with your pleading
On Agamemnon's behalf. If you're his friend          630
You're no longer mine, although I love you.
Hate him because I hate him. It's as simple as that.
You're like a second father to me. Stay here,
Be king with me and share half the honor.
These others can take my message. Lie down
And spend the night on a soft couch. At daybreak
We will decide whether to set sail or stay."

And he made a silent nod to Patroclus
To spread a thick bed for Phoenix. It was time
For the others to think about leaving. Big Ajax,　　　640
Telamon's godlike son, said as much:

"Son of Laertes in the line of Zeus,
Resourceful Odysseus—it's time we go.
I do not think we will accomplish
What we were sent here to do. Our job now
Is to report this news quickly, bad as it is.
They will be waiting to hear. Achilles
Has made his great heart savage.
He is a cruel man, and has no regard
For the love that his friends honored him with,　　　650
Beyond anyone else who camps with the ships.
Pitiless. A man accepts compensation
For a murdered brother, a dead son.
The killer goes on living in the same town
After paying blood money, and the bereaved
Restrains his proud spirit and broken heart
Because he has received payment. But you,
The gods have replaced your heart
With flint and malice, because of one girl,
One single girl, while we are offering you　　　660
Seven of the finest women to be found
And many other gifts. Show some generosity
And some respect. We have come under your roof,
We few out of the entire army, trying hard
To be the friends you care for most of all."

And Achilles, the great runner, answered him:

"Ajax, son of Telamon in the line of Zeus,
Everything you say is after my own heart.
But I swell with rage when I think of how
The son of Atreus treated me like dirt　　　670
In public, as if I were some worthless tramp.
Now go, and take back this message:
I won't lift a finger in this bloody war

Until Priam's illustrious son Hector
Comes to the Myrmidons' ships and huts
Killing Greeks as he goes and torching the fleet.
But when he comes to my hut and my black ship
I think Hector will stop, for all his battle lust."

He spoke. They poured their libations
And headed for the ships, Odysseus leading.　　　　　680
Patroclus ordered a bed made ready
For Phoenix, and the old man lay down
On fleeces and rugs covered with linen
And waited for bright dawn. Achilles slept
In an inner alcove, and by his side
Lay a woman he had brought from Lesbos
With high, lovely cheekbones, Diomede her name,
Phorbas' daughter. Patroclus lay down
In the opposite corner, and with him lay Iphis,
A silken girl Achilles had given him　　　　　　690
When he took steep Scyrus, Enyeus' city.

By now Odysseus and Ajax
Were in Agamemnon's quarters,
Surrounded by officers drinking their health
From gold cups and shouting questions.
Agamemnon, the warlord, had priority:

"Odysseus, pride of the Achaeans, tell me,
Is he willing to repel the enemy fire
And save the ships, or does he refuse,
His great heart still in the grip of wrath?"　　　　700

Odysseus, who endured all, answered:

"Son of Atreus, most glorious Agamemnon,
Far from quenching his wrath, Achilles
Is filled with even more. He spurns you
And your gifts, and suggests that you
Think of a way to save the ships and the army.
He himself threatens, at dawn's first light,
To get his own ships onto the water,

And he said he would advise the others as well
To sail for home, since there is no chance now                    710
You will storm Ilion's height. Zeus has stretched
His hand above her, making her people bold.
This is what he said, as these men here
Who came with me will tell you, Ajax
And the two heralds, prudent men both.
Phoenix will spend the night there. Tomorrow
He sails with Achilles on his voyage home,
If he wants to. He will not be forced to go."

They were stunned by the force of his words
And fell silent for a long time, hushed in grief,               720
Until at last Diomedes said in his booming voice:

"Son of Atreus, glorious Agamemnon,
You should never have pleaded with him
Or offered all those gifts. Achilles
Was arrogant enough without your help.
Let him do what he wants, stay here
Or get the hell out. He'll fight later, all right,
When he is ready or a god tells him to.
Now I want everyone to do as I say.
Enjoy some food and wine to keep up                             730
Your strength, and then get some sleep.
When the rosy light first streaks the sky
Get your troops and horses into formation
Before the ships. Fight in the front yourselves."

The warlords assented, taken aback
By the authority of Diomedes' speech.
Each man poured libation and went to his hut,
Where he lay down and took the gift of sleep.

# ILIAD 10

$A$ll the other leaders of the Greek alliance
Dozed through the night, subdued by soft sleep.
But not Agamemnon. Sleep had no hold
On the troubled mind of the army's commander.

*Think of lightning: Hera's rich hair streams*
*In the sky when her husband builds storms—*
*Heavy rain, or unspeakable hail, or snow*
*That sifts down over cultivated land,*
*Or the barbed-wire mouth of a battlefield.*

Thus Agamemnon, the density of the groans       10
From his heart's deep core, his visceral fear.

Whenever he looked out over the Trojan plain
He marvelled at how many fires burned
Before Ilion's walls, and at the din of flutes
And pipes, and the dull roar of humanity.
And whenever he looked at the Greek ships
He pulled clumps of his hair out from the roots
In appeal to Zeus on high, and his heart ached.
Nestor came to mind. He would go to Nestor
And the two would find some way to save the army.       20
He sat up and pulled on his tunic,

[1–21]

Then laced on his sandals and threw a lion skin
Over his shoulders, a fiery, reddish thing
That reached down to his feet. And he took his spear.

Menelaus was just as troubled and sleepless.
What would happen to all the Argives
Who had crossed the water for his sake
And come to Troy with war in their hearts?
He drew around his shouders the dappled pelt
Of a leopard, put a bronze helm on his head,                    30
And gripping his spear he went through camp
To waken his brother, the great warlord
Whom the common folk honored as a god.
He found Agamemnon by the stern of his ship,
Putting on his armor and glad to see his brother.
Menelaus, good at the war cry, said to him:

"Brother, why are you arming yourself?
To rouse someone to scout out the Trojans?
I am afraid you will find few volunteers
For this mission. To go alone by night                    40
And spy on the enemy would take a brave man indeed."

The warlord Agamemnon answered:

"You and I need a plan, Menelaus,
A good one, to save the army and the ships,
Now that Zeus has turned away from us.
He seems to prefer Hector's sacrifices to ours.
I have never seen or heard of any one man
Ever doing as much harm in a single day
As Hector has done today to our boys
By himself alone—and he is not even the son                    50
Of a goddess or god! Go now, run quickly
Through the ships and summon Ajax
And Idomeneus, while I go to Nestor
And see if he will go to the sentinels
And alert them. They would listen to him,
For his son is captain of the guard,

He and Meriones, Idomeneus' comrade.
It was to them especially we gave this command."

And Menelaus, good at the war cry:

"What are you telling me to do?                    60
To wait there with them until you come?
Or run back after I have delivered your orders?"

And the warlord Agamemnon:

"Wait there, or we may miss each other
As we cross the camp with all its paths.
But give a shout wherever you go
And wake the men up. Call each man by name
And by his father's name, honoring them all.
Let's you and I not be too proud to work.
Zeus gave us this burden when we were born."                    70

And so Agamemnon sent his brother off
But went himself to visit Nestor,
A shepherd to his people, and found him
Lying on a soft bed next to his hut
And black ship. Beside him lay his rich gear—
Shield, two spears, and gleaming helmet—
And the shimmering belt he always wore
When he armed to lead his men into battle.
Nestor just didn't give in to grievous old age.
He rose on his elbow and lifted his head,                    80
And asked these questions of Atreus' son:

"Who are you, going alone through camp
In the dead of night when everyone's asleep?
Are you looking for one of your mules
Or one of your friends? Speak out,
And don't sneak up on me. What do you want?"

And Agamemnon, the great warlord:

"Nestor, son of Neleus, our great glory,

You will know Agamemnon, Atreus' son,
The man whom Zeus besets with more troubles          90
Than any man alive, as long as I draw my breath
And my knees still bend. I'm roaming like this
Because sleep won't come, so worried am I
About the war and the Achaeans' troubles.
I'm so afraid for the army I'm losing my mind.
I toss and turn, my heart pounds through my chest,
And I can't stop trembling. If you want to help,
Since it seems you can't sleep either,
Come with me and let's go to the sentinels
So we can make sure they haven't fallen asleep          100
From fatigue and forgotten their watch.
The enemy are bivouacked close by,
And for all we know they might attack by night."

And Nestor, the old Gerenian horseman:

"Most glorious son of Atreus, lord Agamemnon,
Zeus in his wisdom will not fulfill
All of Hector's hopes. No, his troubles
Will be worse than ours, if only Achilles
Would have a change of heart and give up his grudge.
Of course I will go with you, but we should          110
Wake up some others—Tydeus' son,
And Odysseus, and the swift Ajax,
And Meges too. And someone should go
And summon the godlike Ajax as well,
And Idomeneus, for their ships are the farthest.
As for Menelaus, dear and honored as he is,
And even if it makes you angry, I will not shrink
From having a word with him myself, for sleeping
At a time like this and leaving you all the work.
He should be hard at work beseeching all our best.          120
This is a crisis we can no longer ignore."

The warlord Agamemnon answered him:

"You may remind him of his responsibilities
Another time, old sir, and with my blessings.

He is often unwilling to exert himself,
Not through sloth or lack of discernment,
But in deference to my leadership.
Just now, though, he awoke before I did
And came to me, and I sent him out
To summon the men you are asking for.                    130
But we should go. We will find them at the gates
Among the guards, where I said they should gather."

And Nestor, the old Gerenian horseman:

"This is how he will earn the army's respect
And their compliance when he issues commands."

So saying he pulled on his tunic,
Laced sandals onto his supple feet,
And buckled around him a purple cloak,
Two-ply and broad, with a thick nap.
He grasped a mighty spear, tipped with honed bronze,        140
And went off through the ships.
                                        Odysseus,
Who could match wits with Zeus, was the first
The old Gerenian horseman woke up.
His voice echoed in Odysseus' dreaming mind,
And the Ithacan came out of the hut and said:

"Why are you going alone through the camp
In the dead of night? What's the emergency?"

And Nestor, the horseman of Gerenia:

"Son of Laertes in the line of Zeus,                          150
Odysseus the strategist, don't be angry.
We are under great duress. Come with us
So we can rouse another whom we should consult
As we decide whether to fight or flee."

And Odysseus, the master strategist,
Got a shield from his hut and went with them.

They came to Diomedes, son of Tydeus,
And found him outside his hut with his gear.
His men were sleeping all around him
Using their shields for pillows, their spears          *160*
Driven upright in the ground on their spikes.
The bronze glittered like summer lightning.
The hero was asleep on an oxhide,
A bright rug under his head. Nestor woke him,
Rolling him over with his heel, and scolded:

"Up, son of Tydeus. Are you going to sleep all night?
Don't you know the Trojans are encamped
On the rising ground close by the ships?"

Diomedes was awake and up in an instant,
And his words flew fast as he said to Nestor:          *170*

"You're tough, old man, and you never quit.
Couldn't one of the younger generation
Make the rounds waking up captains
All through camp? You're impossible, though."

And Nestor, the horseman of Gerenia:

"That was well said, friend. I myself have
Perfectly good sons, and there are many others
Who could make the rounds and do the summoning.
But we are very hard-pressed. It all stands
On a razor's edge now for the entire army,          *180*
Ruin or survival. Now go rouse swift Ajax
And Meges—if you really feel sorry for me."

Thus spoke Nestor. And Diomedes threw
Over his shoulders a tawny lion skin
That reached to his feet. Grasping his spear
He went off to rouse and fetch the warriors.

When they joined the sentinels they found them
Wide awake, crouching down with their gear.

*Dogs will watch a sheepfold all night long*
*With bloodshot eyes, but when they hear*                    *190*
*A predator approaching through the woods*
*And then the noise of men and hounds around it,*
*Their sleepiness completely disappears.*

So too these human eyes as the sentinels
Kept watch through the night, turning
Toward the plain over and over again
Whenever they thought they heard Trojans coming.

It warmed Nestor's heart, and the old man
Encouraged them with winged words:

"Just so, my boys, keep your watch. Stay awake,        *200*
Or we will become sport for our enemies."

And he hurried on through the trench, followed
By all the captains summoned to this council,
And by Meriones and Nestor's glorious son,
Whom they invited also. So they went through
And up from the trench and sat themselves down
In an open spot where the ground was clear
Of dead bodies, the very spot where Hector
Had turned back from slaughtering the Greeks
When night enfolded him. Sitting down there      *210*
They held council, and Nestor began:

"Well, my friends, is no one man enough
To go among the Trojans and take captive
Some straggler, or otherwise overhear
What the enemy intends? Will they stay put
Out here by the ships, or withdraw to the city
Now that they have beaten the Achaeans back?
A man might learn all this and return
Unscathed, and his glory among men
Would reach the sky—and he would get gifts       *220*
From every leader commanding ships here,
From each a black ewe with a lamb beneath.

What could be finer? And he would forever be
Invited to feasts and to drinking parties."

He finished, and they were hushed in silence.
Then Diomedes rose to the occasion:

"Nestor, my pride as a man urges me
To go into the enemy camp over there,
But if another were to go with me
It would help, and I would be more confident.                    230
When you work as a team, your partner helps see
What will work out best. Solo, you might see,
But not as much, and you're short on wits."

There was no shortage of volunteers
To accompany Diomedes. Both Ajaxes
Were ready, those servants of War,
Ready was Meriones, and Nestor's son,
Ready Menelaus, the son of Atreus,
And Odysseus, who could endure anything,
Ready to infiltrate the Trojan lines.                           240
Then the warlord Agamemnon spoke out:

"Diomedes, son of Tydeus, dear to my heart,
Choose as your comrade whomever you want,
The best of all these who put themselves forth.
Do not, out of deference, choose a lesser man
And leave a better behind, deferring to birth
And seniority, even if one is more royal."

In truth, he was afraid for red-haired Menelaus.
Diomedes, good at the battle cry, said:

"If you really want me to make my own choice,                   250
How could I pass over godlike Odysseus,
Who has what it takes for any kind of work,
The heart, the courage—and is Athena's friend.
If he goes with me we could make it back
Through blazing fire. He doesn't miss a thing."

And Odysseus, who had endured many campaigns:

"Diomedes, don't overrate my merits or my faults.
You're talking to Greeks who know what's what.
We'd better head out. It's very late,
Getting on toward dawn. The stars have shifted                    260
And more than two-thirds of the night is gone."

With that they put on their formidable gear.
Thrasymedes gave Diomedes a sword—
He had left his own at his ship—and a shield.
On his head he put a leather helmet
Without horn or crest, the kind they call
A skullcap and that young warriors wear.
Meriones gave to Odysseus a bow,
A quiver, and a sword, while on his head
He put a helmet made of hide, stiffened                    270
With numerous taut leather thongs inside
And faced outside with the gleaming white teeth
Of a tusker boar set thick in alternate rows
Cunningly and well. It was lined with felt.
This helmet had been stolen by Autolycus
From Amyntor's palace in Eleon,
And he gave it to Amphidamas of Cythera
To take to Scandeia, and Amphidamas
Gave it as a guest gift to Molus,
Who gave it to his son Meriones to wear.                    280
Now it protected Odysseus' head.

When the two of them had all their gear on
They headed out. Hard on their right
Pallas Athena sent a heron flying,
And although they couldn't see the bird in the dark
They heard its night cry. Glad at the omen
Odysseus said a prayer to Athena:

"Hear me, child of Zeus Aegis-Holder.
You are ever by my side

In all my troubles, and you look over me                    *290*
Wherever I go. Be my friend
Once more, Athena, as never before.
Grant that we return to the ships in glory,
Having done great deeds to confound the Trojans."

And Diomedes, good at the battle cry:

"Hear me also, mystic Daughter of Zeus.
Go with me now even as you went
With my noble father Tydeus to Thebes
When he went as envoy of the Achaeans.
Leaving them by the river Asopus,                           *300*
He bore to the Cadmeians peaceful words
But on his return did violent deeds
With you, divine one, standing beside him.
Be thou willing to stand by me now,
And I will sacrifice upon my return
A sleek heifer, broad-browed, unbroken,
That man has not yet put under the yoke,
And I will goldleaf her horns."

Thus the heroes, and Athena heard them.
Their prayers said, the two moved forward             *310*
Like two lions at midnight, picking their way
Through corpses, weapons, and crusted black blood.

   Hector did not allow the Trojans
To sleep either. He called together all their great,
All of the Trojan leaders and chieftains,
And laid before them this stratagem:

"Who will volunteer for special duty
And a hefty reward? I will guarantee
A chariot and two high-maned horses,
The best in the Achaean beachhead camp,                *320*
To the man who will dare to win himself glory
By going close to the ships and spying out

Whether they are still guarded as they used to be,
Or whether our enemies, having suffered defeat
At our hands, are planning their escape
And are too fatigued to watch through the night."


He finished, and they were all hushed in silence.
Among the Trojans was a certain Dolon,
Son of Eumedes, the godly herald, a man rich
In gold and bronze, ill-favored, but fast.                        330
He was the only brother among five sisters,
And the only Trojan to respond to Hector:


"Hector, my pride as a man urges me
To go close to the ships and scout around.
But lift your staff and swear me an oath
That you really will give me the horses
And chariot, tricked in bronze, that carry
The peerless Achilles. And I will not be
A disappointment to you as a scout
But will go straight through their camp until I reach         340
Agamemnon's ship, where their leaders will be
Deciding in council whether to fight or flee."


So Hector took his staff and swore:


"Zeus be my witness, Hera's thundering lord,
That no other Trojan will drive these horses,
But you alone will enjoy them forever."


He swore an empty oath. Dolon, excited,
Slung his curved bow around his shoulders,
Cloaked himself in a grey wolf skin
And put on a weasel cap. Taking a javelin                     350
He left for the ships, but he never returned
To bring any information to Hector.
He had passed the crowd of horses and men
And was moving eagerly along when Odysseus
Saw him coming and said to Diomedes:

"There's someone coming from their camp,
I don't know whether to spy on our ships
Or to strip one of the corpses. Let him get past
And down the plain a little. Then we can take him.
If he starts to outrun us, hem him in                          360
Toward the ships and away from his camp.
We don't want him to escape toward the city."

So the two of them lay down among the dead
Just off the path. Dolon ran by unaware
And had gone about the length of a furrow
A mule plows—they are better than oxen
At pulling the plow in deep fallow land—
When the two Greeks ran after him.
He stopped when he heard the sound, assuming
They were friends sent from the Trojan camp                    370
To call him back, and that Hector had called a retreat.
They were within a spearcast before he realized
They were hostile. He started to run.
Diomedes and Odysseus picked up their speed

   *Like a pair of hounds on a hare or a doe*
   *That goes bleating before it out in the woods.*


They had him cut off and were hard in pursuit.
When Dolon was coming up to the sentinels
Athena put a burst of strength into Diomedes
So that no other Achaean would be able to score              380
The first blow and Tydeus' son arrive too late.
Diomedes closed the gap and called out:
"Hold it. You're in spear range, and as good as dead."
And he threw as he spoke, but purposely missed,
The point of the polished spear sailing
Over the Trojan's right shoulder and into the ground.
Dolon stopped in his tracks, terrified, stammering,
His teeth chattering, and pale with fear.

His two pursuers came up, panting for breath,
And seized his hands. Bursting into tears he said:          390

"Take me alive. I'm good for the ransom. At home
We have bronze and gold and well-wrought iron,
And my father would give you unlimited ransom
If he heard I was alive at the Achaean ships."

And Odysseus, as wily as they come:

"Get a grip, man. No one's going to kill you.
But tell me this, and give me a straight answer:
What are you doing out here by the ships
Alone at night when everyone's sleeping?
Do you have a mind to strip a corpse or two?                         400
Did Hector send you out on espionage
Or are you acting on your own volition?"

Dolon's knees were shaking as he answered:

"Hector lured me into this, filling my mind
With foolish hopes. He promised to give me
Achilles' horses and his chariot,
And he sent me out into the dead of night
To sneak up close to the enemy's ships
To find out whether they are guarded still,
Or whether the Greeks, having suffered defeat                        410
At our hands, are planning their escape
And are too fatigued to watch through the night."

Odysseus smiled at him wisely and said:

"Your heart was set on a truly great reward,
Achilles' horses. But they are difficult
For mortal men to control. Only Achilles,
Born of a goddess, can master them.
But tell me this, and give it to me straight:
Where did you leave Hector when you left?
Where is his battle gear and where are his horses?                   420
How are the Trojans encamped and guarded?
And what is their plan? Will they stay put

Out here by the ships, or withdraw to the city
Now that they have beaten the Achaeans back?"

And Dolon, Eumedes' only son:

"I'll tell you everything straight. Hector
Is holding council at the tomb of Ilus,
Away from the turmoil. As for sentinels,
None have been posted to guard the camp.
The Trojans keep watch around their fires,                    430
Urging one and another to stay awake,
But the allies, coming from many lands,
Are all asleep, leaving it to the Trojans
To keep watch, since their own children
Are nowhere near, nor their women."

Odysseus, full of cunning, continued:

"Then are the allies camped with the Trojans
Or apart by themselves? I want the details."

Dolon, son of Eumedes, responded:

"I'll tell you everything straight. Toward the sea          440
Are the Carians and Paeonians, archers,
Along with the Leleges, Cauconians,
And the Pelasgi. Over toward Thymbre
Is the Lycian sector. The Mysians are there too,
Along with the charioteers from Phrygia
And Maeonia. But why all these details?
If you want to infiltrate the Trojan camp,
The Thracians are here at this edge, just arrived
With their king Rhesus, son of Eïoneus.
He has the finest horses I ever saw, the greatest,          450
Whiter than snow and as fast as the wind.
His chariot is done in silver and gold,
And he came with this massive gold armor,
Amazing to see, not what mortal men wear,
But what you'd expect on the deathless gods.

But look, take me to the ships now
Or leave me tied up here, so you two can go
And see for yourselves if I'm telling the truth."

Diomedes looked at him darkly and said:

"Don't even think about getting off, Dolon—            *460*
Although you've been a fine messenger.
You've fallen into our hands. If we let you go
You'll come to the Greeks' ships another time,
Either to spy on us or to fight in combat.
If I take care of you now and make sure you're dead,
You'll never worry the Greeks again."

Dolon was reaching up to Diomedes
In supplication—had almost touched his chin—
When Diomedes sprang and with his sword
Severed the tendons at the nape of his neck.            *470*
He was still shrieking when his mouth caught the sand.
They stripped the ferret-skin cap from his head
And took the wolf's hide, the recurved bow,
And the long spear. Odysseus held these up
And prayed to Athena the Despoiler:

"Rejoice in these, Goddess, first of Olympians
To receive our offerings. Guide us once more,
Now to where the Thracians and their horses sleep."

With that, he hoisted the gear into a tamarisk
And stashed it there, leaving as a marker            *480*
A bundle of branches that they couldn't miss
On their way back through the black rush of night.
Then they went forward through the carnage and weapons
Until they came to their goal: the Thracian camp.
The exhausted soldiers were sound asleep, their gear
In three neat rows on the ground around them,
And by each man stood his chariot team.
Rhesus slept in the middle, his thoroughbreds
Tethered by the reins to the chariot's deck.
Odysseus pointed him out to Diomedes:            *490*

"There he is, Diomedes, with his horses,
The man that Dolon told us about.
Well? Don't just stand there
Slouching in your armor. Untie his horses.
Or you kill the men and leave the horses to me."

The Grey-Eyed One breathed into Diomedes,
And he went up and down the row of Thracians
Killing them one by one. Their groans were ugly
When the sword struck. The ground turned to red mud.

   *A lion comes to an unguarded pen*            500
   *Of sheep or goats and leaps in with malice.*

So Tydeus' son went through the Thracians
Until he had killed twelve. Odysseus, always thinking,
Pulled each body out of the way by the feet
As soon as Diomedes did his work with the sword,
So that the combed horses would have an easy path
And not be spooked by having to step over
Dead bodies, which they were as yet unused to.
The thirteenth was Rhesus. As Tydeus' son
Separated him from the sweetness of life,       510
He gasped for breath. Diomedes stood over him
That night, in a bad dream sent by Athena.

By now Odysseus had the horses free
And roped together with the reins.
He drove them out of the Trojan camp
With his bow, not having noticed
The gleaming whip in the chariot.
He whistled over to Diomedes,
Who was pondering his next reckless move.
Should he pull the chariot out by its pole,     520
Or dump the gear piled in it and carry it out?
Or should he just kill more Thracians?
While he was weighing his options, Athena
Stood near to him and said to the hero:

"Time to get back, son of great Tydeus,

To the hollow ships, before some other god
Rouses the Trojans and you are chased back."

He knew it was the voice of the goddess
And quickly mounted the horses. Odysseus
Smacked them with his bow, and they made for the ships.     530

Apollo was out that night too,
And when he saw Athena helping Diomedes
He made his silver presence felt in the camp
And awakened Hippocoön, a Thracian lord,
One of Rhesus' high-born kinsmen.
He started from his sleep, and when he saw
The place empty where the horses had stood
And the men gasping in pools of blood,
He groaned and called his old friend by name.
Then everything was confusion and noise,                   540
The Trojans running up from all over the camp
To view the havoc wreaked by the warriors
Who by now were halfway back to the ships.
   When they reached the spot where they had killed
Hector's spy, Odysseus reined in the horses.
Diomedes jumped down and handed up to him
The bloody spoils, then mounted again
And lashed the horses, who flew on to the ships.

Nestor heard the sound first and said:

"Friends, Argive commanders and counsellors,             550
I may be mistaken but still I must speak.
The sound of horses' hooves strikes my ears.
Let us hope that Odysseus and strong Diomedes
Have rustled some horses away from the Trojans.
But I fear in my heart that the best of the Argives
Have come to harm in the enemy camp."

He was hardly finished when they arrived.
They got down and were welcomed warmly
With handclasps and gentle words.
Gerenian Nestor was first with his questions:           560

"Praise be, Odysseus, glory of the Greeks,
Where did you two come by these horses?
In the Trojan camp? Or did you meet some god
Who gave them to you? They shine like the sun.
I'm always among the Trojans. Old I may be
For a warrior, but I don't stay with the ships.
But I never saw such horses as these.
No, I think a god met you and gave them to you.
Zeus in the clouds loves you both, as does
His grey-eyed daughter who bears the aegis."                570

And Odysseus, wise in every way:

"Nestor, son of Neleus, glory of the Greeks,
A god could easily give us, if he wanted,
Even better horses. Such is heaven's power.
No, these horses, old sir, have just come
From Thrace. Diomedes killed their master
And twelve of his comrades, all their best.
And we got one more, a scout near the ships,
Somebody Hector and the Trojan lords
Sent out to spy on our beachhead camp."                580

And he drove the horses across the trench,
Roaring with laughter. The others followed
In high spirits, and when they came to Diomedes'
Well-built shelter they bound them with thongs
At the stall where his horses stood champing grain.
And on the stern of his ship Odysseus placed
The bloody spoils of Dolon, until such time
As they could prepare a sacrifice for Athena.
Then they waded into the sea and let the waves
Wash the thick sweat from their legs and necks                590
Until they felt refreshed. Then they went to the tubs.
After their bath they rubbed on rich oil
And sat down to eat, drawing off wine
From the brimming bowl to pour to Athena.

# ILIAD 11

Dawn left her splendid Tithonus in bed
And rose to bring light to immortals and men,
As Zeus launched Eris, the goddess Strife,
Down to the Greek ships, a talisman of War
Clutched in her hands. She took her stand
Near the great black hull of Odysseus' ship,
Which lay in the middle, so a shout could reach
Ajax's huts on one end of camp and Achilles'
On the other. These two had beached their ships
On the flanks, confident in their manhood.                    10
Standing there, she emitted a yell that rose
In volume and pitch until it seemed to each Greek
That fighting to the death was far preferable
To sailing home in their hollow ships.

Agamemnon boomed out a command
For his men to arm, and did so himself,
Strapping on sunlit bronze, his greaves first,
Works of art, trimmed with silver at the ankles.
Then he covered his chest with a corselet,
A gift from the Cypriot king, Cinyras.                        20
News had reached Cyprus that the Greeks
Were launching a fleet for Troy, and Cinyras
Sent this corselet as homage to the warlord.
It had ten bands of dark blue enamel,
Twelve of gold, and twenty of tin.

On either side were three enameled dragons
With arching necks—iridescent as rainbows
That Zeus anchors in cloud as portents for men.
And he slung a sword around his shoulders,
Golden bolts shining in the hilt. The sheath                    30
Was silver, fitted with golden straps.
Then he took up his shield, a crafted glory
Of metalwork, ringed with bronze, bossed
With white tin, and inlaid with dark cyan,
A Gorgon flanked by Terror and Rout
Glaring out of the midnight blue center.
The shield was hung with a baldric of silver
Upon which writhed an enameled dragon
With three heads twisting from a single neck.
He set upon his head a two-horned helmet                        40
With four bosses and a horsehair plume
That nodded menacingly on its crest.
The spears that he took tapered to bronze points
Honed with light. The sky caught their glare,
And Hera and Athena thundered in response,
Honoring the lord of gold-crusted Mycenae.

The drivers had orders to keep their horses
In a steady line up and down the trench
While the heroes moved forward on foot
In full battle gear. The shout the troops gave                  50
When they finally charged filled the dawn sky.
The charioteers let them have a long lead
And then closed the gap from behind. Thunder
Rolled up from the plain like black dust, and Zeus,
Soon to be pitching strong souls into Hades,
Rained drops of blood from the crystal air.

Opposite them the Trojans, on rising ground,
Gathered around their heroes, great Hector,
Polydamas, Aeneas, and Antenor's three sons,
Polybus, Agenor, and young Acamas—                              60
All of whom could have passed as immortal gods.
Hector, behind the perfect circle of his shield,
Shone like a death star in a bank of clouds,

Sometimes passing behind them as he moved
From the front lines to the rear, issuing commands,
And his bronze flashed like Zeus' lightning.

*Reapers are working toward each other*
*In a rich man's field, cutting huge swaths*
*Of barley or wheat, and the grain falls in piles.*

The Greeks and Trojans kept coming on.                    70
Turning their backs would have meant
A disastrous rout. They fought on equal terms,
Head to head, going after each other
Like rabid wolves. Eris looked on rejoicing,
The only god who took the field that day.
All of the others kept their peace,
Idle in their homes on Olympus' ridges,
Sulking because the Dark Cloud, Zeus,
Meant to cover the Trojans with glory.
The Patriarch paid them no mind. He sat        80
Apart from the others in glorious solitude,
Looking down at Troy and the Achaean ships,
The flash of bronze, men killing and being killed.

As long as the holy light climbed toward noon,
Men were hit and fell on both sides of battle.

*Toward evening, the woodsman turns home,*
*His hands sore from swinging his axe*
*And his heart weary from felling tall trees,*
*And all his desire is for the sweetness of food.*

About that time in the long afternoon        90
The Danaans broke through, their captains calling,
Calling each other through the ranks of men,
Until their valor split the enemy lines.
Agamemnon led the way, taking out Bienor,
A Trojan commander, and his driver, Oïleus.
Oïleus at least had the chance to jump down
And face Agamemnon, but as he charged
The warlord's spear drove into his forehead.

Oïleus' heavy bronze helm had little effect
On the spear's sharp point, which penetrated                    100
Not only the helmet's rim but the skull's bone,
Scrambling the grey stuff inside. So much
For these two. The warlord left them there,
Their naked chests gleaming in the level light,
And went on to kill Isus and Antiphus,
Two sons of Priam, bastard and legitimate,
Riding in one car. The bastard held the reins
And Antiphus stood by. Achilles once
Had bound these two with willow branches,
Surprising them as they watched their sheep            110
On Ida's hills, and later released them for ransom.
Now Agamemnon, Atreus' wide-ruling son,
Hit Isus with his spear above the nipple
And Antiphus with his sword beside his ear,
Knocking both from the car. As he was busy
Stripping their armor he recognized their faces
From the time when Achilles had brought them
Down from Ida and to the beachhead camp.

*Imagine how easily a lion crushes*
*A pair of fawns in his powerful jaws.*                 120
*He has come to where they lie huddled together*
*On the forest floor, and has ripped out their hearts.*
*And though their mother is near she can do*
*Nothing to save them. Trembling herself,*
*She bolts through the thick woods, and sweat*
*Glazes her skin as she flees the great cat.*

The Trojans were chased off, none of them able
To help Agamemnon's two victims.

Peisander and Hippolochus were next,
Battle-hardened sons of Antimachus,                    130
Who in the shrewdness of his heart
And in consideration of Paris' substantial gifts
Had argued against surrendering Helen
To blond Menelaus. Agamemnon now took
His two sons instead. Together in one car

They were trying to get their rearing horses
Under control—the reins had slipped from their hands—
When Agamemnon charged them like a lion.
They fell to their knees in their chariot's basket:

"Take us alive, son of Atreus, for ransom.　　　　　　　140
Antimachus' palace is piled high with treasure,
Gold and bronze and wrought iron our father
Would give you past counting once he found out
We were alive and well among the Greek ships."

Sweet words, and they salted them with tears.
But the voice they heard was anything but sweet:

"Your father Antimachus—if you really are
His sons—once urged the Trojan assembly
To kill Menelaus on the spot
When he came with Odysseus on an embassy.　　　　　150
Now you will pay for his heinous offense."

He spoke, and knocked Peisander backward
Out of his chariot with a spear through his chest
And sent him sprawling on the ground.
Hippolochus leapt down. Agamemnon
Used his sword to slice off both arms
And lop off his head, sending his torso
Rolling like a stone column through the crowd.
He didn't bother them further, but pressed on
To where the fighting was thickest, Greeks　　　　　160
In their leg-armor crowding in behind him,
Killing Trojans on foot, from chariots,
Dust rolling up from the plain like thunder
Under the horses' hooves, and all the while
In the blood-red bronze, Agamemnon killing,
Calling to his Greeks, the great warlord

> *Like fire consuming dry manzanita*
> *When the winds rise up*
> *And the scrub forest is burned to its roots,*

The Trojans falling as they fled,                            170
And the horses, arching their necks,
Rattled empty cars along the lanes of war,
Feeling the absence of their faultless masters
Who lay sprawled on the ground
Dearer now to vultures than to their wives.

Zeus drew Hector out of the boiling dust,
Out of the blood, out of the noise and the slaughter,
While Agamemnon pressed on,
Howling to his Greeks to follow him.
Past the ancient tomb of Ilus,                               180
Over the middle of the plain,
Beyond the windy fig tree
They rushed toward the city,
Yearned for it, the son of Atreus calling them,
Calling, his hard hands spattered with gore.
But when they came to the Western Gate
And the oak tree there, the two armies halted,
Waiting. There were still some Trojan stragglers
Being driven across the plain like cattle.

> *In the dead of night a lion rushes a herd,*          190
> *Scattering them all, though only one heifer will die.*
> *He crushes her neck first in his teeth,*
> *Then greedily laps up all her soft insides.*

Agamemnon picked off the hindmost Trojans
One by one, toppling them from their chariots,
And was coming up to Ilion's steep wall
When the Father of Gods and Men
Came down from heaven and onto Ida's peaks
In one step, a thunderbolt in his hands,
And sent gold-winged Iris off with a message:     200

"Go, swift Iris, and take word to Hector
That as long as he sees Lord Agamemnon
Storming through the ranks and laying them low
He should hold back and order other troops

To engage the enemy. But when at last
Agamemnon is wounded by an arrow or spear
And mounts his chariot, then will I
Loan Hector strength to kill and keep killing
Until he comes to the thwarted ships
And the sun sets and sacred darkness falls."                    *210*

Thus Zeus, and Iris moved like rain
Down from Ida's hills and to holy Ilion
Seeking Hector, splendor of Priam's house,
And found him standing in his chariot.
Iris hovered nearby on windy feet:

"Hector, son of Priam, Father Zeus
Has sent me here with a message for you.
As long as you see Lord Agamemnon
Storming through the ranks and laying them low
You should hold back and order other troops               *220*
To engage the enemy. But when at last
Agamemnon is wounded by an arrow or spear
And mounts his chariot, then will Zeus
Loan you the strength to kill and keep killing
Until you come to the thwarted ships
And the sun sets and sacred darkness falls."

Iris spoke and was gone, and Hector
Vaulted from his chariot with all his gear.
Brandishing a pair of spears he toured the troops
And worked them into a frenzy for battle.                  *230*
A ripple moved through their lines as they turned
And faced the Greeks. Over against them
The Achaean forces stiffened their lines.
The two armies were poised for battle, but one man,
Agamemnon, charged forward first,
Determined to fight far in advance of all.

And now, Muses, who reside on Olympus,
Tell me who came, of all the Trojans
And their famed allies, to face Agamemnon.
It was Iphidamas, one of Antenor's sons,                   *240*

A good man, tall, bred on Thracian farmland.
His mother was Theano, and her father,
Cisseus, raised the boy from infancy.
When he came of age, Cisseus gave him
His own daughter in marriage to keep him there.
But Iphidamas left her in the bridal chamber
And went chasing after glory when he heard
The Achaeans were coming. He sailed
With twelve trim ships, left them at Percote,
And came overland to Troy. Now he faced                    250
Agamemnon, son of Atreus. When they closed
To within range of each other, Agamemnon
Cast and missed. Iphidamas stepped in
And stabbed him just beneath the corselet,
Putting his weight behind the thrust
And trusting his strong wrist to drive the spear home
Through the glittering belt, but the point
Bent like lead as soon as it hit the silver.
The great warlord seized the spear's haft
And with a lion's ferocity pulled it toward him          260
And out of Iphidamas' hands. A sword stroke
To the neck made his body go slack,
And Iphidamas fell in a sleep of bronze,
The town hero, far from his wedded wife,
Who gave him no joy, though he gave much for her,
A hundred head of cattle, a thousand sheep and goats
On promise from his countless herds.
Agamemnon stripped his costly armor
And paraded it through the Achaean troops.

When Antenor's eldest son, Coön,                            270
Saw his brother fall, his eyes stung with grief.
Working his way to Agamemnon's blind side
He lunged with his spear and hit him
Below his left elbow, the point piercing
The forearm's sinew. The great warlord
Shuddered, but without missing a step
Jumped at Coön, who was now hauling
His brother Iphidamas away by his foot.
The son of Atreus' wind-hardened spear

Caught him under his shield, and as his limbs                    *280*
Went slack, Agamemnon reached over
His brother's body to sever his head.
So Antenor's two sons fulfilled their destiny
Under the warlord's hands and sank into the gloom.

Agamemnon continued his killing rampage
With spear, sword, and chunks of rock
As long as blood flowed warm from the wound.
But when the wound dried and the blood caked,
The pain set in, needling and sharp,

> *As if he were a woman in labor*                               *290*
> *Struggling with the stabbing pain*
> *Hera's daughters dispense*
> *When they preside at a childbirth.*

Agamemnon, in agony, leapt onto his chariot
And told the driver to make for the ships,
Then boomed out a final order to his men:

"Commanders of Greece, the battle is yours!
Keep the war from our ships. Zeus almighty
Has not seen fit to let me fight the whole day."

And the charioteer lashed the horses on                         *300*
To the beached ships. Manes streaming,
Chests flecked with foam, bellies dust-stained,
They bore the wounded warlord from battle.

When Hector saw Agamemnon leaving,
He called to the Trojans and Lycians:

"Trojans and Lycians, Dardanian warriors,
Be men, my friends, and remember your valor.
Their best man is gone, and Zeus has granted me
A great victory. Drive your horses
Directly at them and win the power and glory."        *310*

And he set them on the Greeks
The way a hunter sets his grinning dogs
On a boar or a lion, leading the way himself,
Hector, son of Priam, peer of Ares, bane of mortals,
Falling on the conflict the way a windstorm
Falls on the sea and churns the violet water.

He killed Asaeus first, and Autonous,
And not a few other Danaan leaders—
Dolops, son of Clytius, Opheltius,
Agelaus, Aesymnus, Orus, Hipponous—                    320
Then fell on the common soldiery.

> *Imagine the westerly squalls you have seen*
> *Battering clouds in a silver sky.*
> *The waves curl and blister on the sea below,*
> *And lines of spray shear off in the wind.*

Hector's assault was much like this,
With Greek heads toppling everywhere.
He might have driven them once and for all
Back to their ships in a final rout,
Had not Odysseus called to Tydeus' son:                    330

"Diomedes, what's the matter with us? Have we
Forgotten how to fight? Take a stand here with me.
There'll be hell to pay if Hector takes the ships."

And Diomedes, tough as nails:

"I'm in it for the long haul. But our fun
Won't last long. The god in the clouds
Has decided to boost the Trojans, not us."

With that, he knocked Thymbraeus from his chariot—
A spearcast to his left nipple—while Odysseus
Took out Molion, his godlike protégé.                    340
They left them there with no more fight in them

And moved on, working as a team, spilling guts
Like a pair of boars that fall on a pack of dogs,
Turning the Trojans back and giving the Greeks
A welcome respite from Hector's onslaught.
Two of their more notable victims
Were from Percote, sons of Merops,
A skilled prophet who would not allow
His sons to go to war. They went anyway,
Led on by Death's blackness. Diomedes                       350
Robbed them of their lives and armor. Odysseus
Did the same for Hippodamus and Hypeirochus.

Zeus, observing from Ida, reached down
And stretched the battle line out evenly.

The killing continued. Diomedes
Wounded the hero Agastrophus, Paeon's son,
On the hip with a thrust of his spear.
Agastrophus looked for his horses,
Forgot where his driver was holding them,
And lost his head. He was dead before long.                 360

When Hector spotted Odysseus and Diomedes
Across the ranks, he mounted a charge.
His shout brought with him battalions of Trojans.
Diomedes, always there when you needed him,
Shuddered when he saw Hector coming on
And said to Odysseus, who was a few yards away:

"Here comes Hector, like a damned avalanche.
Let's hold our ground and beat him off."

He spoke, poised his long-shadowed spear,
And cast, a good, hard shot to Hector's head.              370
The spearpoint ricocheted off the helmet's rim,
Bronze off bronze (Apollo had given him
This three-ply crest), and never touched his skin.
But Hector bounded back an amazing distance
And took cover in the crowd, down on his knees
With one hand on the ground. He blacked out

For some time, and then, while Diomedes
Was tracking down his spear, revived again,
Mounted his chariot, and drove off
Through the throng, escaping a darker fate.     380
Diomedes ran after him with his spear, shouting:

"Got away again, didn't you, you dog?
By the skin of your teeth! Apollo
Has bailed you out once more. You must be
A regular devotee, praying each time you go out.
I'll finish you off next time we meet,
If I have a god on my side. Meanwhile,
Let's see who gets my business now."

He spoke, and proceeded to strip the armor
From Agastrophus. But Alexander,     390
Helen's fair-haired lord, was aiming an arrow
At the son of Tydeus, bracing himself
Against a pillar on the tomb of Ilus,
A Trojan elder in days gone by.
Diomedes had unstrapped the gleaming corselet
From Agastrophus' torso and was busy
Removing the shield and heavy helmet
When Paris drew the arrowhead back to the grip,
Released the shaft, and scored a hit, the arrow
Passing through the instep of Diomedes' right foot     400
And sticking in the ground. Paris laughed
And, jumping out of his blind, crowed:

"You're hit! My arrow didn't miss!
I wish it had gone in your gut and killed you
So the Trojans could have some breathing room.
They're trembling like goats before a lion."

There was no hint of fear in Diomedes' response:

"You sissy, curly-haired pimp of a bowman!
Why don't you come down and fight me man to man
And see how far your bow and arrow get you?     410
Boasting because you scratched my foot!

I might as well have been hit by a woman
Or imbecile child. A weakling's weapon is blunt.
When *I* throw a spear it kills you on contact—
My throw *makes* it sharp—and your widow's cheeks
Are torn with grief, your children are fatherless,
Your blood reddens the earth, and you rot,
With more birds than women around you."

When Diomedes finished, Odysseus
Stepped in front of him with his spear.                                    420
Diomedes sat down behind him and pulled
The arrow from his foot. The pain
Was sickening. He limped onto his chariot
And told the driver to head for the ships.

This left Odysseus alone. Every Greek
In the vicinity had fled in fear. Troubled,
Odysseus said to no one but himself:

"Now what? It will be bad enough
If I lose my nerve and run, but worse yet
If I am caught here alone, as I will be,                                    430
Since Zeus has scattered all the Danaans.
But why am I talking to myself like this?
I know only cowards depart from battle.
A real warrior stands his ground
Whether he is hit or hits another."

While he thought it over, the Trojans closed in,
Encircling their own peril.

> Dogs and hunters will go after a boar
> From all sides, and when he comes out
> Of the deep brush, whetting his white tusks                              440
> In his curving jaws, they charge at him,
> And although the sound of his gnashing tusks
> Inspires sheer terror, they keep coming at him.

So too around Odysseus, dear to Zeus,
The Trojans rushed in. Odysseus sprang

And hit Deiopites first, coming down
With his sharp spear onto his shoulder.
Thoön and Eunomus were no great trouble,
And then he stabbed Chersidamas in his navel,
Under his shield, as he leapt from his chariot.     450
Chersidamas fell and clawed at the dust.
Paying these no mind, he put his spear through
A man named Charops, whose brother, Socus,
Now came up to help him. Socus was rich
And well-born, a man the equal of a god.
He put his face in Odysseus' and said:

"So this is Odysseus, who can't get enough
Of cunning and trouble. Today you will either
Boast you have killed Hippasus' two sons
Or go down yourself under my spear."     460

And he hit the circle of Odysseus' shield
With such force that the spear fought its way
All the way through, penetrated the metal
Of the ornamented corselet, and ripped the flesh
From the side of his ribs, but Pallas Athena
Would not let it pierce his inner organs.
Odysseus knew the wound was not fatal.
He pulled back a step and said to Socus:

"You're as good as dead, you sorry bastard.
You may have put me out of commission,     470
But this is the last day on earth for you.
Flattened by my spear you will give glory to me
And your life to Hades, famed for his horses."

This was enough for Socus. He turned to run,
But as he was turning, Odysseus
Rammed his spear between his shoulders,
And drove it all the way through to his chest.
He fell with a thud, and Odysseus exulted:

"Ah, Socus, Death was too quick for you
And you couldn't dodge it. Your parents     480

Will not close your eyes on a bier. No, birds
Will eat your flesh raw, fanning their wings.
But if I die, the Greeks will give me burial."

So saying, he drew Socus' spear
Out of his flesh and from his bossed shield.
Blood spurted out; the pain tore at his heart.
The Trojans, watching, signalled each other
And advanced in a body. Odysseus gave ground,
Shouting to his comrades still on the field.
Menelaus heard each call, and said to Ajax:                          490

"Telamonian Ajax, that is Odysseus shouting.
The Trojans must have cut him off.
We've got to get over and lend a hand
Or the Trojans may overpower him.
Think what his loss would mean to the Greeks."

With that he led the way through the turmoil, and Ajax,
Who was something more than human, followed.
They found Odysseus beset by a crowd of Trojans.

> *Yellow jackals in the mountains*
> *Chase down an antlered stag wounded*                            500
> *By a hunter's arrow. The stag*
> *Has escaped the human and runs quickly*
> *As long as the blood flows warm*
> *And his knees have spring. Eventually,*
> *The arrow defeats him, and the jackals*
> *Tear him to pieces in the green shade,*
> *But then a mountain god brings a lion*
> *To raven them all, and the jackals scatter*
> *While the lion settles down to his meal.*

With Trojans all over him, Odysseus                                 510
Fell back on experience and instinct
To keep himself alive, shooting his spear out
Whenever one of his assailants got too close.
Then Ajax was there, planting himself
With his wall of a shield, and the Trojans

Slunk off by ones and twos. Menelaus
Led Odysseus away, holding him by his hand
Until his driver wheeled the chariot up.

Then Ajax attacked, killing Dorycles,
One of Priam's bastard sons, and likewise                          520
Lysander, Pyrasus, and Pylartes.

*A mountain stream swollen by winter rains*
*Empties onto level ground, sweeping along*
*Desiccated oaks and pines and other flotsam*
*That it finally dumps into the spreading sea.*

So too Ajax in spate across the plain,
Killing horses as well as men.
       And Hector?
As yet he knew nothing of all this.
He was doing his fighting on the left flank                        530
By the banks of the Scamander, where
The fighting was thickest, that is to say
Around great Nestor, and Idomeneus.
It was there that Hector was engaged,
Using his chariot and spear to terrible effect
On the Trojan lines. Even so,
The Greeks would not have backed up
Had not Helen's fair-haired husband Paris
Stopped Machaon from his valorous exploits
With a three-pronged arrow into his shoulder.                      540
The Greeks held their breath, terrified
That the battle would turn and Machaon be killed.
Idomeneus called over to Nestor:

"Nestor, son of Neleus, mount your chariot
And take Machaon back to the ships.
A medic is worth a battalion of men
In pulling out arrows and dressing wounds."

The old horseman did not need any urging.
He mounted his chariot, and Machaon,
Asclepius' son and an inspired physician,                          550

Got in beside him. At a touch of the lash
The horses stretched their necks toward the ships.

Cebriones saw that on the other side of the plain
The Trojans were in rout, and he said to Hector:

"While we dally with the Greeks over here
On the battle's edge, there are Trojans
Beating a hasty retreat, men and horses,
Before Ajax, son of Telamon. I know him
From that wide shield of his that stretches
Around his shoulders. Let's drive over there                    560
To where the real killing is going on."

His lash whistled in the air, and the horses,
Their manes streaming, pulled the chariot
At top speed over the corpses and shields,
Their hooves gouging the dead. The axle
Beneath and the chariot's rails above
Were spattered with blood kicked up by the horses
And turning wheels.

                    Hector yearned
To penetrate the wall of Greek flesh                    570
And shatter it to bits. The battle noise rose,
And a moment later Hector was everywhere
Making lethal circles with his spear and sword
And massive stones, and avoiding only
A single man, Telamonian Ajax.

But Zeus, from his high vantage point,
Had decided it was time for Ajax to withdraw.
As if in a trance, Ajax swung his seven-ply shield
Behind him, and with an anxious glance
Over his shoulder, slunk away like a wild animal,                    580
Turning around again and again in his slow retreat.

  *Dogs and country folk sometimes drive*
  *A tawny lion away from a cattle pen.*
  *They watch the whole night through to stop him*

*From sinking his teeth into the herd's fattest bull,*
*But the ravenous beast advances anyway,*
*Only to be met with spears and firebrands*
*Which he cannot face, for all his hungry power.*
*At dawn the lion departs in a sullen mood.*

So too Ajax, resenting every step he took                        590
Back from the Trojans. He feared for the ships.

*A donkey is usually too strong for boys*
*Who try to keep him out of a wheat field*
*And will wade right in although they break their sticks*
*On his ribs. The boys keep beating him*
*As he wastes the deep grain, but their childish strength*
*Can barely drive him out even after he is full.*

The Trojans and their allies kept up the pressure
On Ajax, hitting his shield with their polished spears.
Every now and again Ajax would remember                          600
Who he was, and turn on them, pushing back
Entire phalanxes of horse-taming Trojans.
Then he would give ground, but even in retreat
It was big Ajax who kept the enemy from the ships,
Big Ajax who stood between the Trojans and the Greeks,
Collecting the spears that were thrown hard enough
To reach his enormous shield. Many fell short,
Sticking in sand instead of the flesh they yearned for.

Eurypylus, Euaemon's glorious son,
Saw the thicket of spears surrounding Ajax                       610
And moved over to help. His first throw
Hit Apisaon, Phausius' son, in the liver.
The man crumpled, and Eurypylus
Leapt upon him to unstrap his armor,
But as he was doing so, Paris Alexander
Saw him and drew his bow. The arrow
Hit Eurypylus in his right thigh. The shaft
Broke off, but it was all he could do
To drag his leg along as he made his way
Back to the Greek lines, shrinking from death.                   620

Then his shout rang in every Danaan ear:

"Achaean captains! Rally around Ajax
And see to it that this day is not his last.
He's under pressure from all sides
And won't pull through without our help.
Make a stand for great Ajax, son of Telamon!"

Thus the wounded Eurypylus, who was soon
Surrounded by Greek troops leaning their shields
On their shoulders and holding their spears high.
Ajax managed to get over to this group,                          630
And when he did, turned and took his stand.

So the fight went on, like wildfire burning.

M eanwhile, the sweat-glazed mares of Neleus
Had pulled Nestor, and Machaon with him,
Out of the battle and into the Greek camp,
And Achilles saw them as they went by.
Achilles was standing on the stern of his ship
Gazing out at the blood, sweat, and tears
Of the Greeks in rout. And the great runner
Called to his comrade Patroclus from the ship,                   640
And Patroclus heard him and came out of the hut
Like the god Ares. This was the beginning of evil
For Menoetius' strong son, who now asked:

"Why have you called me, Achilles? What do you want?"

And Achilles, the great runner, answered:

"Son of Menoetius, my heart's companion,
If I have it right, the Greeks will soon be
Grovelling before me. They've reached their limit.
But I want you to go now and ask Nestor
Whom he is bringing wounded from battle.                         650
From behind, it looked just like Machaon,
Son of Asclepius, but I didn't see his face.

The horses went by at a pretty good clip."

Patroclus did as his beloved friend asked
And sprinted through the camp.

                    Nestor had just reached his hut
And was stepping down from the chariot
With Machaon. His squire Eurymedon
Unhitched the old man's horses,
And the two dried the sweat from their tunics                    660
By standing in the onshore breeze for a while.
Then they went into the hut and sat on chairs
While Hecamede prepared a drink for them.
This woman, who had long, beautiful hair,
Nestor had taken out of Tenedos
When Achilles sacked it. She was the daughter
Of a great man, Arsinous, and the Greeks
Had chosen her for Nestor, their best in council.
She now drew up for them a polished table
With blue enamelled feet, and set on it                    670
A bronze basket, and next to it an onion
Grated for their drink, and pale green honey,
And sacred barley meal. Then she set down
A magnificent cup the old man had brought from home,
Studded with gold rivets. It had four handles,
With a pair of golden doves pecking at each,
And a double base beneath. Anyone else
Would have strained to lift the cup from the table
When full, but old Nestor raised it easily.
Into this cup Hecamede, beautiful as a goddess,                    680
Poured Pramnian wine, grated goat cheese into it
With a brazed grater, and sprinkled white barley on top.
She motioned for them to drink. They did so,
And when they had slaked their parching thirst,
They began to swap tales and were enjoying themselves
When Patroclus stood in the door, more like a god
Than a man. Seeing him, the old man jumped up
From his gleaming chair, took him by the hand,
Led him inside, and asked him to sit down.

Patroclus refused, in no uncertain terms:                    *690*


"No thank you, venerable sir, no seat for me.
I have too much respect for Achilles, who sent me
To ask you whom you have brought back wounded.
But I see for myself it is Machaon,
And I will bring this news back to Achilles now.
You know, sir, what a hard man he is,
Quick to blame even the blameless."


And Nestor, the horseman from Gerenia:


"And why does Achilles feel any sorrow
For wounded Greeks? He has no idea                           *700*
Of the grief that has spread through the army.
Our best men have been hit and are lying
Wounded in camp. Diomedes is out,
And Odysseus, a good man with a spear,
Even Agamemnon has taken a hit.
Eurypylus, too, an arrow in his thigh.
Machaon here I have just brought back
With an arrow wound. But Achilles
For all his valor has no feeling for us.
Is he waiting until our ships go up in flames             *710*
On the shore of the sea, in spite of our efforts,
And we are all killed in a row? For my strength
Is not as it once was in my knotted limbs.
Oh to be young again, with my strength firm,
As I was in the cattle wars with the Eleans
When I killed Itymoneus, the valiant son
Of Hypeirochus, a man of Elis,
During the drive back. Leading the charge
In the fight for his cattle, he was hit by my spear
And fell, and the country folk all fled in terror.         *720*
The spoils we corralled from out of the plain!
Fifty herds of cattle and as many flocks of sheep,
As many droves of pigs, as many herds of goats.
And one hundred and fifty chestnut horses,

All mares, many with foals underneath.
We drove them all into Pylos by night,
Up to the citadel. And Neleus was glad
I had done so well, going to war as a boy.
At the crack of dawn the heralds invited
Anyone who was owed a debt in Elis                    730
To step forth. So the Pylians assembled
And divided the spoils. Most claimed debts,
Since we in Pylos were few and hard-pressed,
For Heracles had come in recent years
And brought us grief, killing our best.
I was one of the twelve sons of Neleus,
And I alone was left; the others had perished.
Emboldened at this, the Epeians in Elis
Campaigned against us with reckless violence.
Well, old Neleus chose a herd of cattle                740
And a great flock of three hundred sheep,
Herdsmen and all. For he was owed
A great debt in Elis, four champion horses,
A chariot team that had gone to the games
To race for a tripod, but which King Augeias
Had kept, sending the forlorn driver back.
Old Neleus was angry because of this
And took high compensation. The rest he gave
For his folk to divide into equal shares.
We were in the midst of all this distribution        750
And offering sacrifice throughout the city
When on the third day the Epeians arrived,
Infantry and horse, at breakneck speed,
And with them were the two Moliones brothers,
Still just boys who didn't really know war.
Now there is a town, Thryoessa, a steep hill
Way down the Alpheius, Pylos' last outpost.
There they encamped, with a mind to destroy it.
When they were through the plain, Pallas Athena
Sped down to us from Olympus by night              760
And told us to arm. The army she assembled
From all Pylos was more than eager, but Neleus
Would not allow me to arm, and hid my horses,
For he did not think I understood warfare.

Even so, on foot, I distinguished myself
Among our horsemen, as Athena would have it.
There is a river Minyeius that hits the sea
Close to Arene. There we waited for dawn,
The Pylian horsemen and all the tribes on foot.
We marched out on the double with all our gear                    770
And at midday reached Alpheius' sacred stream.
There we offered sacrifice to Zeus Almighty,
A bull to Alpheius, a bull to Poseidon,
And a heifer of the herd to the Grey-eyed One.
Then we had our supper by platoons
And settled down to sleep in full battle gear
Along the river banks. The Epeians were deployed
Around the city, determined to destroy it,
But before they could a great battle loomed.
We attacked at daybreak, saying our prayers                       780
To Zeus and Athena, and in that conflict
I was first to kill my man and take his horses.
This was Mulius, Augeias' son-in-law,
Husband of his eldest daughter, blonde Agamede,
Who knew every medicinal plant on earth.
I hit him with my bronze-tipped spear as he charged,
And he fell in the dust. I leapt on his chariot
And took my stand with the foremost fighters.
The Epeians fled when they saw him fallen,
The leader of their horse and best man in battle.                 790
I went after them like a black hurricane
And took fifty chariots, and beside each one
Two men felled by my spear bit the dust.
And I would have killed the two Moliones also
Had not their father, the wide-ruling Earthshaker,
Saved them from war in a thick shroud of mist.
Then Zeus granted the Pylians great power.
We followed in pursuit across the broad plain,
Killing men and culling their fine battle gear,
Driving all the way to Buprasium's wheat fields,                  800
And the rock of Olen, and the hill that is called
Alesium, where Athena again turned back the foe.
Then I killed the last man and left him. Our men
Drove their horses from Buprasium to Pylos

Praising Zeus among gods, and among men Nestor.
   That is the sort of man I was. But Achilles?
His valor is for himself alone. And yet I think
He will sorely lament the army's destruction.
Ah yes, my young friend—Menoetius,
On the day he sent you forth from Phthia                     810
To join Agamemnon, laid a charge on you.
Mustering the army throughout Achaea,
We had come to the well-built house of Peleus,
And we found the hero Menoetius inside
With you and Achilles. The old horseman Peleus
Was burning a bull's fat thighbones to Zeus
Out in the courtyard. He held a golden cup
And poured flaming wine as the sacrifice blazed.
You two were busy with the flesh of the bull
When we appeared in the doorway. Achilles                    820
Jumped up in astonishment, took us by the hand,
And led us inside. He had us sit down,
Then set before us all that guests should have.
When we had our fill of food and drink
I began to speak, urging that you come with us.
You were both right eager, and your fathers
Laid on you both many commands. Old Peleus
Told Achilles to be preeminent always,
But to you Menoetius gave this command:
'My son, Achilles is higher born than you,                   830
But you are older, though he is much stronger.
Advise him, speak to him wisely, direct him,
And he will be better off for obeying.'
Thus spoke the old man, but you have forgotten.
Still, you should speak to Achilles.
It is not too late, and he just might listen.
Who knows but that with the help of some god
You might rouse his spirit? You are his friend,
And it is good for friends to persuade each other.
If some oracle, or a secret his mother                       840
Has learned from Zeus, is holding him back,
Let him send *you* out, let *you* lead a troop
Of Myrmidons and light the way for our army.
If you wear his armor, and the Trojans think

You are he, they will back off and give the Greeks
Some breathing space, what little there is in war.
Our rested men will turn them with a shout
And push them back from our ships to Troy."

This speech put great notions in Patroclus' head,
And he went sprinting down the line of ships                         *850*
To Achilles. But when he reached Odysseus' hulls,
Where the assembly grounds and altars stood,
He ran into Eurypylus limping in from battle
With an arrow in his thigh. Sweat poured down
His neck and shoulders, and black blood pulsed
From his terrible wound, but his spirit was strong.
When Patroclus saw him he cried out in dismay:

"Ah, you Greek heroes, you were all destined
To die far from home and glut Trojan dogs
With your white fat. Eurypylus, tell me,                            *860*
Is there any way to hold back Hector now,
Or will we all go down beneath his spear?"

And the wounded Eurypylus:

"We'll all be piling into our black ships soon.
We have no defense left. All our best
Have been hit and are laid up in camp,
And the Trojans only get stronger.
Lend me a hand here. Lead me back to my ship
And cut this arrow out of my thigh.
Wash the blood off in warm water                                    *870*
And put some soothing poultices on it,
The good stuff. They say Achilles taught you
And that he learned from Chiron, the just centaur.
Our medics, Podalirius and Machaon—
One is laid up wounded and needs a doctor himself,
And the other is out there fighting the Trojans."

Menoetius' valiant son answered:

"What are we going to do, Eurypylus?

I am on my way to Achilles now
With a message from Lord Nestor.                          *880*
But you're hurting, and I won't let you down."

He put his arm around Eurypylus' chest
And helped him to his hut. His attendant,
When he saw them, spread hides on the floor.
Patroclus had him lie down, and with a knife
Cut from his thigh the barbed arrow.
He washed the wound off with warm water
And patted into it a bitter root
That he had rubbed between his hands,
An anodyne that took away the pain.                      *890*
The bleeding stopped, and the wound was dry.

# ILIAD  12

<sup></sup>

While Patroclus doctored Eurypylus
The battle raged on. The Greeks
Still had the protection of their trench
And the wide wall above it they had built
As the last line of defense for their ships—
For the time being. When they built that wall
And drove the trench around it to protect their ships
And all their plunder, they neglected to offer
Formal sacrifice to the immortal gods.
Built against the will of the immortals,                    10
The wall could not endure for long.
While Hector lived and Achilles raged
And the city of Priam was still unpillaged,
The great wall of the Greeks stood firm.
But when all the best Trojans had died
And many Greeks had fallen or had left
And after ten years Priam's city had fallen
And the Greeks had sailed back to their native land,
Then Poseidon and Apollo conspired
To sweep away the wall, bringing against it            20
The might of all the rivers that flow down
From Ida's mountains to the sea—
Rhesus and Heptaporus, Caresus and Rhodius,
Granicus and Aesepus, shining Scamander
And Simois, along the banks of which

Many bullhide shields and helmets fell in the dust,
And a generation of men who were half-divine.
Phoebus Apollo turned all their mouths together
And for nine days sent their flood against the wall.
Zeus poured down rain continually, the sooner                    30
To wash the wall into the sea. The Earthshaker
Led the way, holding a trident in his hands,
And pushed into the waves all the foundations
Of beams and stones the Greeks had laid with toil.
He made all smooth along the mighty Hellespont
And again covered the great shore with sand.
The wall was gone. He turned the beautiful rivers
Back to flow in their original channels.

This Poseidon and Apollo were to do
In time to come. But now the battle raged                        40
On both sides of the well-built wall. The beams
Rang as they were struck, and the Greeks,
Whipped back by Zeus, were penned in with their ships,
Terrified of Hector, who had engineered the rout
And who still fought like a howling wind.

> When hunters are out with their dogs,
> Their prey, a wild boar or a lion,
> Will suddenly feel its strength and turn.
> The men close their ranks like a wall
> And throw their javelins thick and fast,                       50
> But the valiant animal stands its ground,
> And though its bravery will be its death,
> It charges the ranks of men, testing them,
> And where it charges, the men fall back.

Hector kept urging his troops to cross the ditch.

His horses stood at its edge, whinnying,
But would not advance, spooked by the trench,
Too broad to leap and too difficult to drive over.
The banks hung over the sides, and sharp stakes
Were planted in the farther, higher edge,                        60

A formidable obstacle for a horse and chariot.
But the foot soldiers were eager to give it a try.
To that end Polydamas drew up to Hector and said:

"Hector, and Trojan commanders all:
It's not very smart of us to drive our horses
Across this trench, not with those sharp stakes
Set in it, and the Greek wall just a little beyond.
There's not enough space to dismount and fight,
And we'll suffer heavy casualties if we try.
If the high lord of thunder has turned against them          70
And it is his will to help the Trojans,
I would gladly see the Argives blotted out.
But if they rally and we have to retreat
And crash into the ditch, there won't be a man left
Even to bring the news back to the city.
So this is what I say we should do.
Let the squires hold the horses by the trench
While the rest of us advance on foot in full armor,
Massed behind Hector. The Greeks will not
Withstand us if the noose is tight around them."          80

It was sound advice, and Hector took it.
He vaulted to the ground in his armor,
And the other Trojans followed his example.
They instructed their drivers to keep the horses
In good order by the ditch.

    The troops divided
Into five companies behind their commanders.

  Hector and Polydamas stood at the head
Of the two largest contingents, elite troops
Eager to break the wall and fight by the ships.          90
Cebriones joined them in command (Hector
Stationed a lesser man with his chariot).
    The second company was led by Paris

Along with Agenor and Alcathous.
   Helenus and Deïphobus, sons of Priam,
Led the third contingent, joined by Asius,
Hyrtacus' son, whose huge stallions
Brought him from Arisbe and the river Selleis.
   Aeneas led the fourth contingent,
Anchises' son with the sons of Antenor,                    100
Archelochus and Acamas, as his lieutenants.
   Sarpedon commanded the allies
And picked Glaucus and Asteropaeus
As his lieutenants, judging them to be the best
Next to himself. Sarpedon knew no peer.

Massed behind their leather shields
The Trojans attacked, confident
That nothing could stop them now
From falling on the black ships.

All of them followed Polydamas' strategy                    110
Except for Asius. This man, Hyrtacus' son,
Had no intention of leaving his horses
Behind with his squire, but chariot and all
Drove toward the ships, and to his fate,
Never in his glory as charioteer
To drive back to windy Ilion again
With his proud horses. No, his destiny lay
On the bronze point of Idomeneus' spear.
Making for the left wing of the beachhead camp,
Where the Greeks returning from battle entered                    120
With their horses and cars, Asius drove up to
The wide gate and found the doors
Not yet shut and barred, but held open by men
Whose comrades were still returning from battle.
Asius drove straight for the gates, followed by
His howling soldiers, confident that no Greek
Could keep them from the black ships now.
This was all childishness, for at the gates
They found two of Greece's finest warriors,

Lapith spearmen, one a son of Peirithous,                      *130*
Polypoetes by name, and the other,
Leonteus, a match for brutal Ares himself.

> *They were like a pair of oak trees*
> *Planted before the high gates, these two,*
> *Trees that withstand wind and rain*
> *Day after day, with roots deep and strong.*

They met Asius' charge without a tremor,
These two Lapiths, trusting the strength of their hands
To beat off not only Asius but all his men too,
Who were lifting their leather shields high                    *140*
Around their warlord and his captains—
Iamenus and Orestes and Adamas
(Who was Asius' son), Thoön and Oenomaus.
The Lapiths had been inside for some time
Rousing the Greeks to fight in defense
Of their ships, but when they saw the Trojans
Attacking the wall and the Greeks in loud retreat,
They rushed out to fight in front of the gate.

> *They fought like a pair of wild boars*
> *Holding off men and dogs in the mountains.*          *150*
> *Slanting in, they slash through trees,*
> *Cutting them off at the root, and the clashing noise*
> *Of their tusks rises above the general tumult*
> *Until someone gets lucky with a spear.*

The polished bronze clashed on the Lapiths' chests
As they took hits face on from the enemy.

They fought strongly, confident in their might
And in the support from those on the wall above
Who rained down stones from the fortifications
In defense of their own lives, their huts,                    *160*
And their seafaring ships.

                    The stones fell like snow

*Down to the ground, falling, falling, like flakes*
*A cold wind from the shadowy clouds*
*Drives thick and fast upon the bountiful earth.*

Not only stones, but everything that is thrown
By men in war, a steady stream of missiles,
Flowed from the hands of Greeks and Trojans alike.
Helmets and bossed shields rang hoarsely,
Like bells struck by rough stones.                                    *170*
                                  And Asius,
Son of Hyrtacus, groaned, smacked his thighs,
And like a man who has been wronged, spoke:

"Father Zeus, or should I call you the Arch Deceiver?
I never thought the Greeks had a chance against us.
They're like a swarm of wasps or bees, holed up
In a hive they have built near a trail through cliffs
And defending their young against hunters.
These men, even though they are only two,
Will not yield the gate until they kill or are killed."     *180*

These words had no effect upon the mind of Zeus,
Who had decided to give all the glory to Hector.

Other battles were being fought around other gates.

Even if I were a god I could not tell you all.
Suffice it to say there was a firestorm of stone
All around the wall, that the Greeks were hard-pressed
To defend their ships, and that those gods
Who abetted the Greeks were sorely distressed.

Over on the left, the Lapiths were fighting.

Polypoetes, Peirithous' son, threw his spear            *190*
Through the bronze cheek piece of Damasus' helmet.
The point splintered the bone and scrambled
The grey stuff inside. He had been eager to fight.
Polypoetes killed Pylon and Ormenus next.

Leonteus meanwhile was doing his own damage,
Hitting Hippomachus in the belt with his spear,
Then darting through the crowd with sword drawn
And stabbing Antiphates in close fighting,
Sending him sprawling backward on the ground.
Then, in order, he brought Menon, Iamenus,                    200
And Orestes down to earth's bounty.

   While the Lapiths stripped their victims' bronze,
The troops with Hector and Polydamas,
For all their numbers and valor, and their eagerness
To break through the wall and fight by the ships,
Hesitated on the brink of the trench,
Paralyzed by an omen, an eagle overhead
That skirted their front lines from right to left,
Clutching in its talons a huge scarlet snake,
Still alive and with plenty of fight left.                    210
Curling around, the snake struck at the eagle
Just below its neck, and, in a spasm of pain,
The great bird dropped it in the Trojan ranks
And flew off shrieking on a blast of wind.
The soldiers shuddered at the glistening coils
Lying in their midst, a portent from heaven.
Polydamas turned to Hector and said:

"Hector, you always lay into me in assembly,
Even when I give sound advice, since it will not do
For a man of the people to cross you in council                    220
Or in battle, instead of adding to your strength.
Even so, I will speak now as seems best to me.
We should not fight the Danaans for their ships.
It will turn out for us just as with this bird
That came to the Trojans as they were eager to cross.
It skirted their front lines from right to left
Clutching in its talons a huge scarlet snake,
But then let it fall before reaching its nest
And never brought it home to give to its young.
It will be the same with us. Even if our forces                    230
Break through the Greek wall and its gates
And the enemy falls back, we will find ourselves

Beating a disorderly retreat from the ships
And leaving behind us many Trojans
Killed by the Achaeans in defense of their ships.
This is how a soothsayer would respond, one who
Knows omens well and has the people's trust."

Hector's bronze mask leaned toward Polydamas:

"I don't like the way you're talking now.
You know how to speak better than this,                    240
But if you really mean what you say,
The gods themselves must have addled your wits,
Telling me to ignore what thundering Zeus
Has assented to and held out to me.
Birds? You want me to obey birds,
Polydamas? I don't care which way birds fly,
Right to the sunrise or left into the dusk.
All we have to do is obey great Zeus,
Lord of mortals and immortals alike.
One omen is best: to fight for your country.             250
Why should you be afraid of combat?
Even if all the rest of us are killed
At the Argive ships, you will be safe,
Since you don't have an ounce of fight in you.
But if I catch you holding back from battle
Or talking anybody else out of fighting,
You lose your life on the point of my spear."

And he led them across the trench.

To the noise of their advance Zeus now added
A wind from Ida's mountains that blew dust               260
Straight at the ships and the bewildered Greeks.
The sky god was giving the glory to the Trojans
And to Hector.

                    Trusting these portents
And their own strength, the Trojans did their best
To breach the wall. Pulling down pickets
And battlements, they threw them to the ground

And set to work prying up the huge beams
The Greeks had used to reinforce the wall.
They were dragging these out, hoping to topple                    270
The entire structure, but even then the Greeks
Refused to give way, patching the battlements
With bullhide and beating off the invaders.

Both Ajaxes were on the wall, patrolling it
And urging on the troops, using harsh words,
Gentle words, whatever it took
To get the men back into the fight:

"Friends!—and I mean everyone from heroes
To camp followers—no one ever said
Men are equal in war. There is work for us all.            280
You know it yourselves. I don't want a single man
To return to the ships now that you have heard
The rallying cry. Keep the pressure on.
Olympian Zeus may still grant us
To drive the enemy back to the city."

And they roused the Greeks to battle.

*Snow flurries fall thick on a winter's day*
*When Zeus in his cunning rouses himself*
*To show humans the ammunition he has.*
*He lulls the winds and he snows and snows*            290
*Until he has covered all the mountain tops,*
*Headlands and meadows and men's plowed fields.*
*And the snow falls over the harbors*
*And the shores of the grey sea, and only*
*The waves keep it off. The rest of the world*
*Is enveloped in the winter tempest of Zeus.*

The stones flew thick upon the Trojans
And upon the Greeks, and the wooden wall
Was beaten like a drum along its whole length.

For all this, though, Hector and his Trojans            300
Would never have broken the barred gate

Had not Zeus roused his own son, Sarpedon,
Against the Greeks, as a lion against cattle.
Sarpedon held before him a perfect shield,
Its bronze skin hammered smooth by the smith,
Who had stitched the leather beneath with gold
All around the rim. Holding this shield
And brandishing two spears, Sarpedon advanced.

> *The mountain lion has not fed for days*
> *And is hungry and brave enough to enter*                310
> *The stone sheep pen and attack the flocks.*
> *Even if he finds herdsmen on the spot*
> *With dogs and spears to protect the fold,*
> *He will not be driven back without a try,*
> *And either he leaps in and seizes a sheep*
> *Or is killed by a spear, as human heroes are.*

Godlike Sarpedon felt impelled
To rush the wall and tear it down.

He turned to Glaucus and said:

"Glaucus, you know how you and I                          320
Have the best of everything in Lycia—
Seats, cuts of meat, full cups, everybody
Looking at us as if we were gods?
Not to mention our estates on the Xanthus,
Fine orchards and riverside wheat fields.
Well, now we have to take our stand at the front,
Where all the best fight, and face the heat of battle,
So that many an armored Lycian will say,
'So they're not inglorious after all,
Our Lycian lords who eat fat sheep                        330
And drink the sweetest wine. No,
They're strong, and fight with our best.'
Ah, my friend, if you and I could only
Get out of this war alive and then
Be immortal and ageless all of our days.
I would never again fight among the foremost
Or send you into battle where men win glory.

But as it is, death is everywhere
In more shapes than we can count,
And since no mortal is immune or can escape,                340
Let's go forward, either to give glory
To another man or get glory from him."

Thus Sarpedon. Glaucus nodded, and the two of them
Moved out at the head of a great nation of Lycians.
Menestheus, Peteos' son, saw them and shuddered,
For they were advancing toward his part of the wall
And bringing ruin with them. Menestheus
Looked along the wall for a Greek captain
Who would be able to avert this disaster.
He saw both Ajaxes, who never seemed to tire,              350
And Teucer, who had just come from his hut.
They were near enough, but there was no way
To make a shout reach them, with all the noise
Filling the air, the crash of shields and helmets
And the pounding on the gates, which were all closed now
And before each one of which the enemy stood,
Trying their best to break them and enter.
So Menestheus turned to the herald Thoötes:

"Run, Thoötes, and call Ajax, or better yet
Call both of them. All hell is going to break loose here.    360
The Lycian leaders are bearing down on us,
And they've been awfully tough in the big battles.
If the fighting is too heavy for them both to come,
At least get Telamonian Ajax here,
And Teucer too, who is good with a bow."

And the herald was off, running along the wall
Until he came to the two Ajaxes, to whom he said:

"My lords Ajax, captains of the Achaeans,
The son of Peteos, nurtured of Zeus,
Bids you come make a stand, however briefly,               370
In the battle there—both of you would be best—

Since all hell is going to break loose there.
The Lycian leaders are bearing down on us,
And they've been awfully tough in the big battles.
If the fighting is too heavy for both of you to leave,
At least let Telamonian Ajax come,
And Teucer too, who is good with a bow."

Telamonian Ajax heard the herald out
And said to his Oïlean counterpart:

"Ajax, stay here with Lycomedes                         380
And keep these Danaans in the fight.
I'm going to make a stand over there.
When I've helped them out I'll come back here."

Big Ajax left, and with him Teucer,
His natural brother, and Pandion,
Who carried Teucer's curved bow.
Moving along the inside of the wall
They came to Menestheus' sector—
And to men hard-pressed. The Lycians
Were swarming up the battlements                         390
Like black wind. The Greeks pushed back
With a shout. In the combat that ensued
It was Telamonian Ajax who first killed his man,
Sarpedon's comrade Epicles, hitting him
With a jagged piece of marble that lay on top
Of the heap of stones inside the wall there.
You couldn't find a man alive now
Who could lift that stone with both hands,
But Ajax swung it high and hurled it
With enough force to shatter the four-horned helmet      400
And crush Epicles' skull inside. He fell
As if he were doing a high dive from the wall,
And his spirit left his bones. Then Teucer hit
A fast charging Glaucus with an arrow
Where he saw his arm exposed. This stopped him cold,
And he leapt back from the wall, hiding his wound

From Greek eyes and his pride from their taunts.
It pained Sarpedon to see Glaucus withdraw
But it didn't take away any of his fight.
He hit Alcmaon, son of Thestor, with his spear,                    410
Jabbing it in, and as he pulled it out again
Alcmaon came forward with it, falling headfirst
And landing with a clatter of finely tooled bronze.
Sarpedon wrapped his hands around the battlement
And pulled. The whole section gave way, exposing
The wall above and making an entrance for many.

Ajax and Teucer attacked him together.
Teucer's arrow hit his shield's bright belt
Where it slung across his chest, but Zeus
Beat off the death spirits. He would not allow                    420
His son to fall by the ships. Big Ajax
Leapt upon him at the same moment,
Thrusting his spear into Sarpedon's shield,
But could not push the point through.
He did make him reel backward, though.
Sarpedon collected himself a short distance
Back from the wall. He was not giving up.
His heart still hoped to win glory here.
Wheeling around he called to his godlike Lycians:

"Lycians! Why are you slacking off from the fight?                    430
Do you think I can knock this wall down alone
And clear a path to the ships? Help me out here.
The more men we have the better the work will go."

The Lycians cowered before their warlord's rebuke,
Then tightened the ranks around him even more.
The Greeks strengthened their positions on the wall
And steeled themselves for a major battle.
For all their strength the Lycians were unable
To break the wall, nor could the Greek spearmen
Push them back once they were close in.                    440
They fought at close quarters,

                              *like two men*
*Disputing boundary stones in a common field*
*And defending their turf with the measuring rods*
*They had brought with them to stake their claims.*

Likewise the Trojans and Greeks, separated
By the palisade and reaching over it
To hack away at each other's leather shields.
Many were wounded, mostly those who turned
Their unprotected backs to the enemy,                    450
But many through their shields too, until
The whole wooden wall dripped with the blood
Of soldiers from both sides. But the Trojans
Could do nothing to drive the Greeks back.

    *An honest woman who works with her hands*
    *To bring home a meager wage for her children*
    *Will balance a weight of wool in her scales*
    *Until both pans are perfectly level.*

  So too this battle,
Until Zeus exalted Priam's son Hector,                   460
First to penetrate the Achaean wall.

His shout split the air:

                    "Move, Trojans!
Let's tear down this Greek fence
And make a bonfire out of their ships!"

They heard him, all right, and swarmed
Right up the wall, climbing to its pickets
With spears in their hands, while Hector
Scooped up a stone that lay by the gates,
A massive boulder tapering to a point.                   470
It would take two men to heave it onto a cart—
More than two as men are now—but Hector
Handled it easily alone. Zeus

Lightened it for him, so that the stone
Was no more to Hector than the fleece
Of a ram is to a shepherd who carries it
Easily in his free hand. This was how
Hector carried it up to the gates,
A set of heavy double doors, solidly built
And bolted shut by interlocked inner bars.                    480
Standing close to these towering doors, Hector
Spread his feet to get his weight behind the throw
And smashed the stone right into the middle.
The hinges broke off, and the stone's momentum
Carried it through, exploding the doors
And sending splintered wood in every direction.
Hector jumped through, a spear in each hand.

His face was like sudden night,
And a dark gold light played about the armor
That encased his zealous bones. No one                        490
Could have stopped him, except the gods,
In his immortal leap through the ruined gate,
And his eyes glowed with fire.
                              Wheeling around
In the throng, Hector called to his Trojans,
Who needed no persuasion, to scale the wall.
Those who couldn't swarmed through the gate.
And the Greeks? In rout to their hollow ships,
With a noise like the damned stampeded into hell.

# ILIAD 13

After Zeus had brought Hector and the Trojans
To the Greek ships, he left the combatants
To their misery and turned his luminous eyes
Far away, scanning the horse country of Thrace,
The Mysians, who fight in tight formation,
The Hippemolgi, whose diet is mares' milk,
And the Abii, most righteous of humans,
And turned his eyes no more to Troy.
He never dreamed that any of the immortals
Would go to help the Trojans or the Greeks.           10

But Poseidon wasn't blind. He sat high
On the topmost peak of wooded Samothrace,
Marvelling at the war going on beneath him.
He could see all of Ida, and Priam's city,
And the Greek ships, from where he sat.
The sea crawled beneath him. He pitied
The Greeks being beaten by the Trojans,
And he was furious with Zeus.

Three enormous strides took him down
The craggy mountain, and each footfall                 20
Sent tremors through the wooded massif
As the immortal sea god descended.
A fourth step took him to his goal, Aegae,
Where his fabulous palace was built,

Shimmering gold in the depths of the bay.
He harnessed to his chariot a team of horses,
Bronze-hooved, gold-maned, and swift,
And clothed himself in gold, and gripped
His golden whip, and stepped onto his chariot
And went driving over the waves. The sea                    30
Parted in joy before him, and all its denizens
Frolicked beneath him, acknowledging their lord.
The chariot flew on—the bronze axle below
Never got wet—and the prancing horses
Took Poseidon to the Achaean ships.

A wide cave is submerged in the deep water
Midway betweeen Tenedos and rocky Imbros.
The Earthshaker reined in his horses there,
Unhitched them, and threw out ambrosial fodder
For them to eat. And he put hobbles of gold                    40
On their feet so that they would wait there until
Their master returned. Then he went off to the Greeks.

The Trojans were swarming behind Hector
Like flame or rumbling wind, and their howls
Expressed their belief they would take the ships
Of the Greeks and kill beside them all their best.
But Poseidon, who circles the earth and shakes it,
Had emerged from the sea to urge on the Argives.
He assumed the form and voice of Calchas
And spoke to the Ajaxes, who were ready to hear:                    50

"You two men will save the Greek army
If you just summon your strength and don't panic.
The Trojans aren't invincible. The Greek line
Will hold everywhere else they've climbed the wall.
It's only here that I have a premonition
We might be hurt, where a firestorm rages
In the person of Hector, son of Zeus, as he says.
May some god put in your hearts the will
To stand firm yourselves and encourage the others.
You could force Hector back from the ships then,                    60
Even if the Olympian is behind his charge."

And the Lord of Earthquake struck them both
With his staff and pumped strength into them,
Lightening their limbs and their hands and feet.

> And the god himself rose like a hawk
> That lifts itself from a sheer precipice
> And soars downwind after another bird.

So Poseidon was gone across the dusty plain.

Oïlean Ajax took all this in first                                    70
And said to Ajax, son of Telamon:

"That was one of the Olympian gods, Ajax,
Disguised as the seer, ordering us to fight,
Not Calchas himself, who reads birds for us.
I could tell from the tracks he made when he left.
Gods are easy to recognize. As for me,
I never felt readier for battle. I'm itching to fight
All the way down to my fingers and toes."

Telamonian Ajax answered him:

"Me too. I can't wait to wrap my hands                                80
Around a spear. I'm all pumped up, and my feet
Are flying beneath me. Bring on Hector,
Just me and Priam's fighting machine."

That was how they talked to each other,
Feeling the joy the god put in their hearts.

Meanwhile the Earthshaker was rousing the Greeks
Who were catching their breath to the rear by the ships.
They were all done in by the hard fighting
And couldn't take it when they saw the Trojans
Clambering over the wall in droves.                                   90
They watched helplessly, tears in their eyes,
And thought it was the end. But the Earthshaker
Slipped in among them and gave heart to the troops—
Teucer first, then Leitus, the hero Peneleus,

Thoas and Deipyrus, Meriones and Antilochus—
He came to them all, and his words had wings:

"Shame on you, Argives. To think I trusted
You raw recruits to fight for our ships.
If you're backing off when the going gets tough
Then this is the day we get beaten by the Trojans.          100
I can't believe what is before my eyes,
A disaster I thought would never happen—
The Trojans going for our ships. Up until now
They've been like spooked deer that dodge through the woods
To become dinner for jackals, panthers, and wolves,
Totally defenseless, no fight in them.
That's how the Trojans have been with us,
Unwilling to offer the slightest resistance.
But now they're out fighting for our hollow ships
Because, thanks to our leader's cowardice          110
And dissension in the ranks, we would rather be killed
Beside our seagoing vessels than defend them.
But even if Agamemnon is completely to blame
For all this, because he dishonored Achilles,
That's no reason for us go slack in war.
Let's do what good men do and make amends.
It's no longer right for you to slough off,
Not you, our army's best. I wouldn't bother
With some sad sack who was sitting out the war,
But with you I couldn't be angrier.          120
You've gone soft! And the upshot of your laxness
Is going to be worse trouble to come, and soon.
Don't you remember what shame is, or retribution?
Do you think this is some minor skirmish?
This is Hector, showing his strength. He's smashed
The gates open and has taken the war to our ships."

In this way the Earthshaker roused the Achaeans.

The columns that formed around the two Ajaxes
Were so tight they could have passed inspection
From Ares, or from Athena, the soldiers' goddess.          130
These were hand-picked troops, Greece's best,

Who awaited the Trojans and godlike Hector.
Spear on spear, shield overlapping shield,
They stood helmet to helmet, the horsehair plumes
On the burnished crests brushing each other
When they nodded, and when they shook their spears
The shafts tickered against each other. Their minds
Were fixed on the fight ahead of them.

The Trojans closed ranks and charged. Hector led them,
Driving straight ahead like a boulder from a cliff.                    140

> *A river swollen by winter rains*
> *Will push a stone from a high crest,*
> *Breaking it loose from its foundation*
> *By the sheer force of the water. The stone*
> *Knows no shame as it caroms downstream,*
> *Bounding high. The woods echo its sound,*
> *And nothing can stop it until it reaches*
> *Level ground. But then it rolls no more.*

So too with Hector.
                    For a while he threatened                          150
To cut his way to the sea through the ships and huts,
Killing as he went, but when he hit the Greek line
He was stopped cold, and the sons of the Achaeans,
Thrusting with swords and spears, pushed him back.
Shaken, Hector gave way, but his voice boomed out
To the Trojans and their Lycian allies:

"Stand your ground, men. This tight Greek formation
Cannot contain me. They'll fall back under my spear
All right, if it is true that the best of the gods,
Hera's thundering husband, has urged me on."                          160

Hector's speech aroused their enthusiasm.
Deïphobus, Priam's son, strode out,
Almost danced out, behind the disk of his shield.
Meriones took aim at him with a polished spear,
And cast. The spear hit the taut bull's hide
But didn't pierce it, the long shaft shattering

At its metal socket. Deïphobus held the shield
At arm's length, afraid the point would come through.
Meriones made his way back to his own people,
Angry because he had been cheated of victory                    170
And had broken his spear. He made his way
Back through camp to retrieve a spare from his hut.

The others fought on in the eye of war.
Teucer, son of Telamon, killed his man first,
The spearman Imbrius. His father Mentor
Raised horses, and he lived in Pedaeum
Before the war with his wife, Medicaste,
One of Priam's bastard daughters.
When the Danaans came with their curved ships
He moved back to Ilion and had quarters                         180
In the house of Priam, who accorded him
The same honor as his own natural children.
Teucer jabbed his spear into his jaw,
And when he pulled it out, Imbrius fell.

> *He fell as an ash tree falls, a tree*
> *That is a landmark on a mountain crest,*
> *And when it is cut through with bronze axes,*
> *It brings all its soft leafage down to the ground.*

Imbrius' tooled bronze clattered around him,
And Teucer rushed up to relieve him of it.                      190
Hector cast at the moving target he made,
But Teucer had his eye on the bright spear
And managed to dodge it. No matter.
It hit Amphimachus instead, whose lineage
Went back through Cteatus to Poseidon,
Square in the chest as he entered battle.
He crashed to the ground, bronze clattering,
And Hector ran up to rip the helmet
From Amphimachus' noble head.
But he didn't get that far. Big Ajax                            200
Lunged with his spear as Hector charged.
The point never reached his bronze-cased skin
But it struck Hector's shield with enough force

To drive him back from both fallen bodies,
Which the Greeks proceeded to drag away.
Two Athenians, Stichius and Menestheus,
Hauled Amphimachus off to the Greek side,
While the two Ajaxes did the same for Imbrius.

> *Two lions have snatched a goat from snarling dogs*
> *And are carrying it off through thick underbrush,*                210
> *Holding it in their jaws high above the ground.*

They held Imbrius high and stripped him.

When they got the armor off, Oïlean Ajax,
Angry for Amphimachus, lopped off his head
And whirled it like a ball through the crowd.
It fell in the dust before Hector's feet.

Poseidon was pulsing with anger. His son's son
Had fallen in the hard fighting.
He went through the ships and huts to rally                         220
The Greeks and to build trouble for the Trojans.
Idomeneus, the great spearman, bumped into him
As he came from a friend who had been wounded—
A gash in the knee—and carried out of battle.
He had just briefed the medics and was going
Back to his hut, anxious to return to the fight,
When the Earthshaker spoke to him,
Likening his voice to that of Andraemon's son,
Thoas, lord in Pleuron and steep Calydon
And honored as a god by the Aetolians there:                        230

"Idomeneus, you, the Cretan commander,
What has happened to all the threats
The Greeks once issued against the Trojans?"

And Idomeneus, commander of the Cretans:

"Thoas, there's not a Greek here at fault,
As far as I know. We're all experienced.
No one has panicked; no one has deserted.

My guess is that it is great Zeus' pleasure
That the Achaeans die a nameless death here,
Far from Argos. But look, Thoas,                                    240
You have always held your own in battle,
And now you're rallying others. Keep it up.
Don't let anyone hang back from the fight."

And Poseidon, who shakes the continents:

"Idomeneus, may the man who willingly
Shirks battle today never return from Troy
But become a ragbone for the dogs of Ilion.
Get your armor on and let's head out.
We have to work together and do our best
To help out, even though we are only two.                          250
Teamwork makes even riffraff do well,
And you and I know how to fight with the best."

He spoke and returned, a god, to men's toil.

When Idomeneus reached his well-built hut
He strapped on his armor, took two spears,
And walked out like a lightning bolt

   *That Zeus shakes down from Olympus' glare*
   *As a sign to humans, blinding forks of light,*

The bronze on this hero's chest as he ran.
Meriones, his second-in-command, met him                           260
Near the hut, where he was going to get a spear
For himself. Idomeneus boomed out at him:

"Meriones, son of Molus, old friend,
What's this sprint away from the battle?
Are you wounded? Were you nicked?
Or do you have a message for me? Myself,
I'm not for sitting in the huts but for fighting."

And Meriones, who knew what to say:

"I came here for a spear, Idomeneus,
If there are any left in your hut. The one I had          *270*
Shattered when it hit Deïphobus' shield."

And Idomeneus, the Cretan commander:

"Spears? You can have twenty if you want,
Standing along the white plaster wall
As you go in, spears I take off Trojans
I kill in close combat. I have plenty,
Shields too, and helmets, and breastplates."

Meriones knew how to respond:

"The hut by my tarred ships is also filled
With Trojan spoils, but it's not close by.                *280*
I know what it means to fight up front
And win my share of glory in war.
There might be one or two Greeks around
Who haven't noticed, but not you."

And the Cretan commander:

"I know you're good. Why talk about it?
Look. Suppose we were all lined up
For an ambush. At times like that it's obvious
Who has what it takes and who doesn't.
Your coward will turn ten shades of green.                *290*
He's unsteady, shifting his weight
From one foot to another. His heart thumps
So loud you can hear it, and his teeth chatter
As he keeps imagining his death.
The brave man, though, doesn't blanch
And is not too afraid when he gets in position.
His only prayer is to get on with the battle.
At a time like that no one would slight you.
If you were hit in battle or took a shot,
It wouldn't be in the back or the neck                    *300*
But in your chest or belly as you came on hard

In the front lines. Come on, though,
Let's not stand around talking like kids.
Someone might see us and really blow up.
Go on in and get yourself a spear."

Meriones ducked into the hut, got a spear,
And followed Idomeneus, intent on war.

*Ares himself sometimes goes to war*
*And takes with him his son, Rout,*
*Who is as valiant as his father* 310
*And can turn even the bravest man to flight.*
*They arm themselves and go forth from Thrace*
*To join either the Ephyri or Phlegyes,*
*But do not really care which side wins.*

Thus the two human captains
Going to battle in their bronze,
Meriones saying to Idomeneus:

"Where to, son of Deucalion?
Should we enter on the right, center, or left,
Where the Greeks will likely need help the most?" 320

And Idomeneus, the Cretan commander:

"We have some good defense in the central ships,
Both Ajaxes and Teucer, our best bowman
And a good man in hand-to-hand combat.
These will give Hector all he wants and more,
No matter how tough he is. He'll be fighting
Uphill all day trying to beat them back
And burn the ships, and won't be able to
Unless Zeus himself throws a torch on the hulls.
Ajax won't yield to anything human, 330
That's for sure, anything that eats bread,
Can be split with bronze, or crushed with stones.
He wouldn't even give way to Achilles,
Not in a close fight anyway, although no one

Could touch Achilles in the open field.
As for us, let's do as you suggest
And go left, so we can find out whether
We'll give glory to another or another to us."

He spoke, and Meriones, moving like Ares,
Led the way to the left side of the camp.                      340

When the Trojans saw Idomeneus
And his lieutenant in their buffed armor
It was as if they had spotted a fire.
Calling to each other, they converged on the pair,
Another knot in the battle by the sterns of the ships.

*Howling winds with gusts up to fifty*
*On a day when the gravel roadbeds are dry*
*Will raise up indiscriminate clouds of dust.*

That was how they closed with each other,
And all their blind desire was to shred flesh                  350
With stropped bronze, eyes squinting against the glare
Of helmets and corselets—just polished that morning—
And the confusion of shields, like so many suns
Shining through a bristling forest of spears.
It was glorious to see—if your heart were iron,
And you could keep from grieving at all the pain.

There were two strong sons of Cronus
Out that day, with opposing purposes
As to which human heroes they should afflict.
Zeus planned victory for Hector and the Trojans—              360
To honor Achilles. He had no desire
To destroy the Greeks on Troy's dusty plain,
But meant only to honor Thetis and her son.
Poseidon, rising secretly from the grey salt sea,
Went among the Greeks, urging them on,
Hating to see them beaten by the Trojans,
And was strongly resentful of his brother, Zeus.
They were born of the same stock, but Zeus

Was born first, and he knew more, and so
Poseidon avoided giving aid openly,                        370
But spurred on the Greeks disguised as a man.

So these two tightened the cords of war
And tied around each army in turn
A knot that brought many down to their knees.

Idomeneus, hair flecked with grey and yelling
For Greeks to back him up, jumped at the Trojans
And scattered them with his first kill.
This was Othryoneus, who, though from Cabesus,
Was one of Troy's inner circle. Smelling war,
He had come to the capital and asked to marry        380
Priam's most beautiful daughter, Cassandra herself,
Promising no wedding gifts, but one great deed—
That he would drive the Greeks from Trojan soil.
Old Priam promised her with a nod of his head,
And Othryoneus, putting his faith in promises,
Went out to fight. Swaggering along,
He made a perfect target for Idomeneus' spear,
Which lodged in his belly under his useless corselet.
He fell heavily, and Idomeneus taunted him:

"You'll be the happiest man on earth,                     390
Othryoneus, if you accomplish all you promised
Dardanian Priam. We hear he promised you
His own daughter. We could match his offer, you know,
And give you Agamemnon's loveliest daughter,
Ship her here from Argos for the wedding,
If only you'd switch to our side and conquer Troy.
Come on over to the ships so we can negotiate
This marriage. You'll find we offer easy terms."

And he started to drag him off by one leg
Through the crowd, but Asius came to the dead man's aid,   400
Advancing on foot just in front of his horses,
Which his charioteer drove so closely behind him
That their breath warmed his neck. He never got off

The shot he wanted. Idomeneus was too quick,
Catching him in the throat beneath the chin
And slicing the bronze clean through. Asius fell.

> *A tree, oak, say, or poplar, or spreading pine,*
> *Falls in the forest when carpenters cut it down*
> *With their bright axes, to be the beam of a ship.*

Asius lay before his horses and chariot,                        410
Groaning heavily and clawing the bloody dust.

His charioteer lost his wits completely
And in his terror didn't even have enough nerve
To turn the horses around and run for it.
Antilochus stitched him through the belly,
A neat shot just below his corselet,
And he fell gasping from his crafted chariot.
Antilochus drove the horses back to the Greeks.

Deïphobus took Asius' death hard.
He closed in on Idomeneus and cast,                             420
But Idomeneus saw his shot all the way
And ducked behind his shield, a huge
Double oval of leather and bronze,
Fitted with two rods. Deïphobus' spear
Grated on the rim and sailed over,
But, with all of Deïphobus' weight behind it,
Kept going and hit Hypsenor, Hippasus' son,
In the liver. His knees buckled,
And Deïphobus crowed over him:

"Asius is avenged. When he goes down                            430
To Hades' cold gates he can be glad
That at least I have sent him some company."

The Greeks winced at this boast,
And no one more so than Antilochus,
Who did what he could for his fallen comrade,
Standing over him and sheltering him

With his shield until two of his men,
Mecisteus and Alastor, bore Hypsenor,
Groaning heavily, to the hollow ships.

Idomeneus was still going strong,                                    440
Doing his best to get the drop on some Trojan
Or just pound himself against their general menace,
When the hero Alcathous appeared before him.
This man, son of Aesytes, beloved of Zeus,
Had married Anchises' eldest daughter,
Hippodameia, darling of both her parents,
Beautiful, clever with her hands, and wise,
And now wife of the best man in all Troy.
This Alcathous Poseidon now mastered,
Putting a spell on his shining eyes                                  450
And paralyzing him so that he stood
Rooted to the spot like a gravestone or tree,
Unable to move or dodge the spear
That Idomeneus now put through his chest,
Cleaving the bronze breastplate that had always
Protected his flesh from fatal harm
But that now rasped dryly around the wooden shaft.
He fell backward, the spear's point
Fixed deep in the still beating heart
So that the upright shaft quivered a while                          460
Until at last Ares put its fury at ease.
Idomeneus gloated over him loud and long:

"Are we even yet, Deïphobus, three deaths
For one? Do you want to boast some more?
Why don't you get out here and face me
So you can see a true descendant of Zeus.
Minos, my grandfather, was his son,
Overlord of Crete by his divine will,
And his son Deucalion fathered me,
Lord over many in the wide land of Crete.                           470
And now the ships have brought me here
As a curse to your father and the other Trojans."

He spoke, and Deïphobus couldn't decide
Whether he should step back and get help
Or take Idomeneus on by himself.
He decided he'd better go get Aeneas,
And found him in the rear, the last man there,
Angry as always with Priam,
Who utterly failed to honor his worth.
Deïphobus drew near, and his words flew fast:                    *480*

"Aeneas, counsellor of the Trojans,
Alcathous is down and you have to help
If you have any feeling at all for a kinsman,
Your sister's husband, who cared for you
When you were little. Come on, let's go.
Idomeneus has killed him with his spear."

This wrung Aeneas' heart, and he moved up
To find Idomeneus. The war mattered to him now,
A great deal. Idomeneus was not one to run
Like a spoiled child, but stood his ground.                     *490*

> *A boar in the mountains is sure of his strength,*
> *And when gangs of hunters try to flush him out*
> *In some desolate spot, he waits as they come,*
> *Bristling his back, eyes blazing, whetting the tusks*
> *He will use to scatter the men and their dogs.*

Idomeneus, famed for his spear, waited
As Aeneas came on.
                        He didn't yield an inch,
But he called to his friends—Ascalaphus,
Aphareus, Deïpyrus, Meriones,                                    *500*
And Antilochus, masters of the war cry.
His words flew out to them as he urged:

"Come help me out, friends. I'm by myself
And scared to death of this Aeneas,
Who's closing in fast. He's a hell of a fighter

And in his prime. If we were his age
And in the mood we're in, it'd be over fast.
He might still win big, but so might I."

And they closed ranks, locking their shields.
Opposite them, Aeneas called to his comrades,                510
To Deïphobus and Paris and Agenor,
His peers in the Trojan command.
Their troops flocked behind them,

> *Sheep following rams from pasture*
> *To water, the shepherd's joy,*

Aeneas that glad when he saw
A nation of soldiers at his back.

They fought over Alcathous with their long pikes,
And the bronze plate on their chests rang like gongs,
And above them all two men,                                  520
Idomeneus and Aeneas, like gods of war,
Strained to shred each other's flesh with cold metal.
Aeneas cast first, but Idomeneus,
Watching him all the way, sidestepped the missile,
Which, launched by a strong arm but with nowhere to go,
Burrowed, quivering, into the earth.
Idomeneus' throw hit Oenomaus
Full in the belly, smashing the plates on his corselet
And letting his entrails gush through the hole.
He fell, clawing at the dust, Idomeneus' spear             530
Casting a long shadow on the plain. He pulled it
From the corpse but could not get the armor off
With all the pressure he was under. The veteran
Could no longer trust his feet in a charge,
Either to follow his own throw or dodge another's,
And so, unable also to get away quickly,
He had no choice but to stand and fight
And beat off the pitiless day of doom.
As he inched his way back, Deïphobus,
Whose anger toward him had not lost its edge,              540

Took a shot at him. His spear burned the air
But missed Idomeneus again, hitting instead
Ascalaphus, Ares' son, stitching his shoulder.
He fell to the ground and clawed at the dust.
Ares as yet knew nothing of his son's fall.
The blaring god sat under golden clouds
On Olympus' peak, constrained from war
By Zeus' will, along with the other immortals.

The fighting began over Ascalaphus' body.
Deïphobus managed to tear off his helmet                        550
But dropped it when he was hit in the arm
By Meriones' spear. It fell with a clang.
Meriones sprang again, like a vulture,
Pulled his spear out of Deïphobus' arm,
Then drifted back into the ranks. Polites,
Deïphobus' brother, wrapping his arms
Around his waist, escorted him out of harm's way
And to the rear, where his horses stood waiting
To pull him groaning in his ornamented chariot
Back to the city, blood dripping from his arm.                  560

The rest fought on, drowning in their own noise.

Aeneas jumped Aphareus, Caletor's son,
And, having a good angle on his throat,
Sliced through it with his spear. Aphareus' head
Sank to one side, and his helmet clanged on his shield
As death hammered at his soul like a tinsmith.

Antilochus, waiting for his moment,
Caught Thoön turning his back. His quick thrust
Severed the vein that runs up to the neck,
And Thoön was left supine in the dust                           570
Stretching his arms out to his comrades.
Antilochus leapt on top of him
And began unbuckling the armor from his shoulders,
Keeping an eye on the Trojans who circled him.
They kept poking at his big, bright shield

From every direction but couldn't stick a point
Into his flesh, this the doing of Poseidon,
Who guarded Nestor's son with all his power
No matter the spearpoints around him. Antilochus
Was constantly engaged with the enemy,                               580
His spear never at rest but always quivering
With his desire to cast or thrust it home.
He was taking dead aim at someone in the throng
When Adamas, Asius' son, zeroed in on him
And hit his shield from point-blank range.
The blue-maned sea god cancelled the shot
And denied it the life of Antilochus.
Half the spear stuck in the shield like a charred stake,
The other half lay on the ground. Adamas
Knew fate when he saw it and backed away.                            590
But Meriones went after him, and his throw
Caught Adamas where Ares hurts men worst,
Sticking him between the navel and the genitals.
He doubled over, leaning into the shaft,
And writhed and twisted the way a bull will
When mountain men tie it and drag it along.
So too Adamas, but only for a while, until
The hero Meriones drew the spear from his gut.
Then darkness drifted like a veil on his eyes.

In the hand-to-hand fighting, Helenus hit                            600
Deïpyrus' temple with a huge Thracian sword,
Ripping the helmet from his head and sending it
Rolling through the combatants' feet
Until one of the Greeks scooped it up.
By then Deïpyrus' eyes had gone black.
The son of Atreus took his death hard—
Menelaus, good at the war cry—and he strode
Menacingly toward the Trojan hero,
Brandishing his sharp spear as Helenus
Drew back his bow. They each shot at once,                           610
The spear and arrow crossing in mid-air,
Helenus' needling arrow going on to hit
Menelaus' breastplate and clang off the bronze.

*Think of dark beans, or lentils, bounding up*
*From the broad shovel a winnower wields*
*In a great threshing floor swept by shrill winds.*

Thus the arrow that ricocheted off
Menelaus' corselet and went flying away.
But Menelaus' own shot wasn't wasted,
The sharp spearpoint hitting Helenus' bow hand          620
And going through it into the polished wood.
He fell back among his comrades, avoiding death,
The ash-wood spear trailing from his hand,
Until great Agenor pulled it out for him
And bound the hand with a strip of twisted wool,
A sling actually, from his squire's kit.

Peisander now made straight at Menelaus,
Death drawing him on toward his fated end,
To be killed by you, Menelaus, in the mêlée.
When they were within range of each other          630
They each cast, Menelaus' spear missing wide,
Peisander's hitting his shield but shattering
At the socket against its metal face.
Peisander still had hope for victory,
And when the son of Atreus leapt at him
With his silver-studded sword, Peisander drew
From beneath his shield an axe of fine bronze
With a long haft of polished olive wood.
They struck each other at the same moment,
Peisander's axe hitting Menelaus' helmet          640
On the horn, just beneath the horsehair plume,
Menelaus' sword smashing Peisander's brow
Just above the nose. The bones snapped, both eyeballs
Popped out in blood and dropped at his feet
In the dust, and Peisander doubled over and fell.
Menelaus put his foot on his chest, and as he
Ripped off his armor and gloated over him:

"All you Trojans will be leaving our ships like this,
You arrogant bastards! You can't get enough

Of fighting, can you? Can't get enough                                            650
Of abusing people, as you've abused me,
No room in your heart for the anger of Zeus,
The Lord of Thunder, god of host and guest,
Whose wrath will destroy your towering city.
You came and took my bride, made off
With all my stuff—and after you were her guest!
And now you're all hot to burn our ships,
Cut us off from the sea, and kill our men.
But you won't, for all your eagerness to fight.
Father Zeus, they say you are the wisest                                          660
Of gods and men. Yet all this is from you.
Somehow you honor these violent men,
These Trojans, with their reckless strength
And insatiable appetite for the horrors of war.
When it comes to getting enough, everyone else
Would rather have all they want of sleep or love,
Of sweet song or fine dancing. But the Trojans
Are gluttons for war, and cannot get enough."


Thus Menelaus, as he stripped off
The last bit of bloody gear and gave it to his men,                              670
Then went back and took his place in the front.


He was attacked immediately by Harpalion,
Who followed his father, king Pylaemenes,
To Troy and the war, but never returned home.
His spear hit Menelaus' shield from close range,
But not hard enough to go through. Unnerved,
Harpalion drifted back to his comrades,
Glancing warily over his shoulder,
Half expecting to feel bronze in his skin.
As he retreated Meriones shot at him.                                            680
The bronze-tipped arrow hit his right buttock, sliding
Beneath the bone and into his bladder.
Harpalion sank into his comrades' arms
And breathed out his life stretched on the ground
Like an earthworm in a pool of black blood.

The Paphlagonians tended to him
And took him on a chariot to sacred Ilion
In sorrow. His father went with them, weeping.
Nothing would ever replace his dead son.

Paris was enraged at his killing.                               690
Among the Paphlagonians Harpalion
Had been his host, and in anger for his sake
He let fly an arrow tipped with bronze,
And a man named Euchenor got in its way.
He was the son of the prophet Polyidus,
Rich, with estates in Corinth, a good man.
When he boarded ship for Troy he knew well
He was embarking on death, for his father,
Old Polyidus, had told him often
That he must die of painful disease at home          700
Or be killed by Trojans amid Achaean ships.
He chose to avoid both the heavy Greek fine
For avoiding service and the loathsome disease.
Paris' arrow hit him behind his jawbone.
His soul crawled out and the world went dark.

The fight went on, like wildfire burning.
Hector, whom Zeus loved, did not know
That on the left side of the ships his army
Was succumbing to the Greeks, who were not far
From winning the day. The god who laps the earth    710
And makes it tremble was urging them on
And adding his own strength to their efforts.
Hector was still where he had first burst through
The gate and shattered the Greek ranks,
Close to where Ajax's and Protesilaus' ships
Were drawn up on the beach of the grey salt sea
And the wall was lowest. Horses and men
Fought furiously there, in the vortex of battle.

There the Boeotians and fringed Ionians,
The Locrians, Phthians, and proud Epeians            720
Had their hands full trying to repel

Hector's attack on the ships. Hector
Was like a bright flame and could not be stopped,
Not even by the Athenian elite,
Whose captain was Menestheus, Peteos' son,
And who had with him men like Pheidas,
Stichius, and valiant Bias. The Epeians
Were led by Meges, son of Phyleus,
And by Amphius and Dracius; the Phthians
By Medon and steady Podarces.                                    730
Medon was a bastard son of Oïleus
And Ajax's brother, but he lived in Phylace,
Far from his homeland, because he had killed
A relative of Eriopis, his stepmother,
Whom Oïleus had married. Podarces
Was Iphiclus' son and Phylacus' grandson.
Armed and in the front of the Phthian forces
They fought alongside the Boeotians
To defend their ships. Oïleus' other son,
The swift Ajax, was inseparable                                  740
From Telamonian Ajax and would not
Leave his side even for an instant.

> *A team of oxen with faces dark as wine*
> *Strain together at the jointed plow, pulling it*
> *Through a field that has not been worked in years.*
> *Sweat oozes up from the roots of their horns,*
> *And only the polished yoke holds them apart*
> *As they cut the furrow to the field's far edge.*

The two Ajaxes stood side by side in battle.

Telamonian Ajax had his cadres with him,                         750
And there was always someone to relieve him
Of his heavy shield when he began to tire.
But the Locrians commanded by Oïlean Ajax
Were not at his side. They were not trained
To stand and fight at close range, nor equipped:
They had no bronze, plumed helmets, no shields,

No ash-wood spears, but trusting to the bows
And twisted wool slings they had brought
When they followed him to Troy, they now shot
Thick and fast, trying to break the Trojan lines.        760
In the front: troops in full battle gear
Engaging Hector and his Trojans;
In the rear: archers. And the Trojans, confounded
By their arrows, were losing the will to fight.

They would have been beaten miserably
From the beachhead camp back to windy Ilion
Had not Polydamas approached Hector and said:

"Hector, you are a difficult man to persuade.
Because Zeus has made you preeminent in war
You want to excel in counsel too.                        770
But you can't have everything. Zeus makes
One man a warrior, another a dancer,
Another a singer, and in another's heart
He puts wisdom, by which many profit
And which saves many, as the god himself knows best.
So I will say to you what seems best to me.
All around you blazes a ring of war.
The Trojans have passed over the wall,
But some are standing on the sidelines
And others are fighting in skirmishes                    780
Throughout the ships against superior numbers.
Let's fall back and regroup, weigh our options,
And decide whether to attack the ships
In the hope of victory from the god
Or at least a safe retreat. As for myself,
I fear the Greeks will pay us back for yesterday.
He is still waiting back there, you know, and he loves
To fight. He won't sit out the whole war."

This seemed like sound advice to Hector.
He leapt to the ground with his gear                     790
And his words flew to Polydamas:

"Draw back all our best and keep them here
While I go off to pass the word.
I'll be back as fast as I can."

And he went off like an avalanche
Down a mountain, speeding through the Trojans
And their allies and shouting as he went.
At the sound of his voice they all went back
Toward Polydamas. Hector moved up
To the fighters at the very front.                                          800
He was looking for Deïphobus, for Helenus,
For Adamas and Adamas' father Asius,
And hardly found them unscathed.
They were either dead beside the Greek ships
Or nursing wounds inside the city walls.
He did find Paris, though, Helen's lord,
Urging on his men at the left side of battle,
And started in on him with abusive epithets:

"Paris, you desperate, preening pretty boy—
Where is Deïphobus, and where are Helenus                                    810
And Adamas and Adamas' father Asius?
And where is Othryoneus? Troy is doomed,
The whole towering city as good as gone."

And Paris, who could have passed for a god:

"I see you're in a testy mood, Hector.
I may have held back from battle before,
But not now. My mother didn't raise
A total weakling. Ever since you started
This attack on the ships we've been right here
Engaging the Greeks. As for our comrades                                     820
You're asking about, they are dead,
Except for Deïphobus and Helenus,
Who have gone off with spear wounds
In their arms, saved by Zeus from death.
Now, lead on wherever you will,
And we will follow. I don't think you will find us

Lacking in determination, and we will fight
To the best of our ability. No man can do more."

Spoken like a hero. Hector calmed down,
And they plunged into the brutal eye of combat,          830
Which was around Cebriones and Polydamas
And Phalces and Arthaeus, godlike Polyphetes,
Ascanius and Morys, son of Hippotion.
These had come from Ascania's farmland
The morning before, as replacement troops,
And now Zeus roused them on to battle.

> *Aching winds sweep down to the ground*
> *Under rolling thunder from the patriarch Zeus*
> *And then clash with the sea. The water moans*
> *And is whipped into wave after wave of arching,*          840
> *Seething breakers capped with white foam.*

The Trojans kept coming, rank on rank
Flashing with bronze, behind their captains.

Hector, son of Priam, led them all,
And he was like the War God himself
Behind his balanced shield, thick with hide
And layered with welded bronze, and on his head
The crest of his helm rippled in shining wind.
He kept testing the Greek lines here and there
To see if they would yield before him          850
As he came on behind his shield, but the Greeks
Didn't flinch. Then big Ajax strode forward:

"Come closer, sweetheart. No need to be coy.
We're not exactly inexperienced in war,
You know. It was Zeus who whipped us before.
I'm sure you'd like to rip our ships apart,
But be just as sure we have hands to defend them.
Your city, with all its people, will likely fall
A lot sooner, captured by us and plundered.
As for you, the day will soon be here          860

When you pray to Zeus and all immortals
For your combed horses to outfly falcons
And take you through the dusty plain to Troy."

His words were not out before a bird flew past
On the right, a high-soaring eagle.
The Achaeans shouted, taking heart
At the omen. But Hector answered him:

"You bumbling ox, what a stupid thing to say.
I wish it were as certain that I were Zeus' son
And Hera my mother, and that I were honored                    870
Equally with Apollo and Athena
As it is that this day will bring doom
To every last Greek, and you among them,
Killed by my long spear, if you have the guts
To wait for it to pierce your lily-white skin
And leave your larded flesh to glut the dogs and birds
Of Troy, after you have fallen amid the ships."

With that he led the charge, followed by
Trojans shrieking at the top of their lungs.
The Greeks answered with cries of their own,                    880
Digging in their heels as Troy's best came on,
And the noise from both armies blended together
And rose through the air to the brightness of Zeus.

# ILIAD 14

Nestor, drinking wine with Machaon,
Could not help but hear the screaming, and said:

"Son of Asclepius, what do you make of this?
Our boys are shouting much louder by the ships.
Now don't get up. Just keep sipping that wine
Until pretty Hecamede heats up a warm bath
And washes off all that clotted blood.
Myself, I'll go to a lookout point now."

With that, he picked up a metal-plated shield,
One of Thrasymedes' that was lying in the hut,                    10
And a heavy spear with a honed bronze point.
He stepped outside and saw an ugly scene,
The Greeks in rout and behind them
The high-hearted Trojans, pouring through the wall.

 *As the dark sea broods with a silent swell*
 *And only a faint premonition of wind*
 *Is traced on its surface, and no crest forms*
 *Until a decisive breeze comes down from Zeus,*

So the old man pondered which way to go—
To join the Greek troops or to get Agamemnon,                    20
The son of Atreus, shepherd of his people.

He thought it over and went for Agamemnon.

The fighting continued, and the killing.
Armor rang under sword blades
And spearpoints nosed busily past plated shields.

The wounded kings were coming up
From their ships—Diomedes, Odysseus,
And Agamemnon—and met Nestor on the way.
Their ships were drawn up far from the battle
On the sand by the grey sea, in the first row,                    30
And the wall was built near the last row, inland.
The beach was wide but could not hold all the ships
So they were drawn up in rows toward the plain
And filled the space between the two headlands.

So the kings were coming up together,
Leaning on their spears, to see the fighting,
And their hearts were grieved. Old Nestor
Met them, and was hailed by Agamemnon:

"Nestor, son of Neleus, glory of our army,
Why have you left the battle and come here?                    40
I fear that Hector will make good on the threats
He levelled against us in the Trojan muster—
That he would not return to Ilion until
He had burnt our ships and killed our men.
It's all coming true, just as he said.
And the worst part is that all of the Greeks
Are angry with me, just like Achilles.
None of them is willing to defend our ships."

And Nestor, the Gerenian horseman, answered:

"Yes, this is how things are, and Zeus himself,                    50
The thunder lord, could not make them otherwise.
For the wall is down. We put our trust in it
As a bulwark for our ships, and now the enemy
Is at our ships, fighting relentlessly.
You cannot even tell in which direction

Our men are retreating, so confused
Is their slaughter, the air so filled
With the noise of battle, up to the sky.
We must take counsel in this situation,
Not enter the battle ourselves.                              60
It is not possible for wounded men to fight."

And Agamemnon, the warlord:

"Well then, Nestor, the ships are under attack,
And neither the wall nor the trench,
Which we trusted to be a bulwark
For our beachhead camp, has been of any avail.
It must be the pleasure of Zeus Almighty
For us to die here, nameless and far from Argos.
I knew it when he was favoring the Greeks,
And I know now that he is giving the Trojans             70
Glory from above and has tied our hands.
So this is what I say we should all do now:
Let's haul the first line of ships to the water,
Get them afloat and moor them with anchors
Until darkness comes. If and when the Trojans
Stop for the night, we can drag down the rest.
It is no shame to flee ruin, even by night.
Better to give evil the slip than be caught by it."

Odysseus looked him up and down, and said:

"What kind of thing is that to say?                          80
You're a ruined man, son of Atreus, fit to command
Some ragtag army, but not to rule over men like us,
To whom Zeus has granted just one thing in life:
To wind up wars like skeins of wool,
From youth to old age, until the last of us dies.
Do you really want to leave Troy behind,
The great city that we've suffered so much for?
Stop that talk before somebody hears you.
Words like that should never make it past your mouth.
You're a sceptered king commanding the loyalty          90

Of an army of Greeks. You must have lost your mind,
Ordering us to launch ships while the battle is raging.
The Trojans, who are winning as it is,
Will have all their prayers answered, and our army
Will be utterly crushed. Draw the ships
To the sea, and the Greeks will be looking
Over their shoulders and give up the fight.
Your plan will ruin us, Lord Agamemnon."

To which Agamemnon briefly replied:

"That cuts deep, Odysseus. I am not suggesting        100
That the ships be launched against the Achaeans' will.
I wish there were someone, young or old,
With a better plan than mine. I would welcome that."

Diomedes, the bull-roarer, had a response:

"The man is here, no need for a long search,
If you are willing to listen, and if none of you
Will be upset because I am the youngest in years.
There's nothing wrong with my lineage. My father
Was Tydeus, who lies buried at Thebes.
My great-grandfather Portheus had three peerless sons        110
Who lived in Pleuron and steep Calydon,
Agrios, Melas, and the horseman Oineus,
My father's father, the bravest of the three.
My father left home and wandered to Argos,
As Zeus and the other gods no doubt willed.
He married one of Adrastus' daughters
And lived in a rich house with many acres
In wheat and orchards, and many sheep.
And he was the best spearman in all Argos.
You will have heard of all this and know it is true.        120
So don't think I'm a coward by birth
And reject anything worthwhile I might have to say.
We must go down to the battle, injuries and all,
Not to fight—we will stay out of range
To avoid taking wounds on top of wounds—

But to spur the others on and send them in,
Those who have been on the sidelines
Nursing their resentment and failing to fight."

They heard him out and agreed.
Agamemnon led the way as they started out.                    *130*

Poseidon was not blind to any of this
But went with them disguised as an old man.
He took Agamemnon by his right hand
And spoke to him words that winged home:

"Well, son of Atreus, Achilles' dark heart
Must be laughing now, as he sees
The panic and slaughter of the Greeks.
The man hasn't a shred of sense left, none,
Damn him! May some god cripple him.
But the blessed ones aren't angry with you,                    *140*
Not yet. There's still a chance you will see
The Trojan generals raise dust on the wide plain
As they beat a retreat from your ships and huts."

And as he sped over the plain, Poseidon yelled,
So loud it seemed that ten thousand warriors
Had been enlisted by Ares and shouted at once.
And the god's yell put into each Greek's heart
The strength to fight and battle on without pause.

   Standing on a crag of Olympus
Gold-throned Hera saw her brother,                             *150*
Who was her husband's brother too,
Busy on the fields of human glory,
And her heart sang. Then she saw Zeus
Sitting on the topmost peak of Ida
And was filled with resentment. Cow-eyed Hera
Mused for a while on how to trick
The mind of Zeus Aegis-Holder,
And the plan that seemed best to her
Was to make herself up and go to Ida,

Seduce him, and then shed on his eyelids                              160
And cunning mind a sleep gentle and warm.
She went to the bedroom her darling son
Hephaestus had built for her, and closed
Behind her the solid, polished doors
He had fitted out with a secret latch
And that no other god could open.
First she cleansed her lovely skin
With ambrosia, then rubbed on scented oil
So immortally perfumed that if the jar
Were just shaken in Zeus' bronze-floored house          170
The fragrance would spread to heaven and earth.
She rubbed this into her beautiful skin,
And she combed her hair and plaited
The lustrous, ambrosial locks that fell
Gorgeously from her immortal head.
Then she put on a robe that Athena
Had embroidered for her, pinning it
At her breast with brooches of gold.
A sash with a hundred tassels
Circled her waist, and in her pierced ears             180
She put earrings with three mulberry drops
Beguilingly bright. And the shining goddess
Veiled over everything with a beautiful veil
That was as white as the sun, and bound
Lovely sandals on her oiled, supple feet.
When everything was perfect, she stepped
Out of her room and called Aphrodite
And had a word with her in private:


"My dear child, will you do something for me,
I wonder, or will you refuse, angry because            190
I favor the Greeks and you the Trojans?"


And Zeus' daughter Aphrodite replied:


"Goddess revered as Cronus' daughter,
Speak your mind. Tell me what you want

And I'll oblige you if I possibly can."

And Hera, with every intention to deceive:

"Give me now the Sex and Desire
You use to subdue immortals and humans.
I'm off to visit the ends of the earth
And Father Ocean and Mother Tethys          200
Who nursed and doted on me in their house
When they got me from Rhea, after Zeus
Had exiled Cronus to the regions below.
I'm going to see them and try to resolve
Their endless quarrel. For eons now
They've been angry and haven't made love.
If I can talk to them and have them make up—
And get them together in bed again—
They will worship the ground I walk on."

And Aphrodite, who loved to smile:          210

"How could I, or would I, refuse someone
Who sleeps in the arms of almighty Zeus?"

And with that she unbound from her breast
An ornate sash inlaid with magical charms.
Sex is in it, and Desire, and seductive
Sweet Talk, that fools even the wise.
She handed it to Hera and said:

"Here, put this sash in your bosom.
It has everything built in. I predict
You will accomplish what your heart desires."          220

She spoke, and ox-eyed Hera,
Smiling, tucked the sash in her bosom.

Then Zeus' daughter Aphrodite went home,
But Hera streaked down from Olympus' peak,
Used Pieria and Emathia as stepping stones,

And sped over the snowcapped mountains
Of Thrace. Her feet never touched earth.

At Athos she stepped on the billowing sea
And so came to Lemnos, Thoas' city,
Where she met Sleep, the brother of Death.          230
She took Sleep's hand, and said to him:

"Sleep, lord of all, mortal and immortal,
If ever you've listened to me before,
Listen now, and I will be grateful forever.
Lull Zeus' bright eyes to sleep for me
As soon as I lie beside him in love.
I will give you gifts: a handsome throne
Of imperishable gold that Hephaestus,
My strong-armed son, will build you.
It comes with a stool to rest your feet on          240
As you sit at banquet and sip your wine."

Sweet Sleep answered her:

"Goddess revered as Cronus' daughter,
If this were any other of the gods eternal
I'd lull him to sleep without any trouble,
Even if it were the River Ocean,
Which was the origin of them all.
But not Zeus. I wouldn't go near
The son of Cronus, much less lull him
To sleep, unless he himself asked me.          250
I learned my lesson from your last request,
That day Heracles, Zeus' high-hearted son,
Sailed from Troy, having wasted the city.
Yes, I slipped my sweet self around the mind
Of Zeus Aegis-Holder, while you brewed up
Storms at sea to drive his son Heracles
Off course to Cos, far from his friends.
And when Zeus woke up was he angry!
Throwing gods all over the house, and looking
For me especially. He would have pitched me          260

From aether to sea, no more to be seen,
If Night, the Mistress, had not saved me.
I ran to her, and he relented, reluctant
To do anything to offend swift Night.
And now this, another impossible mission."


Hera, the ox-eyed Lady, said to him:


"Sleep, what are you worried about?
Do you think that Zeus will help the Trojans
And be as angry now as he was then
For Heracles, his own son? Come on.                     270
Look, I'll give you one of the young Graces
To have and to hold and be called your wife,
Pasithea, the object of all your desire."


Sleep's mood brightened at this. He said:


"Swear by the inviolable water of Styx,
One hand on fertile Earth and the other
On glistering Sea, so that all the gods
Below with Cronus will be witnesses,
That you will give me one of the Graces,
Pasithea, the object of all my desire."                 280


The white-armed goddess Hera agreed
And swore the oath, naming all the gods
In Tartarus below. Titans they are called.
When she had sworn and finished the oath,
The two of them left Lemnos and Imbros
And came like swirling fog to Ida,
A mountain wilderness dotted with springs.
They left the sea at Lecton and headed inland.
The treetops quivered under their feet.
Sleep halted before Zeus could see him,                 290
Perching in the highest fir tree on Ida
That rose through mist to pure bright air.

Sleep nestled in its long-needled branches
And looked just like the shrill mountain owl
Gods call Chalcis, and men Cymindis.

Hera was fast approaching Gargarus,
Ida's highest peak, when Zeus saw her.
And when he saw her, lust enveloped him,
Just as it had the first time they made love,
Slipping off to bed behind their parents' backs.          300
He stood close to her and said:

"Hera, why have you left Olympus?
And where are your horses and chariot?"

And Hera, with every intention to deceive:

"I'm off to visit the ends of the earth
And Father Ocean and Mother Tethys
Who nursed and doted on me in their house.
I'm going to see them and try to resolve
Their endless quarrel. For eons now
They've been angry and haven't made love.                310
My horses stand at the foot of Ida,
Ready to bear me over land and sea.
I came here from Olympus for your sake,
So you wouldn't be upset that I left
To visit Ocean without a word to you."

And Zeus, clouds scudding about him:

"You can go there later just as well.
Let's get in bed now and make love.
No goddess or woman has ever
Made me feel so overwhelmed with lust,                    320
Not even when I fell for Ixion's wife,
Who bore Peirithous, wise as a god;
Or Danae, with lovely, slim ankles,
Who bore Perseus, a paragon of men;
Or the daughter of far-famed Phoenix,
Who bore Minos and godlike Rhadamanthus;

Or Semele; or Alcmene in Thebes,
Who bore Heracles, a stouthearted son;
And Semele bore Dionysus, a joy to humans;
Or Demeter, the fair-haired queen;                           330
Or glorious Leto; or even you—
I've never loved anyone as I love you now,
Never been in the grip of desire so sweet."

And Hera, with every intention to deceive:

"What a thing to say, my awesome lord.
The thought of us lying down here on Ida
And making love outdoors in broad daylight!
What if one of the Immortals saw us
Asleep, and went to all the other gods
And told them? I could never get up                          340
And go back home. It would be shameful.
But if you really do want to do this,
There is the bedroom your dear son Hephaestus
Built for you, with good solid doors. Let's go
There and lie down, since you're in the mood."

And Zeus, who masses the clouds, replied:

"Hera, don't worry about any god or man
Seeing us. I'll enfold you in a cloud so dense
And golden not even Helios could spy on us,
And his light is the sharpest vision there is."               350

With that he caught his wife in his arms.
Beneath them the shining soil sprouted
Fresh grass, and dewy lotus, and crocus,
And hyacinth, soft and thick, that kept them
Up off the ground. And as they lay there
A beautiful, golden cloud enfolded them
And precipitated drops of glimmering dew.

And so the Father slept soundly on Gargaron's peak,
Mastered by Sleep and Love, and held his wife close.
But sweet Sleep ran down to the Achaean ships                 360

With a message for Poseidon the Earthshaker.
He stood close to him, and his words winged home:

"Help the Greeks all you want now, Poseidon,
And give them their glory, however brief,
While Zeus still sleeps, for Hera has bedded him,
And I have wrapped him in downy slumber."

Saying this, Sleep went off to the human world,
Leaving Poseidon more determined than ever
To aid the Greeks. He sprang to the front and cried:

"Achaeans! Are we going to concede victory to Hector          370
So he can take our ships and claim the glory?
That's how he's talking, now that Achilles
Is nursing his wrath on the beach by his hulls.
But we won't miss him too much if the rest of us
All pull together and help each other.
Now here's what I want all of us to do.
Get the biggest and best shields in the army,
Strap on full-metal helmets, arm yourselves
With the longest spears you can find,
And let's move out! You have my word that Hector,        380
No matter how eager he is, won't hold his ground.
Now let's go—and exchange gear if you have to,
So that our best fighters have the biggest shields."

He spoke, they listened, and they did as he said.
And the kings, though wounded—Diomedes,
Odysseus, and Agamemnon—marshalled them,
Going through the ranks and switching armor,
So that the best men were using the best gear.
When their bodies were covered with burnished bronze,
They moved out, led by Poseidon,                          390
Who held in his clenched fist a terrible sword,
Its long edge like lightning, a weapon outlawed
In mortal combat, sheer terror for men.

Opposite him, Hector marshalled the Trojans,
And the two of them tightened the cords of war,

Poseidon tossing his dark-blue mane and Hector
Standing in a cone of cold light, while the sea
Surged up to the Greek ships and huts.

The two sides closed with a pulsating roar.

> *The pounding of surf when arching breakers*                    400
> *Roll in from the deep under painful northern winds,*
> *Or the hissing roar of a forest fire*
> *When it climbs the hills to burn all the woods,*
> *Or the howling of wind when it is angry with oaks*
> *And moans and shrieks through their leafy branches*

Will give you some idea of the uncanny noise
The Greeks and Trojans made when they clashed.

Hector struck first, a spearcast at Ajax,
Who was in his line of fire. He didn't miss,
But the spear hit Ajax where his two belts,                      410
One for his shield, one for his silver-studded sword,
Formed a protective cross over his skin.
Angry that he had made a good throw for nothing,
Hector backstepped into the ranks of his army,
Avoiding fate. But as he withdrew, big Ajax
Picked up one of the stones that had rolled underfoot—
There were many of these, used as chocks for the ships—
And caught Hector on the chest, above his shield's rim
Just under the neck, and sent him spinning like a top.

> *He fell as a tree falls, an oak tree blasted*                  420
> *By lightning from Zeus. The tree is uprooted*
> *And the air reeks of brimstone, and no one*
> *Who sees this from close up has any desire*
> *To be near Zeus' thunderbolts ever again.*

So Hector fell to the ground in the dust.
The spear was knocked from his hand, but his shield
And helmet flew up in the air and then came down
Clattering on the rest of his embellished armor.
The Greeks ran up screaming with delight,

Hurling javelins thick and fast, and hoping                     430
To drag him off. But they couldn't touch him.
All Troy's best crowded around their hero—
Polydamas, Aeneas, Agenor, Glaucus,
Sarpedon, the Lycian commander—
No one neglected Hector. They circled him with shields
And lifted him up and away from war's toil
Until they brought him to the rear of the battle
Where his horses stood with his charioteer and rig,
Which took him groaning back toward the city.
But when they reached the ford of the Xanthus,               440
The beautiful, swirling river that Zeus begot,
They lifted him from the chariot to the ground
And poured water on him. This brought him around.
His eyes opened, and kneeling on his knees,
He vomited up a cloud of black blood.
Then he sank back to the ground, and darkness
Covered his eyes. The blow still mastered his spirit.

When the Greeks saw that Hector was gone,
They remembered how much they loved to fight.

First to draw blood was Oïlean Ajax.                         450
A quick leap and thrust of his spear
Brought down Satnius, son of Enops
And a peerless Naiad who lived in the river,
The Satnioeis, where he tended his flocks.
When Ajax's spear hit him on the flank
He fell on his back and became the center
Of some hard fighting. Polydamas,
Panthous' son, came up to help him
And put his spear through the right shoulder
Of Prothoënor, Areïlycus' son.                              460
The spear's weight carried it clear through,
And he fell to the earth clawing at the dust.
Polydamas gloated over him loudly:

"Hah! Another great throw from the strong hand
Of the heroic son of Panthous,
And another Greek has my spear in his flesh!

Use it as a crutch on your way down to hell."

This boast pained the Greeks, no one more so
Than Telamonian Ajax, who was closest
To the man when he fell. Ajax's bright spear            470
Was in the air instantly, hurtling at Polydamas,
Who managed to dodge both its point and his death.
No matter. The spear lodged in Archelochus,
Antenor's son, whom the gods wanted to die.
Just where the neck splices into the spine,
At the topmost vertebra, the spearblade sheared
Through the double tendon. His mouth and nose
Hit the earth before his legs and knees.
It was Ajax's turn to call to Polydamas:

"What do you think, Polydamas? Was this man           480
Worthy to be killed in return for Prothoënor?
He wasn't simply a nobody, was he?
Looks like he might be Antenor's brother
Or his son. There's a family resemblance."

He knew perfectly well who it was. The Trojans
Felt their chests tighten. Then Acamas, straddling
His brother's body, stitched his spear
Through Promachus, the Boeotian,
Who was trying to drag the corpse by its feet
Into the clear. Acamas was exultant:                   490

"Try fighting sometime instead of issuing threats!
We're not going to be the only side to suffer.
We're going to give as good as we get.
How do you like the nap Promachus is taking,
Courtesy of my spear? I didn't waste any time
Collecting the price for my brother's blood.
That's what family is for—to beat off ruin."

The Greeks winced when they heard this,
No one more so than the warrior Peneleos.
He charged, and when Acamas did not wait              500
For his onslaught he hit Ilioneus instead.

This man's father was Phorbas, whom Hermes loved
More than any other Trojan and who had the flocks
And wealth to prove it, but only one child,
Ilioneus. Peneleos' spear
Went through his eye socket, gouging out the eyeball
And going clear through the nape of the neck.
Ilioneus stretched out his hands as he settled
Slowly to earth. Peneleos took out his sword
And hacked at his neck, severing the head,                        510
Helmet and all. The great spear was still stuck
In the eye socket. Peneleos held it up
Like a poppy, and showing it to the Trojans, said:

"Kindly take word to Ilioneus' parents
To lament their prince in his family's halls,
As the wife of Promachus, Alegenor's son,
Will lament the absence of her cherished husband
When the Greeks return on their ships from Troy."

He spoke, and the Trojans began to tremble,
Eyes searching for an escape from death.                          520

  Muses who dwell on Olympus, tell me,
Who was the first Greek to bear away spoils
Once Poseidon had turned the battle's tide?
Telamonian Ajax, who wounded Hyrtius,
Son of Gyrtius, leader of the Mysians.
And Antilochus despoiled Phalces and Mermerus,
And Meriones slew Morys and Hippotion,
And Teucer stripped Prothoön and Periphetes,
And the son of Atreus wounded Hyperenor
In the flank, and when the bronze clove through            530
All the bowels spilled out, and his soul rushed
Through the gaping wound, and night covered his eyes.
But Ajax, Oïleus' swift son, killed the most.
No one could chase down men in a rout
Faster than he, when Zeus makes them panic.

# ILIAD 15

The Trojans had retreated through the palisade
And trench, a beaten army, and had halted
Beside their chariots, their faces pale
With terror, when Zeus awoke
On Ida's summit with Hera by his side.
He jumped to his feet and saw the Trojans
Being routed by howling Greeks
With Poseidon Lord among them,
And Hector lying on the plain, his friends
Crouched around him while he gasped for breath          10
In a haze of pain, and vomited blood.
It was no flyweight Greek who had hit him.
The Father of Gods and Men felt pity for him
And, scowling at Hera, delivered this speech:

"Hera, you scheming bitch, this trick of yours
Has taken Hector out and routed his army.
And you may be the first to profit from your plot—
When I whip the living daylights out of you.
Or don't you remember when I strung you up
With anvils hanging from your feet and gold          20
Unbreakable bands on your wrists? You dangled
In the air among the clouds, and all the gods
On high Olympus protested, but none
Could come to your rescue. If anyone tried

I'd send him sailing off our balcony—
There wouldn't be much left when he hit the ground.
Even so, my heart still ached for Heracles.
You and Boreas, whose squalls you suborned,
Had maliciously driven him over the desert sea
And brought him later to the great city of Cos.                    30
I got him out of there and led him back
To bluegrass Argos, after many labors.
I remind you of this so you'll quit playing games
And see where this gets you, making love to me
The way you did just now, and tricking me."

The ox-eyed lady Hera stiffened at this,
And she feathered her words home carefully:

"All right. I swear by Earth and Heaven above,
And the subterranean water of Styx, the greatest
And the most awesome oath a god can swear,                    40
By your sacred head and by our marriage couch,
Upon which I would never perjure myself—
That it is not by my will that Poseidon
Is hurting the Trojans and helping the Greeks.
He's acting of his own free will, out of pity
For the beating the Greeks are taking by their ships.
But I would advise even him to toe the line
And follow wherever you lead, Dark Cloud."

Zeus, the Father of Gods and Men,
Smiled at this and issued a swift reply:                    50

"Well, my ox-eyed Lady, if your mind
Really were to be the same as mine, Poseidon
Would find it difficult not to follow us.
So if you mean what you say, go back now
To the gods and send Iris here, and Apollo,
She to go down to the bronze-coated Greeks
And tell Lord Poseidon to desist from the war;
And Phoebus Apollo to rouse Hector to fight,
Breathe strength into him again, so that he may

Forget the pain that now distresses him and                    *60*
Drive the Achaeans back once more in flight.
So shall they flee in panic and fall dead among
The hollow ships of Peleus' son Achilles,
Who will send forth his comrade Patroclus,
Whom illustrious Hector will kill with his spear
Before Ilium, after Patroclus himself has killed
Many a youth, among them Sarpedon, my son.
In wrath for Patroclus Achilles will kill Hector.
From that time on I shall cause the Trojans
To be driven back from the ships, until the Greeks          *70*
Capture steep Ilion through Athena's counsel.
But until that time comes I will not cease
From my wrath or allow any immortal
To bear aid to the Danaans until the desire
Of the son of Peleus is fulfilled, as I
Promised at the first with a nod of my head
On the day when Thetis begged me by my knees
To honor Achilles, sacker of cities."

White-armed Hera was obedient to his word
And went from Ida's mountains to long Olympus.              *80*

> The thought of a man who has seen the world
> Travels quickly to any spot on the globe
> When he wishes he were there—

So Hera flew with the speed of desire
And came to Olympus.

She found the immortal gods assembled
In the house of Zeus. When they saw her
They were quick to toast her arrival.
She ignored them all, but did take a cup
From lovely Themis, who had run up to greet her            *90*
And who now addressed her with winged words:

"Hera, why have you come? You look so upset. Zeus
Must have really frightened you—your own husband!"

The goddess, ivory-armed Hera, replied:

"Don't get me started, Themis. You know yourself
What a bully he is, and how stubborn. No,
Let's get on with the feast, and you will hear
Along with the others what Zeus means to do.
It's not very pretty, and I rather doubt
That anyone, mortal or god, will be pleased—                    100
Or if anyone will still have an appetite left."

Hera composed herself and sat down.
The gods' mood darkened. Hera smiled
With her lips, but her dark brows were tense,
And at last she burst out indignantly:

"We're all simpering idiots to be angry with Zeus!
We all want to get to him, to talk him down,
To beat some sense into him, but does he care?
He doesn't even notice! No, he sits apart,
Secure in his supreme, almighty power.                    110
You'll just have to take whatever grief
He dishes out to you. I'm afraid that now
It's Ares' turn to suffer, seeing that his son,
Whom he loves more than any mortal man,
His dear Ascalaphus, has died in battle."

When Ares heard this he smacked his muscled thighs
With the flat of his hands and wailed out loud:

"None of you Olympians can blame me now
If I go to the Greek ships and avenge my son,
Not even if I am to be blasted by Zeus                    120
And lie among corpses in the blood and dust."

And he ordered his sons, Panic and Rout,
To yoke his team while he buckled on armor.
The hostility between the gods and Zeus
Would have reached new heights then,

Had not Athena, afraid for them all,
Jumped from her throne, sped through the door,
And disarmed Ares. She plucked the helmet
From his head, the shield from his shoulders,
Took the stiff, bronze spear from his hands,                    130
And gave the furious War God a tongue-lashing:

"Are you out of your mind? Didn't you hear
What Hera just said, or don't you care?
Do you want more trouble than you can handle,
Forced to crawl back to Olympus yourself
And sowing disaster for the rest of us?
He'll leave the Trojans and Greeks, you know,
And come back here to raise hell with us,
Mauling us all in turn, guilty or not.
So please get over your anger for your son.                    140
Better men than he have been killed or will be.
Human offspring are hard to save."

Ares gave in, and sat back down on his throne.
Then Hera called Apollo out of the palace,
And Iris, too, the immortals' messenger,
And said to them in a quick flurry of words:

"Zeus wants you to go to Ida immediately.
When you arrive you will look upon his face
And do whatever he orders you to do."

Having said that, Lady Hera turned away                        150
And sat down on her throne.
                              The pair darted off
And came to Ida, mountain mother of beasts,
And found Cronus' son on Gargaron Peak,
Sitting in a wreath of fragrant cloud.
They stood respectfully before the face of Zeus,
And his mood brightened when he saw how promptly
The two of them had obeyed his wife's words.
He addressed Iris first, with words on wings:

"Go, swift Iris, to Lord Poseidon                                    *160*
And tell him this as true messenger.
Bid him cease from war and battle
And go off to the other gods, or to the bright sea.
If he is inclined to disregard my words
Have him consider in his mind and heart
That strong as he is he cannot withstand
My onset, since I am mightier by far
And elder born. Yet he has the gall to claim
He is equal to me, whom all the gods dread."

He spoke, and Iris was off in a blur of wind,                        *170*
Moving down Ida's mountain to holy Troy

> *Like snow or hail flying from the clouds*
> *Under a cold blast from the brilliant North.*

So Iris flew with the speed of desire
And confronted the glorious Shaker of Earth:

"A message for you, blue-maned Sea God.
I come here from Zeus who bears the aegis
And who bids you cease from war and battle
And go off to the other gods, or to the bright sea.
If you are inclined to disregard his words,                          *180*
He threatens to come here himself and wage war
Against you, and he strongly advises you
To avoid his hands, since he is mightier by far
And elder born. Yet you have the gall to claim
You are equal to him, whom all the gods dread."

The Earthshaker made this angry reply:

"He may be strong, but this is outrageous,
To force me, his peer, to stop against my will.
We three brothers, whom Rhea bore to Cronus,
Zeus, myself, and Hades, lord of the dead,                           *190*
Divided up the universe into equal shares.
When we shook the lots, I got the grey sea
As my eternal domain; Hades, the nether gloom;

Zeus, the broad sky with clouds and bright air.
Earth and high Olympus remain common to all.
I will not follow Zeus' whims. Mighty as he is,
Let him remain content with his third share,
And not try to frighten me as if I were a coward.
Better for him to threaten his own children
With abusive language, the sons and daughters          *200*
He begot himself, who will listen because they must."

And Iris, her feet soft in the offshore wind:

"Is this the message, blue-maned Sea God,
I should take to Zeus, this hard, unyielding speech?
Will you not relent, as noble hearts often do?
You know how the Furies always side with the elder."

And Poseidon Earthshaker answered her:

"That is very well spoken, Iris. It is good
When a messenger understands how things are.
But bitter pain comes to my heart and soul                *210*
Whenever anyone attacks an equal,
A peer of equal status, with angry words.
Although I am offended, I will yield for now.
But I will say this, and make this threat from my heart:
If in spite of me and Pallas Athena,
And Hera and Hermes and Hephaestus Lord,
He spares steep Ilion, and is not willing
To lay it waste, nor give power to the Greeks,
He can be sure of eternal strife between us."

And with that Poseidon left the Greek army              *220*
And dove into the sea. They missed him sorely.

Cumulus clouds piled high on Ida's summit.

Zeus turned and spoke to Apollo:

"Go now, Phoebus, to bronze-clad Hector.
Tremendous Poseidon has gone into the sea

That laps the earth, avoiding my precipitous
Wrath. Too bad. The fight would have been legend,
Even among the gods below with Cronus.
But it was better for us both that he yielded
Before me, angry and indignant as he was.                              230
It would not have been settled without some sweat.
At any rate, take the tasselled aegis in your hands
And shake it over the Greeks to rout their heroes.
And see to Hector yourself. Fortify him
Until the Greeks have run back to their ships
On the Hellespont. I'll take it from there
And see the Achaeans get some breathing space."

Apollo did not disobey his father's words.
He came down from Ida's peaks like a falcon
That bloodies doves in flight, swift on the wing,                      240
And found Hector, light of Troy, sitting up—
He no longer lay down—and catching his breath.
He recognized his friends, and his gasping
And sweating had stopped, since Zeus now had
A mind to revive him. Apollo stood close and said:

"Hector, son of Priam, why are you sitting here
Apart from the rest, scarcely alive? What is wrong?"

Hector's helmet shone in the light. He said weakly:

"Which god are you, questioning me face to face?
Haven't you heard that while I was killing his friends             250
At the rear of the ships, booming Ajax hit me
In the chest with a stone and took the fight out of me?
I thought I would see the dead in Hades' house
This very day, after I had breathed forth my last."

And Apollo, Lord of bright distances:

"Courage. The Son of Cronus has sent me from Ida
To help and stand by you—no one less than me,
Phoebus Apollo, the Gold Sword, who has in the past

Saved both you and your steep citadel.
Come now and rally your many charioteers                    260
To drive their horses against the hollow ships.
I will go ahead and smooth all the ground
For the chariots, and I will turn the Greek heroes."

And he breathed strength into the man
Who tended Troy's army as a shepherd his flock.

*Picture a horse that has eaten barley in its stall*
*Breaking its halter and galloping across the plain,*
*Making for his accustomed swim in the river,*
*A glorious animal, head held high, mane streaming*
*Like wind on his shoulders. Sure of his splendor*       270
*He prances by the horse-runs and the mares in pasture.*

That was Hector, knees and feet like wind,
As he rallied the chariots. He had heard the god's voice.

And the Greeks?

*Hunters and hounds have been hot on the trail*
*Of an antlered stag or a mountain goat,*
*But a sudden sheer rock or a tangled wood*
*Saves the animal, which was not theirs to catch,*
*And their shouting brings a bearded lion*
*Into their path. Then the eager hunters turn back.*      280

Hordes of Greeks had been advancing relentlessly,
Carving their way forward with spears and swords.
But when they saw Hector patrolling the ranks,
They tensed up with fear and stopped in their tracks.

Thoas assessed the situation for them. This man,
Son of Andraemon and by far the best of the Aetolians,
Was not only good with javelin and sword,
But very few Greeks of his generation

Could vie with him when the young men debated.
Now he addressed the Greek command:                          *290*

"Is this a miracle my eyes are seeing?
Hector has risen from the dead. At least,
We all hoped he had died under Ajax's hands.
One of the gods has delivered Hector again
And he's going to go doing what he's always done—
Cut the legs out from under many Danaans—
Since he's not standing out there as a champion
Contrary to the will of thundering Zeus.
Now listen to what I say we should do.
Let's have the troops fall back to the ships          *300*
And have all of our best take a stand here
So we can hit him first and push him back
With a phalanx of spears. That should stop him
From being so eager to get to our troops."

They heard him out and did as he said.
The leaders of this action were big Ajax,
Idomeneus, Teucer, Meriones,
And Meges. Collecting a few good men
They took up a position opposite Hector
As the main troops fell back to the ships.              *310*

The Trojans attacked en masse, Hector out front
Advancing with long strides, and before him Apollo,
Shining, his shoulders capped with cloud, the aegis
He bore in his hands a shaggy, electric glow,
This the craft of Hephaestus and given to Zeus
For the routing of armies, but now Apollo
Bore it in his hands before the Trojan army.

The tight knot of Greeks met them, and a shrill cry
Rose from each side. Arrows jumped from bowstrings,
And spears hurled by bold hands either stuck        *320*
In young men fast (but not fast enough) in battle
Or stopped halfway before touching white skin
And stood quivering in the ground, lusting for flesh.

As long as Apollo held the aegis still,
Soldiers on both sides were hit and went down.
But when he looked the Greeks full in the face
And shook the aegis, and yelled as only a god can,
He shrivelled their hearts, and they lost their nerve.

*They became like cattle or a flock of sheep*
*When a pair of wolves attacks them at midnight*　　　　330
*Out of the darkness, and no herdsman is near,*

These pathetic, running Greeks, panicked by Apollo,
Who gave all the glory to the Trojans and Hector.

The fighting was scattered, man to man.
Hector took out Stichius and Arcesilaus.
One was leader of the bronze-shirted Boeotians,
The other a comrade of the hero Menestheus.
　Aeneas' victims were Medon and Iasus.
Medon was a bastard son of Oïleus
And Ajax's brother, but he lived in Phylace,　　　　340
Far from his homeland, because he had killed
A relative of Eriopis, his stepmother,
Whom Oïleus had married. Iasus,
An Athenian captain, was son of Sphelus Boukolides.
　Polydamas took out Mecisteus, Polites
Killed Echius in the forefront of the fighting,
And Clonius fell to brilliant Agenor.
Paris got Deïochus from behind,
Hitting him below the shoulder as he ran back
Through the front lines, and driving the bronze home.　　　　350

While they were stripping the armor from these,
The Greeks were crowding madly into the trench,
Against the stakes, and, by sheer pressure, through the wall.
Hector called to the Trojans, making his voice carry:

"Forget the spoils and go for the ships!
If I catch any man hanging back on this side
He's dead on the spot with no family funeral.
Dogs will tear his body apart before the city."

He brought the whip down on his horses' backs
And called to the Trojans along the ranks.                    360
They answered his shout and held their horses
Even with his. The noise was deafening.
Before their rolling chariots Phoebus Apollo
Danced on the banks of the trench and pushed the earth
Into the cavity, making for them a causeway
As wide as a field for the javelin throw.
They poured over it, rank after rank, Apollo
Leading the way with the priceless aegis
And casting down the Achaean wall with ease.

> *A child playing on the seashore*                            370
> *Will build the sand into fantastic shapes,*
> *Then gleefully knock them down with his feet.*

Yes, Apollo, all that Achaean toil
Went down like sand, and you made them run
All the way back to their ships.
Stopped by the line of vessels, they cried out
To each other, but mostly to the gods,
Lifting their hands, each man praying,
And Nestor of Gerenia praying the hardest,
Hands outstretched to the starry sky:                        380

"Father Zeus, if ever any man of us
Burned to thee in wheat-bearing Argos
Fat thigh-bones of bulls and of rams
And prayed to return, and thou didst promise
And nod thy head, remember it now
And deliver us, O God of Olympus,
From the day of doom, nor allow the Achaeans
Thus to be vanquished by the men of Troy."

Zeus heard the old man's prayer
And the sky pealed with thunder.                             390
But when the Trojans heard the rumbling overhead,
They redoubled their efforts against the Greeks.

*Far out at sea a huge wave washes over*
*The gunnels of a ship driven by a gale,*
*And the wind is whipping the waves even higher.*

The Trojans shrieked as they rushed over the wall,
Driving their chariots into the Greek camp
To fight at the ships' sterns with bladed spears,
They from their cars, the Greeks from the decks
Of the tarred ships to which they had climbed                 400
And from which they fought with the long naval pikes
They had on board for battles at sea—
Huge jointed poles armed with bronze tips.

  And Patroclus, all during the fight for the wall,
Which took place some distance from the beached ships,
Sat in the hut of Eurypylus, his wounded host,
Cheering him up with small talk and rubbing ointments
Onto his ugly wound to ease his dark pangs.
But when he saw the Trojans rushing onto the wall
And the Greeks beating a noisy retreat, he groaned            410
And slapped his thighs with his hands, saying:

"Eurypylus, I know you're hurting,
But I can't stay with you here any longer.
A big fight is brewing. Have your man
Take care of you. I'm off to see Achilles,
To try to talk him into fighting.
God willing, I may be able to persuade him.
Persuasion works when it comes from a friend."

As Patroclus ran off, the Greeks withstood
The Trojan onslaught, but could not push them back          420
From the ships, even with their superior numbers.
Nor could the Trojans break their resistance
And get into the middle of the ships and huts.

  *The battle was stretched as taut as a carpenter's cord*
  *Snapped onto a beam to mark a straight line.*

So even was the tension along the line of ships,
Though at each ship there were different engagements.

Hector had made straight for Ajax. Ajax stood,
As if scissored out of the sky, on a black ship,
And he and Hector now fought for that ship,                    430
Hector trying to push him back and burn it,
Ajax holding him off. Neither could do much
About the other, so Ajax cast and hit Caletor,
Son of Clytius, who was bringing up fire.
He fell heavily, the torch dropping from his hand.
He was Hector's cousin, and when Hector
Saw him go down in the sand before the ship,
He called to the Trojans and Lycians:

"Stand your ground and fight for Clytius' son.
Don't let the Greeks strip him of his armor                    440
Just because he has fallen by the ships."

As he spoke his spear flashed toward Ajax,
Missing him but hitting Lycophron,
Mastor's son and one of Ajax's lieutenants
Who lived with him because he had killed a man
In sacred Cythera. Hector's spear caught him
Above the ear as he stood near Ajax,
And he fell backward from the ship's stern.
He was dead when he hit the ground.
Ajax stiffened, and he said to his brother:                    450

"Teucer, we've lost a true friend, Lycophron,
Whom we honored as we did our parents
When he came from Cythera to live with us.
Hector killed him. Where are your arrows
And the bow that Phoebus Apollo gave you?"

Teucer lost no time in coming up to him
With his strung bow and quiver of arrows.
Shooting rapid-fire at the Trojans,

He hit Cleitus, who was the son of Peisenor
And Polydamas' friend, as he drove,                              *460*
Busy with the reins, into the thick of battle,
Rendering service to Hector and the Trojans,
None of whom could help him now.
The arrow whizzed into his neck from behind,
And he fell from the chariot. The horses swerved,
Rattling the empty car. Polydamas
Saw it all and got to the horses first,
Handing them over to Astynous,
Son of Protiaon, with strict orders
To hold them close and keep an eye on them.                      *470*
Polydamas then returned to the front.

Teucer drew out another arrow,
This one for Hector, and it would have stopped
That hero from fighting by the ships
If it had only hit him and taken his life.
But Zeus, who protected Hector,
Was watching closely and robbed Teucer
Of his glory, breaking his twisted bowstring
Just as he was drawing it against Hector.
The bronze-armored arrow was shunted aside,                      *480*
And the bow dropped from his hand.
Teucer shuddered, and he said to his brother:

"Damn! So much for our battle plans.
Some god is cutting them pretty short,
Knocking the bow from my hands and snapping
The new string I tied on this morning
So it would hold up to repeated rounds."

Telamonian Ajax answered him:

"That's too bad. But leave your bow
And stash of arrows here, since a god                            *490*
Has tampered with them and begrudged us their use.
Pick up a spear, get a shield on your shoulders,

And battle the Trojans that way. They may beat us,
But they're not going to take our ships without a fight.
Let's keep our minds on what we have to do."

So Teucer laid his bow up in his hut.
He put a four-ply shield around his shoulders,
And on his mighty head a helmet crafted
With a horsehair plume that nodded grimly.
And he took a stout spear tipped with bronze                    500
And ran to take his place at Ajax's side.

When Hector saw Teucer's arrows fail,
He called to his men and made his voice carry:

"Trojan, Lycian, and Dardanian soldiers,
Remember to be the warriors that you are
In this fight for the ships! My eyes have seen
The shafts of one of their best blasted by Zeus.
It is easy to see whom Zeus protects,
To whom he gives glory and grants the victory,
And whom he lays low and will not protect,                      510
Even as now he lays low the Argives
And gives his protection to us. So close your ranks
And fight along the ships, and if any of you
Is hit and dies, then so be it. Death
In defense of your homeland is no dishonor.
Your wife is safe and your children's future,
Your house and estate are inviolate—
If the Greeks sail off to their own native land."

With these words he raised their spirits,
And Ajax did the same for the Greeks:                           520

"Shame on you, Argives! It's do or die now.
If Hector takes the ships, do you think
We'll all be walking home? Didn't you hear him
Screaming at his men to burn our fleet?
He's not inviting them to a dance, you know.
Our only strategy is this: to take them on

Hand to hand, our muscle against theirs.
Better to get it over with, live or die,
Than to be strung out here along the ships,
Pecked to death by inferior men."                              530

This bolstered their spirits,
And the killing began. Hector took out
A Phocian commander named Schedius,
Perimedes' son, and Ajax killed
Laodamas, an infantry captain
And son of Antenor. Polydamas
Laid low Otus of Cyllene, a comrade
Of Meges, the Epeian commander.
Meges saw this and jumped at him,
But Polydamas ducked and Meges missed:                         540
Apollo would not allow Polydamas
To be killed in the front lines. But Meges
Did kill Croesmus with a thrust to the chest.
Croesmus fell heavily, and as Meges
Got busy stripping his armor, Dolops,
Who knew what to do with a spear,
Rushed at him. This man was the grandson
Of Laomedon and the son of Lampus,
His bravest son and a furious fighter.
His spear ground through Meges' shield                         550
From close range, but the corselet saved him,
The intricate, plated corselet he wore.
His father Phyleus had brought it home
From Ephyre, on the river Selleïs,
Having received it from lord Euphetes,
A guest-friend, to protect him in war.
It now saved his son's life. Meges thrust back
And got his spear onto Dolops' bronze helmet,
Shearing the horsehair plume from its socket.
The whole plume, bright with its fresh scarlet dye,            560
Fell in the dust. Meges continued fighting
His still confident opponent until Menelaus
Came up to help him, unnoticed by Dolops.
Standing slightly behind him, Menelaus
Heaved his spear through Dolops' shoulder,

And the spear, with an eager life of its own,
Punctured his sternum. Dolops fell on his face,
And his two antagonists moved to strip him.
But Hector called to his many kinsmen,
Beginning with Melanippus, Hicetaon's son.                          570
This man used to pasture his shambling cattle
Off in Percote when there was no enemy near.
But when the curved prows of the Danaans appeared
He moved back to Ilion, a distinguished Trojan,
And lived in the house of Priam, who treated him
As a son of his own. Hector prodded him now:

"Melanippus, are we going to slack off like this?
Don't you have any feeling for your dead kinsman?
Look at how they are handling Dolops' armor.
Come on. We can no longer fight the Greeks                          580
From long range. Either we kill them or they
Take Ilion's heights and murder our people."

Melanippus went with him, moving like a god,
And Telamonian Ajax urged on the Greeks:

"Be men, my friends, and show some shame.
You should feel shame before each other in battle.
More men with shame are saved than are slain.
There's no glory or power in shameless flight."

They were already eager to ward off the enemy,
But they took his words to heart and fenced in the ships           590
With a hedge of bronze, against which Zeus
Urged on the Trojans. Then Menelaus,
Good at the war cry, shouted to Antilochus:

"Antilochus, there is none of us younger,
Faster, or braver than you in battle.
Get moving and take some Trojan out."

Menelaus melted back into the ranks
When he had said this, but he inspired
Antilochus, who jumped out into no-man's-land.

With a quick look around he hurled his spear.                    *600*
The Trojans recoiled from the flare it made,
But the throw was not wasted. It hit Melanippus,
Hicetaon's high-hearted son, right in the chest,
Beside his nipple, as he came into battle.
He fell heavily, and the light left his eyes.
Antilochus was all over him.

> *A dog goes after a wounded fawn a hunter hits*
> *With unerring aim as it jumps from its lair.*

That was how Antilochus leapt
At you, Melanippus, to strip off your armor.                    *610*
But Hector saw him and came running over
To meet him in battle, and Antilochus,
For all his speed as a combatant, fled.

> *A marauding animal that has killed a hound,*
> *Or a drover beside his herd, will sometimes flee*
> *Even before the crowd of men has gathered.*

As Nestor's son Antilochus was running,
Hector and the Trojans showered him
With a whining barrage of missiles.
He didn't turn and stand until he reached his own lines.        *620*

It was then that the Trojans, like lions
Who have tasted raw meat, charged the ships
And completed this part of Zeus' design.
He steadily turned up the Trojans' intensity
And softened the Greeks' resolve to win.
Hector would win all the glory for now,
Priam's son would burn the beaked ships
With fire from heaven, and so fulfill
The last syllable of Thetis' prayer.
It was for this that Zeus waited,                               *630*
The glare from a burning ship. From then on
He would will the Trojans back from the ships
And shift glory to the Greeks. With this intent
He roused Hector against the hollow ships,

And Hector needed no urging. Hector
Raged like the War God, the Spear Wielder,

    *Fire that consumes a wooded mountainside,*

Foam flecking his mouth, eyes burning
Under fierce brows, and the helmet
Encasing his face a sinister glitter                                    640
As Hector fought, as Zeus himself
Shed a cone of light from the aether
Around the solitary warrior, but only
For this brief moment. Pallas Athena
Was hastening his doom under Achilles' hands.
Yes, Hector was eager, but for all his efforts,
Probing the Greek lines where he saw
The greatest concentration of fine weapons,
He could not break their ranks.
They were as solid as a wall,                                           650

    *Or an iron cliff that drops sheer*
    *Into the grey sea and withstands*
    *Whistling winds and swollen waves*
    *That break against its rock face.*

The Greeks were not going to budge,
So Hector, with a nimbus of fire about him,
Leapt high and fell upon their bulk.

    *Waves driven by winds sometimes reach*
    *Tsunami proportions. When one breaks over*
    *A ship, the entire vessel is hidden by foam*     660
    *And the wind roars like devils in the sail.*
    *The crew shudders and their hearts turn to ice,*
    *So narrow is their passage out of Death.*

So too the Greeks under Hector's charge.

    *A maleficent lion charges a herd of cows*
    *Grazing in the bottom land of a great marsh,*
    *There is no counting how many, and with them*

*Is only a single herdsman, inexperienced*
*At contesting a heifer's carcass with a wild beast.*
*The herdsman walks at the front or rear,*                    *670*
*But the lion attacks in the middle and is soon*
*Feeding on its kill. The others stampede off.*

It was marvelous to see, the Greeks
Scattering before Hector—and Father Zeus—
Even though Hector killed only one man,
Periphetes of Mycenae, the son of that Copreus
Who used to shuttle messages from Eurystheus
To Heracles. His son was better in every way,
Whether it came to running or fighting,
And he had one of the best minds in Mycenae.          *680*
Now he yielded the glory to Hector.
As he turned, he tripped on the rim of his own shield,
A Mycenaean style that went down to his feet
And protected him from spears, but not from himself
As he stumbled and fell backward, his helmet
Ringing like a gong in his astonished ears.
Hector was quick to take advantage, putting a spear
Into his chest before his watching comrades
Were able to react. They grieved for their friend
But were too afraid of shining Hector to help him.     *690*

The Greeks regrouped within the ships' perimeter,
But the Trojans kept coming. The outermost ships
Were conceded, but the Greeks did take a stand
By their huts. They were massed now,
Too afraid to spread out through the camp,
And they kept calling back and forth to each other.
Nestor of Gerenia, the old general,
Implored them all in the name of their parents:

"Fight like the men that you are, my friends,
And feel some shame before the men around you.        *700*
Remember your children, your wives, your possessions,
And your parents, whether they are dead or alive.
For the sake of those who are not here I beseech you
To stand firm and fight, and not retreat."

This helped, but Athena helped them more,
Pushing aside the wondrous cloud of mist
From their eyes. Light flooded in from both sides,
From the ships behind and the battlefield in front.
They could all see Hector now, and his men.
The entire Greek army, from the idle in the rear                    710
To the champions in front, could see the enemy.

Ajax decided it was time to make his move.
Separating himself from the rest of the Greeks
He boarded a ship and strode along its deck
Wielding a long pike made for naval warfare,
Some forty feet in length, jointed with iron rings.
And then,

> *as skillfully as a stunt rider*
> *Jumps from horse to horse as his chariot,*
> *Drawn by a team of hand-picked thoroughbreds,*                    720
> *Speeds from plain to city down a highway*
> *Lined with spectators, who cheer him on,*

Ajax leapt from ship to ship, and his voice,
Like a shock wave from the wide, blue sky,
Admonished the Greeks to defend their ships
And the huts clutched beneath them. Hector
Reacted quickly, a streak of bronze armor
Flashing out from the general sea of bronze

> *Like a golden eagle dive-bombing down*
> *To a river bank where a flock of wild geese,*                     730
> *Or cranes, or long necked swans are feeding.*

Hector made like that for a dark-prowed ship,
And a great hand reached down from Ida
And pushed him on, and his army with him.

The fighting began again beside the ships,
So keenly you would have thought the troops
On both sides were fresh and had just entered battle.

Their minds were different, though. The Greeks fought
As if they would never get out of this battle alive,
While every Trojan heart beat with the hope                    740
Of burning the ships and killing Greek heroes.
Such were their thoughts as they faced off in battle.

Hector laid hold of the stern of a ship,
A beautiful vessel that had brought Protesilaus
Over to Troy, but would not bring him back home.
It was about this ship that the Greeks and Trojans
Fought in close combat. Instead of withstanding
Assaults from arrows and javelins in flight,
They fought toe to toe here, of one heart in battle,
Hacking at each other with axes and hatchets,              750
Enormous swords and double-edged spears.
Many fine blades with black leather ferrules
Fell to the ground, some from the hands,
Others from the shoulders of men as they fought.
The earth flowed black with their blood. Hector,
Once he had grasped the horn of the ship's stern,
Would not let go, and he called to the Trojans:

"Fire! Bring fire! And raise the war cry
All together! Zeus has given us this day
As payment for everything—to seize the ships          760
That came here against the gods' will
And have brought us endless trouble
Because of the cowardice of our elders,
Who, when I wanted to bring the fight here,
Kept me back and withheld the army.
But if Zeus clouded our minds then,
There is no doubt he is urging us on now."

At this, the Trojans intensified their attack.
Ajax, battered by everything they could throw,
And sensing death if he stayed where he was,          770
Inched back along the seven-foot cross-plank
He had been standing on and jumped from the deck.
He took up a position guarding the ship,

His spearpoint menacing any Trojan
Who tried to bring up fire, and his voice
Kept booming out alarms to his compatriots:

"Soldiers of Greece—be men, my friends!
We have to dig in on defense now.
Do you think we have allies to back us up,
Or some stronger wall that will protect us?                    780
There's no fortified city behind us now,
With reinforcements there to turn the tide.
We're out here on the plain of Troy
With the sea at our backs, far from home,
Surrounded by armed men. If there's a way out,
It's in our own hands, not in slacking off."

And as Ajax spoke his spear carved holes
In the various Trojans who thought that they
Might please Hector by bringing fire to the ship.
He mangled a good dozen at close range like this.        790

# ILIAD 16

While they fought for this ship, Patroclus
Came to Achilles and stood by him weeping,
His face like a sheer rock where the goat trails end
And dark springwater washes down the stone.
Achilles pitied him and spoke these feathered words:

"What are all these tears about, Patroclus?
You're like a little girl, pestering her mother
To pick her up, pulling at her hem
As she tries to hurry off and looking up at her
With tears in her eyes until she gets her way.          10
That's just what you look like, you know.
You have something to tell the Myrmidons?
Or myself? Bad news from back home?
Last I heard, Menoetius, your father,
And Peleus, mine, were still alive and well.
Their deaths would indeed give us cause to grieve.
Or are you broken-hearted because some Greeks
Are being beaten dead beside our ships?
They had it coming. Out with it, Patroclus—
Don't try to hide it. I have a right to know."          20

And with a deep groan you said to him,
Patroclus:
                "Achilles, great as you are,
Don't be vengeful. They are dying out there,

All of our best—or who used to be our best—
They've all been hit and are lying
Wounded in camp. Diomedes is out,
And Odysseus, a good man with a spear,
Even Agamemnon has taken a hit.
Eurypylus, too, an arrow in his thigh.                        30
The medics are working on them right now,
Stitching up their wounds. But you are incurable,
Achilles. God forbid I ever feel the spite
You nurse in your heart. You and your damned
Honor! What good will it do future generations
If you let us go down to this defeat
In cold blood? Peleus was never your father
Or Thetis your mother. No, the grey sea spat you out
Onto crags in the surf, with an icy scab for a soul.
    What is it? If some secret your mother               40
Has learned from Zeus is holding you back,
At least send *me* out, let *me* lead a troop
Of Myrmidons and light the way for our army.
And let me wear your armor. If the Trojans think
I am you, they'll back off and give the Greeks
Some breathing space, what little there is in war.
Our rested men will turn them with a shout
And push them back from our ships to Troy."

    That was how Patroclus, like a child
Begging for a toy, begged for death.                         50

And Achilles, angry and deeply troubled:

"Ah, my noble friend, what a thing to say.
No, I'm not in on any divine secret,
Nor has my mother told me anything from Zeus.
But I take it hard when someone in power
Uses his authority to rob his equal
And strip him of his honor. I take it hard.
The girl the Greeks chose to be my prize—
After I demolished a walled city to get her—
Lord Agamemnon, son of Atreus, just took              60
From my hands, as if I were some tramp.

But we'll let that be. I never meant
To hold my grudge forever. But I did say
I would not relent from my anger until
The noise of battle lapped at my own ships' hulls.
So it's on your shoulders now. Wear my armor
And lead our Myrmidons into battle,
If it is true that a dark cloud of Trojans
Has settled in over the ships and the Greeks
Are hemmed in on a narrow strip of beach.                    70
The Trojans have become cocky, the whole city,
Because they do not see my helmeted face
Flaring close by. They would retreat so fast
They would clog the ditches with their dead—
If Lord Agamemnon knew how to respect me.
As it is they have brought the war to our camp.
So Diomedes is out, eh? It was his inspired
Spear work that kept the Trojans at arm's length.
And I haven't been hearing Agamemnon's battle cry,
As much as I hate the throat it comes from—only            80
Hector's murderous shout breaking like the sea
Over the Trojans, urging them on. The whole plain
Is filled with their whooping as they rout the Greeks.
   Hit them hard, Patroclus, before they burn the ships
And leave us stranded here. But before you go,
Listen carefully to every word I say.
Win me my honor, my glory and my honor
From all the Greeks, and, as their restitution,
The girl Briseis, and many other gifts.
But once you've driven the Trojans from the ships,        90
You come back, no matter how much
Hera's thundering husband lets you win.
Any success you have against the Trojans
Will be at the expense of my honor.
And if you get so carried away
With killing the Trojans that you press on to Troy,
One of the immortals may intervene.
Apollo, for one, loves them dearly.
So once you have made some daylight for the ships,
You come back where you belong.                           100
The others can fight it out on the plain.

O Patroclus, I wish to Father Zeus
   And to Athena and Apollo
That all of them, Greeks and Trojans alike,
Every last man on Troy's dusty plain,
Were dead, and only you and I were left
   To rip Ilion down, stone by sacred stone."

And while they talked, Ajax retreated.

Zeus saw to it that everything the Trojans threw
At Ajax hit him, and his helmet tickered and rang          110
From all the metal points its bronze deflected
From his temples and cheeks. His left arm was sore
From holding up his shield, but the Trojans could not,
For all their pressure, force it aside.
Gulping in air, sweat pouring down his limbs,
He could scarcely breathe and had nowhere to turn.

Tell me now, Muses, who dwell on Olympus,
How fire first fell on the Achaean ships.

It was Hector who forced his way
To Ajax's side, and with his heavy sword                    120
Lopped through the ash-wood shaft of his spear
At the socket's base, sending the bronze point
Clanging onto the ground far behind him
And leaving in Ajax's hands a blunted stick.
Ajax knew that this was the work of the gods,
That Zeus had cancelled Ajax's battle plans
And planned instead a Trojan victory.
No one could blame him for getting out of range,
And when he did, the Trojans threw their firebrands
Onto the ship, and she went up in flames.                   130

Achilles slapped his thighs and said:

"Hurry, Patroclus! I see fire from the ships.
Don't let them take the fleet and cut off our escape.
Put on the armor while I gather the troops."

And so Patroclus armed, putting on
The bronze metalwork tailored to the body
Of Aeacus' swift grandson: the greaves
Trimmed with silver at the ankles, the corselet
Spangled with stars, the silver-studded sword,
The massive shield, and the crested helmet     140
That made every nod a threat.
He took two spears of the proper heft,
But left behind the massive battle pike
Of Aeacus' incomparable grandson.
No one but Achilles could handle this spear,
Made of ash, which the centaur Chiron
Had brought down from Mount Pelion and given
To Achilles' father to be the death of heroes.
Patroclus left the horses to Automedon,
The warrior he trusted most, after Achilles,     150
To be at his side in the crush of battle.
Automedon led beneath the yoke
The windswift horses Xanthus and Balius,
Immortal horses the gods gave to Peleus
When he married silver Thetis.
The Harpy Podarge had conceived them
When the West Wind blew through her
As she grazed in a meadow near Ocean's stream.
As trace horse Automedon brought up Pedasus,
Whom Achilles had acquired in the raid     160
On Eëtion's city. This faultless animal,
Though mortal, kept pace with immortal horses.

Achilles toured the rows of huts
That composed the Myrmidons' camp
And saw to it the men got armed.

> Think of wolves
> Ravenous for meat. It is impossible
> To describe their savage strength in the hunt,
> But after they have killed an antlered stag
> Up in the hills and torn it apart, they come down     170
> With gore on their jowls, and in a pack

*Go to lap the black surface water in a pool*
*Fed by a dark spring, and as they drink,*
*Crimson curls float off from their slender tongues.*
*But their hearts are still, and their bellies gorged.*

So too the Myrmidon commanders
Flanking Achilles' splendid surrogate,
And in their midst stood Achilles himself,
Urging on the horses and the men.

Achilles had brought fifty ships to Troy.                    180
Each ship held fifty men, and the entire force
Was divided into five battalions
Whose five commanders answered to Achilles.
  Menesthius led the first battalion.
His mother, Polydore, a daughter of Peleus,
Had lain with the river god Spercheius,
Whose sky-swollen waters engendered the child.
His nominal father was a man called Boros,
Who gave many gifts to marry Polydore.
  The second battalion was led by Eudorus,                   190
Polymele's bastard son. This woman
Once caught Hermes' eye as she danced
In Artemis' choir, and the god later
Went up to her bedroom and slept with her.
The son she bore shone like silver in battle.
After childbirth Actor's son Echecles
Led her to his house in marriage,
And her father, Phylas, kept the boy
And brought him up as if he were his own.
  Peisander led the third contingent.                        200
He was, next to Patroclus, the best
Of all the Myrmidons with a spear.
  Old Phoenix led the fourth contingent,
And Alcimedon, Laerces' son, the fifth.

When Achilles had the troops assembled
By battalions, he spoke to them bluntly:

"Myrmidons! I would not have a man among you forget

The threats you have been issuing against the Trojans—
From the safety of our camp—while I was in my rage.
All this time you have been calling me                          *210*
The hard-boiled son of Peleus and saying to my face
That my mother must have weaned me on gall
Or I wouldn't keep my friends from battle.
That, together with hints you'd sail back home
If all I was going to do was sit and sulk. Now, however,
That there *is* a major battle to hold your interest,
I hope that each of you remembers what it means to fight."

The speech steeled their spirit. The Myrmidons
Closed ranks until there was no more space between them
Than between the stones a mason sets in the wall            *220*
Of a high house when he wants to seal it from the wind.
Helmet on helmet, shield overlapping shield, man on man,
So close the horsehair plumes on their bright crests
Rubbed each other as their heads bobbed up and down.
And in front of them all, two men with one heart,
Patroclus and Automedon made their final preparations
To lead the Myrmidons into war.
                              But Achilles
Went back to his hut and opened the lid
Of a beautiful, carved chest his mother Thetis            *230*
Had put aboard his ship when he sailed for Troy,
Filled with tunics and cloaks and woolen rugs.
And in it too was a chalice that no one else
Ever drank from, and that he alone used for libation
To no other god but Zeus. This chalice
He now took from the chest, purified it
With sulfur crystals, washed it with clear water,
Then cleansed his hands and filled it with bright red wine.
And then he prayed, standing in his courtyard
Pouring out the wine as he looked up to heaven.           *240*
And as he prayed, Zeus in his thunderhead listened.

"Lord Zeus, God of Dodona, Pelasgian God
Who dwells afar in the snows of Dodona
With your barefoot priests who sleep
On the ground around your sacred oak:

As you have heard my prayer before
And did honor me and smite the Achaeans,
So now too fulfill my prayer.
As I wait in the muster of the ships
And send my Patroclus into battle with my men,      250
Send forth glory with him.
Make bold the heart in his breast
So that Hector will see that my comrade
Knows how to fight and win without me.
And when he has driven the noise of battle
Away from our ships, may he come back to me
Unharmed, with all his weapons and men."

Zeus in his wisdom heard Achilles' prayer
And granted half of it. Yes, Patroclus
Would drive the Trojans back from the ships,         260
But he would not return from battle unharmed.

Achilles placed the chalice back in the chest
And stood outside his hut. He still longed to see
The grim struggle on Troy's windswept plain.

The Myrmidons under Patroclus
Filed out and swarmed up to the Trojans.

*Boys will sometimes disturb a hornets' nest*
*By the roadside, jabbing at it and infuriating*
*The hive—the little fools—*
*Until the insects become a menace to all*          270
*And attack any traveller who happens by,*
*Swarming out in defense of their brood.*

So too the Myrmidons.
Patroclus called to them over their shouts:

"Remember whose men you are
And for whose honor you are fighting.
And fight so that even wide-ruling Agamemnon
Will recognize his blind folly

In not honoring the best of the Achaeans.
  FOR ACHILLES!"                                          280

This raised their spirits even higher.
They were all over the Trojans,
And the ships' hulls reverberated
With the sounds of their battle cries.
The Trojans, when they saw Patroclus
Gleaming in his armor, fell apart,
Convinced that Achilles had come out at last,
His wrath renounced and solidarity restored.
Each of them looked for a way to save his skin.

Patroclus' spear shot out like stabbing light          290
To where the Trojans were clustered
Around the stern of Protesilaus' ship
And hit a certain chariot commander
Named Pyraechmes, a Paeonian
Who had led a contingent of chariots
From the Axius river in Amydon.
He went down now, groaning in the dust
With Patroclus' spear in his right shoulder.
Having lost their leader and best fighter
The Paeonians panicked, and Patroclus                   300
Drove them from the ships and doused the fire.

The half-burnt ship was left there.

                              The Trojans,
Frantic and screaming, were on the run,
And the Greeks poured in with an answering roar.

  *Zeus will at times rein in his lightning*
  *And remove a dense cloud from a mountain top,*
  *And all the crests and headlands and high glades*
  *Break into view, and brightness falls from the air.*

The Greeks had repelled the enemy fire                  310
From the ships and could catch their breath,

But only for a while. The battle was not over.
The Trojans had withdrawn from the black ships,
But were not giving up. They had taken a stand
And would have to be pushed back by force.

The fighting was scattered at first, as heroes
Killed each other in individual combat.

Menoetius' brave son struck first, hitting
Areïlycus in the thigh just as he turned.
The bronze sheared through the flesh                    320
And shattered the bone. He pitched forward
Into the dirt.
                Then the warrior Menelaus
Drove his spear into Thoas' chest
Where it was unprotected by his shield.
As Thoas sagged to the earth, Phyleus' son
Was watching Amphiclus bear down on him,
But beat him to the punch, getting his spear
Into the thick muscle at the base of his thigh.
The point skewered the sinews and split them,                    330
And Amphiclus blacked out.
                        Then Nestor's son,
Antilochus, sliced into Atumnius' flank
With his bronze spear and drove it through,
Sending him sprawling. Maris wasted no time
Getting his spear between Antilochus
And his brother's corpse, but Thrasymedes,
Another of Nestor's sons, was even quicker.
Thrasymedes' spearblade cut through Maris' arm
Where it joined the shoulder, neatly flaying                    340
The muscle off and crushing the bone.
He fell heavily, eyes leaning into the dark.
So these two brothers, killed by brothers,
Entered the undergloom, comrades of Sarpedon,
Spearmen sons of Amisodarus, who had reared
The raging Chimaera, an evil for many.
  In the confusion Oïlean Ajax
Jumped Cleobulus, taking him alive
And in the same instant ending his life

With a sword stroke to the neck. The blade                    *350*
Ran warm with blood up to the hilt,
And death's haze lay heavy on his eyes.
  Peneleos and Lycon both cast, both missed,
Both drew their swords and charged each other.
Lycon's sword landed hard on Peneleos' helmet
But the heavy crest shattered the blade to the hilt.
Peneleos' sword caught Lycon under the ear
And sliced through the neck, leaving only
A ribbon of skin from which the head dangled.
Lycon collapsed in a heap.
                    Meanwhile, Meriones,                      *360*
Sprinting hard, caught up with Acamas
As he was mounting his chariot and nailed him
In his right shoulder. He fell from the rig
And mist poured over his eyes.
                    Idomeneus
Plugged Erymas' mouth with cruel bronze,
The spearpoint passing beneath the brainpan,
Shattering all the bones. His teeth rattled out,
His eyes filled with blood, and he spurted blood          *370*
Out through his nostrils and gaping mouth
Until death's black nimbus enveloped him.

In this way, each Greek leader took out his man.

> Wolves will unerringly pick off lambs or kids
> That have become separated from the flock
> Through the shepherd's lack of attention,
> The marauding predators making swift havoc
> Of the defenseless young animals.

So too the Greeks had their way with the Trojans,
Whose only tactic now was dishonorable flight.            *380*

All this time big Ajax was trying
To get a shot off at Hector, who,
Knowing the ways of war, kept his shoulders
Under his oxhide shield and listened
For the whistling of arrows and thud of spears.

NOTE: detail of gore, the immense amount of death, and the eloquent way in which it is described / written

He knew the fight was not going his way,
But he held his ground and tried to save his friends.

*A cloud detaches itself from Olympus*
*And moves across the clear blue sky*
*When Zeus is about to unleash a storm.*                    390

The rout from the ships had begun,
And in no good order. Hector's horses
Got him across the trench, but he left
His army behind it. The Trojans drove
Team after team into the trench
Only to see the horses break their poles,
Struggle free, and leave their lords
Stranded in their chariots. Patroclus
Called his men in for the kill. The Trojans
Were screaming and running                    400
In every direction, while a cloud of dust
Rose high over their horses as they left
The ships behind and strained for the city.
Patroclus drove his chariot to wherever
The routed Trojans were thickest,
Shouting as he plowed over broken chariots
And the drivers who fell beneath his wheels.
The horses the gods had given to Peleus
Jumped the trench in one immortal leap,
And Patroclus steered them after Hector,                    410
In whose back he longed to plant his spear,
But Hector's horses had too big a lead.

*When the storm finally breaks, on a day*
*During harvest, the black earth is soaked*
*Until it can hold no more, and still the rain*
*Comes down in sheets as Zeus' judgment*
*On men who govern by violence*
*And drive Justice out with their crooked verdicts,*
*As if they have never heard of an Angry God.*
*All the rivers flood their banks, and every hill*                    420
*Is rutted with torrents that feed the rivers,*

*And down from the mountains the waters roar*
*And sweep men's tillage into the shining sea.*

The Trojan mares were thundering down the plain.

Patroclus let them go. But when he had cut off
The foremost battalions, he hemmed them back
Toward the ships, blocking their frantic retreat
Toward the city, and in the space defined
By the ships, the river, and Troy's high wall,
    He made them pay in blood.                                     430

Pronous was first, Patroclus' spear hitting him
Like searing light where his shield left part
Of his chest exposed. His limbs were unstrung,
And he fell with a thud.
                          Thestor, son of Enops,
Was next, crouching in his polished chariot basket,
Half out of his mind with terror, the reins slack
And trailing out of his hands. Patroclus eased up
Alongside him and shattered his right jaw
With his spear, driving the point through his teeth,          440
Then, gripping the shaft, levered him up
And over his chariot rail, the way a man
Sitting on a jutting rock with a fishing rod
Flips a flounder he has hooked out of the sea.
So Thestor was prised gaping from his chariot
And left flat on his face. His soul crawled off.
    Erylaus Patroclus got with a stone
As he charged, crushing helmet and skull.
Death sifted around him as he pitched to earth.
And then, and in quick succession, Patroclus killed:          450
Erymas, Amphoterus, Epaltes, Echius,
Pyris, Tlepolemus, son of Damastor, Ipheus,
Euippus, and Polymelus, Argeas' son—
Making Troy's rich earth fat with their blood.

Sarpedon saw his comrades running
With their tunics flapping loose around their waists

And being swatted down like flies by Patroclus.
He called out, appealing to their sense of shame:

"Why this sudden burst of speed, Lycian heroes?
Slow down a little, while I make the acquaintance          460
Of this nuisance of a Greek who seems by now
To have hamstrung half the Trojan army."

And he stepped down from his chariot in his bronze
As Patroclus, seeing him, stepped down from his.

> *High above a cliff vultures are screaming*
> *In the air as they savage each other's craws*
> *With their hooked beaks and talons.*

    And higher still,
Zeus watched with pity as the two heroes closed
And said to his wife Hera, who is his sister too:          470

"Fate has it that Sarpedon, whom I love more
Than any man, is to be killed by Patroclus.
Shall I take him out of battle while he still lives
And set him down in the rich land of Lycia,
Or shall I let him die under Patroclus' hands?"

And Hera, his lady, her eyes soft and wide:

"Son of Cronus, what a thing to say!
A mortal man, whose fate has long been fixed,
And you want to save him from rattling death?
Do it. But don't expect all of us to approve.             480
Listen to me. If you send Sarpedon home alive,
You will have to expect other gods to do the same
And save their own sons—and there are many of them
In this war around Priam's great city.
Think of the resentment you will create.
But if you love him and are filled with grief,
Let him fall in battle at Patroclus' hands,
And when his soul and life have left him,
Send Sleep and Death to bear him away

To Lycia, where his people will give him burial          *490*
With mound and stone, as befits the dead."

The Father of Gods and Men agreed
Reluctantly, but shed drops of blood as rain
Upon the earth in honor of his own dear son
Whom Patroclus was about to kill
On Ilion's rich soil, far from his native land.

When they were close, Patroclus cast, and hit
Not Prince Sarpedon, but his lieutenant
Thrasymelus, a good man—a hard throw
Into the pit of his belly. He collapsed in a heap.          *500*
Sarpedon countered and missed. His bright spear
Sliced instead through the right shoulder
Of Pedasus, who gave one pained, rasping whinny,
Then fell in the dust. His spirit fluttered off.
With the trace horse down, the remaining two
Struggled in the creaking yoke, tangling the reins.
Automedon remedied this by drawing his sword
And cutting loose the trace horse. The other two
Righted themselves and pulled hard at the reins,
And the two warriors closed again in mortal combat.          *510*
Sarpedon cast again. Another miss. The spearpoint
Glinted as it sailed over Patroclus' left shoulder
Without touching him at all. Patroclus came back,
Leaning into his throw, and the bronze point
Caught Sarpedon just below the rib cage
Where it protects the beating heart. Sarpedon fell

*As a tree falls, oak, or poplar, or spreading pine,*
*When carpenters cut it down in the forest*
*With their bright axes, to be the beam of a ship,*

And he lay before his horses and chariot,          *520*
Groaning heavily and clawing the bloody dust,

*Like some tawny, spirited bull a lion has killed*
*In the middle of the shambling herd, groaning*
*As it dies beneath the predator's jaws.*

Thus beneath Patroclus the Lycian commander
Struggled in death. And he called his friend:

"Glaucus, it's time to show what you're made of
And be the warrior you've always been,
Heart set on evil war—if you're fast enough.
Hurry, rally our best to fight for my body,                    530
All the Lycian leaders. Shame on you,
Glaucus, until your dying day, if the Greeks
Strip my body bare beside their ships.
Be strong and keep the others going."

The end came as he spoke, and death settled
On his nostrils and eyes. Patroclus put his heel
On Sarpedon's chest and pulled out his spear.
The lungs came out with it, and Sarpedon's life.
The Myrmidons steadied his snorting horses.
They did not want to leave their master's chariot.            540

Glaucus could hardly bear to hear Sarpedon's voice,
He was so grieved that he could not save him.
He pressed his arm with his hand. His wound
Tormented him, the wound he got when Teucer
Shot him with an arrow as he attacked the wall.
He prayed to Apollo, lord of bright distances:

"Hear me, O Lord, wherever you are
In Lycia or Troy, for everywhere you hear
Men in their grief, and grief has come to me.
I am wounded, Lord, my arm is on fire,                         550
And the blood can't be staunched. My shoulder
Is so sore I cannot hold a steady spear
And fight the enemy. Sarpedon is dead,
My Lord, and Zeus will not save his own son.
Heal my wound and deaden my pain,
And give me the strength to call the Lycians
And urge them on to fight, and do battle myself
About the body of my fallen comrade."

Thus Glaucus' prayer, and Apollo heard him.

He stilled his pain and staunched the dark blood          560
That flowed from his wound. Glaucus felt
The god's strength pulsing through him,
Glad that his prayers were so quickly answered.
He rounded up the Lycian leaders
And urged them to fight for Sarpedon's body,
Then went with long strides to the Trojans,
To Polydamas, Agenor, Aeneas,
And then saw Hector's bronze-strapped face,
Went up to him and said levelly:

"Hector, you have abandoned your allies.          570
We have been putting our lives on the line for you
Far from our homes and loved ones,
And you don't care enough to lend us aid.
Sarpedon is down, our great warlord,
Whose word in Lycia was Lycia's law,
Killed by Patroclus under Ares' prodding.
Show some pride and fight for his body,
Or the Myrmidons will strip off the armor
And defile his corpse, in recompense
For all the Greeks we have killed by the ships."          580

This was almost too much for the Trojans.
Sarpedon, though a foreigner, had been
A mainstay of their city, the leader
Of a large force and its best fighter.
Hector led them straight at the Greeks,
    "For Sarpedon!"
And Patroclus, seeing them coming,
Urged on the already eager two Ajaxes:

"Let me see you push these Trojans back
With everything you've ever had and more.          590
Sarpedon is down, first to breach our wall.
He's ours, to carve up his body and strip
The armor off. And all his little saviors
Are ours to massacre with cold bronze."

They heard this as if hearing their own words.

The lines on both sides hardened to steel.
Then Trojans and Lycians, Myrmidons and Greeks
Began fighting for the corpse, howling and cursing
As they threw themselves into the grinding battle.
And Zeus stretched hellish night over the armies
So they might do their lethal work over his son.

The Trojans at first pushed back the Greeks
When Epeigeus was hit, Agacles' son.
This man was far from the worst of the Myrmidons.
He once lived in Boudeum, but having killed
A cousin of his, came as a suppliant
To Peleus and silver-footed Thetis,
Who sent him with Achilles to fight at Troy.
He had his hand on the corpse when Hector
Brought down a stone on his head, splitting his skull          610
In two inside his heavy helmet. He collapsed
On Sarpedon's body, and death drifted over him.
Patroclus ached for his friend and swooped
Into the front like a hawk after sparrows—
Yes, my Patroclus—and they scattered like birds
Before your anger for your fallen comrade.
Sthenelaos, Ithaemenes' beloved son,
Never knew what hit him. The stone Patroclus threw
Severed the tendons at the nape of his neck.
The Trojan champions, including Hector,                         620
Now withdrew, about as far as a javelin flies
When a man who knows how throws it hard
In competition or in mortal combat.

The Greeks pressed after them, and Glaucus,
The Lycian commander now, wheeled around
And killed Bathycles, a native of Hellas
And the wealthiest of the Myrmidons.
He was just catching up with Glaucus
When the Lycian suddenly pivoted on his heel
And put his spear straight into Bathycles' chest.              630
He fell hard, and the Greeks winced.
A good man was down, much to the pleasure
Of the Trojans, who thronged around his body.

But the Greeks took the offensive again,
And Meriones killed Laogonus,
A priest of Idaean Zeus who was himself
Honored as a god. Meriones thrust hard
Into his jaw, just beneath the ear,
And he was dead, in the hated dark.
Aeneas launched his spear at Meriones,                    *640*
Hoping to hit him as he advanced
Under cover of his shield, but Meriones
Saw the spear coming and ducked forward,
Leaving it to punch into the ground and stand there
Quivering, as if Ares had twanged it
So it could spend its fury. Aeneas fumed:

"That would have been your last dance, Meriones,
Your last dance, if only my spear had hit you!"

And Meriones, himself famed for his spear:

"Do you think you can kill everyone                    *650*
Who comes up against you, Aeneas,
And defends himself? You're mortal stuff too.
If I got a solid hit on you with my spear
You'd be down in no time, for all your strength.
You'd give me the glory, and your life to Hades."

Patroclus would have none of this, and yelled:

"Cut the chatter, Meriones. You're a good man,
But don't think the Trojans are going to retreat
From the corpse because you make fun of them.
Use hands in war, words in council.                    *660*
Save your big speeches; we've got fighting to do."

And he moved ahead, with Meriones,
Who himself moved like a god, in his wake.

*Woodcutters are working in a distant valley,*
*But the sound of their axes, and of trees falling,*
*Can be heard for miles around in the mountains.*

The plain of Troy thrummed with the sound
Of bronze and hide stretched into shields,
And of swords and spears knifing into these.
Sarpedon's body was indistinguishable                                          670
From the blood and grime and splintered spears
That littered his body from head to foot.

>   *But if you have ever seen how flies*
>   *Cluster about the brimming milk pails*
>   *On a dairy farm in early summer,*

You will have some idea of the throng
Around Sarpedon's corpse.

                        And not once did Zeus
Avert his luminous eyes from the combatants.
All this time he looked down at them and pondered                              680
When Patroclus should die, whether
Shining Hector should kill him then and there
In the conflict over godlike Sarpedon
And strip the armor from his body, or whether
He should live to destroy even more Trojans.
And as he pondered it seemed preferable
That Achilles' spendid surrogate should once more
Drive the Trojans and bronze-helmed Hector
Back to the city, and take many lives.
And Hector felt it, felt his blood turn milky,                                 690
And mounted his chariot, calling to the others
To begin the retreat, that Zeus' scales were tipping.
Not even the Lycians stayed, not with Sarpedon
Lying at the bottom of a pile of bodies
That had fallen upon him in this node of war.

The Greek stripped at last the glowing bronze
From Sarpedon's shoulders, and Patroclus gave it
To some of his comrades to take back to the ships.

Then Zeus turned to Apollo and said:

"Sun God, take our Sarpedon out of range.                    *700*
Cleanse his wounds of all the clotted blood,
And wash him in the river far away
And anoint him with our holy chrism
And wrap the body in a deathless shroud
And give him over to be taken swiftly
    By Sleep and Death to Lycia,
Where his people shall give him burial
With mound and stone, as befits the dead."

And Apollo went down from Ida
Into the howling dust of war,                    *710*
And cleansed Sarpedon's wounds of all the blood,
And washed him in the river far away
And anointed him with holy chrism
And wrapped the body in a deathless shroud
And gave him over to be taken swiftly
    By Sleep and Death to Lycia.

Patroclus called to his horses and charioteer
And pressed on after the Trojans and Lycians,
Forgetting everything Achilles had said
And mindless of the black fates gathering above.                    *720*
Even then you might have escaped them,
Patroclus, but Zeus' mind is stronger than men's,
And Zeus now put fury in your heart.

Do you remember it, Patroclus, all the Trojans
You killed as the gods called you to your death?
Adrastus was first, then Autonous, and Echeclus,
Perimas, son of Megas, Epistor, Melanippus,
Elasus, Mulius, and last, Pylartes,
And it would have been more, but the others ran,
Back to Troy, which would have fallen that day                    *730*
By Patroclus' hands.

                    But Phoebus Apollo
Had taken his stand on top of Troy's wall.

                    Three times Patroclus
Reached the parapet, and three times
Apollo's fingers flicked against the human's shield
And pushed him off. But when he came back
A fourth time, like a spirit from beyond,
Apollo's voice split the daylight in two:

"Get back, Patroclus, back where you belong.          740
Troy is fated to fall, but not to you,
Nor even to Achilles, a better man by far."

And Patroclus was off, putting distance
Between himself and that wrathful voice.

   Hector had halted his horses at the Western Gate
And was deciding whether to drive back into battle
Or call for a retreat to within the walls.
While he pondered this, Phoebus Apollo
Came up to him in the guise of Asius.
This man was Hector's uncle on his mother's side,    750
And Apollo looked just like him as he spoke:

"Why are you out of action, Hector? It's not right.
If I were as much stronger than you as I am weaker,
You'd pay dearly for withdrawing from battle.
Get in that chariot and go after Patroclus.
Who knows? Apollo may give you the glory."

Hector commanded Cebriones, his charioteer,
To whip the horses into battle. Apollo melted
Into the throng, a god into the toil of men.
The Greeks felt a sudden chill,                       760
While Hector and the Trojans felt their spirits lift.
Hector was not interested in the other Greeks.
He drove through them and straight for Patroclus,
Who leapt down from his own chariot
With a spear in one hand and in the other
A jagged piece of granite he had scooped up

And now cupped in his palm. He got set,
And without more than a moment of awe
For who his opponent was, hurled the stone.
The throw was not wasted. He hit Hector's                          770
Charioteer, Cebriones, Priam's bastard son,
As he stood there holding the reins. The sharp stone
Caught him right in the forehead, smashing
His brows together and shattering the skull
So that his eyeballs spurted out and dropped
Into the dirt before his feet. He flipped backward
From the chariot like a diver, and his soul
Dribbled away from his bones. And you,
Patroclus, you, my horseman, mocked him:

"What a spring the man has! Nice dive!                             780
Think of the oysters he could come up with
If he were out at sea, jumping off the boat
In all sorts of weather, to judge by the dive
He just took from his chariot onto the plain."

And with that he rushed at the fallen warrior

> *Like a lion who has been wounded in the chest*
> *As he ravages a farmstead, and his own valor*
> *Destroys him.*

                    Yes, Patroclus, that is how you leapt
Upon Cebriones.                                                   790
                    Hector vaulted from his chariot,
And the two of them fought over Cebriones

> *Like a pair of lions fighting over a slain deer*
> *In the high mountains, both of them ravenous,*
> *Both high of heart,*

                    very much like these two
Human heroes hacking at each other with bronze.
Hector held Cebriones' head and would not let go.

Patroclus had hold of a foot, and around them
Greeks and Trojans squared off and fought.                    *800*

> *Winds sometimes rise in a deep mountain wood*
> *From different directions, and the trees—*
> *Beech, ash, and cornelian cherry—*
> *Batter each other with their long, tapered branches,*
> *And you can hear the sound from a long way off,*
> *The unnerving splintering of hardwood limbs.*

The Trojans and Greeks collided in battle,
And neither side thought of yielding ground.

Around Cebriones many spears were stuck,
Many arrows flew singing from the string,                      *810*
And many stones thudded onto the shields
Of men fighting around him. But there he lay
In the whirling dust, one of the great,
    Forgetful of his horsemanship.


While the sun still straddled heaven's meridian,
Soldiers on both sides were hit and fell.
But when the sun moved down the sky and men
All over earth were unyoking their oxen,
The Greeks' success exceeded their destiny.
They pulled Cebriones from the Trojan lines                    *820*
And out of range, and stripped his armor.

And then Patroclus unleashed himself.

Three times he charged into the Trojan ranks
With the raw power of Ares, yelling coldly,
And on each charge he killed nine men.
But when you made your fourth, demonic charge,
Then—did you feel it, Patroclus?—out of the mist,
Your death coming to meet you. It was
Apollo, whom you did not see in the thick of battle,

Standing behind you, and the flat of his hand                    830
Found the space between your shoulder blades.
The sky's blue disk went spinning in your eyes
As Achilles' helmet rang beneath the horses' hooves,
And rolled in the dust—no, that couldn't be right—
Those handsome horsehair plumes grimed with blood,
The gods would never let that happen to the helmet
That had protected the head and graceful brow
Of divine Achilles. But the gods did
Let it happen, and Zeus would now give the helmet
To Hector, whose own death was not far off.                    840

Nothing was left of Patroclus' heavy battle spear
But splintered wood, his tasselled shield and baldric
Fell to the ground, and Apollo, Prince of the Sky,
Split loose his breastplate. And he stood there, naked,
Astounded, his silvery limbs floating away,
Until one of the Trojans slipped up behind him
And put his spear through, a boy named Euphorbus,
The best his age with a spear, mounted or on foot.
He had already distinguished himself in this war
By knocking twenty warriors out of their cars                    850
The first time he went out for chariot lessons.
It was this boy who took his chance at you,
Patroclus, but instead of finishing you off,
He pulled his spear out and ran back where he belonged,
Unwilling to face even an unarmed Patroclus,
Who staggered back toward his comrades, still alive,
But overcome by the god's stroke, and the spear.

Hector was watching this, and when he saw
Patroclus withdrawing with a wound, he muscled
His way through to him and rammed his spearhead                    860
Into the pit of his belly and all the way through.
Patroclus fell heavily. You could hear the Greeks wince.

  *A boar does not wear out easily, but a lion*
  *Will overpower it when the two face off*

*Over a trickling spring up in the mountains*
*They both want to drink from. The boar*
*Pants hard, but the lion comes out on top.*

So too did Hector, whose spear was draining the life
From Menoetius' son, who had himself killed many.

His words beat down on Patroclus like dark wings:                    870

"So, Patroclus, you thought you could ransack my city
And ship our women back to Greece to be your slaves.
You little fool. They are defended by me,
By Hector, by my horses and my spear. I am the one,
Troy's best, who keeps their doom at bay. But you,
Patroclus, the vultures will eat you
On this very spot. Your marvelous Achilles
Has done you no good at all. I can just see it,
Him sitting in his tent and telling you as you left:
'Don't bother coming back to the ships,                    880
Patroclus, until you have ripped Hector's heart out
Through his bloody shirt.' That's what he said,
Isn't it? And you were stupid enough to listen."

And Patroclus, barely able to shake the words out:

"Brag while you can, Hector. Zeus and Apollo
Have given you an easy victory this time.
If they hadn't knocked off my armor,
I could have made mincemeat of twenty like you.
It was Fate, and Leto's son, who killed me.
Of men, Euphorbus. You came in third at best.                    890
And one more thing for you to think over.
You're not going to live long. I see Death
Standing at your shoulder, and you going down
Under the hands of Peleus' perfect son."

Death's veil covered him as he said these things,
And his soul, bound for Hades, fluttered out

Resentfully, forsaking manhood's bloom.
He was dead when Hector said to him:

"Why prophesy my death, Patroclus?
Who knows? Achilles, son of Thetis,                          *900*
May go down first under my spear."

And propping his heel against the body,
He extracted his bronze spear and took off
After Automedon. But Automedon was gone,
Pulled by immortal horses, the splendid gifts
  The gods once gave to Peleus.

# ILIAD 17

When Menelaus saw Patroclus go down,
He shouldered his way through the heroes in front
And stood over the body

                    *the way a lowing heifer*
    *Stands over the first calf she has given birth to,*

Red-haired Menelaus above Patroclus
With his spear out and shield over him,
Determined to kill anyone who approached.

Panthous' son Euphorbus was still interested
In the fallen Patroclus. He came up,                              10
Planted himself close to Menelaus, and said:

"Back off, son of Atreus, leave the corpse
And forget the blood-soaked spoils.
No Trojan or Trojan ally hit Patroclus
Before I did in the heat of battle.
So let me have the glory that is mine
If you value your sweet life."

This was too much for Menelaus, who said:

"It's not good to boast beyond your strength,
Euphorbus. Leopards and lions                                    20

332                                                           [1–20]

And razorback boars, the wildest of beasts,
May be nothing compared to Panthous' sons,
But mighty Hyperenor did not live
To enjoy his youth when he made light of me
As the weakest warrior in all of Greece.
He's not going home under his own power
To gladden his wife and devoted parents.
I'll unstring you too if you stand against me.
Take my advice and get back to your troops
Before you get hurt. Fools learn the hard way."                    *30*

Euphorbus was not convinced. He answered:

"Now, Menelaus, you're going to pay the price
For killing my brother—and boasting about it—
And for widowing his young bride
And causing our parents unspeakable pain.
But I could relieve their suffering for a while
By bringing back your head and armor
And placing them in Panthous' and Phrontis' hands.
But it won't take long to settle this.
Either put up a fight or clear out of here."                       *40*

His ash spear hit the disk of Menelaus' shield,
But the point bent and didn't break through
The heavy bronze. Menelaus charged
With a prayer to Zeus, and as Euphorbus stepped back,
Put his spear through the base of his neck,
Leaning into the thrust with a strong grip on the shaft.
The point passed right through his soft neck
And he fell heavily with a clatter of armor.
His hair, braided like twisted myrtle
With gold and silver, was drenched with blood.                     *50*

*A man has been rearing an olive sapling*
*In a lonely place, where it has enough water.*
*It is beautiful and growing well, quivering*
*In the breeze, its white buds blossoming.*
*One day a storm comes with violent winds,*
*Tears it from its trench, and leaves it on the ground.*

So too Panthous' son, Euphorbus.

Menelaus moved in to strip off the armor.

> *A mountain lion, supremely confident,*
> *Has seized the finest heifer in the grazing herd.* 60
> *First he crunches her neck in his strong jaws,*
> *Then greedily laps her blood and soft innards.*
> *The herdsmen and their hounds shout at him*
> *From a safe distance, but, pale with fear,*
> *They lack the will to take him on.*

Not a single Trojan opposed Menelaus,
And he would have carried off Euphorbus' armor
Easily, had not Apollo begrudged it.
Taking the form of Mentes, a Ciconian commander,
He went to work on Hector, and his words flew fast: 70

"Hector, you're chasing something you'll never catch,
The horses of Peleus, a team hard to handle
For any mortal except Achilles, a goddess's son.
Meanwhile, Atreus' son Menelaus
Has gotten in position over Patroclus
And killed the best man we've got, Euphorbus,
Panthous' son, stopped him cold."

And the god went back into the toil of men.
A dark shadow of grief passed over Hector.
He scanned the lines and saw one figure 80
Bending over another, stripping off armor,
The other beneath him in a pool of blood.
He strode forward though the men in front,
His armor blazing, and the cry from his lips
Was like Hephaestus' inextinguishable flame.
Atreus' son heard it and said to himself:

"Ah me, if I leave behind the fine armor
And Patroclus too, who fought for my honor,

All of the Greeks will hold it against me.
But if I fight Hector and the Trojans alone 90
Out of a sense of shame, I'll be surrounded,
One against many. Hector is leading
The whole Trojan army in this direction.
But why am I talking to myself this way?
There's nothing but trouble in bucking heaven
And fighting a man with a god on his side.
No Greek looking on will hold it against me
If I pull back from Hector, who has divine help.
But if I could just find Ajax, the two of us
Could go back in and think about fighting, 100
Even against heaven's will, make the best
Of a bad situation, and see if we can save
Patroclus' corpse for the son of Peleus."

While he thought it over the Trojan ranks
Closed in behind Hector. Menelaus pulled back,
Leaving the corpse and constantly turning around

*Like a bearded lion that men with dogs*
*Drive from a pen with spears and shouts.*
*His heart is like ice, and he leaves reluctantly.*

Red-haired Menelaus left Patroclus, 110
But when he reached his own lines
He looked around for Telamonian Ajax
And spotted him on the army's left flank,
Cheering on his men and urging them to fight,
For Phoebus Apollo had panicked them.
Menelaus ran over and said to him:

"Ajax, old friend, Patroclus is dead.
We'll have to hurry if we're going to get
His body back to Achilles—that is,
The naked corpse. Hector has the armor." 120

Ajax was moved when he heard this. He strode
To the front, Menelaus at his side.

Hector had stripped the armor from Patroclus' body
And was pulling at the corpse—he meant to sever
The head and feed the trunk to the dogs of Troy—
When Ajax stood before him like a city wall.
Hector gave ground and vaulted into his chariot,
Handing the exquisite gear to some Trojans
To take back to town, where he could glory in it.

Ajax covered Menoetius' son with his shield.                    130

> *A lioness stands over her cubs. She had been leading*
> *The little ones through the forest when hunters*
> *Came across her, and now, savoring her strength,*
> *She narrows her eyes to cold yellow slits.*

Ajax stood over the fallen hero, and Menelaus
Came up beside him, nursing his grief.

Then Glaucus, the Lycian captain,
Glared at Hector and said angrily:

"You're all good looks, Hector, and no fight,
Just another big name attached to a quitter.                    140
Well, you'd better think now how to save your city
With home-grown Trojans and nobody else.
No Lycians, at least, are going to fight the Greeks
To rescue Troy, since there's no gratitude
For nonstop combat with the enemy forces.
Are you likely to save an ordinary soldier
In the press of battle when you left Sarpedon,
Your comrade and guest, as pickings for the Greeks?
After all he'd done for you and your city
While he was still alive, you didn't have the heart            150
To keep the dogs off his head. That's why now,
If any of the Lycians will listen to me,
We're heading home. Then Troy will be done for.
If only the Trojans showed the sort of courage
Real men have when they fight for their country
Against foreign invaders, laying it all on the line,
We would drag Patroclus to Troy in no time.

And if we did, if we got that man's corpse
Out of battle and into Priam's great city,
The Greeks would give back Sarpedon's armor,                    160
And we could bring his body into Ilion.
That's how great a man the dead Patroclus served,
The best of the Achaeans, and his soldiers too.
But you didn't have the guts to stand up to Ajax
And look him in the eye just now, much less fight him,
The reason being that he's stronger than you."

Hector, helmet shimmering, responded:

"Glaucus, this insolence is not like you at all.
I've always thought you were the most intelligent
Of all the Lycians, but I have no use                           170
For nonsense like this. What a thing to say,
That I wouldn't take on big hulking Ajax.
I don't rattle, Glaucus, or freeze up in combat.
Sure, Zeus can overpower the greatest hero,
Make him panic, and rob him of victory,
Just as he can make men get up and fight.
So come along if you want to see how I do
All day long—whether I'm the coward you say I am,
Or stop a Greek or two cold, for all their fury,
From fighting in defense of Patroclus' corpse."                 180

Then Hector made his voice carry:

"Trojan, Lycian, and Dardanian soldiers,
Be men, my friends, and remember your strength
While I put on Achilles' resplendent armor
That I took off Patroclus when I cut him down."

And his helmet flashed gold as he turned and ran
Out of the battle. He soon caught his comrades—
They were not far, and he was running hard—
As they carried Achilles' gear back to Troy.
There, on the edge of war's horrors, he changed armor.          190
He gave his own to be carried back to the city
By his fighting men, and he put on the inhuman gear

Of Peleus' son Achilles that the gods of heaven
Had given to his father, and he to his son
When he had grown old in them, as his son would not.

Zeus saw him from his seat high in the clouds
As he buckled on Achilles' armor.
Shaking his head the god said to himself:

"Unhappy man, you have no thought of death,
Yet death is close. You are putting on                           200
The immortal armor of a man who makes you
And many others tremble. You killed his comrade,
Gentle and strong, and you violated the order of things
When you took the armor from his shoulders and head.
Yet I will grant you strength in recompense for this:
Andromache will never welcome you home
Wearing the glorious armor of Achilles."

And the Son of Cronus nodded, his brows
Darkening the air. He made the armor
Fit Hector like his own skin, and Ares                           210
In all his dread power entered into him,
Packing every muscle in his body with strength.
Hector returned to the field with a great shout
And went among his allied forces,
A gleaming image in Achilles' armor.
He encouraged them all, singling them out,
Speaking to Mesthles and Glaucus and Medon,
Thersilochus, Asteropaeus, and Deisenor,
Hippothous, Phorcys, and Chromius,
And to Ennomus who read the flight of birds,                     220
Giving them heart with these soaring words:

"Hear me, my valiant allies and neighbors!
I did not invite you to come here from your cities
Because I was looking for or needed a crowd,
But because I thought you would fight with willing hearts
To save the Trojan women and children
From these war-mongering Greeks. This is why
I have been feeding you at our expense

And giving you gifts to keep up your morale.
So face the enemy and fight! Maybe you'll pull through          230
And maybe you won't. That's the charm of battle.
Whoever gets Patroclus, mere corpse that he is,
Back to our lines, and makes Ajax give in,
Gets half the spoils. I'll split them with him
Right down the middle—and he'll have glory like mine."

This inspired them to charge the Greeks en masse,
Spears held high, thinking they would surely
Pull the corpse from under Telamonian Ajax,
The fools. Ajax killed many over that corpse,
But finally turned to Menelaus and said:                       240

"Menelaus, old friend, I don't have much hope
Of us two getting out of this battle alive.
I'm not only afraid that Patroclus' body
Is soon going to glut Trojan dogs and birds,
But that you and I are going to get it in the neck.
There's a cloud of war covering everything—
Hector—with one thing clear, our sudden death.
Call in our heroes. Maybe someone's within earshot."

And Menelaus, who had a good battle cry,
Split the air with a shout to the Greeks:                      250

"Argive leaders! Everyone who drinks
At Agamennon's table, commands a troop,
And has honor and glory from Zeus—
I can't make out every single captain
In this battle's firestorm, but get out here
On your own, out of shame that Patroclus
Is becoming a ragbone for Trojan dogs."

The Ajax that was Oïleus' swift son
Heard him clearly and was the first man out.
Sprinting behind him were Idomeneus                            260
And his comrade Meriones, a real killer.
As for the rest, who could remember
All of the Greeks who swarmed into battle?

Bunched behind Hector the Trojans struck.

> *A great wave sometimes rolls into the mouth*
> *Of a swollen river, pushing against its current.*
> *The headlands resound as the sea roars to get in.*

The Trojans came on, but the Greeks stood firm
Around Menoetius' son, their hearts united,
Their bronze shields locked.                                     270
                              And from above
Zeus poured over their dark gold helmets
A profound mist, for Menoetius' son
Had been far from hateful when in life he was
Achilles' companion. Now he loathed the thought
Of his enemies' dogs playing with his body,
And so he roused his comrades to fight for him.

At first the Trojans drove the wild-eyed Greeks
Back from the body, and although for all their efforts
And high spirits they failed to land a spear on anyone,           280
They started to pull the corpse away. The Greeks,
However, were back soon, rallied by Ajax,
Who looked and acted more like a hero
Than any living Greek, except peerless Achilles.

Ajax split the Trojan front lines

> *as a wild boar*
> *In the mountains tosses dogs and men*
> *When he turns on them in a clearing.*

This was the son of Telamon, glorious Ajax,
Scattering the Trojan platoons that stood                         290
Around Patroclus and wanted nothing else more
Than the glory of dragging him back to their city.
Hippothous, a Pelasgian, had tied his war belt
Around the corpse's ankles and was hauling it
Inch by inch through the fierce fighting,
Much to the satisfaction of Hector and the Trojans.
None of them could have stopped what happened next,

Ajax's spear coming from nowhere
And smashing through his plumed helmet.
Hippothous' brains, clotted with blood,                    300
Spurted out from the wound along the spear's socket.
He dropped Patroclus' foot and then fell himself
Face down on the corpse, far from Larissa
And his father Lethus, his debt to his parents
Unpaid, his life cut short by great Ajax's spear.
Hector countered, but Ajax kept his eye
On the bright flare his spear made and managed,
Although just barely, to dodge the bronze point.
Hector's spear went on to kill Schedius,
Son of Iphitus and the best of the Phocians,                    310
Who ruled over many from his home in Panopeus.
The bronze point passed through his collarbone
And went straight through to the base of his shoulder.
He fell with a heavy clanging of armor.
Ajax then hit Phorcys, Phaenops' son,
Right in the belly as he straddled Hippothous.
The spearpoint broke the corselet plate,
And his guts oozed through the bronze.
After he had fallen his hand still clawed at the dust.
The Trojan champions, including Hector,                    320
Had enough. They backed off, and howling Greeks
Dragged off the dead, Phorcys and Hippothous,
And got busy stripping off their armor.

It would have been another defeat for the Trojans—
Driven by the Greeks, with Ares on their side,
Back to Ilion—and an Argive victory,
Power and glory beyond Zeus' allotment,
Had not Apollo himself aroused Aeneas,
Assuming the form of a herald, Periphas,
Son of Ephytos, a courteous man                    330
Who had grown old in Anchises' service.
Apollo, a son of Zeus, spoke in his guise:

"Aeneas, admittedly you will never defend
Steep Ilion in defiance of a god, although indeed
I have seen other men trust their prowess and strength,

Their courage and their superior numbers,
And defend their people against all odds.
But in our case Zeus wants victory for us,
Not for the Greeks. And yet you hang back in fear."

Aeneas knew it was the god Apollo                               340
When he looked him in the face. He called to Hector:

"Hector, Trojan leaders, and allied commanders!
Shame on us all if we are beaten back to Ilion
By the Achaeans without defending ourselves.
One of the gods has just whispered in my ear
That Zeus on high is on our side in this fight.
Let's go straight at the Danaans! Don't let them take
Dead Patroclus to their ships at their leisure!"

With that, he bounded to the front of the fight
And took his stand. The Trojans rallied                        350
And faced the Greeks. Then Aeneas thrust,
Getting his spear into Leocritus, Arisbas' son
And worthy comrade of Lycomedes.
When his friend went down, Lycomedes
Felt for him and, standing right beside him,
Cast his bright spear and hit Apisaon,
Son of Hippasas, under the ribs in the liver.
The man crumpled, the best warrior
In deep-soiled Paeonia, after Asteropaeus,
Who watched him fall, pitied him,                              360
Then charged the Greeks with everything he had.
But there was nothing he could do. The Greeks
Had formed around Patroclus a wall of shields
Forward from which they held their spears.
Ajax was everywhere among them, seeing to it
That not a man took one step backward
From the body, or went out in front to show off,
But that all stood together and fought close in.
That was how big Ajax managed it, and the earth
Grew wet with dark blood as the dead fell              370
Thick and fast on both sides, Trojans, allies,

Greeks too, who shed blood, but less of it,
And with fewer casualties, because they fought
In a tight group and protected each other.

So the battle burned on, but you would have thought
The sun had gone out, and the moon too,
For they fought in dark air, all the heroes
Clustered around Menoetius' slain son.
The rest of the Trojans and Greeks had their war
Under the open sky and in brilliant sunlight,                    380
Not a cloud on the horizon. They took breaks
From the fighting, avoiding each other's
Groaning shafts, making some open space in battle.
But those in the center suffered the agony
Of combat in darkness with merciless bronze.
All the best were there, except for two Greeks,
Thrasymedes and Antilochus. They did not know
Blameless Patroclus was dead, and assumed
He was still alive and fighting the Trojans in front.
These two were struggling to keep their men alive            390
And in combat, fighting off at some distance
Where Nestor had ordered them when they left the ships.

The day was passing. Men hacked slowly at each other
In pain, the sweat from their labor coating
Their thighs and knees, pooling under their feet,
Spattering from their arms into their glazed eyes,
As the two armies fought over Achilles' surrogate.

> *A tanner gives his men an oxhide to stretch,*
> *Having first drenched it in oil. They stand in a circle*
> *And pull at it until its moisture is squeezed out*         400
> *By all of their tugging and the oil has a chance*
> *To penetrate the taut leather's pores.*

So too the tight circle of men on either side
Tugging at the corpse, the Trojans with high hopes
Of dragging it back to Ilion, the Greeks
With their own hopes of getting it back to the ships.

It was a savage fight, and not even Ares
Or Athena, in their most belligerent moods,
Could have watched it with disdain.

Such was the labor for men and horses                    410
Zeus stretched over Patroclus that day.
                              But all this time
Achilles did not know Patroclus was dead,
For they were fighting far from the ships
Under Troy's walls, and Achilles never dreamed
He would die there, but thought he would return alive
After he reached the gates. Nor did he think
Patroclus would take Troy without him,
Or with him for that matter. He had heard this
Many times from his mother when they had their talks     420
And she would tell him the intentions of Zeus.
But his mother did not tell him now
Of this great evil, his dearest friend dead.

Around the corpse they kept pressing hard
With sharp spears and killing each other.
Some Greek would say from his bronze mask:

"Friends, there's no point in returning
To the hollow ships. It would be better
For the black earth to swallow us here
If we're going to let the Trojans haul him              430
Back to the city and win all the glory."

Or some Trojan would say:

"Friends, even if we're all fated to die
By this body, don't take a step back."

These words would lift everyone's strength.

While they fought on, and as the iron noise
Rose through the barren air to the bronze sky,
Achilles' horses, some distance from the battle,
Were weeping, and had been since first they learned

That their charioteer had fallen in the dust                    440
Under the hands of man-slaying Hector.
Automedon, Diores' valiant son,
Was doing everything he could with lash,
Gentle words, and curses to get them moving,
But the pair would not go back to the ships
By the level sea, or back into battle
With the Achaeans. They stood still as stone,
Still as a post on a man's or woman's tomb,
There in front of the beautiful chariot,
Their heads bowed to the earth, their tears             450
Rolling warm from their eyes to the ground
As they wept in longing for their charioteer,
And their lustrous manes were fouled in the dust
As they streamed to either side of the yoke.
When he saw them mourning the son of Cronus
Felt pity. He shook his head and said to himself:

"Ah, why did we give you to lord Peleus,
To a mortal, while you are deathless and ageless?
Was it so you could share men's pain?
Nothing is more miserable than man                          460
Of all that breathes and moves upon earth.
But Priam's son Hector will not drive you
Or your wrought chariot. That I will not allow.
Is it not enough that he has the armor
And struts vainly in it? No, in your knees
And in your heart I will put strength
So you may bear Automedon out of the war
To the hollow ships. For I will continue to give
The Trojans glory to kill, until they reach the ships,
And the sun sets, and sacred darkness comes on."          470

And he breathed into the horses great strength.
The two shook the dust from their manes
And raced with the chariot through the combatants.
Automedon kept trying to fight, though grieving
For his comrade, swooping with the horses
Like a vulture on a flock of geese, easily
Leaving the clamor of the Trojans behind

And just as easily bearing down on them,
But he could not kill any of his quarry
Since he was alone in the haunted chariot                        480
And could not handle a spear and drive too.
Finally a friend saw him and caught his eye,
Alcimedon, son of Laerces Haemonides,
Who now stood behind the chariot and said:

"Automedon, which god has put this bad idea
Into your head and robbed you of your good sense,
Fighting the Trojans up here in the thick of things
All alone? Your companion is dead, and Hector
Is strutting around in old Peleus' armor."

Diores' son Automedon answered:                                   490

"Alcimedon, is there a man in the army
Who could control these immortal horses
Besides Patroclus? He had a will like a god's
While he lived. Now death has caught up with him.
But take the lash anyway, and the reins,
And I will dismount so I can fight."

Alcimedon swung into the fast war chariot
And took the reins and lash in his hands.
Automedon jumped off. Hector saw the move
And said to Aeneas, who was at his side:                          500

"Aeneas, I've just spotted Achilles' horses
Coming into battle with a pair of weak drivers.
I think I could take them, if you would help.
Their drivers couldn't stand up to men like us."

Aeneas was willing, and the two went forward,
Shoulders hunched behind their shields,
Pounds of bronze welded to hardened leather.
With them went Chromius and godlike Aretus,
Who fully expected they would kill the men
And drive off the high-necked horses,                            510
But Automedon would extract blood

For these childish hopes. He prayed to Lord Zeus,
And felt a dark surge of power within him,
Then spoke quickly to his trusted driver:

"Alcimedon, keep the horses close enough
That I can feel their breath on my back.
Hector won't stop until he he mounts the chariot
Behind Achilles' horses, with us dead
And the rest of the Argive army in rout,
Or until he himself goes down in the front."                    520

And he called to both Ajaxes and to Menelaus:

"Ajax, both of you, and Menelaus too,
Leave the body for the best men you have
To defend it against the Trojan onslaught,
And come help us out while we're still alive.
Hector and Aeneas have weighed in here,
The best Troy has. Well, it's in the gods' laps.
I'll do what I can and leave the rest to Zeus."

He balanced his long-shadowed spear and threw,
Hitting Aretus' shield, which did not stop                      530
The bronze point from penetrating all the way through
And into his belly just below his belt.

> When a strong man swings a sharp ax
> Onto a bull's neck just behind the horns
> And cuts through all the sinews there,
> The animal pitches forward as it falls.

Aretus pitched forward and fell on his back,
Undone by the razor-sharp spear that stuck
Quivering in his entrails. Hector rifled
His polished spear at Automedon,                                540
But Automedon saw it all the way and ducked,
Leaving it to punch into the ground and stand there
Trembling, until Ares finally stilled its fury.
They would have closed on each other with swords,
But the two Ajaxes, responding to their comrade's call

Stepped between them, sending cold chills
Through Hector, Aeneas, and Chromius,
Who all withdrew, letting Aretus lie there
Mangled and dead. As Automedon stripped him,
He said with grim satisfaction:                                    550

"This makes up for the death of Patroclus,
Though it is a lesser man I have killed."

And he swung the bloody spoils into the chariot
And mounted, his feet and arms smeared with gore,
Like a lion that has just eaten a bull.

The tense fight over Patroclus went on,
Made even more tense now by Athena,
Who stepped down from the sky, sent by Zeus.

*Zeus sometimes sends a shimmering arc from the sky*
*As a portent of war, or of a cold rainstorm*                      560
*That brings men in from the fields and vexes the flocks.*

Athena wrapped herself in an iridescent mist
And entered the Greek throng, urging on each man,
Beginning with Atreus' son, Menelaus,
Standing by his side and speaking to him
In the guise of Phoenix and using his voice:

"The shame and dishonor will be mostly yours,
Menelaus, if lord Achilles' faithful comrade
Is savaged by dogs under Ilion's walls.
Hold your ground and urge on the army!"                           570

Menelaus, good at the war cry, answered:

"Phoenix, old sir! If only Athena
Would give me strength and shield me from spears,
I would stand by Patroclus and protect him all day.
I take his death hard. But Hector is on fire,
Just carving us up with his bronze.
Zeus is giving him all the glory."

Athena, eyes glinting in the sun, was glad
That Menelaus had put her first in his prayers.
She put power into his shoulders and knees,                    *580*
And into his breast the boldness of a horsefly
That however often it is flicked away
From human flesh, persists in biting,
For human blood is sweet. Menelaus felt
That kind of boldness in his dark heart
As he straddled Patroclus and threw his bright spear.
There was among the Trojans a certain Podes,
A son of Eëtion, a rich, valiant man
Whom Hector honored with a place at his table.
Menelaus' spear hit him on the belt                            *590*
As he turned to run. The metal point went through
And he fell with a thud. Atreus' red-haired son
Dragged the body to the main group of Greeks.

Then Apollo stood close to Hector,
Seeming to be Asius' son Phaenops,
A dear family friend who lived in Abydos.
In his likeness the Archer urged him on:

"Hector, is there any Greek who will fear you now?
Look how you lost your nerve before Menelaus,
A well-known weakling. He's taken the corpse                   *600*
Out from under our noses all by himself
And is gone. And he's killed your true friend
And great hero Podes, son of Eëtion."

A black cloud of grief enveloped Hector,
And he strode forward in a blaze of bronze.

At the same moment the Son of Cronus took his aegis,
A fringed glare in the sky, and wrapped Ida in clouds.
He thundered and lightened and shook the aegis,
Giving victory to the Trojans and routing the Greeks.

Peneleos the Boeotian bolted first.                            *610*
A spear grazed his shoulder as he faced the enemy,
But the blade sliced through to the bone,

A lucky throw by Polydamas from close range.
Leitus was next, nicked on the wrist
By Hector, enough to make him quit the fight,
Seeing he couldn't grip a spear properly.
This man was the son of Alectryon.
As he withdrew, wide-eyed and apprehensive,
Hector chased him, and Idomeneus
Took a shot at the Trojan, hitting him                           620
On the breastplate right by the nipple,
But the spear's shaft shattered in its socket.
The Trojans cheered. Hector returned the favor,
His javelin just missing Idomeneus
As he stood in his chariot but hitting Coeranus,
Meriones' charioteer and comrade from Lyctus.
Idomeneus had set out from the ships on foot
And would have handed the Trojans a great coup
Had not Coeranus driven his fast horses by
And given him some daylight. He saved the day             630
But lost his life to man-slaughtering Hector,
Whose spear got him behind the jaw, under the ear,
Plowing out his teeth and slicing his tongue lengthwise.
He fell from the car and dropped the reins to the ground.
Meriones bent over and scooped them up
From the dirt, and said to Idomeneus:

"Lay on the lash until you get back to the ships.
You know as well as I do the Greeks are washed up."

He spoke, and Idomeneus, in a panic now,
Lashed the maned horses back to the hollow ships.         640

Not even Ajax and Menelaus failed to notice
That Zeus had shifted the momentum to the Trojans.
Big Ajax turned to his companion and said:

"Any fool can see that Father Zeus himself
Is helping the Trojans. Everything they throw
Hits home. It doesn't matter who throws it,
Brave man or coward, Zeus guides them all straight.
But we can't hit anything but the ground.

Let's try to come up with the best plan we can
To haul the corpse out and build morale                          *650*
By getting ourselves back to our comrades.
They must feel despair when they look this way.
I doubt if they think Hector can be stopped
Before he lays his hands on our black sailing ships.
If only one of our men could get a message through,
Fast, to Achilles. I don't think he's heard
The bad news, that his best friend is dead.
But I can't see any Greek who could do that job.
They're all lost in dark mist, their horses too.
Father Zeus, deliver the Greeks from the dark.                   *660*
Make the sky clear. Allow us to see with our eyes.
Destroy us in the light, since destroy us you will."


He spoke, and the Father had pity for his tears.
Instantly he dispersed the darkness and mist,
And the sun shone, and all the battle was clear.
Then Ajax turned to Menelaus and said:


"Menelaus, see if you can spot Antilochus
Still alive, Nestor's son. Have him go quickly
To Achilles and tell him his best friend is dead."


Menelaus, who was good at the war shout,                         *670*
Couldn't argue with this, and started to leave,

> Very much like a lion that leaves a corral
> After it is tired of vexing the men and dogs
> Who, standing guard all night, will not allow it to seize
> The herd's prime bull. Lusting for flesh,
> The lion charges, but gets nothing for it
> But a rain of javelins launched by bold hands
> And flaming torches that stop it in its tracks.
> At dawn the lion goes off in a sullen mood.

Menelaus was just as reluctant to leave                          *680*
Patroclus' body, afraid of a general rout
That would leave him stranded behind enemy lines.
He lingered to remind his comrades of their duty:

"Both you Ajaxes, and Meriones too,
Everyone should keep in mind what a good man
Our Patroclus was, gentle and kind to all
When he was alive. And now death has taken him."

Finally, Menelaus left,
Glancing every which way.

> *An eagle, whose eyesight is the keenest*                    690
> *Of all the birds in the sky, can spot*
> *From high altitude a rabbit crouching*
> *Under a leafy bush and, swooping down,*
> *Catch it and instantly rip out its life.*

Yes, Menelaus, that's how your bright eyes
Swept everywhere through the allied troops
Searching for Nestor's son—was he still alive?—
And, yes, spotted him on the battle's left,
Encouraging his men and urging them to fight.
Menelaus made his way to his side and said:                    700

"I have bad news, Antilochus. You know
Some god has turned the tide against us.
Well, now the best of the Achaeans is dead,
Patroclus. God, that it were not true.
Run to the ships and tell Achilles.
If he acts quickly he might still save the body—
Naked, though. Hector has the armor."

He spoke, and Antilochus was choked with horror.
He was speechless, astounded; his eyes
Welled with tears; his voice stuck in his throat.                    710
But he did not disregard Menelaus' orders.
He started to run, giving his armor
To his charioteer, who drove beside him.
He left the battlefield on foot and in tears,
With a grim report for Achilles, son of Peleus.

Menelaus had no intention of staying to help
The sore-pressed troops from Pylos,

Who already missed their commander Antilochus.
He dispatched Thrasymedes in his place
And ran back to take his stand over Patroclus,                    720
Next to the Ajaxes, to whom he said at once:

"I've sent Antilochus there ahead to the ships
To go to Achilles, but we can't count on Achilles
Coming any time soon. He may want Hector badly,
But he can't fight the Trojans unarmed and naked.
We have to come up with the best plan we can
To get the body out and escape ourselves
From this deafening battle without any casualties."

It was big Ajax who came up with the plan:

"Right, Menelaus. You and Meriones                                730
Get the body up on your shoulders
And carry it out. We'll be behind you
Holding off the Trojans and Hector.
We have the same name and the same heart,
And we've stuck with each other in battle before."

They got their arms round the corpse and raised it
High off the ground. The Trojans shouted out
When they saw the Greeks lift the body, and charged.

> *Hunting dogs after a wounded boar*
> *Will run up in front of the hunters*                           740
> *And for a while threaten to tear the boar apart.*
> *But when the boar pivots and trusts its strength,*
> *The dogs quail and slink back one by one.*

So too the Trojans, who would launch mass attacks,
Thrusting with swords and double-edged spears.
But when the two Ajaxes wheeled and made a stand,
They would all turn pale, not a single man willing
To make a quick move and contend for the corpse.

In this way, this little knot of Greeks
Did their best to carry Patroclus' body                          750

Out of combat and back to their ribbed ships,
While against them the battle strained and coiled,

> As wild as fire when it engulfs a city
> Suddenly, and sets it aflame, and the houses
> Shrivel in the heat and the wind roars like thunder.

So too, as they went on, the eternal din
Of horses, cars, and spearmen, noise like heat.

> Or think of a team of mules, matched in strength,
> Dragging a load down a craggy mountain path,
> A beam, say, or a huge ship timber. Their spirits          760
> Flag with the toil and sweat, but they push on.

So these two Greeks pushed on with the corpse,
And the two Ajaxes held the enemy off.

> A wooded ridge that lies across a plain
> Will check the cruel currents of swollen rivers,
> Turning them back to spread over the plain,
> And the floods, though strong, never break through.

So the two Ajaxes contained the Trojans'
Offensive push. But the Trojans kept coming,
And two among them especially,                               770
Aeneas, Anchises' son, and glorious Hector.

> A cloud of starlings or jackdaws will loop around
> Shrieking doom when they see ahead of them
> A falcon, which brings death to smaller birds.

So too before Aeneas and Hector the Greeks
Ran shrieking, as if it were the end of the world.
The trench was littered with their beautiful,
Discarded weapons. But there was no armistice.

# ILIAD 18

The fight went on, like wildfire burning.
Antilochus, running hard like a herald,
Found Achilles close to his upswept hulls,
His great heart brooding with premonitions
Of what had indeed already happened.

   "This looks bad,
All these Greeks with their hair in the wind
Stampeding off the plain and back to the ships.
God forbid that what my mother told me
Has now come true, that while I'm still alive          10
Trojan hands would steal the sunlight
From the best of all the Myrmidons.
Patroclus, Menoetius' brave son, is dead.
Damn him! I told him only to repel
The enemy fire from our ships,
And not to take on Hector in a fight."

Antilochus was in tears when he reached him
And delivered his unendurable message:

"Son of wise Peleus, this is painful news
For you to hear, and I wish it were not true.         20
Patroclus is down, and they are fighting
For his naked corpse. Hector has the armor."

A mist of black grief enveloped Achilles.
He scooped up fistfuls of sunburnt dust
And poured it on his head, fouling
His beautiful face. Black ash grimed
His fine-spun cloak as he stretched his huge body
Out in the dust and lay there,
Tearing out his hair with his hands.
The women, whom Achilles and Patroclus                           30
Had taken in raids, ran shrieking out of the tent
To be with Achilles, and they beat their breasts
Until their knees gave out beneath them.
Antilochus, sobbing himself, stayed with Achilles
And held his hands—he was groaning
From the depths of his soul—for fear
He would lay open his own throat with steel.

The sound of Achilles' grief stung the air.

Down in the water his mother heard him,
Sitting in the sea depths beside her old father,            40
And she began to wail.
                          And the saltwater women
Gathered around her, all the deep-sea Nereids,
Glaucē and Thaleia and Cymodocē,
Neseia and Speio, Thoē and ox-eyed Haliē,
Cymothoē, Actaeē, and Limnoeira,
Melitē and Iaera, Amphithoē and Agauē,
Doris, Panopē, and milk-white Galateia,
Nemertes, Apseudes, and Callianassa,
Clymenē, Ianeira, Ianassa, and Maera,                         50
Oreithyia and Amatheia, hair streaming behind her,
And all of the other deep-sea Nereids.
They filled the silver, shimmering cave,
And they all beat their breasts.

                          Thetis led the lament:

"Hear me, sisters, hear the pain in my heart.
I gave birth to a son, and that is my sorrow,
My perfect son, the best of heroes.

He grew like a sapling, and I nursed him
As I would a plant on the hill in my garden,    60
And I sent him to Ilion on a sailing ship
To fight the Trojans. And now I will never
Welcome him home again to Peleus' house.
As long as he lives and sees the sunlight
He will be in pain, and I cannot help him.
But I'll go now to see and hear my dear son,
Since he is suffering while he waits out the war."

She left the cave, and they went with her,
Weeping, and around them a wave
Broke through the sea, and they came to Troy.    70
They emerged on the beach where the Myrmidons' ships
Formed an encampment around Achilles.
He was groaning deeply, and his mother
Stood next to him and held her son's head.
Her lamentation hung sharp in the air,
And then she spoke in low, sorrowful tones:

"Child, why are you crying? What pain
Has come to your heart? Speak, don't hide it.
Zeus has granted your prayer. The Greeks
Have all been beaten back to their ships    80
And suffered horribly. They can't do without you."

Achilles answered her:

"Mother, Zeus may have done all this for me,
But how can I rejoice? My friend is dead,
Patroclus, my dearest friend of all. I loved him,
And I killed him. And the armor—
Hector cut him down and took off his body
The heavy, splendid armor, beautiful to see,
That the gods gave to Peleus as a gift
On the day they put you to bed with a mortal.    90
You should have stayed with the saltwater women,
And Peleus should have married a mortal.
But now—it was all so you would suffer pain
For your ravaged son. You will never again

Welcome me home, since I no longer have the will
To remain alive among men, not unless Hector
Loses his life on the point of my spear
And pays for despoiling Menoetius' son."

And Thetis, in tears, said to him:

"I won't have you with me for long, my child,                    100
If you say such things. Hector's death means yours."

From under a great weight, Achilles answered:

"Then let me die now. I was no help
To him when he was killed out there. He died
Far from home, and he needed me to protect him.
But now, since I'm not going home, and wasn't
A light for Patroclus or any of the rest
Of my friends who have been beaten by Hector,
But just squatted by my ships, a dead weight on the earth . . .
I stand alone in the whole Greek army                    110
When it comes to war—though some do speak better.
I wish all strife could stop, among gods
And among men, and anger too—it sends
Sensible men into fits of temper,
It drips down our throats sweeter than honey
And mushrooms up in our bellies like smoke.
Yes, the warlord Agamemnon angered me.
But we'll let that be, no matter how it hurts,
And conquer our pride, because we must.
But I'm going now to find the man who destroyed                    120
My beloved—Hector.
                                        As for my own fate,
I'll accept it whenever it pleases Zeus
And the other immortal gods to send it.
Not even Heracles could escape his doom.
He was dearest of all to Lord Zeus, but fate
And Hera's hard anger destroyed him.
If it is true that I have a fate like his, then I too
Will lie down in death.
                                        But now to win glory                    130

And make some Trojan woman or deep-breasted
Dardanian matron wipe the tears
From her soft cheeks, make her sob and groan.
Let them feel how long I've been out of the war.
Don't try, out of love, to stop me. I won't listen."

And Thetis, her feet silver on the sand:

"Yes, child. It's not wrong to save your friends
When they are beaten to the brink of death.
But your beautiful armor is in the hands of the Trojans,
The mirrored bronze. Hector himself                         140
Has it on his shoulders. He glories in it.
Not for long, though. I see his death is near.
But you, don't dive into the red dust of war
Until with your own eyes you see me returning.
Tomorrow I will come with the rising sun
Bearing beautiful armor from Lord Hephaestus."

Thetis spoke, turned away
From her son, and said to her saltwater sisters:

"Sink now into the sea's wide lap
And go down to our old father's house                        150
And tell him all this. I am on my way
Up to Olympus to visit Hephaestus,
The glorious smith, to see if for my sake
He will give my son glorious armor."

As she spoke they dove into the waves,
And the silver-footed goddess was gone
Off to Olympus to fetch arms for her child.

And while her feet carried her off to Olympus,
Hector yelled, a yell so bloodcurdling and loud
It stampeded the Greeks all the way back                     160
To their ships beached on the Hellespont's shore.
They could not pull the body of Patroclus
Out of javelin range, and soon Hector,
With his horses and men, stood over it again.

Three times Priam's resplendent son
Took hold of the corpse's heels and tried
To drag it off, bawling commands to his men.
Three times the two Ajaxes put their heads down,
Charged, and beat him back. Unshaken, Hector
Sidestepped, cut ahead, or held his ground                    170
With a shout, but never yielded an inch.

   *It was like shepherds against a starving lion,*
   *Helpless to beat it back from a carcass,*

The two Ajaxes unable to rout
The son of Priam from Patroclus' corpse.
And Hector would have, to his eternal glory,
Dragged the body off, had not Iris stormed
Down from Olympus with a message for Achilles,
Unbeknownst to Zeus and the other gods.
Hera had sent her, and this was her message:                    180

"Rise, son of Peleus, most formidable of men.
Rescue Patroclus, for whom a terrible battle
Is pitched by the ships, men killing each other,
Some fighting to save the dead man's body,
The Trojans trying to drag it back
To windy Ilion. Hector's mind especially
Is bent on this. He means to impale the head
On Troy's palisade after he strips off its skin.
And you just lie there? Think of Patroclus
Becoming a ragbone for Trojan dogs. Shame                    190
To your dying day if his corpse is defiled."

The shining sprinter Achilles answered her:

"Iris, which god sent you here?"

And Iris, whose feet are wind, responded:

"None other than Hera, Zeus' glorious wife.
But Zeus on high does not know this, nor do
Any of the immortals on snow-capped Olympus."

And Achilles, the great runner:

"How can I go to war? They have my armor.
And my mother told me not to arm myself          200
Until with my own eyes I see her come back
With fine weapons from Hephaestus.
I don't know any other armor that would fit,
Unless maybe the shield of Telamonian Ajax.
But he's out there in the front ranks, I hope,
Fighting with his spear over Patroclus dead."

Windfoot Iris responded:

"We know very well that they have your armor.
Just go to the trench and let the Trojans see you.
One look will be enough. The Trojans will back off          210
Out of fear of you, and this will give the Greeks
Some breathing space, what little there is in war."

Iris spoke and was gone. And Achilles,
Whom the gods loved, rose. Around
His mighty shoulders Athena threw
Her tasselled aegis, and the shining goddess
Haloed his head with a golden cloud
That shot flames from its incandescent glow.

> *Smoke is rising through the pure upper air*
> *From a besieged city on a distant island.*          220
> *Its soldiers have fought hard all day,*
> *But at sunset they light innumerable fires*
> *So that their neighbors in other cities*
> *Might see the glare reflected off the sky*
> *And sail to their help as allies in war.*

So too the radiance that flared
From Achilles' head and up to the sky.
He went to the trench—away from the wall
And the other Greeks, out of respect
For his mother's tense command. Standing there,          230
He yelled, and behind him Pallas Athena

Amplified his voice, and shock waves
Reverberated through the Trojan ranks.

*You have heard the piercing sound of horns*
*When squadrons come to destroy a city.*

The Greek's voice was like that,
Speaking bronze that made each Trojan heart
Wince with pain.
                                    And the combed horses
Shied from their chariots, eyes wide with fear,                    240
And their drivers went numb when they saw
The fire above Achilles' head
Burned into the sky by the Grey-Eyed One.
Three times Achilles shouted from the trench;
Three times the Trojans and their confederates
Staggered and reeled, twelve of their best
Lost in the crush of chariots and spears.
But the Greeks were glad to pull Patroclus' body
Out of range and placed it on a litter. His comrades
Gathered around, weeping, and with them Achilles,                    250
Shedding hot tears when he saw his loyal friend
Stretched out on the litter, cut with sharp bronze.
He had sent him off to war with horses and chariot,
But he never welcomed him back home again.

And now the ox-eyed Lady Hera
Sent the tireless, reluctant sun
Under the horizon into Ocean's streams,
Its last rays touching the departing Greeks with gold.
It had been a day of brutal warfare.

After the Trojans withdrew from battle,                    260
They unhitched their horses from the chariots
And held an assembly before thinking of supper.
They remained on their feet, too agitated to sit,
Terrified, in fact, that Achilles,
After a long absence, was back.
Polydamas was the first to speak, prudent

Son of Panthous, the only Trojan who looked
Both ahead and behind. This man was born
The same night as Hector, and was his comrade,
As good with words as Hector was with a spear.          270
He had their best interests at heart when he spoke:

"Take a good look around, my friends. My advice
Is to return to the city and not wait for daylight
On the plain by the ships. We are far from our wall.
As long as this man raged against Agamemnon,
The Greeks were easier to fight against.
I too was glad when I spent the night by the ships,
Hoping we would capture their upswept hulls.
That hope has given way to a terrible fear
Of Peleus' swift son. He is a violent man          280
And will not be content to fight on the plain
Where Greeks and Trojans engage in combat.
It is for our city he will fight, and our wives.
We must go back. Trust me, this is how it will be:
Night is holding him back now, immortal night.
But if he finds us here tomorrow
When he comes out in his armor in daylight,
Then you will know what Achilles is,
And you will be glad to be back in sacred Ilion—
If you make it back, and are not one          290
Of the many Trojans the dogs and vultures
Will feast upon. I hope I'm not within earshot.
But if we trust my words, as much as it may gall,
We will camp tonight in the marketplace, where
The city is protected by its towers, walls,
And high gates closed with bolted, polished doors.
At dawn we take our positions on the wall
In full armor, and so much the worse for him
If he wants to come out from the ships and fight us
For our wall. He will go back to the ships          300
After he has had enough of parading
His high-necked prancers in front of the city.
He will not have the will to force his way in.
Dogs will eat him before he takes our town."

And Hector, glaring at him under his helmet:

"Polydamas, I don't like this talk
About a retreat and holing up in the city.
Aren't you sick of being penned inside our walls?
People everywhere used to talk about how rich
Priam's city was, all the gold, all the bronze.                310
Now the great houses are empty, their heirlooms
Sold away to Phrygia, to Maeonia, since Zeus
Has turned wrathful. But now—when the great god,
Son of Cronus, has vouchsafed me the glory
Of hemming the Greeks in beside the sea—
Now is no time for you to talk like a fool.
Not a Trojan here will listen. I won't let them.
  Now hear this! All troops will mess tonight
With guards posted and on general alert.
If any of you are worried about your effects,                 320
You can hand them over for distribution!
Better our men should have them than the Greeks.
At first light we strap on our armor
And start fighting hard by the ships.
If Achilles really has risen up again
And wants to come out, he'll find it tough going,
For I will be there. I, for one,
Am not retreating. Maybe he'll win, maybe I will.
The War God doesn't care which one he kills."


Thus Hector, and the Trojans cheered,                         330
The fools, their wits dulled by Pallas Athena.
Hector's poor counsel won all the applause,
And not a man praised Polydamas' good sense.
Then the troops started supper.

                              But the Greeks
Mourned Patroclus the whole night through.
Achilles began the incessant lamentation,
Laying his man-slaying hands on Patroclus' chest
And groaning over and over like a bearded lion

Whose cubs some deer hunter has smuggled out                    *340*
Of the dense woods. When the lion returns,
It tracks the human from valley to valley,
Growling low the whole time. Sometimes it finds him.

Achilles' deep voice sounded among the Myrmidons:

"It was all for nothing, what I said that day
When I tried to hearten the hero Menoetius,
Telling him I would bring his glorious son
Home to Opoeis with his share of the spoils
After I had sacked Ilion. Zeus does not fulfill
A man's every thought. We two are fated                        *350*
To redden the selfsame earth with our blood,
Right here in Troy. I will never return home
To be welcomed by my old father, Peleus,
Or Thetis, my mother. The earth here will hold me.
And since I will pass under the earth after you,
Patroclus, I will not bury you until
I have brought here the armor and head of Hector,
Who killed you, great soul. And I will cut
The throats of twelve Trojan princes
Before your pyre in my wrath. Until then,                      *360*
You will lie here beside our upswept hulls
Just as you are, and round about you
Deep-bosomed Trojan and Dardanian women
Will lament you day and night, weeping,
Women we won with blood, sweat and tears,
Women we cut through rich cities to get."

With that, he ordered his companions
To put a great cauldron on the fire,
So they could wash the gore
From Patroclus' body without further delay.                    *370*
They put a cauldron used for heating baths
Over a blazing fire and poured in the water,
Then stoked the fire with extra wood.
The flames licked the cauldron's belly
And the water grew warm. When it was boiling
In the glowing bronze, they washed the body,

Anointed it with rich olive oil,
And filled the wounds with a seasoned ointment.
Then they laid him on his bed, covered him
From head to foot with a soft linen cloth,                    380
And spread a white mantle above it.
Then the whole night through the Myrmidons
Stood with Achilles, mourning Patroclus.

Zeus said to Hera, his wife and sister:

"So you have had your way, my ox-eyed lady.
You have roused Achilles, swift of foot. Truly,
The long-haired Greeks must be from your womb."

And the ox-eyed lady Hera replied:

"Awesome son of Cronus, what a thing to say!
Even a mortal man, without my wisdom,                         390
Will succeed in his efforts for another man.
How then was I—the highest of goddesses
Both by my own birth and by marriage to you,
The lord and ruler of all the immortals—
Not to cobble up evil for Troy in my wrath?"

While they spoke to each other this way,
Thetis' silver feet took her to Hephaestus' house,
A mansion the lame god had built himself
Out of starlight and bronze, and beyond all time.
She found him at his bellows, glazed with sweat            400
As he hurried to complete his latest project,
Twenty cauldrons on tripods to line his hall,
With golden wheels at the base of each tripod
So they could move by themselves to the gods' parties
And return to his house—a wonder to see.
They were almost done. The intricate handles
Still had to be attached. He was getting these ready,
Forging the rivets with inspired artistry,
When the silver-footed goddess came up to him.
And Charis, Hephaestus' wife, lovely                          410

In her shimmering veil, saw her, and running up,
She clasped her hand and said to her:

"My dear Thetis, so grave in your long robe,
What brings you here now? You almost never visit.
Do come inside so I can offer you something."

And the shining goddess led her along
And had her sit down in a graceful
Silver-studded chair with a footstool.
Then she called to Hephaestus, and said:

"Hephaestus, come here.                                        420
Thetis needs you for something."

And the renowned smith called back:

"Thetis? Then the dread goddess I revere
Is inside. She saved me when I lay suffering
From my long fall, after my shameless mother
Threw me out, wanting to hide my infirmity.
And I really would have suffered, had not Thetis
And Eurynome, a daughter of Ocean Stream,
Taken me into their bosom. I stayed with them
Nine years, forging all kinds of jewelry,                     430
Brooches and bracelets and necklaces and pins,
In their hollow cave, while the Ocean's tides,
Murmuring with foam, flowed endlessly around.
No one knew I was there, neither god nor mortal,
Except my rescuers, Eurynome and Thetis.
Now the goddess has come to our house.
I owe her my life and would repay her in full.
Set out our finest for her, Charis,
While I put away my bellows and tools."

He spoke and raised his panting bulk                          440
Up from his anvil, limping along quickly
On his spindly shanks. He set the bellows
Away from the fire, gathered up the tools

He had been using, and put them away
In a silver chest. Then he took a sponge
And wiped his face and hands, his thick neck,
And his shaggy chest. He put on a tunic,
Grabbed a stout staff, and as he went out
Limping, attendants rushed up to support him,
Attendants made of gold who looked like real girls,                    450
With a mind within, and a voice, and strength,
And knowledge of crafts from the immortal gods.
These busily moved to support their lord,
And he came hobbling up to where Thetis was,
Sat himself down on a polished chair,
And clasping her hand in his, he said:

"My dear Thetis, so grave in your long robe,
What brings you here now? You almost never visit.
Tell me what you have in mind, and I will do it
If it is anything that is at all possible to do."                      460

And Thetis, shedding tears as she spoke:

"Hephaestus, is there a goddess on Olympus
Who has suffered as I have? Zeus son of Cronus
Has given me suffering beyond all the others.
Of all the saltwater women he singled me out
To be subject to a man, Aeacus' son Peleus.
I endured a man's bed, much against my will.
He lies in his halls forspent with old age,
But I have other griefs now. He gave me a son
To bear and to rear, the finest of heroes.                             470
He grew like a sapling, and I nursed him
As I would nurse a plant in my hillside garden,
And I sent him to Ilion on a sailing ship
To fight the Trojans. And now I will never
Welcome him home again to Peleus' house.
As long as he lives and sees the sunlight
He will be in pain, and I cannot help him.
The girl that the army chose as his prize
Lord Agamemnon took out of his arms.
He was wasting his heart out of grief for her,                         480

But now the Trojans have penned the Greeks
In their beachhead camp, and the Argive elders
Have petitioned him with a long list of gifts.
He refused to beat off the enemy himself,
But he let Patroclus wear his armor,
And sent him into battle with many men.
All day long they fought by the Scaean Gates
And would have sacked the city that very day,
But after Menoetius' valiant son
Had done much harm, Apollo killed him                              490
In the front ranks and gave Hector the glory.
So I have come to your knees, to see if you
Will give my son, doomed to die young,
A shield and helmet, a fine set of greaves,
And a corselet too. His old armor was lost
When the Trojans killed his faithful companion,
And now he lies on the ground in anguish."

And the renowned smith answered her:

"Take heart, Thetis, and do not be distressed.
I only regret I do not have the power                              500
To hide your son from death when it comes.
But armor he will have, forged to a wonder,
And its terrible beauty will be a marvel to men."

Hephaestus left her there and went to his bellows,
Turned them toward the fire and ordered them to work.
And the bellows, all twenty, blew on the crucibles,
Blasting out waves of heat in whatever direction
Hephaestus wanted as he hustled here and there
Around his forge and the work progressed.
He cast durable bronze onto the fire, and tin,                     510
Precious gold and silver. Then he positioned
His enormous anvil up on its block
And grasped his mighty hammer
In one hand, and in the other his tongs.

He made a shield first, heavy and huge,
Every inch of it intricately designed.

He threw a triple rim around it, glittering
Like lightning, and he made the strap silver.
The shield itself was five layers thick, and he
Crafted its surface with all of his genius.                                    520

On it he made the earth, the sky, the sea,
The unwearied sun, and the moon near full,
And all the signs that garland the sky,
Pleiades, Hyades, mighty Orion,
And the Bear they also call the Wagon,
Which pivots in place and looks back at Orion
And alone is aloof from the wash of Ocean.

On it he made two cities, peopled
And beautiful. Weddings in one, festivals,
Brides led from their rooms by torchlight                                      530
Up through the town, bridal song rising,
Young men reeling in dance to the tune
Of lyres and flutes, and the women
Standing in their doorways admiring them.
There was a crowd in the market-place
And a quarrel arising between two men
Over blood money for a murder,
One claiming the right to make restitution,
The other refusing to accept any terms.
They were heading for an arbitrator                                            540
And the people were shouting, taking sides,
But heralds restrained them. The elders sat
On polished stone seats in the sacred circle
And held in their hands the staves of heralds.
The pair rushed up and pleaded their cases,
And between them lay two ingots of gold
For whoever spoke straightest in judgment.

Around the other city two armies
Of glittering soldiery were encamped.
Their leaders were at odds—should they                                         550
Move in for the kill or settle for a division

Of all the lovely wealth the citadel held fast?
The citizens wouldn't surrender, and armed
For an ambush. Their wives and little children
Were stationed on the wall, and with the old men
Held it against attack. The citizens moved out,
Led by Ares and Pallas Athena,
Both of them gold, and their clothing was gold,
Beautiful and larger than life in their armor, as befits
Gods in their glory, and all the people were smaller.                    560
They came to a position perfect for an ambush,
A spot on the river where stock came to water,
And took their places, concealed by fiery bronze.
Farther up they had two lookouts posted
Waiting to sight shambling cattle and sheep,
Which soon came along, trailed by two herdsmen
Playing their panpipes, completely unsuspecting.
When the townsmen lying in ambush saw this
They ran up, cut off the herds of cattle and fleecy
Silver sheep, and killed the two herdsmen.                               570
When the armies sitting in council got wind
Of the ruckus with the cattle, they mounted
Their high-stepping horses and galloped to the scene.
They took their stand and fought along the river banks,
Throwing bronze-tipped javelins against each other.
Among them were Hate and Din and the Angel of Death,
Holding a man just wounded, another unwounded,
And dragging one dead by his heels from the fray,
And the cloak on her shoulders was red with human blood.
They swayed in battle and fought like living men,                        580
    And each side salvaged the bodies of their dead.


    On it he put a soft field, rich farmland
Wide and thrice-tilled, with many plowmen
Driving their teams up and down rows.
Whenever they came to the end of the field
And turned, a man would run up and hand them
A cup of sweet wine. Then they turned again
Back up the furrow pushing on through deep soil

To reach the other end. The field was black
Behind them, just as if plowed, and yet                          590
  It was gold, all gold, forged to a wonder.


  On it he put land sectioned off for a king,
Where reapers with sharp sickles were working.
Cut grain lay deep where it fell in the furrow,
And binders made sheaves bound with straw bands.
Three sheaf-binders stood by, and behind them children
Gathered up armfuls and kept passing them on.
The king stood in silence near the line of reapers,
Holding his staff, and his heart was happy.
Under an oaktree nearby heralds were busy                        600
Preparing a feast from an ox they had slaughtered
In sacrifice, and women were sprinkling it
  With abundant white barley for the reapers' dinner.


  On it he put a vineyard loaded with grapes,
Beautiful in gold. The clusters were dark,
And the vines were set everywhere on silver poles.
Around he inlaid a blue enamel ditch
And a fence of tin. A solitary path led to it,
And vintagers filed along it to harvest the grapes.
Girls, all grown up, and light-hearted boys                      610
Carried the honey-sweet fruit in wicker baskets.
Among them a boy picked out on a lyre
A beguiling tune and sang the Linos song
In a low, light voice, and the harvesters
  Skipped in time and shouted the refrain.


  On it he made a herd of straight-horn cattle.
The cows were wrought of gold and tin
And rushed out mooing from the farmyard dung
To a pasture by the banks of a roaring river,
Making their way through swaying reeds.                          620
Four golden herdsmen tended the cattle,
And nine nimble dogs followed along.
Two terrifying lions at the front of the herd
Were pulling down an ox. Its long bellows alerted
The dogs and the lads, who were running on up,

But the two lions had ripped the bull's hide apart
And were gulping down the guts and black blood.
The shepherds kept trying to set on the dogs,
But they shied away from biting the lions
    And stood there barking just out of harm's way.          630


    On it the renowned lame god made a pasture
In a lovely valley, wide, with silvery sheep in it,
    And stables, roofed huts, and stone animal pens.


    On it the renowned lame god embellished
A dancing ground, like the one Daedalus
Made for ringleted Ariadne in wide Cnossus.
Young men and girls in the prime of their beauty
Were dancing there, hands clasped around wrists.
The girls wore delicate linens, and the men
Finespun tunics glistening softly with oil.               640
Flowers crowned the girls' heads, and the men
Had golden knives hung from silver straps.
They ran on feet that knew how to run
With the greatest ease, like a potter's wheel
When he stoops to cup it in the palms of his hands
And gives it a spin to see how it runs. Then they
Would run in lines that weaved in and out.
A large crowd stood round the beguiling dance,
Enjoying themselves, and two acrobats
    Somersaulted among them on cue to the music.          650


    On it he put the great strength of the River Ocean,
Lapping the outermost rim of the massive shield.


And when he had wrought the shield, huge and heavy,
He made a breastplate gleaming brighter than fire
And a durable helmet that fit close at the temples,
Lovely and intricate, and crested with gold.
And he wrought leg-armor out of pliant tin.
And when the renowned lame god had finished this gear,
He set it down before Achilles' mother,
And she took off like a hawk from snow-capped Olympus,     660
Carrying armor through the sky like summer lightning.

# ILIAD 19

Dawn shrouded in saffron
Rose out of the deep water with light
For immortals and humans alike.
                              And Thetis
Came to the ships with Hephaestus' gifts.
She found her son lying beside
His Patroclus, wailing,
And around him his many friends,
Mourning. The silvery goddess
Stood in their midst, took his hand,                          10
Whispered his name, and said to him:

"Achilles, you must let him rest,
No matter our grief. This man was gentled
By the gods. But you, my son, my darling,
Take this glorious armor from Hephaestus,
So very beautiful, no man has ever worn
Anything like it."
                        She spoke,
And when she set the armor down before Achilles,
All of the metalwork clattered and chimed.                    20
The Myrmidons shuddered, and to a man
Could not bear to look at it. But Achilles,
When he saw it, felt his rage seep
Deeper into his bones, and his lids narrowed
And lowered over eyes that glared

374                                                   [1–17]

Like a white-hot steel flame. He turned
The polished weapons the god had given him
Over and over in his hands, and felt
Pangs of joy at all its intricate beauty.
And his words rose on wings                              30
To meet his mother:
                              "My mother,
A god has given me these weapons—no
Mortal could have made them—and it is time
I arm myself in them. But I am afraid
For Patroclus, afraid that flies
Will infest his wounds and breed worms
In his body, now the life is gone,
And his flesh turn foul and rotten."

The silver-footed goddess answered:                     40

"Do not let that trouble you, child.
I will protect him from the swarming flies
That infest humans slain in war.
Even if he should lie out for a full year
His flesh would still be as firm, or better.
But call an assembly now. Renounce
Your rage against Agamemnon.
Arm yourself for war and put on your strength."

Saying this, she multiplied his heroic temper.
Then she dripped ambrosia and ruby nectar              50
Through Patroclus' nostrils, to keep his flesh firm.

And then Achilles went along the shore
Etched in sunlight, and shouted so loud
That not only the heroes came out, but all those too
Who had spent the war among the encamped ships,
All the pilots and oarsmen and stewards and cooks—
They all came to the assembly then, because Achilles,
Who had abstained a long time, was back.
Limping along were the two veterans,
Battle-scarred Diomedes and brilliant Odysseus,        60
Badly wounded, using their spears as crutches.

They came in and sat at the front of the assembly,
And behind them came the warlord, Agamemnon,
Wounded himself (that spear thrust by Coön,
Son of Antenor, in a hard-fought battle).
When all of the Greeks were gathered together,
Swift-footed Achilles rose and addressed them:

"Well, son of Atreus, are either of us better off
For this anger that has eaten our hearts away
Like acid, this bitter quarrel over a girl?                    70
Artemis should have shot her aboard my ship
The day I pillaged Lyrnessus and took her.
Far fewer Greeks would have gone down in the dust
Under Trojan hands, while I nursed my grudge.
Hector and the Trojans are better off. But the Greeks?
I think they will remember our quarrel forever.
But we'll let all that be, no matter how it hurts,
And conquer our pride, because we must.
I hereby end my anger. There is no need for me
To rage relentlessly. But let's move quickly now                    80
To get our troops back into battle
So I can confront the Trojans and test their will
To bivouac among our ships. They will more likely
Be thankful to rest their knees at day's end,
If any of them gets out of this alive."

He spoke, and the Greeks cheered.
Peleus' great son had renounced his rage.

And then the warlord Agamemnon spoke
From where he sat, without rising among them:

"Friends, Danaan heroes, servants of Ares—                    90
It is right to listen to one who stands to speak
And unseemly for even a skilled orator
To interrupt him. Even if he could
Make himself heard above the crowd
He would be at a disadvantage.
What I have to say is for the son of Peleus,

But I want each one of you to mark my words.
There's not a Greek here who has not said
Spiteful things about me. But I am not to blame.
Zeus is, and Fate, and the Dark Avenger,	100
Who put a fit of madness on me, in public,
That day I robbed Achilles of his prize.
But what could I do? Gods decide everything.
Zeus' eldest daughter is the goddess Atê,
Who blinds everyone, a deadly power.
She has delicate feet, not made for the ground
But for treading on the skulls of men as she
Afflicts them. Now and again she pins one down.
Once she even blinded Zeus, who is, they say,
The best of all, human or divine—even him.	110
Hera, being female, hoodwinked him
On the day Alcmena was due to give birth
To mighty Heracles in coronated Thebes.
Zeus had made this boast to all the gods:
'Hear me, all you gods and goddesses,
While I say to you what is on my mind.
This day shall Eileithyia, midwife goddess,
Bring to light a man who shall rule his land,
One of the race of men who are of my own blood.'
And his lady, Hera, said to him craftily:	120
'Liar. You will never make this story come true.
I dare you to swear me a great oath, Olympian,
That whoever shall fall between a woman's legs today,
Provided he is one of your own bloodline,
Really will rule over all his neighbors.'
She spoke, and Zeus did not see through this trick
But swore a mighty oath, blinded as he was.
Hera shot down from the peak of Olympus
And came to Argos in Achaea, where she knew
That the strong wife of Sthenelus, Perseus' son,	130
Was in the seventh month of her pregnancy.
This child Hera brought to light prematurely,
But delayed Alcmena's, holding back the birth-spirits.
Then she brought the news to Zeus herself:
'Father Zeus, Lord of Lightning, important news:

A man has been born who will rule the Argives,
Eurystheus, born to Sthenelus, Perseus' son,
Of your own bloodline, fit to rule the Argives.'
This rankled deep in Zeus' heart. He seized Atê
By her rich bright hair, angry as can be,                           140
And swore a great oath that she would never again
Come to Olympus or to starry heaven.
Whirling her around he threw her from the sky
And she fell quickly to the fields of men.
The very thought of her would make him groan,
Especially when he saw his own dear son
Performing unseemly labors for Eurystheus.
That's how I felt when I saw great Hector
Slaughtering Argives at the sterns of our ships.
I could not forget Atê, who had made me blind.             150
Yes, I was blind. Zeus robbed me of my wits.
But I want to make reparation, generously.
Rouse yourself, and your soldiers, for battle.
I am here to promise you all of the gifts
Odysseus proposed in your hut last night.
Or wait, if you wish, though you are eager for war,
While my men start bringing things from my ship
So you can see that my gifts will please your heart."

And Achilles, strong and swift, answered him:

"Son of Atreus, most glorious Agamemnon,                    160
Whether you offer me gifts, as is right,
Or keep them, is your concern. War is mine.
Let's not waste any more time with speeches.
We have work to do. I want each one of you
To see Achilles fighting on the front line,
Destroying the Trojan ranks with his spear.
Have that image in mind as you fight your man."

Odysseus, the wily thinker, answered him:

"Achilles, we know how good you are,
But don't send our men out to fight the Trojans             170

Without any food in their stomachs.
It's not going to be a short battle
Once the two sides close and start feeling
The god's breath working inside them.
You should have our men go to their ships
For food and wine, and get their strength up.
No one can fight all day until sunset
On an empty stomach. He may have the heart,
But as hunger and thirst creep up on him,
His arms get heavy and his knees go slack.                    *180*
But a man who has had his fill of food and wine
Can fight all day long with confidence,
And stays strong until the last man quits. So come,
Dismiss the troops and have them prepare their meal.
As for the gifts, let Lord Agamemnon
Bring them out here, so that the whole army
Can see them. This will warm your heart.
And he should stand and swear a public oath
That he has not gone to the woman's bed.
You, Achilles, should be gracious about this,                    *190*
And then he should complete his amends
By feasting you richly, so you have all your due.
Next time, son of Atreus, you will act more justly,
But there is no cause at all for offense when kings
Make their amends for unprovoked anger."

And the warlord Agamemnon answered him:

"Son of Laertes, I am glad to hear your words.
You have laid it all out just as it should be.
I am ready and willing to swear this oath,
And I will not perjure myself. But Achilles                    *200*
Should wait here, eager as he is for war.
All should wait here assembled, until the gifts
Come from my hut, and we swear solemn oaths.
And I lay this charge upon you, Odysseus:
Choose the finest young men in all the army
And bring from my ships all the gifts
We promised Achilles yesterday, the women too.

And Talthybius will prepare a boar for me
To sacrifice before the army to Helios and Zeus."

But swift-footed Achilles answered him:                           210

"Son of Atreus, most glorious Agamemnon,
You should do all this at some other time
When there is a break in the war—
And when my rage is not so great.
Hector has beaten these men to death,
They are lying here mangled, he has the glory,
And you two want us to eat? If it were up to me
I'd have the troops out there fighting unfed,
No food all day. When the sun goes down
We can have a big meal, our shame avenged.                        220
Until then no food or drink will pass
My lips at least. My comrade is dead,
Lying in my hut mangled with bronze,
His feet turned toward the door, and around him
Our friends grieve. Nothing matters to me now
But killing, and blood, and men in agony."

And Odysseus, with his many wiles:

"Son of Peleus, strongest of the Achaeans,
Far stronger than me, certainly, with a spear,
Yet I might be better than you in council,                        230
Since I have lived longer and come to know more:
Have the patience to listen to my words.
Men quickly have their fill of battle, where
Moving blades litter the ground with stalks
But there's very little to reap after Zeus decides
The price in human lives with a tip of his scales.
We can't mourn the dead with our bellies.
There are too many corpses, and more each day.
When would anyone get time off from grief?
No, we have to bury all our dead,                                 240
Steel our hearts, and mourn them for a day.
The survivors must remember to eat and drink
So we can go on fighting, day after day, until

We wear out the enemy's bronze skin.

                              Let no man
Hold back awaiting some other call.
This is the call: There will be hell to pay
For any man who stays here with the ships.
Now let's move out. This is War."

Odysseus spoke and was off, taking with him             250
Nestor's sons Antilochus and Thrasymedes,
Along with Meriones and Lycomedes,
Meges the Doulichian, Thoas the Aetolian
And Melanippus. They all went straight
To Agamemnon's hut. No sooner said than done:
They brought out seven tripods, as promised,
A dozen bright cauldrons and as many horses,
And they quickly led out the women, faultless
In their handiwork, seven of these,
And Briseis made eight. Then Odysseus             260
Weighed out the full ten talents of gold
And led back the youths, who carried the gifts
And set them in the middle of the assembly grounds.
Agamemnon rose up, and Talthybius,
Whose voice was like a god's, stood beside him
Holding a boar. The son of Atreus
Drew the knife that hung by his sword scabbard
And cut the boar's hairs, then lifting his hands to Zeus,
He prayed, and all the Greeks sat silently,
In the proper way, each man listening to his king             270
As he spoke in prayer, looking at the sky:

    "Be Zeus my witness first,
    Highest and best of gods,
    And Earth, and Sun,
    And the Furies who underground
    Take vengeance on men
    Who break their oaths:
I swear I never laid a hand on the girl Briseis,
Either to bed her or for anything else,
But that she stayed untouched in my quarters.             280
    If any of what I swear is false

May the gods torment me
As a transgressor of oaths."

And he slashed the boar's throat with ruthless bronze.
Talthybius whirled and threw the carcass
Into the open sea to be food for fish. Then Achilles
Rose and addressed the war-loving Achaeans:

"Father Zeus, great is the blindness you send to men.
Else Atreus' son never would have roused my rage
Or insisted on leading the girl away                              290
Against my will. Somehow it has pleased Zeus
That many Greeks should die.
Now go to your meal, so we can join battle."

  The assembly broke up and the men scattered,
Each to his own ship. The Myrmidons got busy
With the gifts, bringing them to Achilles' ship.
They stored it all in his huts, left the women there,
And proudly drove the horses to the herd.

Briseis stood there like golden Aphrodite.

But when she saw Patroclus' mangled body                          300
She threw herself upon him and wailed
In a high, piercing voice, and with her nails
She tore her breast and soft neck and lovely face.
And this woman, so like a goddess, cried in anguish:

"My poor Patroclus. You were so dear to me.
When I left this hut you were alive,
And now I find you, the army's leader, dead
When I come back. So it is for me always,
Evil upon evil. I have seen my husband,
The man my father and mother gave me to,                          310
Mangled with sharp bronze before my city,
And my three brothers, all from the same mother,
Brothers I loved—they all died that day.
But you wouldn't let me cry when Achilles
Killed my husband and destroyed Mynes' city,

Wouldn't let me cry. You told me you'd make me
Achilles' bride, told me you'd take me on a ship
To Phthia, for a wedding among the Myrmidons.
I will never stop grieving for you, forever sweet."

Thus Briseis, and the women mourned with her,                    320
For Patroclus, yes, but each woman also
For her own private sorrows.

                              Around Achilles
The Achaean elders gathered, begging him to eat,
But he refused them, groaning:

                                "I beg you, my friends—
Aren't any of you listening? Don't keep asking me
To satisfy my heart with food or drink
Before it is time. My grief is too great.
I will stay as I am and endure until sunset."                    330

And he waved them off. Only Atreus' two sons
Remained with him, along with Odysseus,
Nestor, and the old charioteer, Phoenix,
Trying to comfort him in his grief's extremity.
But he could not be comforted. His heart would ache
Until he lost himself in war's blood-stained mouth.
Memories welled up and caught in his throat:

"There was a time, my ill-fated, beloved friend,
You would serve me a fine dinner in this hut,
Deftly and quickly, while the army hurried                       340
To bring war's sorrow to the horse-breaking Trojans.
Now you lie here a mangled corpse, and my heart
Fasts from the food and drink that are here
Out of grief for you. I could not suffer worse,
Not even if I learned my father were dead,
Who perhaps is weeping back in Phthia right now
Because he misses his son who is off fighting
On Trojan soil—for Helen, at whom we all shudder.
Not even if it were my son, Neoptolemus,
Who is being reared for me in Scyrus, if indeed                  350

My dear child is still alive. I had hoped,
Until now, that I alone would perish at Troy,
And that you would return, and take my boy
In your swift black ship away from Scyrus
And show him all my things back home in Phthia.
For Peleus by now must be dead and gone,
Or if he does still live he draws his breath in pain,
Clinging to a shred of life and always expecting
The grim message that will tell him I am dead."

He wept, and the elders added their laments to his,                    360
Each remembering what he had left at home.

Zeus saw them in their grief and, pitying them,
Spoke to Athena these feathered words:

"My child, have you deserted your warrior?
Do you no longer have any thought for Achilles?
He is mourning his friend, sitting there
In front of his upswept hulls. Everyone else
Has gone off to dinner, but he refuses to eat.
Go drip some nectar and savory ambrosia
Into his breast, so he will not weaken with hunger."       370

Athena needed no encouragement. She flew
From the crystal sky like a shrill raptor
And pounced on Achilles. The other Achaeans
Were busy arming for battle. Athena distilled
Nectar and ambrosia into Achilles' chest
So that grim hunger would not weaken his knees,
And then was gone, back to her father's house,
While the Greeks poured out from their beached ships.

> *Snow flurries can come so thick and fast*
> *From the cold northern sky that the wind*                        380
> *That bears them becomes an icy, blinding glare.*

So too the gleaming, polished weaponry—
The helmets, shields, spears, and plated corselets—
All the bronze paraphernalia of war

That issued from the ships. The rising glare
Reflected off the coppery sky, and the land beneath
Laughed under the arcing metallic glow.
A deep bass thrumming rose from the marching feet.

And, like a bronze bolt in the center, Achilles,
Who now began to arm.                                     *390*
                         His eyes glowed
Like white-hot steel, and he gritted his teeth
Against the grief that had sunk into his bones,
And every motion he made in putting on the armor
Forged for him in heaven was an act of passion
Directed against the Trojans: clasping on his shins
The greaves trimmed in silver at the ankles,
Strapping the corselet onto his chest, slinging
The silver-studded bronze sword around a shoulder,
And then lifting the massive, heavy shield                *400*
That spilled light around it as if it were the moon.

*Or a fire that has flared up in a lonely settlement*
*High in the hills of an island, reflecting light*
*On the faces of men who have put out to sea*
*And must watch helplessly as rising winds*
*Bear them away from their dear ones.*

So too the terrible beauty of Achilles' shield,
A fire in the sky.
                    He lifted the helmet
And placed it on his head, and it shone like a star,      *410*
With the golden horsehair Hephaestus had set
Thickly on the crest rippling in waves.
He tested the fit and flex of the armor,
Sprinting on the sand, and found that the metal
Lifted him like wings. He pulled from its case
His father's spear, the massive, heavy
Spear that only Achilles could handle,
Made of Pelian ash, which the centaur Chiron
Had brought down from Mount Pelion and given
To Achilles' father to be the death of heroes.            *420*
Automedon and Alcimus harnessed the horses,

Cinched the leather straps, fit the bits in their jaws
And drew the reins back to the jointed chariot.
Automedon picked up the bright lash
And jumped into the car, and behind him
Achilles stepped in, shining in his war gear
Like an amber Sun, and in a cold voice
He cried to his father's horses:

"Xanthus and Balius, Podarge's famous colts,
See that you bring your charioteer back                    430
Safe this time when we have had enough of war
And not leave him for dead, as you left Patroclus."

And from beneath the yoke Xanthus spoke back,
Hooves shimmering, his head bowed so low
That his mane swept the ground, as Hera,
The white-armed goddess, gave him a voice:

"This time we will save you, mighty Achilles,
This time—but your hour is near. We
Are not to blame, but a great god and strong Fate.
Nor was it slowness or slackness on our part                    440
That allowed the Trojans to despoil Patroclus.
No, the best of gods, fair-haired Leto's son,
Killed him in the front lines and gave Hector the glory.
As for us, we could outrun the West Wind,
Which men say is the swiftest, but it is your destiny
To be overpowered by a mortal and a god."

Xanthus said this; then the Furies stopped his voice.
And Achilles, greatly troubled, answered him:

"I don't need you to prophesy my death,
Xanthus. I know in my bones I will die here                    450
Far from my father and mother. Still, I won't stop
Until I have made the Trojans sick of war."

And with a cry he drove his horses to the front.

# ILIAD 20

While the Greeks armed themselves by their ships
Around you, Achilles, the vortex of war,
And while the Trojans waited for them on the high plain,
Zeus ordered Themis to call the gods to assembly.
She ranged far along Olympus' ridgeline,
Commanding them to come to the house of Zeus.
They all came—every last river (except Ocean)
And every last spirit-woman who ever haunted
A pretty copse, spring, or meadow—
They all came to the house of Zeus in the clouds          10
And sat in the stone colonnades that Hephaestus,
The master architect, had built for his father.
They were all inside when Poseidon came up
From the sea. Not even he could ignore
The goddess' call. He took a seat
In the middle and asked Zeus his purpose:

   "Lord of Lightning,
Why have you assembled the gods?
Are you pondering the Greek-Trojan issue
Now that the fighting has flared up again?"          20

And Zeus, who masses the clouds:

"Earthshaker, you know my purpose.
I care for them, even though they die.

Even so, I will stay in a crevice of Olympus
And sit and watch and take my pleasure.
   The rest of you
Can go out among the Greeks and Trojans
And help whichever side you please.
If Achilles is the only one fighting out there,
The Trojans won't last a minute against him.                        30
The very sight of him used to make them tremble,
And now he is in his passion. I fear
He may exceed his fate and demolish the wall."

With these words Zeus unleashed the war,
And the gods joined the battle on different sides.

On the Greek side were Hera and Pallas Athena,
And Poseidon Earthshaker and Hermes
The Helper, his mind sharp as needles,
And Hephaestus, who exuded strength
Though he limped along on his spindly legs.                        40

The Trojans got Ares, his helmet flashing,
Apollo and the archer goddess Artemis,
Leto, Xanthus, and smiling Aphrodite.

As long as the gods had been on the sidelines,
The Greeks kept on winning: Achilles'
Reappearance after his absence from the war
Had reduced the Trojans to spineless jelly.
They quivered helplessly when they saw the hero
Glowing in metal like the War God himself.
But when the Olympians joined the human fray,                        50
Strife, who drives armies on, lifted her head,
And Athena shouted, now by the trench,
Then long cries from the beach where the surf pounded in.
On the other side Ares responded,
Roaring to the Trojans like a dark whirlwind
On the city's height, then swooping down
Along the Simois' banks and across Callicolonê.

In this way the gods prompted the two armies
To clash in combat. Strife exploded in each camp.
Overhead, the Father of gods and men thundered,                60
And Poseidon shook all the ground underneath,
And the tremors climbed the steep mountain slopes.
Ida shuddered from her roots to her peaks,
Along with Troy herself and the Achaean ships.
And in the world below the Lord of the Shades,
Unseen Hades, leapt from his throne and shrieked,
Terrified that Poseidon would crack open the earth
And his halls would lie open to immortals and men,
The moldering horror loathed even by the gods.

Such was the force of the gods in collision.                   70

       Opposite Lord Poseidon
Stood Phoebus Apollo with fletched arrows.
Taking on Ares was grey-eyed Athena.
Up against Hera went Apollo's sister,
Golden Artemis, the huntress with her bow.
Leto was countered by Hermes the Ally,
And against Hephaestus rolled the deep river
The gods call Xanthus, and men Scamander.

  So god went up against god.

                       Achilles, though,             80
Wanted to take on no one but Hector.
It was Hector's blood that he wanted
To glut Ares' thick belly. But it was Aeneas,
Not Hector, that Apollo put up to fight
Peleus' son, and gave him the courage to do so.
Disguising himself as Lycaon, one of Priam's sons,
And imitating his voice, Apollo said:

"What about all those boasts, Aeneas,
To the Trojan princes over your wine
That you would take on Achilles man to man?"              90

Aeneas had this to say in answer:

"Why ask me to do something I'd rather not—
Fight the hero Achilles, son of Peleus?
This won't be the first time I've faced his speed.
Once before he chased me off with his spear,
From Ida, when he came after our cattle
And wasted Lyrnessus and Pedasus. Zeus
Pulled me out then, put some zip in my knees,
Or Achilles and Athena would have blasted me.
She was there in front of him lighting things up,                     100
Had him skewer Leleges and other Trojans.
There's no way for a man to fight Achilles.
Some god is always there to protect him.
Not that his spear doesn't fly straight by itself
Or doesn't stop until it draws blood. But if a god
Were to level the playing field, he wouldn't beat me
Easily, even if he could brag he were solid bronze."

And Zeus' son, Lord Apollo:

"Why not pray to the gods and get on with it?
You're a hero too. They say Zeus' daughter,                           110
Aphrodite, bore you. He's from a lesser god,
His mother being born from the Old Man of the Sea.
Go right at him with your bronze, and don't let him
Turn you back with all his taunts and threats."

And he breathed strength into the field marshal,
Who strode to the front corseleted in light.
Hera saw Anchises' son as he advanced
Through the throng to confront Achilles.
She huddled her gods and said to them:

"Poseidon and Athena, what about this?                                120
There goes Aeneas in full blazing armor
Against Achilles, and it's Apollo who sent him.
Come on, then, and let's turn him back,

Or let's one of us at least stand by Achilles
And give him strength, keep up his morale,
So he'll know that the best of the gods love *him*
And the others are worthless as wind, all those
Divinities who have protected Troy in this war.
We've all come down from Olympus to fight
So that Achilles will not be hurt by the Trojans                    130
For this one day. Later he must suffer
Whatever Fate has spun at his birth.
If he doesn't hear this from the voice of a god,
He may lose heart when a god attacks him.
Gods are daunting when they appear as they are."

Poseidon Earthshaker answered her:

"There's no need to get all worked up, Hera.
I would not wish to have the gods in conflict.
Let's find some out-of-the-way lookout
And have a seat. Leave the war to men.                              140
If Ares or Phoebus Apollo starts something,
Or holds Achilles back and won't let him fight,
Then we can get involved in the action,
And before long they will take themselves out
And go back to the other gods on Olympus,
Overpowered by our invincible hands."

So saying, the blue-maned god led the way
To that high heap of a wall the Trojans
And Pallas Athena had built for Heracles
To help him escape from the sea monster                             150
When it chased him from shore to plain.
There Poseidon and his companions sat down,
Their shoulders mantled with banks of cloud.


Opposite them the other gods sat
On Callicolonê's brows, around you,
My Lord Apollo, and Ares the Plunderer.

So the two sides sat, planning strategies
But reluctant to commence hostilities,
Even with permission from Zeus on high.

The whole plain was filled with horses and men                    160
And the glint of bronze, and the earth trembled
Under their tramping feet. As the troops advanced,
Two heroes, eager for combat, moved forth
To face each other in no-man's land,
Anchises' son Aeneas and noble Achilles.
Aeneas strode out first, helmet nodding
With every threatening step, war shield
Curved around his chest, bronze spear poised.

Then Achilles began to close ground quickly.

*A marauding lion has been hunted down*                           170
*By an entire village determined to kill him.*
*At first he ignores them and goes his way,*
*But then one of the young men wounds him*
*With a spearcast, and he gathers himself,*
*Crouching with mouth open, foam*
*Flecking his teeth, and, growling deep in his chest,*
*He lashes his flanks and ribs with his tail,*
*Working himself into a frenzy. Eyes glaring,*
*He charges, carried forward by sheer passion,*
*And no one can tell if he will kill or be killed.*                180

Thus were Achilles' mood and temper
As he closed in on great Aeneas.

When they were within each other's range
The shining sprinter was the first to speak:

"Aeneas, what are you doing out here in front?
Have you taken a mind to fight with me
Because you hope to inherit Priam's honor
Among the Trojans? Even if you kill me

Priam's not going to hand his kingship to you.
He has sons of his own, and he's not senile yet.          *190*
Or have the Trojans cut a deal for you,
Some choice real estate in orchards and plowland
For you to possess—if only you kill me.
You won't find that easy. If I remember right,
I've chased you off with my spear once before,
When I made you run from your cattle,
Careening down Ida's slopes. You never looked back,
Ran all the way to Lyrnessus, which I then sacked
By the grace of Athena and Father Zeus.
I took the women captive and led them off,                *200*
But you were saved by Zeus and other gods.
I rather doubt he will save you today,
Which you seem to be counting on. My advice
Is for you to get back to your troops
Before you get hurt. Fools learn the hard way."

Aeneas had this to say in reply:

"Don't think you can scare me off with words,
Son of Peleus, as if I were a child.
I can trade insults pretty well myself. We know
Each other's ancestry, each other's parents                *210*
From hearing the old stories. I've never seen
Your parents, as you have never seen mine,
But men say that Peleus is your father
And Thetis, the saltwater woman, your mother.
I boast that I am the son of great Anchises
And that Aphrodite is my mother.
One set of these parents will mourn a dear son
This day, because we're not going to settle this
With childish words and walk off from battle.
But if you really do want to hear my story,               *220*
You're welcome to listen. Many men know it.
   Cloud-herding Zeus first bore Dardanus,
Who founded Dardania. Sacred Ilion
Was not yet a town on the plain. The people then
All lived on the slopes of spring-dotted Ida.

Dardanus' son was King Erichthonius,
Who became the richest of mortal men,
With three thousand horses in marshland pasture,
All of them fine mares with tender foals.
The North Wind lusted for them as they grazed                230
And mated with them as a blue-maned stallion.
They conceived and gave birth to a dozen fillies
Who could prance over a field of grain
And not ever break a tasselled ear,
Who could bound over the sea's broad back
With their hooves on the crests of the breaking waves.
Erichthonius begot Tros to rule the Trojans,
And then from Tros three peerless sons were born,
Ilus, Assaracus, and Ganymedes,
A godlike man, the most beautiful mortal,                    240
Whom the gods snatched up because of his beauty
To pour for Zeus and live with the immortals.
Then Ilus had a son, peerless Laomedon,
And Laomedon begot Tithonus, Priam,
Clytius, and Hicetaon, a scion of Ares.
Assaracus begot Capys, and he Anchises.
Anchises begot me, and Priam Hector.
These are my bloodlines, my proud lineage.
But Zeus gives men their worth, or lessens it,
As he wills, since he is strongest of all.                   250
At any rate, let's stop talking like children
As we stand here in the heat of battle.
We could trade a boatload of insults
And not reach the end. Men's tongues are glib,
And we have words for everything.
Whatever you say, you'll hear back again.
Why should we wrangle like angry women
Quarreling in the street, all worked up,
Saying anything, whether it's true or not?
Battle is what I want, and nothing you can say            260
Can turn me back from it, man to man with sharp bronze.
Come on, let's see what it tastes like."

With that, he drove his heavy spear
Into the metal circles of Achilles' shield,

Making it clang like a cymbal. Achilles
Tightened his grip and held the shield forward,
Afraid that Aeneas' tree of a spear
Would come all the way through—a foolish notion:
He had forgotten that the gods' gloried gifts
Do not fail, nor do men easily foil them.                           270
Aeneas' war spear broke through
Two layers of the shield, but the gold layer,
Hephaestus' special gift, stopped it.
And there were still two more, for the lame god
Had welded five: two bronze, two tin,
And the gold that stopped the ash-wood spear.

Achilles now threw his long-shadowed spear
And hit the disk of Aeneas' shield
Beneath the outer rim, where the bronze
And oxhide ran thinnest. The Pelian ash                             280
Shot right through. The shield gave a loud crack,
And Aeneas held it away and cringed
While the spear rocketed over his back
And stuck in the earth, taking two circles
Of the shield with it. Having dodged the missile,
Aeneas rose in a state of shock at how close
The spear stood to him. Achilles drew his sword
And leapt at him with a bloodcurdling yell.
Aeneas recovered quickly and picked up a stone
That two men—as men go now—couldn't lift,                          290
But which he handled easily. In an instant
Aeneas would have hit the charging Achilles
With that stone, on his helmet or on the shield
That had just saved him, and Peleus' son
Would have killed Aeneas in close combat,
But Poseidon had all this in sharp focus
And spoke in that moment among the immortals:

"Alas for great-hearted Aeneas, who will now
Be killed by Achilles and go down to Hades
Because he innocently obeyed Apollo,                                300
Who will do nothing to keep him from perishing.
Why should he, a guiltless man, now suffer

For the woes of others, a man who has always
Pleased the gods in heaven with his offerings?
Let us deliver him from the shadow of death.
Zeus will be angry if Achilles kills him,
For it is destined that Aeneas escape
And the line of Dardanus not be destroyed
And disappear without seed—Dardanus,
Whom Zeus loved more than any of the sons                310
Born from his union with mortal women.
The son of Cronus has come to hate Priam's line,
And now Aeneas will rule the Trojans with might,
And the sons born to his sons in the future."

The ox-eyed lady Hera replied:

"As for Aeneas, Earthshaker, you should do
Whatever seems best, whether to save him
Or have Achilles kill him, good man though he be.
But we two, Pallas Athena and I,
Have taken oaths among all the immortals                 320
Never to ward off doom for the Trojans,
Not even when the whole city goes up in flames,
Burned by the warlike youth of Greece."

When he heard this, the earthquaking god
Went his way through the battlefield
And the moving spears until he came
To where Aeneas was, and glorious Achilles.
He poured a mist over Achilles' eyes
And drew his bronze-tipped, ash-wood spear
From the remnants of Aeneas' shield                      330
And placed it before Achilles' feet.
Aeneas he swung up from the ground
And sent sailing over row after row
Of heroes and horses in an immortal vault
From the god's hand, to land finally
On the perimeter of the battlefield,
Where the Caucones were arming themselves.

Poseidon came up very close,
And his words flew into Aeneas' ears:                          340

"Aeneas, what god hoodwinked you
Into fighting with Peleus' high-hearted son,
A better man than you and dearer to the gods?
Draw back whenever you encounter him
Or else enter Hades before your doom.
When Achilles has met his own destined death,
Take courage and fight among the foremost,
For no other Achaean will take your life."

Poseidon left him with this revelation,
Then quickly scattered from Achilles' eyes
The magic mist. Achilles stared hard                           350
And, deeply troubled, said to himself:

"This is a miracle right before my eyes.
My spear's on the ground, but the man I threw it at,
Trying to kill him, is nowhere in sight.
It seems Aeneas really is dear to the gods.
I thought he was just boasting. To hell with him!
He'll never have the guts to face me again,
Glad as he must be to have gotten off this time.
Well, I'd better call up our war-loving troops
And try my hand with the rest of the Trojans."          360

He leapt along the ranks and called to each man:

"Greeks! Close this ground and engage the enemy
Man to man. I want to see some spirit!
Do you think I can fight all those men by myself?
Not even Ares, an immortal, or Athena
Could close this battle's jaws alone.
I'll shoulder as much of this as I can
And I don't think I'll come up short—
Break right through their lines and ruin the day
Of any Trojan who comes close to my spear."             370

That was his exhortation. Hector responded
By promising the Trojans he would face Achilles:

"Trojans! Don't be afraid of Peleus' son.
I could fight the immortals too—with words.
It's harder with a spear. They're much too strong.
Nor will Achilles accomplish all he says.
He'll finish some and leave the rest half done.
I'm going after him, even if he has hands of fire,
Hands of fire, and fury like cold steel."

Thus Hector. The Trojans lifted their spears                    380
In response, and the battle was on. Amid the noise
Phoebus Apollo stood near Hector and said:

"Do not challenge Achilles, Hector.
Wait for him in the throng to lessen the chance
Of being hit by his spear or his sword close in."

Hector fell back when he heard this,
Terrified by the voice of the speaking god.

But Achilles sprinted into the Trojans,
With a cold yell. He first killed Iphition,
Commander of a large contingent.                               390
This man was the son of Otrynteus,
A raider of cities, and a water nymph
Who bore him under snowy Tmolus
In the rich land of Hyde. Achilles' spear
Split his head in two as he came on,
And he fell heavily. Achilles crowed:

"Lie there, son of Otrynteus,
Iphition, most formidable of men.
Dead here, born there—by Lake Gygaea,
Your ancestral land, near the Hyllus, isn't it?—            400
Where the fish teem and the Hermus swirls."

He spoke, but Iphition lay folded in darkness,

And his body was soon shredded
By the metal rims of Greek chariot wheels.

Next came Demoleon, Antenor's son,
A good soldier. Achilles pierced his temple
Through his helmet's bronze cheek pieces.
The spear's business end sheared right through
Bronze and bone, scrambling the skull's contents
And stopping him cold.                                              410

                        Hippodamas had jumped
From his chariot and was running the other way
When Achilles' spear landed in his back.
He gasped and then bellowed,

                                    *the way a bull*
    *Will bellow when dragged by young men*
    *Around Poseidon's altar in Helice,*
    *Making the Earthshaker beam with pleasure.*

Hippodamas' manly spirit left his bones.

Achilles went next after Polydorus,                                420
Priam's son. His father would not allow him
To fight at all, since he was his youngest
And the apple of his eye. He was the fastest too,
And now he was childishly showing off
Just how fast he was, running through the front lines
Until he lost his life. Achilles, the great sprinter,
Hit him in the back as he flashed by,
The spear going through just where the corselet
Folded under the golden clasps of his belt
And exiting just beside his navel.                                 430
He fell to his knees with a groan, and as he sank
In the dark mist, he clutched his bowels to him.

When Hector saw his brother Polydorus
Sinking to the earth with his entrails in his hands
Everything turned hazy. No longer able

To pace the sidelines, he came at Achilles,
His spear like a branch of flame. When Achilles
Saw who he was, he was exultant:

"Here he is, the man who has reamed my heart,
Who has killed my noble friend. Not for long          440
Will we skirt each other in the battle lanes."

And with a dark scowl he called to Hector:

"Keep on coming. You're as good as dead."

And Hector, without a trace of fear:

"Don't think you can scare me off with words,
Son of Peleus, as if I were a child.
I can trade insults with the best of them.
I know you're really good, a lot better than me,
But it is up to the gods to decide whether I,
A lesser man, will rob you of life with my spear.          450
It's been proven to have an edge before."

And he poised his spear and let it fly,
But Athena blew it away from Achilles
Wafting it back with the lightest of breaths
To fall at Hector's feet. Achilles charged
With a terrifying yell, his whole being
Inspired to kill. But the god Apollo
Whisked Hector away, as only a god can,
And swirled fog around him. Three times
The shining sprinter charged with his bronze spear,          460
And three times he struck nothing but deep mist.
On his fourth, last charge he howled to the winds:

"You've escaped death again, dog!
Apollo saved you in another close call.
You must pray to him every time you go out.
But I'll get you yet, next time we meet,
If I have a god to help me too. For now,
I'll make do with whoever comes my way."

And he put his spear through Dryops' neck,
Dropping him at his feet. He left him there                    470
And took out Demuchus, Philetor's tall son,
First hitting him on the knee with his spear,
Then finishing him off with his sword.
Bias' two sons, Laogonus and Dardanus,
He shoved from their chariot, killing one
With a spearcast, the other in close with his sword.
And then Tros, Alastor's son, tried to clasp
Achilles' knees to see if he would spare him,
Take him captive and then let him go
And not kill him because they were the same age.            480
He actually thought he would persuade him,
But this was a man with no gentleness in him,
A man with one purpose. As Tros clasped his knees
In supplication, Achilles shoved his sword
Down into his liver. The liver slid out
Into Tros' lap with a clot of black blood,
And the world went dark as he expired.
Achilles was already upon Mulius,
Putting his bronze javelin through one ear
And all the way out the other, while,                       490
In almost the same motion, he struck
Agenor's son Echeclus full on the head
With his hilted sword. Echeclus' blood
Warmed the whole blade, and death came
In an overpowering violet haze.
Deucalion was next, Achilles' spearpoint
Piercing his elbow just where the sinews join.
His arm hung uselessly as he stood there
Staring death in the face. Achilles closed in
And sliced into his neck, sending the head,                  500
Helmet and all, flying through the air.
Marrow spurted up through his spinal cord,
And then the corpse was lengthwise on the ground.
Rhigmus, Peiros' peerless son, had come
From farm country in Thrace. Achilles' spear
Transfixed him and stuck in his belly.
He fell from his chariot, and as his driver,
Areïthous, was turning the horses around

Achilles hit him in the back, the blow
Pushing him from his car. The horses ran wild.                              510

>    *Fire raging through a parched forest*
>    *In a mountain valley, when the wind rises*
>    *And spirals the flames in every direction*

Will give you some idea of Achilles' presence
As the black earth ran with blood.

>    *A team of broad-browed oxen has been yoked*
>    *And is now treading white barley*
>    *On a solid threshing floor. It does not take long*
>    *For the bellowing bulls to tread out the grain.*

So the hooves of Achilles' horses trampled                                 520
Dead bodies, shields. The chariot's axle
And rails were splashed with blood
Kicked up by the wheels and horses' hooves.
But the son of Peleus pressed on to glory,
His invincible hands spattered with gore.

# ILIAD 21

When they came to the ford of Xanthus,
The eddying river that Zeus begot,
Achilles split the Trojans.

                    Half he chased
Toward the city, across the plain where yesterday
The Greeks had fled from Hector's shining rage.
Hera, to slow this stampede of Trojans,
Spread a curtain of fog before them.

                    The others swerved—
And found themselves herded into the river.                    10
They crashed down into the deep, silver water
As it tumbled and roared through its banks.
You could hear their screams as they floundered
And were whirled around in the eddies.

*Fire will sometimes cause a swarm of locusts*
*To rise in the air and fly to a river. The fire*
*Keeps coming, burning them instantly,*
*And the insects shrink down into the water.*

Just so Achilles. And Xanthus' noisy channel
Was clogged with chariots, horses, and men.                    20

Achilles wasted no time. Leaving his spear
Propped against a tamarisk
And holding only his sword, he leapt from the bank
Like a spirit from hell bent on slaughter.
He struck over and over, in a widening spiral.
Hideous groans rose from the wounded,
And the river water turned crimson with blood.

> *Fish fleeing a dolphin's huge maw*
> *Hide by the hundreds in the harbor's crannies,*
> *But the dolphin devours whatever it catches.*                    30

Likewise the Trojans beneath the riverbanks.

When Achilles' hands were sore from killing,
He culled twelve boys live from the river
To pay for the blood of dead Patroclus.
They were dazed as fawns when he led them out,
Their hands bound behind them with the leather belts
They had been wearing around their corded tunics.
Achilles' men led them back to the ships
And Achilles returned to his killing frenzy.

On the way back he met a son of Priam,                             40
Lycaon by name, running from the river.
This boy Achilles had captured once before
In his father's orchard, where he had come one night
To cut fig saplings for chariot rails
But found Achilles' iron mask in his face.
That time Achilles sold him, for a good price,
To Jason's son on Lemnos, where he had shipped him.
A family friend, Eëtion of Imbros, had ransomed him
For even more money and sent him to Arisbe.
From there he managed to make his way home.                        50
For eleven days he celebrated with friends
His escape from Lemnos. On the twelfth day Zeus
Gave him back to Achilles, who would send him now
Off again against his will, this time to Hades.
He was all but naked when Achilles noticed him,

Having discarded helmet, spear, and shield
Because they made him sweat as he clambered
Up from the river, and his knees were giving out.
Achilles was indignant and said to himself:

"What's this I see? The Trojan princes I've killed          60
Are going to start rising from the moldering gloom,
Judging from how this one has escaped his fate
After being shipped off to Lemnos and sold.
All that grey sea couldn't keep him back.
Let's give him a taste of my spearhead
And see whether he comes back from that
Or stays put in the teeming earth."

And he waited. Lycaon aproached in a daze,
Intent on grasping his knees. All he wanted
Was to wriggle away from death and black fate.          70
All Achilles wanted was to run him through.
His spear flashed out, but Lycaon, stooping
To touch his knees, ducked under it. The spear
Passed over his back and stuck in the earth,
Quivering with desire for a man's flesh.
Lycaon caught Achilles' knees with one hand
And held the pointed spear with the other
And would not let go of either as he begged:

"I am at your knees, Achilles. Pity me.
You have to respect me as your suppliant          80
For I tasted Demeter's holy grain with you
On that day you took me captive in the orchard
And sent me far from my father and friends,
Sold into sacred Lemnos for a hundred oxen.
I ransomed myself for three times that. This morning
Was my twelfth since getting back to Ilion
After many hard turns. And now Fate
Has put me in your hands again. Father Zeus
Must hate me to give me to you twice.
My mother bore me for a shortened life,          90
Laothoë, old Altes' daughter, Altes,

Lord of the Leleges, whose stronghold
Is steep Pedasus on the Satnioeis.
Priam had his daughter as one of his wives,
And we're her two sons, and you'll butcher us both.
Godlike Polydorus you've already killed,
Got him with your spear as he led the charge.
And now this is it for me. I doubt I can escape,
Since it was some god who put me in your hands.
But I'll say this too, and you can think it over:          100
Don't kill me, since I'm not from the same womb
As Hector, who killed your gentle, valiant friend."

Priam's glorious son spoke words of entreaty,
But heard a voice without a trace of softness say:

"Shut up, fool, and stop talking ransom.
Before Patroclus met his destiny
It was more to my taste to spare Trojan lives,
Capture them, and sell them overseas.
But now they all die, every last Trojan
God puts into my hands before Ilion's walls,          110
All of them, and especially Priam's children.
You die too, friend. Don't take it hard.
Patroclus died, and he was far better than you.
Take a look at me. Do you see how huge I am,
How beautiful? I have a noble father,
My mother was a goddess, but I too
Am in death's shadow. There will come a time,
Some dawn or evening or noon in this war,
When someone will take my life from me
With a spear thrust or an arrow from a string."          120

He spoke. Lycaon's knees and heart went slack.
He let go the spear and sat there, both hands
Outstretched. Achilles drew his honed sword
And struck near the collar bone. The whole blade
Sank into his trunk, and he fell prone to the ground,
Black blood trickling out and wetting the dirt.
Achilles slung him into the river by his foot
And crowed over him as the current bore him off:

"Lie there with the fish. They will lick the blood
From your wound, your cold funeral rites. Your mother          *130*
Will not lay you on a bier and lament. No,
Eddying Scamander will roll you out to sea,
And fish will dart up under the black ripples
And nibble at Lycaon's shining fat.
All of you Trojans will die like that,
Die all the way back to Troy's sacred town
As I whittle you down from behind!
Your river won't help you with his silver eddies,
The water you've sanctified no doubt with bulls
And with live horses thrown into his pools.
No, you'll all die, die ugly deaths, until you have paid       *140*
For the Greeks' loss, for Patroclus dead,
Killed by the ships while I was away."

As he spoke the river roiled in wrath
And pondered how to foil Achilles' efforts
And save the Trojans from this pestilence.

Meanwhile Achilles attacked Asteropaeus,
Son of that Pelagon who was born of a river,
The wide Axius, who lay with Periboea,
Eldest of the daughters of Acessamenus.                        *150*
As Achilles charged him, Asteropaeus,
Carrying two spears, stepped from the river
To face him, his courage coming from Xanthus,
Who was angry because of all the young men
Cut down in his stream by Achilles.
When they were within range of each other
The shining sprinter addressed Asteropaeus:

"Who are you, with the nerve to face me,
And where are you from? It's your parents' loss."

Pelegon's glorious son answered him:                           *160*

"Why ask about my lineage, son of Peleus?
I come from Paeonian soil, a distant land,
And I led its spearmen here to Ilion

Eleven days ago. My lineage
Is from wide-flowing Axius, whose river water
Flows loveliest on the face of the earth.
Pelegon was his son and my father, men say.
Now let's do battle, glorious Achilles."

It was a threat, and as Achilles raised high
His spear of Pelian ash, Asteropaeus,                           170
Who was ambidexterous, hurled both his spears.
One hit Achilles' shield but did not penetrate,
Stopped by the layer of god-given gold.
The other spear grazed his raised right forearm,
Drawing a welt of black blood and sailing on
Until it punched into earth unsatisfied.
Then it was Achilles' turn, and he rifled his shaft
At Asteropaeus with murderous aim
But missed the man, the ashen spear
Boring into the bank up to half its length.                     180
Drawing his sharp sword from beside his thigh
The son of Peleus made a furious leap,
And in the space of that leap, Asteropaeus
Tried once, twice, three times
To pull Achilles' spear from the bank
But only got it to quiver. The fourth time
He tried desperately to break the shaft,
But Achilles got to him first with a quick slash
Across his belly. His guts oozed out,
And he went down gasping in darkness.                           190
Achilles jumped on his chest, and as he
Ripped off his armor, his boasts rang out:

"Lie there like that! Sons of Zeus almighty
Are too tough for even a river's offspring.
You say you are born from a wide-flowing river,
But I boast that I am descended from Zeus.
My father rules the Myrmidons, Peleus,
Son of Aeacus, and Aeacus came from Zeus.
And just as Zeus is stronger than any river,

Zeus' sons are stronger than any river's sons.                    *200*
There's a great river beside you right now,
If he can help, but no one fights Zeus,
Not even the great Achelous, not even Ocean,
From whose deeps every river and sea,
Every spring and well flows. Even he fears
The lightning of Zeus and his crackling thunder."

He pulled his bronze spear from the bank
And left Asteropaeus lying in the sand,
Quite dead. The dark water lapped at his body,
And the eels and fish went to work on him,                        *210*
Nibbling at the fat around his kidneys.
Achilles' next move was to go after
The Paeonian charioteers along the river.
They were in shock at what they had just seen,
Their best man and leader utterly destroyed
By one strong swipe of Achilles' sword.
He killed them easily—Thersilochus, Mydon,
Astypylus, Mnesus, Thrasius, Aenius,
Ophelestes—and with his blinding speed
He would have killed more, had not the River,                     *220*
Assuming human semblance, called to Achilles
In a voice that came deep from his eddies:

"Achilles, you are stronger and do more harm
Than any man, for the very gods assist you.
If Zeus has allowed you to kill all the Trojans,
At least drive them from me, and do it on the plain.
My beautiful streams are clogged with dead men,
I can no longer pour my waters into the sea,
Choked with corpses, while you blindly go on killing.
Let it be. I am stunned, O warlord!"                              *230*

And Achilles, the great sprinter:

"As you wish, sky-bred Scamander.
But I will not stop killing these insolent Trojans

Until I have penned them all inside their city
And taken on Hector. It's him or me now."

And he leapt on the Trojans like a god.
Then the swirling River spoke to Apollo:

"Silverbow, child of Zeus! You have not kept
His stern commandment to stand by the Trojans
And aid them until the evening comes on                          240
And shadows darken the planet's deep soil."

He spoke, and Achilles took a flying leap
Off the bank and came down in midstream.
The River rushed upon him in full spate
And with all the force of its current swept along
The bodies of Achilles' many victims
And washed them ashore, roaring like a bull.
At the same time he sheltered the living
In deep pools where his water flowed smooth.
Around Achilles the wall of water arched high                    250
And pushed against his shield. He lost his footing
And grasped at an elm, a tall, stately tree,
But it fell uprooted, and tearing away the bank
Crashed with its thick branches into the water,
Bridging the river's width. Achilles jumped out
And, afraid now, began to sprint across the plain.
But the great god wouldn't stop, chasing him
With a black crest, determined to stop
The shining sprinter and save Troy from ruin.
Achilles got about a spearcast ahead, swooping                   260

> *Like a black eagle, the great raptor*
> *That is strongest and swiftest of all winged things,*

The bronze plate clanging on his chest
As he leaned into his stride to escape the River
That followed him with a tremendous roar.

> *A farmer has dug an irrigation ditch*
> *To lead the water from a dark spring*

Into his garden plots. Now, hoe in hand,
He is knocking out the dams from the channel,
And the water sweeps all the pebbles                         270
Along the bottom as it sluices down,
And the man leading the water is left behind.

So the River kept overtaking Achilles,
Fast as he was: Gods are stronger than men.

Whenever Achilles tried to make a stand
And put up a fight (and see if perhaps
All the gods in heaven weren't pursuing him),
The sky-swollen River would pound
On his shoulders, and Achilles would jump.
His morale was sinking. The strong current                   280
Was wearing his knees out and cutting the ground
From under his feet. With a look at the sky,
The son of Peleus cried out in distress:

"Father Zeus, not a single god is stepping in
To save me from the River, pitiful as I am!
If I escape this, I don't mind dying later.
I blame my mother more than any deity,
With her lullabies that I would meet my death
Under Ilion's walls, shot by Apollo.
Better to be killed by Hector, Troy's best,                  290
One good man killed by another.
As it is, I am doomed to a wretched death,
Caught in this river, like a swineherd boy
Swept away while crossing a winter torrent."

Then Poseidon and Athena were with him,
In human form, clasping his hands
And pledging support, Poseidon saying:

"Fear not, son of Peleus, nor be afraid.
Two gods are with you, with Zeus' consent,
Pallas Athena and I. It is not your doom                     300
To be vanquished by a River.
He will soon relent, as you will see yourself.

We have good counsel for you to accept.
Do not cease from war until you have driven
All the Trojans who escape from your hands
Within Ilion's walls. When you have killed Hector,
Return to the ships. We grant you this glory."

And they were off to the company of spirits,
While Achilles, aroused by the gods' command,
Turned toward the plain. It was all flooded now,          310
Awash with splendid gear and the floating corpses
Of slain young men. Achilles sprinted hard
Straight into the current, and the wide River
Could not hold him back. Athena's strength was in him.
But Scamander was still in spate, and raged
Even more strongly against Peleus' son.
Lifting his waters into an arching wave,
He surged to a crest and called Simois:

"Join with me, brother, to hold in check
This human's strength, or he will soon storm          320
Lord Priam's great city. The Trojans can't stop him.
Help me beat him back now. Fill your currents
With water from your springs, rouse your torrents,
Raise a great wave and make it churn and rumble
With logs and stones so we can stop this wild man
Who thinks he can fight on par with the gods.
His strength will not help him, nor his beauty,
Nor his splendid armor, which will lie deep in slime,
And I will shroud his body in tons and tons
Of pebbly sand, nor shall the Achaeans know          330
Where to find his bones, so deep the silt
I will bury him in. This will be his monument.
No need to heap a mound for his funeral."

And he arched high over Achilles—boiling
And seething with foam, blood, and corpses,
The livid surge of the sky-swollen River
Cresting and poised to overwhelm Peleus' son.
Hera shrieked, terrified that the great River
Would sweep Achilles away in its current.

She called to her son Hephaestus and said:                          *340*

"Let's go, Clubfoot! We thought that you
Were matched up with Xanthus. Hurry up
And show your fire here, and I'll rouse up
Onshore winds from the west and south
To drive your flames over the Trojan dead
And burn them and their gear to a crisp.
You burn the trees around Xanthus' banks
And surround him with fire. Don't back off
No matter how he whines or threatens.
Keep the pressure on until you hear me shout."              *350*

So Hephaestus kindled his fire,
And it swept across the plain, burning the dead,
The many corpses left by Achilles,
And evaporating the glittering water.

> *Late in the summer, the North Wind*
> *Dries out a freshly watered orchard,*
> *And the man who tills the orchard is glad.*

The plain was parched, and the dead consumed.

Then the Fire moved toward the River.
The elms, the willows, and the tamarisks burned,            *360*
The lotus, the rushes, and the galingale
That grew lush on the beautiful riverbanks, burned.
The eels and the fish in the eddying pools,
Tortured by the heat Hephaestus concocted,
Plunged and darted through the glassy currents.
The River itself burned, and pleaded with the god:

"Hephaestus, no god can oppose you,
And I will not fight you in your blaze of fire.
Stop! As for the Trojans, let bright Achilles
Drive them from Ilion. I will not help or hinder."          *370*

And as he spoke, his water seethed

*As if in a cauldron set on a fire*
*Stoked with kindling, boiling to melt*
*Rich hog fat, and bubbling over.*

The River burned, and his water boiled,
Impossible for it to flow any further
In the tormenting blast of Hephaestus' heat.
Then his words rose up on wings to Hera:

"Hera, why has your son singled me out
For punishment. I am not so guilty,                                    380
In your eyes, as Troy's other allies.
But I will stop if you order me to.
Make him stop too. And I will swear
Not to ward off Ilion's doom
On that day when Troy goes up in flames,
Burned by the warlike youth of Greece."

Ivory-armed Hera heard his plea
And spoke to her darling son Hephaestus:

"Hephaestus, my glory, hold back. It is not right
To attack an immortal for the sake of a mortal,"                        390

So Hephaestus quenched his fire,
And the river Xanthus flowed again,
But its fury was quelled. Hera,
Though angry herself, had calmed these two.

The other gods, though, were at each others' throats,
Clashing like contrary winds. At the force
Of their collision the earth clanged like a cymbal
And the sky blared like a trumpet. Zeus,
Sitting on Olympus, took it all in
And laughed with delight at the spectacle                              400
Of the gods closing with each other in combat.

Ares began with an assault on Athena,
Landing in front of her with a bronze spear:

"What are you doing now, dogfly,
Setting the gods against each other
Whatever way your high spirits dictate.
Remember when you goaded on Diomedes
To wound me? With everyone watching
You guided the spear into my noble flesh.
You'll pay the price now for what you did then."          410

And he stabbed at her tasselled aegis,
Which not even Zeus' lightning can pierce.
Athena backpedalled from his bloody snout
And scooped up a jagged piece of black granite
That lay on the plain, a huge boundary stone
From days gone by. It flew from her sculpted hand
And caught Ares on the neck. His knees buckled
And he went down, covering a good acre or two,
Hair grimed with dust, armor clattering around him.
Athena broke into a laugh and crowed:          420

   "You simpleton!
You still haven't learned that I'm too strong
For you, or you wouldn't try to match up with me.
Maybe this is what your mother wanted
When she cursed you for abandoning the Greeks
And giving aid and comfort to the Trojans."

And while she turned her luminous eyes away,
Aphrodite came up and led him off by the hand,
Groaning heavily. He was barely conscious.
Ivory-armed Hera took notice of this,          430
And her words took wing to Pallas Athena:

"Mystic daughter of Zeus, that bloated tick
Is leading Ares out of battle. Get on her!"

Athena was only too glad to comply,
Charging Aphrodite and punching her
In the breast with her clenched fist. Aphrodite
Collapsed in a heap, taking Ares down with her.

The two of them lay on the teeming sod,
And Athena's boast flew up to the sky:

"May everyone who fights for Troy                          440
Against the Greeks wind up like this,
And may they all be as brave as Aphrodite was
When she helped Ares and confronted me.
We would have ended this war a long time ago
And destroyed Ilion's foundation stone."

This brought a smile to Hera's lips.
Then Lord Poseidon spoke to Apollo:

"Phoebus, why are we two holding back?
It's not fitting. All the others have started.
More shame on us if we return to Olympus              450
And cross Zeus' bronze threshold without fighting.
You start, since you're younger. It would not be
Proper for me, since I am older and know more.
Has your mind gone soft? Don't you remember
The suffering we two, alone of all the gods,
Endured at Ilion that time we came here
From Zeus' side and served proud Laomedon
For a year at fixed wages. He was our boss,
And I built for the Trojans their city wall,
Wide and beautiful, to make Ilion invulnerable.        460
And you, Phoebus, herded their cattle
In the wooded foothills of ridged Mount Ida.
But when the year was up and the time came
For us to be paid, Laomedon outrageously
Robbed us of our wages, threatening
To bind us hand and foot and sell us off
To distant islands, and to lop off our ears.
So back we went, angry and disgruntled
Over the wages he promised but did not pay.
It is his people you are favoring now                     470
When you should instead be working with us
For the utter destruction of these insolent Trojans
Together with their children and blushing wives."

And Apollo, Lord of the Distances:

"Earthshaker, you would call me imprudent
If I fought with you for the sake of mortals,
Pitiful creatures who like leaves on a tree
Flame briefly to life, eat the fruit of the fields,
Then wither and die. No, we should desist
Immediately and let them fight on their own."          480

And Apollo withdrew, too well-bred
To slug it out with his paternal uncle.
But his hellcat sister Artemis,
Queen of wild things, reviled him mercilessly:

"Running away, Apollo? What a collapse!
Poseidon can claim an easy victory now.
That bow you carry is as worthless as wind.
Don't let me catch you bragging again,
As you always used to in our father's house,
That you would take on Poseidon in open combat."       490

Apollo turned away without a word,
But Zeus' august wife was furious with her:

"Do you think you can cross me like this,
You bitch? I'm not an easy opponent
For the likes of you, even if you do
Carry a bow—Zeus' little lioness,
With license to kill whatever woman you please.
You'd do better to hunt wild game, deer
In the woods, than tangle with your betters.
But if you want a taste of war, you might as well      500
Find out how undermatched you are against me."

She seized her wrists with her left hand
And ripped the bow from her shoulders
With her right, and with a smile on her face
Used these weapons to beat her about the ears
As she twisted and squirmed, spilling the arrows

Out of her quiver. She finally got away
And fled from Hera, weeping, as a dove
Flies from a falcon into a cleft in the rock,
Leaving her bow and arrows on the ground.                    510
At this, Hermes turned to Leto and said:

"Tell you what, Leto, I won't fight with you.
Zeus' wives are pretty tough customers.
You have my permission to boast openly
That you have beaten the daylights out of me."

Thus Hermes, and Leto gathered up
Her daughter's curved bow and arrows
From the swirling dust, and then withdrew.
Artemis crossed Zeus' bronze threshold
And sat down sobbing on her father's lap,                    520
Her fragrant robe fluttering. He held her tight,
And laughing pleasantly, asked her:

"Which god has done this to you, child?
Outrageous. It's not as if you would misbehave."

And the huntress, ribbons in her hair:

"Your wife Hera beat me up, father.
She's always causing trouble among the gods."

And while they talked in heaven,
Phoebus Apollo entered sacred Ilion,
Afraid that the Greeks would breach its wall                 530
And exceed their destiny that very day.
The other immortals went to Olympus,
Some of them angry and some jubilant,
And they sat down around their father,
The Dark Cloud.

                    Meanwhile, Achilles
Was still killing Trojans, both men and horses.

*When a city burns, the smoke rises*
*To the wide heavens, and the gods' wrath*
*Fans the fire and drives it on.*                                    540
*Everyone suffers, many grievously.*

Such was the suffering Achilles caused the Trojans.

Old Priam stood on Troy's sacred wall.
He saw Achilles as a prodigious force
Before whom the Trojans were being driven
Helplessly. Groaning, he climbed down to the ground
And called to the gatekeepers along the wall:

"Hold the gates wide open until the army
Can run inside the city. Achilles is here
Driving them on, and I fear the worst.                              550
When they are all inside and can rest,
Close the double doors tight. I dread the thought
Of that monster leaping inside the wall."

He spoke, they thrust back the bars,
And light poured from the gates. Apollo
Leapt out to keep Achilles from Troy.

The Trojans were streaming toward the city's high walls,
Parched with thirst and white with dust from the plain,
With Achilles at their backs with his spear,
Maniacal in his rage and lust for glory.                            560

The Greeks would have taken Troy right then
Had not Apollo lifted Antenor's son,
Agenor, to one bright, peerless moment.
He put into his heart the fortitude
To defend himself from Death's heavy hands,
Then stood nearby, leaning on the oak tree
And enfolded in mist. So when Agenor
Caught sight of Achilles, sacker of cities,
He halted. His heart brooded darkly,
And with a sense of great oppression he said:                       570

"Now I'm in for it. If I run from Achilles
The way the others are, like panicked animals,
He'll catch me anyway and butcher me like a lamb.
   But what if I let these others go,
Let them be driven by Achilles, and run myself
Away from the wall, toward the Ilean plain
Until I reach the foothills of Ida
And hide out in the thickets? Toward evening
I could bathe in the river, cool off,
And maybe make it back to Troy.                                580
   Why am I talking to myself like this?
It's all over if he spots me turning off
Away from the city and toward the plain.
He'll chase me down with his great speed
And then there'll be no way to escape from death,
Since he is far stronger than any man alive.
Then why not face him in front of the city?
His skin is not impervious to bronze,
And he only has one life in him.
Everyone says he is human. It's just that                     590
Zeus, son of Cronus, gives him glory."

And he crouched to await Achilles' onset,
Heart pumping, ready for battle.

   *A leopard steps out from the deep bush*
   *In full sight of a hunter, completely unafraid.*
   *Even if she hears the hounds baying,*
   *She will not turn tail and run, and even if*
   *The human is lucky enough to strike first*
   *And hit her with his spear, she will not give up,*
   *But will fight on with the spear in her body*          600
   *Until she is killed—or gets her claws in him.*

So too Agenor, lord Antenor's son,
Would not give up until he had tested Achilles.
He poised his balanced shield before him,
Took aim at Achilles, and shouted:

"I'll bet you hope to capture Troy today,
Don't you, Achilles the Splendid?
You fool! There's still a lot of sorrow
To be endured for her sake, and within her
Our many brave men standing before    610
Our parents, our wives, and our sons
And protecting Ilion. No, it is you
Who will meet your doom today,
I don't care how great a warrior you are."

And the javelin flew from his heavy hand
Hitting Achilles' shin just beneath the knee.
The newly-forged tin greave clanged loudly
And the bronze spearpoint ricocheted off
The armor that the god had given him.
It was Achilles' turn to charge Agenor,   620
But Apollo denied him victory,
Snatching Agenor off in a curtain of mist,
And escorting him softly out of battle.
Then, with a ruse, Apollo got the son of Peleus
Away from the Trojan army. Likening himself
To Agenor in every detail, he stood
Just before Achilles, who gave chase,
Pursuing him across the plain, then turning him
Along the banks of the swirling Scamander.
All the while Apollo, beguiling him,   630
Stayed just out of reach, and Achilles,
With his footspeed, thought he would catch him.

This bought time for the panicked Trojans
To swarm gratefully into the city.
They no longer had the will to wait for each other
Outside the city walls to see who had made it
And who had died in battle. Everyone
Whose legs could carry him stampeded in.

# ILIAD 22

Everywhere you looked in Troy, exhausted
Soldiers, glazed with sweat like winded deer,
Leaned on the walls, cooling down
And slaking their thirst.
                              Outside, the Greeks
Formed up close to the wall, locking their shields.
In the dead air between the Greeks
And Troy's Western Gate, Destiny
Had Hector pinned, waiting for death.

Then Apollo called back to Achilles:                              10

"Son of Peleus, you're fast on your feet,
But you'll never catch me, man chasing god.
Or are you too raging mad to notice
I'm a god? Don't you care about fighting
The Trojans anymore? You've chased them back
Into their town, but now you've veered off here.
You'll never kill me. You don't hold my doom."

And the shining sprinter, Achilles:

"That was a dirty trick, Apollo,
Turning me away from the wall like that!                              20

I could have ground half of Troy face down
In the dirt! Now you've robbed me
Of my glory and saved them easily
Because you have no retribution to fear.
I swear, I'd make you pay if I could!"

His mind opened to the clear space before him,
And he was off toward the town, moving

*Like a thoroughbred stretching it out*
*Over the plain for the final sprint home—*

Achilles, lifting his knees as he lengthened his stride.          30

Priam saw him first, with his old man's eyes,
A single point of light on Troy's dusty plain.

*Sirius rises late in the dark, liquid sky*
*On summer nights, star of stars,*
*Orion's Dog they call it, brightest*
*Of all, but an evil portent, bringing heat*
*And fevers to suffering humanity.*

Achilles' bronze gleamed like this as he ran.

And the old man groaned, and beat his head
With his hands, and stretched out his arms               40
To his beloved son, Hector, who had
Taken his stand before the Western Gate,
Determined to meet Achilles in combat.

Priam's voice cracked as he pleaded:

"Hector, my boy, you can't face Achilles
Alone like that, without any support—
You'll go down in a minute. He's too much
For you, son, he won't stop at anything!
O, if only the gods loved him as I do:

Vultures and dogs would be gnawing his corpse.                    50
Then some grief might pass from my heart.
So many fine sons he's taken from me,
Killed or sold them as slaves in the islands.
Two of them now, Lycaon and Polydorus,
I can't see with the Trojans safe in town,
Laothoë's boys. If the Greeks have them
We'll ransom them with the gold and silver
Old Altes gave us. But if they're dead
And gone down to Hades, there will be grief
For myself and the mother who bore them.                          60
The rest of the people won't mourn so much
Unless *you* go down at Achilles' hands.
So come inside the wall, my boy.
Live to save the men and women of Troy.
Don't just hand Achilles the glory
And throw your life away. Show some pity for me
Before I go out of my mind with grief
And Zeus finally destroys me in my old age,
After I have seen all the horrors of war—
My sons butchered, my daughters dragged off,                      70
Raped, bedchambers plundered, infants
Dashed to the ground in this terrible war,
My sons' wives abused by murderous Greeks.
And one day some Greek soldier will stick me
With cold bronze and draw the life from my limbs,
And the dogs that I fed at my table,
My watchdogs, will drag me outside and eat
My flesh raw, crouched in my doorway, lapping
My blood.
                    When a young man is killed in war,            80
Even though his body is slashed with bronze,
He lies there beautiful in death, noble.
But when the dogs maraud an old man's head,
Griming his white hair and beard and private parts,
There's no human fate more pitiable."

And the old man pulled the white hair from his head,
But did not persuade Hector.

                                    His mother then,
Wailing, sobbing, laid open her bosom
And holding out a breast spoke through her tears:          90

"Hector, my child, if ever I've soothed you
With this breast, remember it now, son, and
Have pity on me. Don't pit yourself
Against that madman. Come inside the wall.
If Achilles kills you I will never
Get to mourn you laid out on a bier, O
My sweet blossom, nor will Andromache,
Your beautiful wife, but far from us both
Dogs will eat your body by the Greek ships."

So the two of them pleaded with their son,               100
But did not persuade him or touch his heart.
Hector held his ground as Achilles' bulk
Loomed larger. He waited as a snake waits,

*Tense and coiled*
*As a man approaches*
*Its lair in the mountains,*
*Venom in its fangs*
*And poison in its heart,*
*Glittering eyes*
*Glaring from the rocks:*                                 110

So Hector waited, leaning his polished shield
Against one of the towers in Troy's bulging wall,
But his heart was troubled with brooding thoughts:

"Now what? If I take cover inside,
Polydamas will be the first to reproach me.
He begged me to lead the Trojans back
To the city on that black night when Achilles rose.
But I wouldn't listen, and now I've destroyed
Half the army through my recklessness.
I can't face the Trojan men and women now,          120
Can't bear to hear some lesser man say,

'Hector trusted his strength and lost the army.'
That's what they'll say. I'll be much better off
Facing Achilles, either killing him
Or dying honorably before the city.
   But what if I lay down all my weapons,
Bossed shield, heavy helmet, prop my spear
Against the wall, and go meet Achilles,
Promise him we'll surrender Helen
And everything Paris brought back with her                        130
In his ships' holds to Troy—that was the beginning
Of this war—give all of it back
To the sons of Atreus and divide
Everything else in the town with the Greeks,
And swear a great oath not to hold
Anything back, but share it all equally,
All the treasure in Troy's citadel.
   But why am I talking to myself like this?
I can't go out there unarmed. Achilles
Will cut me down in cold blood if I take off              140
My armor and go out to meet him
Naked like a woman. This is no time
For talking, the way a boy and a girl
Whisper to each other from oak tree or rock,
A boy and a girl with all their sweet talk.
Better to lock up in mortal combat
As soon as possible and see to whom
God on Olympus grants the victory."

Thus spoke Hector.
                        And Achilles closed in              150
Like the helmeted God of War himself,
The ash-wood spear above his right shoulder
Rocking in the light that played from his bronze
In gleams of fire and the rising sun.
And when Hector saw it he lost his nerve,
Panicked, and ran, leaving the gates behind,
With Achilles on his tail, confident in his speed.

   *You have seen a falcon*
   *In a long, smooth dive*

*Attack a fluttering dove*                           160
*Far below in the hills.*
*The falcon screams,*
*Swoops, and plunges*
*In its lust for prey.*

So Achilles swooped and Hector trembled
In the shadow of Troy's wall.
                         Running hard,
They passed Lookout Rock and the windy fig tree,
Following the loop of the wagon road.
They came to the wellsprings of eddying              170
Scamander, two beautiful pools, one
Boiling hot with steam rising up,
The other flowing cold even in summer,
Cold as freezing sleet, cold as tundra snow.
There were broad basins there, lined with stone,
Where the Trojan women used to wash their silky clothes
In the days of peace, before the Greeks came.

They ran by these springs, pursuer and pursued—
A great man out front, a far greater behind—
And they ran all out. This was not a race           180
For such a prize as athletes compete for,
An oxhide or animal for sacrifice, but a race
For the lifeblood of Hector, breaker of horses.

*But champion horses wheeling round the course,*
*Hooves flying, pouring it on in a race for a prize—*
*A woman or tripod—at a hero's funeral games*

Will give you some idea of how these heroes looked
As they circled Priam's town three times running
  While all the gods looked on.

Zeus, the gods' father and ours, spoke:             190

"I do not like what I see, a man close
To my heart chased down around Troy's wall.
Hector has burned many an ox's thigh

To me, both on Ida's peaks and in the city's
High holy places, and now Achilles
Is running him down around Priam's town.
Think you now, gods, and take counsel whether
We should save him from death or deliver him
Into Achilles' hands, good man though he be."

The grey-eyed goddess Athena answered:                    200

   "O Father,
You may be the Lord of Lightning and the Dark Cloud,
But what a thing to say, to save a mortal man,
With his fate already fixed, from rattling death!
Do it. But don't expect us all to approve."

Zeus loomed like a thunderhead, but answered gently:

"There, there, daughter, my heart wasn't in it.
I did not mean to displease you, my child. Go now,
Do what you have in mind without delay."

Athena had been longing for action                    210
And at his word shot down from Olympus,

As Achilles bore down on Hector.

   *A hunting hound starts a fawn in the hills,*
   *Follows it through brakes and hollows,*
   *And if it hides in a thicket, circles,*
   *Picks up the trail, and renews the chase.*

No more could Hector elude Achilles.
Every time Hector surged for the Western Gate
Under the massive towers, hoping for
Trojan archers to give him some cover,                    220
Achilles cut him off and turned him back
Toward the plain, keeping the inside track.

   *Running in a dream, you can't catch up,*
   *You can't catch up and you can't get away.*

No more could Achilles catch Hector
Or Hector escape.
                And how could Hector
Have ever escaped death's black birds
If Apollo had not stood by his side
This one last time and put life in his knees?      230

Achilles shook his head at his soldiers:
He would not allow anyone to shoot
At Hector and win glory with a hit,
Leaving him only to finish him off.

But when they reached the springs the fourth time,
Father Zeus stretched out his golden scales
And placed on them two agonizing deaths,
One for Achilles and one for Hector.
When he held the beam, Hector's doom sank down
Toward Hades. And Phoebus Apollo left him.      240

By now the grey-eyed goddess Athena
Was at Achilles' side, and her words flew fast:

"There's nothing but glory on the beachhead
For us now, my splendid Achilles,
Once we take Hector out of action, and
There's no way he can escape us now,
Not even if my brother Apollo has a fit
And rolls on the ground before the Almighty.
You stay here and catch your breath while I go
To persuade the man to put up a fight."      250

Welcome words for Achilles. He rested,
Leaning on his heavy ash and bronze spear,
While the goddess made her way to Hector,
The spitting image of Deïphobus.
And her voice sounded like his as she said:

"Achilles is pushing you hard, brother,
In this long footrace around Priam's town.
Why don't we stand here and give him a fight?"

Hector's helmet flashed as he turned and said:

"Deïphobus, you've always been my favorite                    260
Brother, and again you've shown me why,
Having the courage to come out for me,
Leaving the safety of the wall, while all
Priam's other sons are cowering inside."

And Athena, her eyes as grey as winter moons:

"Mother and father begged me by my knees
To stay inside, and so did all my friends.
That's how frightened they are, Hector. But I
Could not bear the pain in my heart, brother.
Now let's get tough and fight and not spare          270
Any spears. Either Achilles kills us both
And drags our blood-soaked gear to the ships,
Or he goes down with your spear in his guts."

That's how Athena led him on, with guile.
And when the two heroes faced each other,
Great Hector, helmet shining, spoke first:

"I'm not running any more, Achilles.
Three times around the city was enough.
I've got my nerve back. It's me or you now.
But first we should swear a solemn oath.               280
With all the gods as witnesses, I swear:
If Zeus gives me the victory over you,
I will not dishonor your corpse, only
Strip the armor and give the body back
To the Greeks. Promise you'll do the same."

And Achilles, fixing his eyes on him:

"Don't try to cut any deals with me, Hector.
Do lions make peace treaties with men?
Do wolves and lambs agree to get along?
No, they hate each other to the core,                   290
And that's how it is between you and me,

No talk of agreements until one of us
Falls and gluts Ares with his blood.
By God, you'd better remember everything
You ever knew about fighting with spears.
But you're as good as dead. Pallas Athena
And my spear will make you pay in a lump
For the agony you've caused by killing my friends."

With that he pumped his spear arm and let fly.
Hector saw the long flare the javelin made, and ducked.     *300*
The bronze point sheared the air over his head
And rammed into the earth. But Athena
Pulled it out and gave it back to Achilles
Without Hector noticing. And Hector,
Prince of Troy, taunted Achilles:

"Ha! You missed! Godlike Achilles! It looks like
You didn't have my number after all.
You said you did, but you were just trying
To scare me with big words and empty talk.
Did you think I'd run and you'd plant a spear     *310*
In my back? It'll take a direct hit in my chest,
Coming right at you, that and a god's help too.
Now see if you can dodge this piece of bronze.
Swallow it whole! The war will be much easier
On the Trojans with you dead and gone."

And Hector let his heavy javelin fly,
A good throw, too, hitting Achilles' shield
Dead center, but it only rebounded away.
Angry that his throw was wasted, Hector
Fumbled about for a moment, reaching     *320*
For another spear. He shouted to Deïphobus,
But Deïphobus was nowhere in sight.
It was then that Hector knew in his heart
What had happened, and said to himself:

"I hear the gods calling me to my death.
I thought I had a good man here with me,
Deïphobus, but he's still on the wall.

Athena tricked me. Death is closing in
And there's no escape. Zeus and Apollo
Must have chosen this long ago, even though　　　330
They used to be on my side. My fate is here,
But I will not perish without some great deed
That future generations will remember."

And he drew the sharp broadsword that hung
By his side and gathered himself for a charge.

> *A high-flying eagle dives*
> *Through ebony clouds down*
> *To the sun-scutched plain to claw*
> *A lamb or a quivering hare*

Thus Hector's charge, and the light　　　　　　340
That played from his blade's honed edge.

Opposite him, Achilles exploded forward, fury
Incarnate behind the curve of his shield,
A glory of metalwork, and the plumes
Nodded and rippled on his helmet's crest,
Thick golden horsehair set by Hephaestus,
And his spearpoint glinted like the Evening Star

> *In the gloom of night*
> *Star of perfect splendor,*

A gleam in the air as Achilles poised　　　　　　350
His spear with murderous aim at Hector,
Eyes boring into the beautiful skin,
Searching for the weak spot. Hector's body
Was encased in the glowing bronze armor
He had stripped from the fallen Patroclus,
But where the collarbones join at the neck
The gullet offered swift and certain death.
It was there Achilles drove his spear through
As Hector charged. The heavy bronze apex

Pierced the soft neck but did not slit the windpipe,                360
So that Hector could speak still.

He fell back in the dust.

And Achilles exulted:

"So you thought you could get away with it
Didn't you, Hector? Killing Patroclus
And ripping off his armor, *my* armor,
Thinking I was too far away to matter.
You fool. His avenger was far greater—
And far closer—than you could imagine,
Biding his time back in our beachhead camp.                370
And now I have laid you out on the ground.
Dogs and birds are going to draw out your guts
While the Greeks give Patroclus burial."

And Hector, barely able to shake the words out:

"I beg you, Achilles, by your own soul
And by your parents, do not
Allow the dogs to mutilate my body
By the Greek ships. Accept the gold and bronze
Ransom my father and mother will give you
And send my body back home to be burned                380
In honor by the Trojans and their wives."

And Achilles, fixing him with a stare:

"Don't whine to me about my parents,
You dog! I wish my stomach would let me
Cut off your flesh in strips and eat it raw
For what you've done to me. There is no one
And no way to keep the dogs off your head,
Not even if they bring ten or twenty
Ransoms, pile them up here and promise more,
Not even if Dardanian Priam weighs your body                390

Out in gold, not even then will your mother
Ever get to mourn you laid out on a bier.
No, dogs and birds will eat every last scrap."

Helmet shining, Hector spoke his last words:

"So this is Achilles. There was no way
To persuade you. Your heart is a lump
Of iron. But the gods will not forget this,
And I will have my vengeance on that day
When Paris and Apollo destroy you
In the long shadow of Troy's Western Gate."        400

Death's veil covered him as he said these things,
And his soul, bound for Hades, fluttered out
Resentfully, forsaking manhood's bloom.

He was dead when Achilles spoke to him:

"Die and be done with it. As for my fate,
I'll accept it whenever Zeus sends it."

And he drew the bronze spear out of the corpse,
Laid it aside, then stripped off the blood-stained armor.
The other Greeks crowded around
And could not help but admire Hector's                410
Beautiful body, but still they stood there
Stabbing their spears into him, smirking.

"Hector's a lot softer to the touch now
Than he was when he was burning our ships,"

One of them would say, pulling out his spear.

After Achilles had stripped the body
He rose like a god and addressed the Greeks:

"Friends, Argive commanders and councillors,
The gods have granted us this man's defeat,

Who did us more harm than all the rest                    420
Put together. What do you say we try
Laying a close siege on the city now
So we can see what the Trojans intend—
Whether they will give up the citadel
With Hector dead, or resolve to fight on?
  But what am I thinking of? Patroclus' body
Still lies by the ships, unmourned, unburied,
Patroclus, whom I will never forget
As long as I am among the living,
Until I rise no more; and even if                    430
In Hades the dead do not remember,
Even there I will remember my dear friend.
  Now let us chant the victory paeon, sons
Of the Achaeans, and march back to our ships
With this hero in tow. The power and the glory
Are ours. We have killed great Hector,
Whom all the Trojans honored as a god."

But it was shame and defilement Achilles
Had in mind for Hector. He pierced the tendons
Above the heels and cinched them with leather thongs    440
To his chariot, letting Hector's head drag.
He mounted, hoisted up the prize armor,
And whipped his team to a willing gallop
Across the plain. A cloud of dust rose
Where Hector was hauled, and the long black hair
Fanned out from his head, so beautiful once,
As it trailed in the dust. In this way Zeus
Delivered Hector into his enemies' hands
To be defiled in his own native land.

Watching this from the wall, Hector's mother           450
Tore off her shining veil and screamed,
And his old father groaned pitifully,
And all through town the people were convulsed
With lamentation, as if Troy itself,
The whole towering city, were in flames.
They were barely able to restrain

The old man, frantic to run through the gates,
Imploring them all, rolling in the dung,
And finally making this desperate appeal:

"Please let me go, alone, to the Greek ships.                460
I don't care if you're worried. I want to see
If that monster will respect my age, pity me
For the sake of his own father, Peleus,
Who is about my age, old Peleus
Who bore him and bred him to be a curse
For the Trojans, but he's caused me more pain
Than anyone, so many of my sons,
Beautiful boys, he's killed. I miss them all,
But I miss Hector more than all of them.
My grief for him will lay me in the earth.                  470
Hector! You should have died in my arms, son!
Then we could have satisfied our sorrow,
Mourning and weeping, your mother and I."

The townsmen moaned as Priam was speaking.
Then Hecuba raised the women's lament:

"Hector, my son, I am desolate!
How can I live with suffering like this,
With you dead? You were the only comfort
I had, day and night, wherever you were
In the town, and you were the only hope                     480
For Troy's men and women. They honored you
As a god when you were alive, Hector.
Now death and doom have overtaken you."

And all this time Andromache had heard
Nothing about Hector—news had not reached her
That her husband was caught outside the walls.
She was working the loom in an alcove
Of the great hall, embroidering flowers
Into a purple cloak, and had just called
To her serving women, ordering them                         490
To put a large cauldron on the fire, so

A steaming bath would be ready for Hector
When he came home from battle. Poor woman,
She had little idea how far from warm baths
Hector was, undone by the Grey-Eyed One
And delivered into the hands of the Greeks.

Then she heard the lamentation from the tower.

She trembled, and the shuttle fell
To the floor. Again she called her women:

"Two of you come with me. I must see                    500
What has happened. That was Hecuba's voice.
My heart is in my throat, my knees are like ice.
Something terrible has happened to one
Of Priam's sons. O God, I'm afraid
Achilles has cut off my brave Hector
Alone on the plain outside the city
And has put an end to my husband's
Cruel courage. Hector never held back
Safe in the ranks; he always charged ahead,
Second to no one in fighting spirit."                   510

With these words on her lips Andromache
Ran outdoors like a madwoman, heart racing,
Her two waiting-women following behind.
She reached the tower, pushed through the crowd,
And looking out from the wall saw her husband
As the horses dragged him disdainfully
Away from the city to the hollow Greek ships.

Black night swept over her eyes.
She reeled backward, gasping, and her veil
And glittering headbands flew off,                      520
And the diadem golden Aphrodite
Gave her on that day when tall-helmed Hector
Led her from her father's house in marriage.
And now her womenfolk were around her,
Hector's sisters and his brother's wives,

Holding her as she raved madly for death,
Until she caught her breath and her distraught
Spirit returned to her breast. She moaned then
And, surrounded by Trojan women, spoke:

"Hector, you and I have come to the grief                    530
We were both born for, you in Priam's Troy
And I in Thebes in the house of Eëtion
Who raised me there beneath wooded Plakos
Under an evil star. Better never to have been born.
And now you are going to Hades' dark world,
Underground, leaving me in sorrow,
A widow in the halls, with an infant,
The son you and I bore but cannot bless.
You can't help him now you are dead, Hector,
And he can never help you. Even if                    540
He lives through this unbearable war,
There's nothing left for him in life but pain
And deprivation, all his property
Lost to others. An orphan has no friends.
He hangs his head, his cheeks are wet with tears.
He has to beg from his dead father's friends,
Tugging on one man's cloak, another's tunic,
And if they pity him he gets to sip
From someone's cup, just enough to moisten
His lips but not enough to quench his thirst.                    550
Or a child with both parents still alive
Will push him away from a feast, taunting him,
'Go away, your father doesn't eat with us.'
And the boy will go to his widowed mother
In tears, Astyanax, who used to sit
In his father's lap and eat nothing but
Mutton and marrow. When he got sleepy
And tired of playing he would take a nap
In a soft bed nestled in his nurse's arms
His dreaming head filled with blossoming joy.                    560
But now he'll suffer, now he's lost his father.
The Trojans called him Astyanax
Because you alone were Troy's defender,
You alone protected their walls and gates.

Now you lie by the curved prows of the ships,
Far from your parents. The dogs will glut
On your naked body, and shiny maggots
Will eat what's left.
                    Your clothes are stored away,
Beautiful, fine clothes made by women's hands—                    *570*
I'll burn them all now in a blazing fire.
They're no use to you, you'll never lie
On the pyre in them. Burning them will be
Your glory before Trojan men and women."

And the women's moans came in over her lament.

# ILIAD 23

While the Trojans lamented throughout the city,
The Greeks came to their beachhead camp
On the Hellespont and dispersed, each man
To his own ship.
                        But Achilles
Did not dismiss the Myrmidons.
He addressed his troops, men who lived for war:

"Myrmidons! I know you love your horses,
But before we unhitch them from the chariots
Let us all stay in armor and drive up close          10
And weep for Patroclus. We owe it to the dead.
After we've indulged in grief and sorrow
We can loosen our horses and eat together."

He spoke, and led them in their lamentation.
Three times they drove their horses round the corpse,
Wailing as they went. Thetis was with them,
And she honed their desire for grief. The sand
Was wet, and the warriors' armor, wet with tears.
They missed him. God, how he could fight!
Achilles' voice rose through their choked sobbing,          20
As he placed his man-slaying hands on his friend's breast:

"I hail you, Patroclus, even in Hades!
I am fulfilling all that I promised before,

440

To drag Hector here and feed him raw to the dogs,
And to cut the throats of twelve fine Trojan boys
Before your pyre, in my rage at your murder."

He spoke, and treated glorious Hector foully,
Stretching him out in the dust before the bier
Of Menoetius' son.

           The men took off their armor,                    30
Bronze gleaming in the dusk, and unhitched
Their whinnying horses, and sat down by the ship
Of Aeacus' swift grandson, too many to count.
And he made a funeral feast to satisfy their hearts.
Many sleek bulls bellowed beneath the knife
As they were slaughtered, many sheep, bleating goats,
And white-tusked boars, rich with fat,
Were skewered to roast over the fire's flame.
The ground around the corpse ran cup-deep with blood.

The other Greek leaders had come for Achilles             40
And were now escorting him to Agamemnon.
It had not been easy to convince him to come—
His heart raged for his friend. When they reached
Agamemnon's hut, they ordered the heralds
To put a cauldron on the fire, hoping to persuade
Achilles to bathe and wash off the gore.
He refused outright and swore this oath:

"By Zeus on high, there will not be
Any washing of my head until I have laid
Patroclus on the fire, and heaped his barrow,           50
And shorn my hair, for never will I grieve
Like this again, while I am among the living.
Now let's force ourselves to eat this feast.
But at the break of dawn, Agamemnon,
Order your men to bring wood and make ready
All that is fit for a dead man to have
When he goes beneath the murky gloom,
So that the fire may burn him quickly out of sight
And the men return to what they have to do."

He spoke, they listened, and they did as he said.    60
They prepared a meal and each man feasted,
And when they all had enough of food and drink,
They went to their huts and took their rest.
But the son of Peleus lay groaning heavily
Among his Myrmidons on the open beach
Where the waves crashed and seethed.
When sleep finally took him, unknotting his heart
And enveloping his shining limbs—so fatigued
From chasing Hector to windy Ilion—
Patroclus' sad spirit came, with his same form    70
And with his beautiful eyes and his voice
And wearing the same clothes. He stood
Above Achilles' head, and said to him:

"You're asleep and have forgotten me, Achilles.
You never neglected me when I was alive,
But now, when I am dead! Bury me quickly
So I may pass through Hades' gates.
The spirits keep me at a distance, the phantoms
Of men outworn, and will not yet allow me
To join them beyond the River. I wander    80
Aimlessly through Hades' wide-doored house.
And give me your hand, for never again
Will I come back from Hades, once you burn me
In my share of fire. Never more in life
Shall we sit apart from our comrades and talk.
The Fate I was born to has swallowed me,
And it is your destiny, though you are like the gods,
Achilles, to die beneath the wall of Troy.
And one thing more, Achilles. Do not lay my bones
Apart from yours, but let them lie together,    90
Just as we were reared together in your house
After Menoetius brought me, still just a boy,
From Opoeis to your land because I had killed
Amphidamas' son on that day we played dice
And I foolishly became angry. I didn't mean to.
Peleus took me into his house then and reared me
With kindness, and he named me your comrade.

So let one coffer enfold the bones of us both,
The two-handled gold one your mother gave you."

And Achilles answered him, saying:                    100

"Why have you come to me here, dear heart,
With all these instructions? I promise you
I will do everything just as you ask.
But come closer. Let us give in to grief,
However briefly, in each other's arms."

Saying this, Achilles reached out with his hands
But could not touch him. His spirit vanished like smoke,
Gone under the earth, with a last, shrill cry.
Awestruck, Achilles leapt up, clapping
His palms together, and said lamenting:                110

"Ah, so there is something in Death's house,
A phantom spirit, although not in a body.
All night long poor Patroclus' spirit
Stood over me, weeping and wailing,
And giving me detailed instructions
About everything. He looked so like himself."

His words aroused in them a longing for grief,
And they were still wailing around the corpse
When Dawn's roselight touched them.

                  Then Lord Agamemnon      120
Sent out from all over the camp a contingent
Of mules and men to gather wood,
Putting a good man in charge, Meriones,
Idomeneus' henchman. The men went out
With axes and ropes, and the mules before them,
Upward, downward, sideways, and slantwise,
Until they came to the spurs of spring-dotted Ida.
There they set to work felling high-crowned oaks
With bronze axes. The trees kept crashing down.
They split the trunks and bound them together        130

Behind the mules, who tore up the ground
As they tramped through underbrush toward the plain.
Meriones ordered the whole crew of woodcutters
To carry back logs, and they cast them down
On the shore in order, where Achilles planned
A great mound for Patroclus and for himself.

When they had laid out an immense amount of wood,
The crowd sat down and waited. Then Achilles
Ordered the Myrmidons to put on their armor
And yoke the horses to the chariots. They armed                140
And mounted, charioteers and warriors both,
And the chariots rolled out, with foot soldiers
Following behind in an endless cloud.
In the middle his comrades bore Patroclus,
Covering his body, as if with a garment,
With hair they sheared off and cast upon it.
Behind them Achilles cradled his head, grieving
For the peerless friend he was sending to Hades.

When they came to the place Achilles had told them,
They put the body down and quickly heaped up             150
Enough wood and plenty. Then Achilles,
Acting on impulse, stood apart from the pyre
And sheared off his hair, the tawny hair
He had been growing long for the River Spercheius.
Brooding, he turned toward the open sea,
The water glinting like wine, and said:

"Spercheius, my father Peleus vowed in vain
That when I had come home to my native land
I would shear my hair for you and sacrifice
Bulls by the hundred and fifty rams unblemished          160
Into your springs, where your precinct is
And your smoking altar. An old man's prayer,
Which you did not fulfill. Since I will never
Return home to my native land, I would give
To the hero Patroclus this lock to bear with him."

And he placed it in his beloved friend's hands.
This started them all weeping, and the sun
Would have set on their lamentation
Had not Achilles said to Agamemnon:

*170*

"Son of Atreus—you have the widest command—
These men can mourn all they want, but for now
Disperse them from the pyre and have them
Prepare their dinner. Those of us who are
Closest to the dead will do everything here.
And we would have all the leaders stay too."

The warlord Agamemnon heard him
And dismissed the troops to the ships.
The funeral party stayed and heaped up wood,
Building a pyre a hundred feet on each side,
And with heavy hearts they set the corpse on top.

*180*

Then they flayed many fine sheep and oxen
And laid them dressed out before the pyre.
Achilles gathered the fat from them all
And enfolded the body from head to foot,
Then heaped around it the flayed carcasses.
Next he set amphoras of honey and oil
Against the bier, and with heavy groans
Quickly cast on the pyre four high-necked horses.
Nine dogs once fed under the prince's table.
Achilles cut the throats of two and cast them on,

*190*

And twelve Trojans also, sons from good families,
Slashing them with bronze in a vengeful spirit.
Then he kindled the fire and let its iron will rage.
With a groan he called his beloved friend's name:

"Hear me, Patroclus, even from Hades.
All that I promised you I am completing now.
Twelve Trojans, sons of good families,
The fire consumes with you. Hector, though,
I will not give to the fire to eat, but to dogs."

Thus went his threat, but no dogs would eat Hector.     200
Aphrodite kept the dogs from his corpse
By day and by night, and she anointed him
With ambrosial oil of rose, so that when Achilles
Dragged his body it would not be torn.
And Phoebus Apollo drew a dark blue cloud
From the sky to the plain, covering the spot
Where the body lay, so that the sun's heat
Would not shrivel the flesh on his bones.

But Patroclus' pyre would not kindle.
Achilles thought of something else to try.     210
Standing apart from the pyre, he prayed
To the North Wind and West Wind, promising
Fine offerings, pouring libations from a gold cup,
And earnestly beseeching them to come and blow
So the wood would kindle and the body burn.
Iris heard his prayer and was off to the Winds
With the message. They were all in the house
Of the brisk West Wind, eating a banquet,
And Iris swooped to a stop on the stone threshold.
When they saw her there, they all whooshed up,     220
And each Wind invited her to sit next to him.
But she refused to sit, and made this speech:

"No seat for me. I'm off to Ocean's streams,
To the Ethiopians. They are offering sacrifices
To the immortals, and I want to get my share.
But Achilles is praying for the Winds to come—
The North Wind and the howling West—
And he is promising fine offerings
If you will raise the fire on Patroclus' pyre,
For whom all the Achaeans are groaning aloud."     230

She spoke and was gone. And the Winds rose
With an eerie noise, driving clouds before them.
They reached the sea quickly, and the waves swelled
Under their whistling blast. When they came to Troy
They fell on the pyre, and the flames roared to life.
The whole night long the shrill winds blew steadily

On the funeral fire, and all the long night Achilles
Drew wine from a golden bowl and poured it out
From a two-handled cup, wetting the earth,
Ever summoning the spirit of forlorn Patroclus.          240

  *A father wails for his son as he burns*
  *His bones, a son newly wed, a son whose death*
  *Has brought his parents inconsolable grief.*

Achilles wailed for his friend as he burned his bones,
Moving slowly about the pyre, groaning heavily.

The morning star rose, speaking light to the earth,
And dawn opened over the sea like a crocus.
The flames died down and the fire subsided.
The Winds left and returned to their home
Over the Thracian sea, and it moaned beneath them.       250
Then the son of Peleus left the pyre
And lay down exhausted. He was soon asleep,
But the men with Agamemnon gathered around,
And the sound of their tramping woke him.
He sat up and spoke to them, saying:

"Son of Atreus and princes of Greece,
First quench the funeral fire with wine,
Wherever it burned. Then gather the bones
Of Patroclus, son of Menoetius. Pick them out
Carefully. They are easily recognized,                   260
For he lay in the middle, while the others burned
Off to the sides, men and horses jumbled.
Then let us wrap the bones in fat and keep them
In a golden bowl, until I am hidden in Hades.
You need not labor over a huge barrow for him,
But only what is seemly. Later the Achaeans
Can build it broad and high, all of you still left
Amid our thwarted ships when I am gone."

Thus Peleus' swift son, and they obeyed him.
First they doused the pyre with wine                     270
Wherever it had burned and the embers were thick.

Then they gathered the bones of their gentle comrade
Into a golden bowl, wrapping them twice in fat,
And they placed the bowl in the hut and covered it
With a soft linen cloth. Then they traced a circle
For a mound and laid a foundation around the pyre
And piled up earth to form a tumulus over it.
Then they started to go back. But Achilles
Kept all the people there and had them sit down.
Then he brought prizes from his ship:                            280
Cauldrons, tripods, horses, mules, oxen,
Silken-waisted women, and grey iron.

First he set out prizes for the chariot race:
A woman whose work was immaculate
And a twenty-two gallon tripod with handles
For first place; for second place, a mare,
Six years old, unbroken, pregnant with a mule foal;
For third place, a beautiful cauldron, unfired,
Holding four gallons, still pristine white;
For fourth place, two bars of gold;                              290
For fifth, a two-handled bowl, unfired.
He put out these prizes, then stood up and said:

"Son of Atreus and Greek heroes all:
These prizes await the charioteers.
If our games were in someone else's honor,
I would win first prize hands down,
For you know how superior my horses are,
Immortal in fact, a gift from Poseidon
To my father Peleus, who gave them to me.
But I will sit this one out, and my horses too,            300
Who have lost the glorious, brave charioteer
Who was so kind to them, who would often
Rub down their coats with soft olive oil
After bathing them with bright water. It is for him
The two of them now stand in grief, their manes
Trailing on the ground, standing there in sorrow.
But this is the call for any other Achaean
Who trusts his horses and jointed chariot."

The charioteers responded quickly.
Eumelus was first up, Admetus' son,      310
A prince and a fine horseman,
Followed by Diomedes, who yoked up
The horses of Tros, which he had taken
From Aeneas (though Apollo saved the man).
Atreus' son Menelaus was next, yoking up
A fast team, Agamemnon's mare, Aethe,
And his own horse, Podargus. The mare
Had been given to Agamemnon
By Echepolus, Anchises' son, as a bribe
So he wouldn't have to go to windy Ilion      320
But could stay at home and enjoy the wealth
Zeus had given him in spacious Sicyon.
The mare, at any rate, was eager to race.
Antilochus was the fourth entry, Nestor's son.
His fleet, combed horses were bred in Pylos,
And as Antilochus was yoking them,
His noble father came up to give him advice,
Well-meant, but his son already understood:

"Antilochus, young as you are, Zeus and Poseidon
Have taught you all there is to know about horses.      330
There is no need for me to teach you
What you already know—how to round a turn
And so forth. However, your horses
Are the slowest in the race, and that spells trouble.
But if the others' horses are faster, that doesn't mean
They know more than you or are better strategists.
Well then, my boy, develop your strategy
So that prizes in games won't elude your grasp.
Strategy makes a better woodcutter than strength.
Strategy keeps a pilot's ship on course      340
When crosswinds blow it over the wine-blue sea.
And strategy wins races for charioteers.
One type of driver trusts his horses and car
And swerves mindlessly this way and that,
All over the course, without reining his horses.
But a man who knows how to win with lesser horses
Keeps his eye on the post and cuts the turn close,

And from the start keeps tension on the reins
With a firm hand as he watches the leader.

350

Now here's a sign you can't possibly miss:
A dry stump stands about a fathom high,
Either oak or pine, something rain won't rot,
With two white stones set close on each side
Where the smooth stretches of the course converge,
Either the grave marker of a man long dead
Or the goal of a race in an earlier age.
Achilles has made this his turning post.
Crowd it when you drive your horses by,
Leaning gently to their left in your leather rig
As you urge your right horse on and give him rein
Have your left horse crimp the turning post
So close that the hub of your well-made wheel
Seems to scrape its edge. But don't touch the stone
Or you'll wreck your chariot and injure your team,
A humiliation for you which the others would love.
So keep your wits about you, my boy.
If you drive past the rest at the turning post
No one will catch you or pass you in a sprint,
Not even if Arion were following your wheel,
Adrastus' swift horse from a breed divine,
Or one of Laomedon's excellent local stock."

360

370

Thus Nestor, son of Neleus, who then sat down,
Having explained to his dear son every last detail.

Meriones was the fifth to enter the race.

They mounted their chariots and cast in their lots.
Achilles shook them and out jumped the lot
Of Antilochus for the pole position.
Eumelus drew the next slot. Then came
Meriones, and after him Menelaus.
Diomedes, the best man in the field,
Drew the last position for his horses.

380

They took their places on the line, and Achilles
Showed them the turning post far off on the plain,
And he posted Phoenix there, his father's comrade,
To monitor the race and report the facts.


They curled their whips above their horses' backs,
Smacked them with the reins, and with hurried yells
They were off, streaking across the plain
And away from the ships, dust rising up under
The horses' chests like a line of thunderheads,                    *390*
Their manes streaming in the jets of wind.
The chariots sometimes rolled, sometimes hurtled
Over the ground, and the drivers stood in them
With their hearts pounding for victory, calling
To their horses, who flew along in the dust.


It was when they were racing down the final stretch
Back toward the grey sea that the men showed their valor
And the horses extended themselves. Eumelus' mares
Jumped into the lead, with Diomedes' stallions
Not far behind, so close in fact they seemed to mount           *400*
Eumelus' chariot, and their breath was warm
On his shoulders and back, their heads inches behind.
Diomedes would have passed him, or drawn up even,
Had not Apollo become peeved with Tydeus' son
And knocked the shining lash from his hands.
Diomedes' eyes filled with angry tears
When he saw the mares pick up their speed
And his own horses hampered, running without a goad.
But Athena saw Apollo cheat Diomedes
And swooped up behind the Greek commander,                     *410*
Returned his lash, and strengthened his horses.
Then the angry goddess went after Eumelus
And broke his horses' yoke. The mares swerved
Off course, and the pole slipped to the ground.
Eumelus rolled from the car alongside one wheel,
Skinning his elbows, mouth, and nose
And bruising his forehead above his eyebrows.

His eyes filled with tears, and his voice choked.
Diomedes steered his horses aside and drove on,
Shooting out far ahead of the rest, for Athena                    420
Bolstered his horses and gave him the power.
Fair-haired Menelaus was in second behind him.
Then Antilochus called to his father's horses:

"Get in there, you two, and give it all you have!
Don't worry about catching those horses up there
That Diomedes is driving. Athena
Has speeded them up and given him glory.
But you'd better catch Menelaus' horses,
And quickly, or be shamed by Aethe, a mare!
Why are you studs being left behind?                               430
I'll tell you something you can count on, though:
Lord Nestor won't put up with you two.
He'll kill you with cold steel in a heartbeat
If you pull in a cheap prize through lack of effort.
So get on it! Pour on all the speed you have,
And I'll take care of the rest, find a spot
Where we can slip past them on the narrow road."

The horses were frightened by their master's rebuke
And ran faster for a short time. Antilochus,
Who was a real fighter, saw that the course narrowed          440
Into a gully just ahead, where the winter torrents
Had washed out the road. Menelaus drove in
So that their wheels wouldn't touch, but Antilochus
Drove off parallel to the road and gave chase.
Menelaus was afraid and shouted over to him:

"Antilochus, you're driving recklessly! Rein in!
You can pass up ahead where the road gets wider.
You'll wreck us both if you graze my car."

But Antilochus drove even harder,
Plying the lash as if he hadn't heard.                             450
They kept on this way about the distance
A discus flies after a good hard throw,
But then Menelaus reined in his mares,

Afraid that the horses would tangle their hooves,
Overturn their rigs, and send them sprawling
Into the dust as they strained for victory.
He had some angry words for Antilochus:

"Out of my way, you malicious brat.
To think we gave you credit for good sense!
But you'll get no prize without going on oath."            460

Then he called to his horses:

"Don't hold back and stand around grieving.
Their feet and knees will tire before yours.
It's been a long time since those horses were young."

Frightened by their master's rebuke, the horses
Picked up the pace and soon closed the gap.

The assembled spectators watched as the horses
Flew across the plain in a cloud of dust.
The first to spot them was Idomeneus,
The Cretan commander, who had taken a seat             470
On a lookout point apart from the crowd.
When he heard Menelaus shout in the distance,
He knew who it was, and he could make out a horse
With distinct markings leading the race,
Bay all over, with a white moon on its forehead.
He stood up and announced to the crowd:

"Friends, Argive commanders and rulers,
Am I the only one or do you see them too?
We've got new horses in the lead now,
A new charioteer. The mares that were in front          480
On the way out must have gotten into trouble
Somewhere on the plain. I saw them swing
Into the turn first, but now I can't see them
Anywhere at all on the Trojan plain.
Maybe the reins slipped, and he lost control
Coming out of the turn. That must be it.
He must have crashed there, and the mares

Must have run off the course wild with terror.
Stand up and have a look. I'm not sure,
But the driver seems to be an Aetolian,                490
Which would make him no other than the son
Of Tydeus, breaker of horses, tough Diomedes."

Oïlean Ajax gave him a hard time:

"Do you always have to mouth off, Idomeneus?
They're still galloping way the hell out there.
You're not so young that your eyesight is perfect,
But you have the biggest mouth, which you
Shouldn't let flap in the presence of your betters.
The same mares are in the lead as were before,
Eumelus', and he's in the car holding the reins."          500

Angry now, the Cretan commander answered:

"You're big on insults, Ajax, but short on brains
And stubborn, which is why you're such a loser.
Why don't we bet something, a tripod or cauldron,
And have Agamemnon decide for us which mares
Are out front, so you can learn by paying."

He spoke, and Ajax jumped up abruptly
In an ugly mood. It would have gone further
Had not Achilles himself stood up and said:

"Let's break it up, Ajax and Idomeneus.                  510
It's unseemly. If you heard someone else arguing
With language like this you would be outraged.
No, sit down now and watch for the horses.
They'll be in the home stretch soon, running to win,
And then each man can see for himself
Which horses are in first place and which in second."

He had just said this when Diomedes
Was almost upon them, pushing hard,
Laying on the lash for all he was worth.

His horses leapt high as they ate up the road,                    520
Kicking flakes of dust back onto their driver,
And the chariot, plated with gold and tin,
Rolled on behind the swift-footed horses,
Their wheels barely tracing a track
In the light dust as the team flew on.
Diomedes stopped in the middle of the crowd,
Sweat pouring from his horses' necks and chests,
And he leapt down from his gleaming chariot
And leaned the lash against the yoke. Sthenelus
Lost no time in collecting the prize for him                      530
And delivering to his proud comrades the woman
And the eared tripod. Then he unyoked the horses.

Antilochus pulled in next, taking second place
From Menelaus, with tactics rather than speed.
Even so, Menelaus was close behind.

> *A horse pulling a chariot across a plain*
> *Can be so close to the wheel that its tail*
> *Scrapes the rim with its hindmost hairs.*

Menelaus was that close behind Antilochus.
Although he had been a discus throw behind,                       540
He made up ground quickly when Aethe,
Agamemnon's pretty mare, began to feel her mettle,
And had the course been longer he would have
Passed Antilochus without any question.
Meriones, Idomeneus' lieutenant,
Was a spearcast behind. His horses were the slowest,
And he was the least skillful driver.
Last of all came the son of Admetus, dragging
His chariot and driving his horses along.
Achilles, the great sprinter, felt sorry for him                  550
And he addressed the crowd with winged words:

"Look, the best man is coming in last.
He should get a prize, the prize for second.
But let Tydeus' son take first prize."

Everyone agreed, and he would have given
The mare to Eumelus—for he had their approval—
But Antilochus, son of great-souled Nestor,
Registered this complaint with Achilles:

"I will be really angry with you, Achilles,
If you do what you say. You're going to rob me                    560
Of my prize, on the grounds that Eumelus
Had an accident with his horses and chariot,
Good as he is. He should have prayed
To the immortals, and he wouldn't have lost.
But if you like him so much and feel so bad for him,
You have enough gold and bronze in your huts,
And sheep and women and solid-hooved horses,
To give him an even better prize later,
Or do it right now so the Greeks can applaud you.
But I'm not giving up the mare. Anybody                           570
Who wants to is welcome to fight me for her."

And swift-footed, godlike Achilles smiled.
He liked Antilochus and was glad for him,
And the onshore breeze carried his answer:

"Antilochus, if you want me to give Eumelus
Something else from my hut, I will do so.
I'll give him the corselet I took from
Asteropaeus. It is bronze plated with circles
Of bright tin, and something he will value."

He asked Automedon to bring it from the hut,                      580
And he went and brought it, and placed it
In Eumelus' hands, who received it gratefully.

Then up rose Menelaus, troubled at heart
And furious with Antilochus. A herald
Put the staff in his hands and asked for silence.
Then the godlike man began to speak:

"Antilochus, you have shown good sense
In the past, but look at what you have done now.

You shamed my valor when you fouled my horses
And forced yours in front though they were not as good.          *590*
Come now, Argive commanders and counsellors,
And judge between us without any bias,
So that no Achaean man at arms can say,
'Menelaus beat out Antilochus with lies
And went off with the mare. His horses were worse
By a long shot, but he had more clout.'
Here's my judgment, and I don't think anyone
Will reproach me for it, because it will be just.
Antilochus, come here, prince, and as is the custom,
Stand before your horses and chariot.                           *600*
Hold in your hand the slender lash you drove with,
And touching your horses swear to the Earthshaker
That you didn't deliberately block my chariot."

And Antilochus very sensibly replied:

"Bear with me now. I am much younger than you,
Lord Menelaus. You are the elder and the better man,
And familiar with the transgressions of youth,
Our impulsive notions and light-headed thoughts.
So please, be tolerant. The mule that I won
I will give to you, and if you should demand                    *610*
Something even better that I have in my house,
I would rather give it to you, my prince,
Than fall out of your good graces all of my days
And become a sinner in the eyes of the gods."

Thus Nestor's son, and he led up the mare
And gave it to Menelaus, whose heart warmed

> *Like morning dew on full ears of wheat*
> *When the sun ripens the bristling crop.*

Yes, Menelaus, your heart warmed,
And your words went to him on wings:                             *620*

"Antilochus, I accept your apology
Although I am angry, for never before

Have you been out of line or malicious.
This time your youth got the better of you.
Just don't try to outsmart your betters again.
There are very few men in this army
Who could have won me over like that,
But you have gone through a lot for my sake,
As have your brave father and brother.
So I not only accept your apology,                              630
But I will give you the mare, which is mine by rights,
To the end that everyone here may know
That my heart is not overbearing or hard."

And he gave the mare to Noëmon,
Antilochus' comrade, and took for himself
The shining cauldron. Meriones took
The two talents of gold for fourth place,
Which was where he finished, but the fifth prize,
The two-handled bowl, was left unclaimed.
This bowl Achilles gave to Nestor,                              640
Bringing it to him through the crowd and saying:

"Take this, reverend sir, as your keepsake
And memorial of Patroclus' burial,
For you will not see him again among the Greeks.
I simply give you this prize, for you will not compete
In boxing or wrestling, or enter the javelin throw,
Or run in the sprints. Old age is heavy upon you."

Nestor took the bowl from his hands and was glad.
Then he addressed Achilles with winged words:

"Yes, my boy, right you are. My limbs                           650
Are no longer firm, my feet, my hands,
And I have no punch left in my arms.
O, if I were young and strong again
As I was on that day when the Epeians
Were burying lord Amarynceus
At Buprasium, and his sons put up prizes
In his honor. Not a man there was my equal,

Not an Epeian, Pylian, or Aetolian hero.
I outboxed Clytomedes, Enops' son,
And in wrestling I threw Ancaeus of Pleuron.                   660
I beat out Iphiclus in the sprint, good as he was,
And outthrew Phyleus and Polydorus both
In the javelin. It was only in the chariot race
That the twin sons of Actor outdrove me,
Crowding me out, jealous for victory
Because the best prizes were left for this race.
They were joined at the hip. One of them drove
Steady as she goes, the other plied the whip.
Well, that was then. I leave such exploits
To younger men now, and yield as I must                       670
To grievous age. But I was the best back then.
Now you bury your friend too with funeral games,
And I am glad to receive this. My heart rejoices
That you are always kind enough to remember me
And do not forget the honor that is my due.
May the gods repay you and grant you grace."

Achilles listened to all that Nestor said,
Then went back again through the great throng.
Then he set out prizes for the boxing match.
He led in a sturdy mule and tethered her                      680
In the assembly ground, a mule of six years,
Unbroken, the hardest kind to tame.
For the loser he set out a two-handled cup.
Then he rose to announce to them all:

"Son of Atreus and Greek heroes all:
We need two men for these prizes, the two best
At trading punches. Whoever Apollo
Gives endurance to as the crowd looks on
Will lead the sturdy mule to his hut.
The loser's prize will be the two-handled cup."               690

At this point a real boxer stood up, Epeius,
Son of Panopeus, tall and well-built,
And laid hold of the sturdy mule, saying:

"Anybody want the cup as his prize?
Because no Greek alive is going to beat me
In boxing and lead away this mule.
I'm the best there is. Isn't it enough
I come up short in war? A man can't be
Good at everything. But let me tell you this,
And it's a sure thing: Anybody fights me,                           700
I'll bust him wide open and crush his bones.
Better have his next of kin standing by
To carry him out when I'm through with him."

Dead silence. Only one man stood up,
A godlike figure, Euryalus, whose father,
Mecisteus, had once come to Thebes
For the burial of Oedipus and beaten all
Of the native sons in the funeral games.
Diomedes badly wanted him to win
And acted as his second. He gave him a pep talk,               710
Then got him a loincloth and oxhide thongs
To strap on his hands. When they were girded up,
They stepped into the middle with hands held high
And were all over each other with flurries
Of hard punches, snapping jabs to the jaw,
And the sweat was flying from their arms and legs.
As his opponent looked for an opening,
Epeius moved in and got him with an uppercut,
And Euryalus' legs were no longer under him.

  *A fish leaps out from wind-rippled shallows*                      720
  *And is just as quickly in the black water again.*

Euryalus made like that when he was hit.
                                        Epeius,
Generous soul, pulled him upright, and his friends
Dragged him through the crowd with feet trailing,
Spitting out clots of blood, head hanging to one side.
They set him down, groggy, among his companions
And went off to claim the two-handled cup.

Then Peleus' son set out the prizes
For the third event, a grueling wrestling match.        *730*
For the winner he displayed a cauldron
Which the spectators guessed to be worth twelve oxen,
And for the loser he put up a woman skilled
In various crafts. They rated her at four oxen.
Then he rose to announce to them all:

"Will the contestants for this event please rise."

Then up rose huge Telamonian Ajax
And wily Odysseus, who knew all the tricks.
They girded themselves, stepped to the middle,
And took their stance, gripping each other        *740*

   *Like crisscrossing rafters set in the gable*
   *Of a high roof built to withstand the wind.*

Their backs creaked under the strain
Of their strong intertwined arms. Sweat
Poured down their bodies, and bloody welts
Rose up on their shoulders and ribs
As they struggled to win the exquisite cauldron.
Odysseus couldn't trip or throw Ajax
Nor Ajax Odysseus, whose strength held firm.
The crowd was getting bored, when Ajax said:        *750*

"Odysseus, either you lift me or let me
Lift you, and let's leave it all up to Zeus."

Ajax spoke and lifted him, but Odysseus
Did not forget his tricks, clipping Ajax
In the back of his knee and sending him down
With Odysseus on his chest. The crowd was amazed.
Then Odysseus tried to lift Ajax. He moved him
A little from the ground but couldn't get him up.
But he did hook his knee around Ajax's leg
So that they went down together. Grimy with dust,        *760*

They were ready to go at it a third time,
But Achilles himself rose and held them back:

"No need to continue and wear yourselves out.
You're both winners. Take equal prizes
And go your way, so others can compete."

Then Peleus' son set out prizes for a sprint.
He had a silver mixing-bowl, highly wrought.
It held six gallons and was the most beautiful
On earth, a masterpiece of Sidonian art.
Phoenician merchants had carried it over                    770
The misty sea to the harbor of Lemnos.
There they gave it as a gift to Thoas,
And Jason's son Euneus gave it as ransom
For Priam's son Lycaon to the hero Patroclus.
This bowl Achilles offered as a prize
To the winning sprinter, in honor of his friend.
For second he put up a great, fattened ox,
And a half talent of gold for third.
Then he stood up and announced:

"Will the contestants for this event please rise."      780

Up rose swift Oïlean Ajax, wily Odysseus,
And Nestor's son Antilochus, the fastest
Of all the army's young men. They lined up,
Achilles showed them the finish line,
And they were off, running flat out from the pole
With Ajax moving quickly into the lead
And Odysseus following close behind.

*A woman weaving pulls the shed rod back*
*Close to her breast and holds it there*
*While she spools the weft through.*                    790

That's how close Odysseus was. His feet landed
In Ajax's tracks before the dust had settled,
And his breath beat down on Ajax's head
As he sped on. The crowd was screaming

For Odysseus to win and kept cheering him on.
When they reached the final stretch, Odysseus
Said a silent prayer to grey-eyed Athena:

"Hear me, goddess, and don't fail my feet now."

Pallas Athena heard his prayer
And made his feet and hands light.           800
But when they were about to make their final spurt,
Ajax slipped as he ran—Athena's doing—
In the dung that was left from all the bulls
Achilles had sacrificed in Patroclus' honor.
Odysseus, finishing first, collected the bowl,
And glorious Ajax, spewing out dung
From his nostrils and mouth, took the ox.
With his hands on one horn, he addressed the crowd:

"Shit! The goddess tripped me up. It's like
She's Odysseus' mother, always at his side."       810

They all had a good laugh at his expense.
Then Antilochus took off the last prize,
Smiling, and addressed the crowd:

"As you all well know, the gods to this day
Still honor the older generation of men.
Ajax is just a little older than I am,
But Odysseus belongs to an older generation—
Old but still with plenty of juice, as they say of him—
And tough to outrun, except for Achilles."

Thus Antilochus, paying a compliment         820
To the great sprinter Achilles, who answered:

"Antilochus, your praise will not go unrewarded.
I will add a half-talent of gold to your prize."

Antilochus received it gladly from his hands.
Then Peleus' son brought onto the field
A long-shadowed spear, a shield, and a helmet,

Gear that Patroclus had stripped from Sarpedon.
And he announced to the crowd:

"We invite two men to compete for these prizes,
Two good men who will fight in full armor                        830
Before the crowd with bronze sharp to the touch.
The first man to reach the other man's skin,
Pierce the armor and draw blood, is the winner
And gets as his prize this silver-studded sword,
Good Thracian work, I took from Asteropaeus.
The two will hold Sarpedon's arms in common,
And we will feast them both well in our quarters."

He spoke, and up rose huge Telamonian Ajax
And Tydeus' son, tough Diomedes.
They armed themselves on opposite sides of the crowd,            840
Then stepped into the middle, eager to fight,
A cold light in their eyes. The crowd was spellbound.
Three times they lunged at each other, and the third time
Ajax hit the disk of his opponent's shield
But did not get through to his corseleted skin.
Diomedes kept trying to get his spear over
Ajax's shield and touch his neck with the point.
The crowd feared for Ajax and wanted them to stop
And take equal prizes, but Achilles gave
The sword to Diomedes with its scabbard and belt.               850

Then Peleus' son set out a rough lump of iron
That mighty Eëtion once used to hurl.
When brilliant, swift-footed Achilles killed him,
He took it to his ship with his other possessions.
Now he rose and announced to the crowd:

"Will the contestants for this event please rise.
The winner here will have enough iron
To last his shepherd and plowman five full years
And not have to send them to town to buy more."

Then up rose the battler Polypoetes,                             860
Along with Leonteus, strong and godlike,

Telamonian Ajax, and resplendent Epeius.
They lined up and Epeius went first,
Whirling around with the lump of iron
And heaving it out. The crowd laughed at his throw.
Leonteus went second, and then big Ajax,
Whose throw went farther than the other marks.
But when Polypoetes heaved the iron
He sent it sailing over the heads of the crowd
Like a cowhand's bolas over a herd of cattle.                    870
The crowd roared, and Polypoetes' men
Carried the prize to their strong king's ship.

Then Achilles set out iron for the archers,
Ten double axeheads and ten single
With a violet sheen. And he set up the mast
Of a tarred ship far off in the sand,
And attached to the top a fine cord
Tied onto the foot of a quivering dove.
He told them this was their target:

"Whoever hits the fluttering dove                    880
Will take home the double axes.
Hitting the cord but not the bird
Gets second place and the single axes."

Then up rose lord Teucer in his might
And Meriones, Idomeneus' comrade.
They put their lots in a bronze helmet
And shook it. Teucer drew first place.
He let fly an arrow, a strong shot,
But he failed to vow to the Archer
A sacrifice of a hundred firstling lambs.                    890
So he missed the bird—Apollo grudged him that—
But he hit the cord close to where it was tied
To the bird's foot, and the keen edge severed it.
The dove soared up to the sky as the cord
Sagged down to earth. Meriones grabbed the bow
From Teucer—he had been holding an arrow
While Teucer aimed—and vowed a sacrifice
Of a hundred firstling lambs to the Archer.

He spotted the dove fluttering overhead
Beneath the clouds, and as she circled there          900
He hit her smack beneath the wing. The arrow
Passed clean through and, falling down,
Stuck in the ground before Meriones' foot.
The dove landed on the mast. She hung her head,
And her plumage drooped. Her life flitted away,
And she dropped to the earth. The spectators
Were lost in wonder and could not believe their eyes.
Meriones scooped up all ten double axeheads,
And Teucer took the singles to his hollow ship.

Then Peleus' son brought out a long-shadowed spear          910
And an unfired cauldron, worth an ox, embossed
With flowers. The javelin throwers rose,
Atreus' son, the warlord Agamemnon,
And Meriones, Idomeneus' comrade.
But Achilles, swift and godlike, addressed them:

"Son of Atreus, we recognize your power
And know you are the best at throwing spears.
Take the prize and return to your hollow ships.
But we will give the spear to Meriones,
With your consent. At least that's how I want it."          920

The warlord did not disagree. He gave
The bronze spear to Meriones, then handed
To his herald Talthybius the beautiful prize.

# ILIAD 24

The funeral games were over.
The troops dispersed and went to their ships,
Where they turned their attention to supper
And a good night's sleep. But sleep
That masters all had no hold on Achilles.
Tears wet his face as he remembered his friend.
He tossed and turned, yearning for Patroclus,
For his manhood and his noble heart,
And all they had done together, the shared pain,
The battles fought, the hard times at sea.                        10
Thinking on all this, he would weep softly,
Lying now on his side, now on his back,
And now face down. Then he would rise
To his feet and wander in a daze along the shore.
Dawn never escaped him. As soon as she appeared
Over the sea and the dunes, he would hitch
Horses to his chariot and drag Hector behind.
When he had hauled him three times around
Patroclus' tomb, he would rest again in his hut,
Leaving Hector stretched face down in the dust.                   20
But Apollo kept Hector's flesh undefiled,
Pitying the man even in death. He kept him
Wrapped in his golden aegis, so that Achilles
Would not scour the skin as he dragged him.

So Achilles defiled Hector in his rage.

The gods, looking on, pitied Hector,
And urged Hermes to steal the body,
A plan that pleased all but Hera,
Poseidon, and the Grey-Eyed One,
Who were steady in their hatred                          30
For sacred Ilion and Priam's people
Ever since Paris in his blindness
Offended these two goddesses
And honored the one who fed his fatal lust.


Twelve days went by. Dawn.
Phoebus Apollo addressed the immortals:


"How callous can you get? Has Hector
Never burned for you thighs of bulls and goats?
Of course he has. But now you cannot
Bring yourselves to save even his bare corpse          40
For his wife to look upon, and his mother,
And child, and Priam, and his people, who would
Burn him in fire and perform his funeral rites.
No, it's the dread Achilles that you prefer.
His twisted mind is set on what he wants,
As savage as a lion bristling with pride,
Attacking men's flocks to make himself a feast.
Achilles has lost all pity and has no shame left.
Shame sometimes hurts men, but it helps them too.
A man may lose someone dearer than Achilles has,       50
A brother from the same womb, or a son,
But when he has wept and mourned, he lets go.
The Fates have given men an enduring heart.
But this man? After he kills Hector,
He ties him behind his chariot
And drags him around his dear friend's tomb.
Does this make him a better or nobler man?
He should fear our wrath, good as he may be,
For he defiles the dumb earth in his rage."

This provoked an angry response from Hera:                    60

"What you say might be true, Silverbow,
If we valued Achilles and Hector equally.
But Hector is mortal and suckled at a woman's breast,
While Achilles is born of a goddess whom I
Nourished and reared myself, and gave to a man,
Peleus, beloved of the gods, to be his wife.
All of you gods came to her wedding,
And you too were at the feast, lyre in hand,
Our forever faithless and fair-weather friend."

And Zeus, who masses the thunderheads:                        70

"Calm down, Hera, and don't be so indignant.
Their honor will not be the same. But Hector
Was dearest to the gods of all in Ilion,
At least to me. He never failed to offer
A pleasing sacrifice. My altar never lacked
Libation or burnt savor, our worship due.
But we will not allow his body to be stolen—
Achilles would notice in any case. His mother
Visits him continually night and day.
But I would have one of you summon Thetis                     80
So that I might have a word with her. Achilles
Must agree to let Priam ransom Hector."

  Thus spoke Zeus,
And Iris stormed down to deliver his message.
Midway between Samos and rocky Imbros,
She dove into the dark sea. The water moaned
As it closed above her, and she sank into the deep

  *Like a lead sinker on a line*
  *That takes a hook of sharpened horn*
  *Down to deal death to nibbling fish.*                      90

She found Thetis in a cave's hollow, surrounded
By her saltwater women and wailing
The fate of her faultless son, who would die
On Trojan soil, far from his homeland.
Iris, whose feet are like wind, stood near her:

"Rise, Thetis. Zeus in his wisdom commands you."

And the silver-footed goddess answered her:

"Why would the great god want me? I am ashamed
To mingle with the immortals, distraught as I am.
But I will go, and he will not speak in vain."                    100

And she veiled her brightness in a shawl
Of midnight blue and set out with Iris before her.
The sea parted around them in waves.
They stepped forth on the beach
And sped up the sky, and found themselves
Before the face of Zeus. Around him
Were seated all the gods, blessed, eternal.
Thetis sat next to him, and Athena gave place.
Hera put in her hand a fine golden cup
And said some comforting words. Thetis drank          110
And handed the cup back. Then Zeus,
The father of gods and men, began to speak:

"You have come to Olympus, Thetis,
For all your incurable sorrow. I know.
Even so, I will tell you why I have called you.
For nine days the gods have argued
About Hector's corpse and about Achilles.
Some want Hermes to steal the body away,
But I accord Achilles the honor in this, hoping
To retain your friendship along with your respect.      120
Go quickly now and tell your son our will.
The gods are indignant, and I, above all,
Am angry that in his heart's fury
He holds Hector by the beaked ships

And will not give him up. He may perhaps fear me
And so release the body. Meanwhile,
I will send Iris to great-souled Priam
To have him ransom his son, going to the ships
With gifts that will warm Achilles' heart."

Zeus had spoken, and the silver-footed goddess          130
Streaked down from the peaks of Olympus
And came to her son's hut. She found him there
Lost in grief. His friends were all around,
Busily preparing their morning meal,
For which a great, shaggy ram had been slaughtered.
Settling herself beside her weeping child,
She stroked him with her hand and talked to him:

"My son, how long will you let this grief
Eat at your heart, mindless of food and rest?
It would be good to make love to a woman.          140
It hurts me to say it, but you will not live
Much longer. Death and Doom are beside you.
Listen now, I have a message from Zeus.
The gods are indignant, and he, above all,
Is angry that in your heart's fury
You hold Hector by these beaked ships
And will not give him up. Come now,
Release the body and take ransom for the dead."

And Achilles, swift of foot, answered her:

"So be it. Let them ransom the dead,          150
If the god on Olympus wills it so."

So mother and son spoke many words
To each other, with the Greek ships all around.

Meanwhile, Zeus dispatched Iris to Troy:

"Up now, swift Iris, leave Olympus
For sacred Ilion and tell Priam

He must go to the Greek ships to ransom his son
With gifts that will soften Achilles' heart.
Alone he must go, with only one attendant,
An elder, to drive the mule cart and bear the man            160
Slain by Achilles back to the city.
He need have no fear. We will send
As his guide and escort Hermes himself,
Who will lead him all the way to Achilles.
And when he is inside Achilles' hut,
Achilles will not kill him, but will protect him
From all the rest, for he is not a fool,
Nor hardened, nor past awe for the gods.
He will in kindness spare a suppliant."

Iris stormed down to deliver this message.                   170
She came to the house of Priam and found there
Mourning and lamentation. Priam's sons
Sat in the courtyard around their father,
Fouling their clothes with tears. The old man,
Wrapped in his mantle, sat like graven stone.
His head and neck were covered with dung
He had rolled in and scraped up with his hands.
His daughters and sons' wives were wailing
Throughout the house, remembering their men,
So many and fine, dead by Greek hands.                       180
Zeus' messenger stood near Priam,
Who trembled all over as she whispered:

"Courage, Priam, son of Dardanus,
And have no fear. I have come to you
Not to announce evil, but good.
I am a messenger from Zeus, who
Cares for you greatly and pities you.
You must go to the Greek ships to ransom Hector
With gifts that will soften Achilles' heart.
You must go alone, with only one attendant,                  190
An elder, to drive the mule cart and bear the man
Slain by Achilles back to the city.

You need have no fear. We will send
As your guide and escort Hermes himself,
Who will lead you all the way to Achilles.
And when you are inside Achilles' hut,
Achilles will not kill you, but will protect you
From all the rest, for he is not a fool,
Nor hardened, nor past awe for the gods.
He will in kindness spare a suppliant."                          200

Iris spoke and was gone, a blur in the air.
Priam ordered his sons to ready the mule cart
And fasten onto it the wicker trunk.
He himself went down to a high-vaulted chamber,
Fragrant with cedar, that glittered with jewels.
And he called to Hecuba, his wife, and said:

"A messenger has come from Olympian Zeus.
I am to go to the ships to ransom our son
And bring gifts that will soften Achilles' heart.
What do you make of this, Lady? For myself,                      210
I have a strange compulsion to go over there,
Into the wide camp of the Achaean ships."

Her first response was a shrill cry, and then:

"This is madness. Where is the wisdom
You were once respected for at home and abroad?
How can you want to go to the Greek ships alone
And look into the eyes of the man who has killed
So many of your fine sons? Your heart is iron.
If he catches you, or even sees you,
He will not pity you or respect you,                             220
Savage and faithless as he is. No, we must mourn
From afar, sitting in our hall. This is how Fate
Spun her stern thread for him in my womb,
That he would glut lean hounds far from his parents,
With that violent man close by. I could rip
His liver bleeding from his guts and eat it whole.

That would be at least some vengeance
For my son. He was no coward, but died
Protecting the men and women of Troy
Without a thought of shelter or flight."                              230

And the old man, godlike Priam:

"Don't hold me back when I want to go,
And don't be a bird of ill omen
In my halls. You will not persuade me!
If anyone else on earth told me to do this,
A seer, diviner, or priest, we would
Set it aside and count it false.
But I heard the goddess myself and saw her face.
I will go, and her word will not be in vain.
If I am fated to die by the Achaean ships,                            240
It must be so. Let Achilles cut me down
As soon as I have taken my son in my arms
And have satisfied my desire for grief."

He began to lift up the lids of chests
And took out a dozen beautiful robes,
A dozen single-fold cloaks, as many rugs,
And added as many white mantles and tunics.
He weighed and brought out ten talents of gold,
Two glowing tripods and four cauldrons with them,
And an exquisite cup, a state gift from the Thracians          250
And a great treasure. The old man spared nothing
In his house, not even this, in his passion
To ransom his son. Once out in the portico,
He drove off the men there with bitter words:

"Get out, you sorry excuses for Trojans!
Don't you have enough grief at home that you
Have to come here and plague me? Isn't it enough
That Zeus has given me the pain and sorrow
Of losing my finest son? You'll feel it yourselves
Soon enough. With him dead you'll be much easier                 260

For the Greeks to pick off. But may I be dead and gone
Before I see my city plundered and destroyed."

And he waded through them, scattering them
With his staff. Then he called to his sons
In a harsh voice—Helenus and Paris,
Agathon, Pammon, Antiphonus, Polites,
Deïphobus, Hippothous, and noble Dius—
These nine, and shouted at them:

"Come here, you miserable brats. I wish
All of you had been killed by the ships                    270
Instead of Hector. I have no luck at all.
I have fathered the best sons in all wide Troy,
And not one, not one I say, is left. Not Mestor,
Godlike Mestor, not Troilus, the charioteer,
Not Hector, who was like a god among men,
Like the son of a god, not of a mortal.
Ares killed them, and now all I have left
Are these petty delinquents, pretty boys, and cheats,
These dancers, toe-tapping champions,
Renowned throughout the neighborhood for filching goats!    280
Now will you please get the wagon ready
And load all this on, so I can leave?"

They cringed under their father's rebuke
And brought out the smooth-rolling wagon,
A beauty, just joinered, and clamped on
The wicker trunk. They took the mule yoke
Down from its peg, a knobbed boxwood yoke
Fitted with guide rings, and the yoke-band with it,
A rope fifteen feet long. They set the yoke with care
Upon the upturned end of the polished pole,               290
Placing the ring on the thole-pin, and lashed it
Tight to the knob with three turns each way,
Then tied the ends to the hitch under the hook.
This done, they brought from the treasure chamber
The lavish ransom for Hector's head and heaped it

On the hand-rubbed wagon. Then they yoked the mules,
Strong-hooved animals that pull in harness,
Splendid gifts of the Mysians to Priam.
And for Priam they yoked to a chariot horses
Reared by the king's hand at their polished stall.                    *300*

So Priam and his herald, their minds racing,
Were having their rigs yoked in the high palace
When Hecuba approached them sorrowfully.
She held in her right hand a golden cup
Of honeyed wine for them to pour libation
Before they went. Standing by the horses she said:

"Here, pour libation to Father Zeus, and pray
For your safe return from the enemy camp,
Since you are set on going there against my will.
Pray to Cronion, the Dark Cloud of Ida,                               *310*
Who watches over the the whole land of Troy,
And ask for an omen, that swiftest of birds
That is his messenger, the king of birds,
To appear on the right before your own eyes,
Something to trust in as you go to the ships.
But if Zeus will not grant his own messenger,
I would not advise or encourage you
To go to the ships, however eager you are."

And Priam, with grave dignity:

"I will not disregard your advice, my wife.                            *320*
It is good to lift hands to Zeus for mercy."

And he nodded to the handmaid to pour
Pure water over his hands, and she came up
With basin and pitcher. Hands washed,
He took the cup from his wife and prayed,
Standing in the middle of the courtyard
And pouring out wine as he looked up to heaven:

"Father Zeus, who rules from Ida,
Most glorious, most great,

Send me to Achilles welcome and pitied.                    330
And send me an omen, that swiftest of birds
That is your messenger, the king of birds,
To appear on the right before my own eyes,
That I may trust it as I go to the ships."

Zeus heard his prayer and sent an eagle,
The surest omen in the sky, a dusky hunter
Men call the dark eagle, a bird as large
As a doorway, with a wingspan as wide
As the folding doors to a vaulted chamber
In a rich man's house. It flashed on the right            340
As it soared through the city, and when they saw it
Their mood brightened.

                          Hurrying now, the old man
Stepped into his chariot and drove off
From the gateway and echoing portico.
In front of him the mules pulled the wagon
With Idaeus at the reins. Priam
Kept urging his horses with the lash
As they drove quickly through the city.
His kinsmen trailed behind, all of them                   350
Wailing as if he were going to his death.
When they had gone down from the city
And onto the plain, his sons and sons-in-law
Turned back to Troy. But Zeus saw them
As they entered the plain, and he pitied
The old man, and said to his son, Hermes:

"Hermes, there's nothing you like more
Than being a companion to men, and you do obey—
When you have a mind to. So go now
And lead Priam to the Achaean ships, unseen             360
And unnoticed, until he comes to Achilles."

Thus Zeus, and the quicksilver courier complied,
Lacing on his feet the beautiful sandals,
Immortal and golden, that carry him over
Landscape and seascape in a rush of wind.

And he took the wand he uses to charm
Mortal eyes asleep and make sleepers awake.
Holding this wand, the tough quicksilver god
Flew down to Troy on the Hellespont,
And walked off as a young prince whose beard          370
Was just darkening, youth at its loveliest.

Priam and Idaeus had just driven past
The barrow of Ilus and had halted
The mules and horses in the river to drink.
By now it was dusk. Idaeus looked up
And was aware of Hermes close by.
He turned to Priam and said:

"Beware, son of Dardanus, there's someone here,
And if we're not careful we'll be cut to bits.
Should we escape in the chariot          380
Or clasp his knees and see if he will pity us?"

But the old man's mind had melted with fear.
The hair bristled on his gnarled limbs,
And he stood frozen with fear. But the Helper came up
And took the old man's hand and said to him:

"Sir, where are you driving your horses and mules
At this hour of the night, when all else is asleep?
Don't you fear the fury of the Achaeans,
Your ruthless enemies, who are close at hand?
If one of them should see you bearing such treasure          390
Through the black night, what would you do?
You are not young, sir, and your companion is old,
Unable to defend you if someone starts a fight.
But I will do you no harm and will protect you
From others. You remind me of my own dear father."

And the old man, godlike Priam, answered:

"Yes, dear son, it is just as you say.
But some god has stretched out his hand
And sent an auspicious wayfarer to meet me.

You have an impressive build, good looks,                    *400*
And intelligence. Blessed are your parents."

And the Guide, limned in silver light:

"A very good way to put it, old sir.
But tell me this now, and tell me the truth:
Are you taking all of this valuable treasure
For safekeeping abroad or are you
All forsaking sacred Ilion in fear?
You have lost such a great warrior, the noblest,
Your son. He never let up against the Achaeans."

And the old man, godlike Priam, answered:                    *410*

"Who are you, and from what parents born,
That you speak so well about my ill-fated son?"

And Hermes, limned in silver, answered:

"Ah, a test! And a question about Hector.
I have often seen him win glory in battle
He would drive the Argives back to their ships
And carve them to pieces with his bronze blade.
And we stood there and marvelled, for Achilles,
Angry with Agamemnon, would not let us fight.
I am his comrade in arms, from the same ship,            *420*
A Myrmidon. My father is Polyctor,
A wealthy man, and about as old as you.
He has six other sons, seven, counting me.
We cast lots, and I was chosen to come here.
Now I have come out to the plain from the ships
Because at dawn the Achaeans
Will lay siege to the city. They are restless,
And their lords cannot restrain them from battle."

And the old man, godlike Priam, answered him:

"If you really are one of Achilles' men,                      *430*
Tell me this, and I want the whole truth.

Is my son still by the ships, or has Achilles
Cut him up by now and thrown him to the dogs?"

And Hermes, limned in silver light:

"Not yet, old sir. The dogs and birds have not
Devoured him. He lies beside Achilles' ship
Amid the huts just as he was at first. This is now
The twelfth day he has been lying there,
But his flesh has not decayed at all, nor is it
Consumed by worms that eat the battle-slain.                    440
Achilles does drag him around his dear friend's tomb,
And ruthlessly, every morning at dawn,
But he stays unmarred. You would marvel, if you came,
To see him lie as fresh as dew, washed clean of blood,
And uncorrupted. All the wounds he had are closed,
And there were many who drove their bronze in him.
This is how the blessed gods care for your son,
Corpse though he be, for he was dear to their hearts."

And the old man was glad, and answered:

"Yes, my boy. It is good to offer                               450
The immortals their due. If ever
There was anyone in my house
Who never forgot the Olympian gods,
It was my son. And so now they have
Remembered him, even in death.
But come, accept from me this fine cup,
And give me safe escort with the gods
Until I come to the hut of Peleus' son."

And Hermes, glimmering in the dark:

"Ah, an old man testing a young one.                            460
But you will not get me to take gifts from you
Without Achilles' knowledge. I respect him
And fear him too much to defraud him.
I shudder to think of the consequences.
But I would escort you all the way to Argos,

With attentive care, by ship or on foot,
And no one would fight you for scorn of your escort."

And he leapt onto the chariot,
Took the reins and whip, and breathed
Great power into the horses and mules.                          470
When they came to the palisade and trench
Surrounding the ships, the guards were at supper.
Hermes sprinkled them with drowsiness,
Then opened the gates, pushed back the bars,
And led in Priam and the cart piled with ransom.
They came to the hut of the son of Peleus
That the Myrmidons had built for their lord.
They built it high, out of hewn fir beams,
And roofed it with thatch reaped from the meadows.
Around it they made him a great courtyard              480
With thick-set staves. A single bar of fir
Held the gate shut. It took three men
To drive this bar home and three to pull it back,
But Achilles could work it easily alone.
Hermes opened the gate for Priam
And brought in the gifts for Peleus' swift son.
As he stepped to the ground he said:

"I am one of the immortals, old sir—the god
Hermes. My father sent me to escort you here.
I will go back now and not come before              490
Achilles' eyes. It would be offensive
For a god to greet a mortal face to face.
You go in, though, and clasp the knees
Of the son of Peleus, and entreat him
By his father and rich-haired mother
And by his son, so you will stir his soul."

And with that Hermes left and returned
To high Olympus. Priam jumped down
And left Idaeus to hold the horses and mules.
The old man went straight to the house              500
Where Achilles, dear to Zeus, sat and waited.

Ｈe found him inside. His companions sat
Apart from him, and a solitary pair,
Automedon and Alcimus, warriors both,
Were busy at his side. He had just finished
His evening meal. The table was still set up.
Great Priam entered unnoticed. He stood
Close to Achilles, and touching his knees,
He kissed the dread and murderous hands
That had killed so many of his sons.                    510

> *Passion sometimes blinds a man so completely*
> *That he kills one of his own countrymen.*
> *In exile, he comes into a wealthy house,*
> *And everyone stares at him with wonder.*

So Achilles stared in wonder at Priam.
Was he a god?
                    And the others there stared
And wondered and looked at each other.
But Priam spoke, a prayer of entreaty:

"Remember your father, godlike Achilles.                    520
He and I both are on the doorstep
Of old age. He may well be now
Surrounded by enemies wearing him down
And have no one to protect him from harm.
But then he hears that you are still alive
And his heart rejoices, and he hopes all his days
To see his dear son come back from Troy.
But what is left for me? I had the finest sons
In all wide Troy, and not one of them is left.
Fifty I had when the Greeks came over,                    530
Nineteen out of one belly, and the rest
The women in my house bore to me.
It doesn't matter how many they were,
The god of war has cut them down at the knees.
And the only one who could save the city
You've just now killed as he fought for his country,
My Hector. It is for him I have come to the Greek ships,
To get him back from you. I've brought

A fortune in ransom. Respect the gods, Achilles.
Think of your own father, and pity me.                    *540*
I am more pitiable. I have borne what no man
Who has walked this earth has ever yet borne.
I have kissed the hand of the man who killed my son."

He spoke, and sorrow for his own father
Welled up in Achilles. He took Priam's hand
And gently pushed the old man away.
The two of them remembered. Priam,
Huddled in grief at Achilles' feet, cried
And moaned softly for his man-slaying Hector.
And Achilles cried for his father and                     *550*
For Patroclus. The sound filled the room.

When Achilles had his fill of grief
And the aching sorrow left his heart,
He rose from his chair and lifted the old man
By his hand, pitying his white hair and beard.
And his words enfolded him like wings:

"Ah, the suffering you've had, and the courage.
To come here alone to the Greek ships
And meet my eye, the man who slaughtered
Your many fine sons! You have a heart of iron.
But come, sit on this chair. Let our pain                 *560*
Lie at rest a while, no matter how much we hurt.
There's nothing to be gained from cold grief.
Yes, the gods have woven pain into mortal lives,
While they are free from care.
                              Two jars
Sit at the doorstep of Zeus, filled with gifts
That he gives, one full of good things,
The other of evil. If Zeus gives a man
A mixture from both jars, sometimes                       *570*
Life is good for him, sometimes not.
But if all he gives you is from the jar of woe,
You become a pariah, and hunger drives you
Over the bright earth, dishonored by gods and men.
Now take Peleus. The gods gave him splendid gifts

From the day he was born. He was the happiest
And richest man on earth, king of the Myrmidons,
And although he was a mortal, the gods gave him
An immortal goddess to be his wife.
But even to Peleus the god gave some evil:                     580
He would not leave offspring to succeed him in power,
Just one child, all out of season. I can't be with him
To take care of him now that he's old, since I'm far
From my fatherland, squatting here in Troy,
Tormenting you and your children. And you, old sir,
We hear that you were prosperous once.
From Lesbos down south clear over to Phrygia
And up to the Hellespont's boundary,
No one could match you in wealth or in sons.
But then the gods have brought you trouble,                   590
This constant fighting and killing around your town.
You must endure this grief and not constantly grieve.
You will not gain anything by torturing yourself
Over the good son you lost, not bring him back.
Sooner you will suffer some other sorrow."

And Priam, old and godlike, answered him:

"Don't sit me in a chair, prince, while Hector
Lies uncared for in your hut. Deliver him now
So I can see him with my own eyes, and you—
Take all this ransom we bring, take pleasure in it,           600
And go back home to your own fatherland,
Since you've taken this first step and allowed me
To live and see the light of day."

Achilles glowered at him and said:

"Don't provoke me, old man. It's my own decision
To release Hector to you. A messenger came to me
From Zeus—my own natural mother,
Daughter of the old sea god. And I know you,
Priam, inside out. You don't fool me one bit.
Some god escorted you to the Greek ships.                     610
No mortal would have dared come into our camp,

Not even your best young hero. He couldn't have
Gotten past the guards or muscled open the gate.
So just stop stirring up grief in my heart,
Or I might not let you out of here alive, old man—
Suppliant though you are—and sin against Zeus."

The old man was afraid and did as he was told.

The son of Peleus leapt out the door like a lion,
Followed by Automedon and Alcimus, whom Achilles
Honored most now that Patroclus was dead.                    620
They unyoked the horses and mules, and led
The old man's herald inside and seated him on a chair.
Then they unloaded from the strong-wheeled cart
The endless ransom that was Hector's blood price,
Leaving behind two robes and a fine-spun tunic
For the body to be wrapped in and brought inside.
Achilles called the women and ordered them
To wash the body well and anoint it with oil,
Removing it first for fear that Priam might see his son
And in his grief be unable to control his anger             630
At the sight of his child, and that this would arouse
Achilles' passion and he would kill the old man
And so sin against the commandments of Zeus.

After the female slaves had bathed Hector's body
And anointed it with olive, they wrapped it 'round
With a beautiful robe and tunic, and Achilles himself
Lifted him up and placed him on a pallet
And with his friends raised it onto the polished cart.
Then he groaned and called out to Patroclus:

"Don't be angry with me, dear friend, if somehow            640
You find out, even in Hades, that I have released
Hector to his father. He paid a handsome price,
And I will share it with you, as much as is right."

Achilles reentered his hut and sat down again
In his ornately decorated chair
Across the room from Priam, and said to him:

"Your son is released, sir, as you ordered.
He is lying on a pallet. At dawn's first light
You will go see him yourself.
  Now let's think about supper.    650
Even Niobe remembered to eat
Although her twelve children were dead in her house,
Six daughters and six sturdy sons.
Apollo killed them with his silver bow,
And Artemis, showering arrows, angry with Niobe
Because she compared herself to beautiful Leto.
Leto, she said, had borne only two, while she
Had borne many. Well, these two killed them all.
Nine days they lay in their gore, with no one
To bury them, because Zeus had turned    660
The people to stone. On the tenth day
The gods buried them. But Niobe remembered
She had to eat, exhausted from weeping.
Now she is one of the rocks in the lonely hills
Somewhere in Sipylos, a place they say is haunted
By nymphs who dance on the Achelous' banks,
And although she is stone she broods on the sorrows
The gods gave her.
                  Well, so should we, old sir,
Remember to eat. You can mourn your son later    670
When you bring him to Troy. You owe him many tears."


A moment later Achilles was up and had slain
A silvery sheep. His companions flayed it
And prepared it for a meal, sliced it, spitted it,
Roasted the morsels and drew them off the spits.
Automedon set out bread in exquisite baskets
While Achilles served the meat. They helped themselves
And satisfied their desire for food and drink.
Then Priam, son of Dardanus, gazed for a while
At Achilles, so big, so much like one of the gods,    680
And Achilles returned his gaze, admiring
Priam's face, his words echoing in his mind.

When they had their fill of gazing at each other,
Priam, old and godlike, broke the silence:

"Show me to my bed now, prince, and quickly,
So that at long last I can have the pleasure of sleep.
My eyes have not closed since my son lost his life
Under your hands. I have done nothing but groan
And brood over my countless sorrows,
Rolling in the dung of my courtyard stables.                    690
Finally I have tasted food and let flaming wine
Pass down my throat. I had eaten nothing till now."

Achilles ordered his companions and women
To set bedsteads on the porch and pad them
With fine, dyed rugs, spread blankets on top,
And cover them over with fleecy cloaks.
The women went out with torches in their hands
And quickly made up two beds. And Achilles,
The great sprinter, said in a bitter tone:

"You will have to sleep outside, dear Priam.                    700
One of the Achaean counselors may come in,
As they always do, to sit and talk with me,
As well they should. If one of them saw you here
In the dead of night, he would tell Agamemnon,
And that would delay releasing the body.
But tell me this, as precisely as you can.
How many days do you need for the funeral?
I will wait that long and hold back the army."

And the old man, godlike Priam, answered:

"If you really want me to bury my Hector,                    710
Then you could do this for me, Achilles.
You know how we are penned in the city,
Far from any timber, and the Trojans are afraid.
We would mourn him for nine days in our halls,
And bury him on the tenth, and feast the people.

On the eleventh we would heap a barrow over him,
And on the twelfth day fight, if fight we must."

And Achilles, strong, swift, and godlike:

"You will have your armistice."

And he clasped the old man's wrist                           720
So he would not be afraid.
                              And so they slept,
Priam and his herald, in the covered courtyard,
Each with a wealth of thoughts in his breast.
But Achilles slept inside his well-built hut,
And by his side lay lovely Briseis.

Gods and heroes slept the night through,
Wrapped in soft slumber. Only Hermes
Lay awake in the dark, pondering how
To spirit King Priam away from the ships          730
And elude the strong watchmen at the camp's gates.
He hovered above Priam's head and spoke:

"Well, old man, you seem to think it's safe
To sleep on and on in the enemy camp
Since Achilles spared you. Think what it cost you
To ransom your son. Your own life will cost
Three times that much to the sons you have left
If Agamemnon and the Greeks know you are here."

Suddenly the old man was afraid. He woke up the herald.
Hermes harnessed the horses and mules              740
And drove them through the camp. No one noticed.
And when they reached the ford of the Xanthus,
The beautiful, swirling river that Zeus begot,
Hermes left for the long peaks of Olympus.

Dawn spread her saffron light over earth,
And they drove the horses into the city
With great lamentation. The mules pulled the corpse.

No one in Troy, man or woman, saw them before
Cassandra, who stood like golden Aphrodite
On Pergamon's height. Looking out she saw
Her dear father standing in the chariot                    *750*
With the herald, and then she saw Hector
Lying on the stretcher in the mule cart.
And her cry went out through all the city:

"Come look upon Hector, Trojan men and women,
If ever you rejoiced when he came home alive
From battle, a joy to the city and all its people."

She spoke. And there was not a man or woman
Left in the city, for an unbearable sorrow
Had come upon them. They met Priam by the gates          *760*
As he brought the body through, and in the front
Hector's dear wife and queenly mother threw themselves
On the rolling cart and pulled out their hair
As they clasped his head amid the grieving crowd.
They would have mourned Hector outside the gates
All the long day until the sun went down,
Had not the old man spoken from his chariot:

"Let the mules come through. Later you will have
Your fill of grieving, after I have brought him home."

He spoke, and the crowd made way for the cart.           *770*
And they brought him home and laid him
On a corded bed, and set around him singers
To lead the dirge and chant the death song.
They chanted the dirge, and the women with them.
White-armed Andromache led the lamentation
As she cradled the head of her man-slaying Hector:

"You have died young, husband, and left me
A widow in the halls. Our son is still an infant,
Doomed when we bore him. I do not think
He will ever reach manhood. No, this city                *780*
Will topple and fall first. You were its savior,

And now you are lost. All the solemn wives
And children you guarded will go off soon
In the hollow ships, and I will go with them.
And you, my son, you will either come with me
And do menial labor for a cruel master,
Or some Greek will lead you by the hand
And throw you from the tower, a hideous death,
Angry because Hector killed his brother,
Or his father, or son. Many, many Greeks          790
Fell in battle under Hector's hands.
Your father was never gentle in combat.
And so all the townspeople mourn for him,
And you have caused your parents unspeakable
Sorrow, Hector, and left me endless pain.
You did not stretch your hand out to me
As you lay dying in bed, nor did you whisper
A final word I could remember as I weep
All the days and nights of my life."

The women's moans washed over her lament,          800
And from the sobbing came Hecuba's voice:

"Hector, my heart, dearest of all my children,
The gods loved you when you were alive for me,
And they have cared for you also in death.
My other children Achilles sold as slaves
When he captured them, shipped them overseas
To Samos, Imbros, and barren Lemnos.
After he took your life with tapered bronze
He dragged you around Patroclus' tomb, his friend
Whom you killed, but still could not bring him back.   810
And now you lie here for me as fresh as dew,
Although you have been slain, like one whom Apollo
Has killed softly with his silver arrows."

The third woman to lament was Helen.

"Oh, Hector, you were the dearest to me by far
Of all my husband's brothers. Yes, Paris

Is my husband, the godlike prince
Who led me to Troy. I should have died first.
This is now the twentieth year
Since I went away and left my home,                              *820*
And I have never had an unkind word from you.
If anyone in the house ever taunted me,
Any of my husband's brothers or sisters,
Or his mother—my father-in-law was kind always—
You would draw them aside and calm them
With your gentle heart and gentle words.
And so I weep for you and for myself,
And my heart is heavy, because there is no one left
In all wide Troy who will pity me
Or be my friend. Everyone shudders at me."                       *830*

And the people's moan came in over her voice.

Then the old man, Priam, spoke to his people:

"Men of Troy, start bringing wood to the city,
And have no fear of an Argive ambush.
When Achilles sent me from the black ships,
He gave his word he would not trouble us
Until the twelfth day should dawn."

He spoke, and they yoked oxen and mules
To wagons, and gathered outside the city.
For nine days they hauled in loads of timber.                    *840*
When the tenth dawn showed her mortal light,
They brought out their brave Hector
And all in tears lifted the body high
Onto the bier, and threw on the fire.

Light blossomed like roses in the eastern sky.

The people gathered around Hector's pyre,
And when all of Troy was assembled there
They drowned the last flames with glinting wine.
Hector's brothers and friends collected

His white bones, their cheeks flowered with tears.                    850
They wrapped the bones in soft purple robes
And placed them in a golden casket, and laid it
In the hollow of the grave, and heaped above it
A mantle of stones. They built the tomb
Quickly, with lookouts posted all around
In case the Greeks should attack early.
When the tomb was built, they all returned
To the city and assembled for a glorious feast
In the house of Priam, Zeus' cherished king.

That was the funeral of Hector, breaker of horses.                   860

# MAJOR CHARACTERS

## Gods and Goddesses

**Aphrodite** (A-fro-deye'-tee): Goddess of love and beauty. Daughter of Zeus and Dione in the *Iliad*. Aphrodite is pro-Trojan, due in part to her affinity for Paris Alexander, who in other versions awarded her the prize of the Golden Apple for being the most beautiful of the goddesses. — *also, how-trojan son Aereas (shot by Diomedes)*

**Apollo** (A-pol'-oh): Patron god of many areas, including music and the arts. Son of Zeus and Leto; brother of Artemis. Also known as Phoebus Apollo, Lord of the Silver Bow, and the Far-Shooter (for his role in bringing death by natural causes to men). Apollo is pro-Trojan in the *Iliad*.

**Ares** (Ai'-reez): God of war. Son of Zeus and Hera. Ares is pro-Trojan in the *Iliad*, although at times he appears as an impartial representative of bloodshed and the cruelties of war. *Sometimes, wants anyone to die*

**Artemis** (Ar'-te-mis): Goddess of the hunt and the moon. Daughter of Zeus and Leto; sister of Apollo. Like her brother, Artemis brings natural death to mortals, although she is the slaughterer of female mortals in particular. She is pro-Trojan in the *Iliad*.

**Athena** (A-thee'-na): Goddess of wisdom, crafts, and battle. Daughter of Zeus, usually said to have sprung from his head. Also called Pallas Athena. Athena is powerfully pro-Achaean in the *Iliad* and has particular favorite heroes on that side. *♡ Odysseus and Achilles*

**Charis** (Ka'-ris): One of the Graces, goddesses of beauty and grace. Wife of Hephaestus in the *Iliad*.

**Cronion** (Kro'-nee-on): Son of Cronus. See Zeus.

**Cypris** (Si'-pris): See Aphrodite.

**Dione** (Deye-oh'-nee): A goddess of the early generation, either a Titan or an Oceanid. Mother of Aphrodite in the *Iliad*.

**Hades** (Hay-deez): God of the Underworld, sometimes synonymous with death. Son of Cronus and Rhea; brother of Zeus,

Poseidon, and Hera; husband of Persephone. Hades shows no partiality to the Achaeans or the Trojans.

**Hebe** (Hee'-bee): Goddess of youth and beauty. Daughter of Zeus and Hera. She serves as a palace helper to the gods on Olympus.

**Hephaestus** (He-fees'-tus): God of fire and patron of metalworkers. Son of Zeus and Hera; husband of Charis in the *Iliad*. Hephaestus is pro-Achaean, although his major roles are to make peace between his parents and to create magically endowed objects, in particular Achilles' armor. *married to an unfaithful Aphrodite later, crippled by Zeus*

**Hera** (Heer'-a): Queen of the Olympian gods. Daughter of Cronus and Rhea; wife of Zeus; mother of Ares, Hephaestus, and Hebe. Hera is powerfully pro-Achaean in the *Iliad*, to the extent that she is at war with her husband. *She is a fighter and a submitter*

**Hermes** (Hur'-meez): God who serves as messenger for the Olympians. Son of Zeus and Maia. Hermes is technically pro-Achaean, but has a larger role as a messenger and guide, including guiding Priam, the Trojan king, to the Achaean camp.

**Iris** (Eye'-ris): Goddess of the rainbow and a messenger for the Olympians. Daughter of the Titan Thaumas and the Oceanid Electra.

**Leto** (Lee'-toh): A Titan goddess. Daughter of Coeus and Phoebe; mother of the twins Apollo and Artemis, sired by Zeus. Leto is pro-Trojan, given that her beloved children are strong allies of the Trojans.

**Poseidon** (Po-seye'-don): God of the sea. Son of Cronus and Rhea; brother of Zeus, Hades, and Hera. In the *Iliad*, Poseidon is generally pro-Achaean, although at times he favors certain Trojans. *father of Polyphemos in Odyssey (cyclops)*

**Themis** (The'-mis): Titan goddess of law and order. Daughter of Uranus and Gaia.

**Thetis** (The'-tis): A sea goddess, one of the Nereids. Daughter of Nereus and Doris; wife of Peleus; mother of Achilles. Thetis' main concern in the *Iliad* is watching out for her mighty son and securing his desires. *creates political war between Zeus and Hera*

**Xanthus** (Xan'-thus): God of the river near Troy, called by men Scamander. In the battle of the gods, Xanthus fittingly takes his place on the Trojan side.

**Zeus** (Zyoos): The supreme god of Olympus, known as the father of gods and men. Son of Cronus and Rhea; husband of Hera; father of Athena, Aphrodite, Ares, Apollo, Artemis, Hephaestus, and others. Zeus' position in the *Iliad* is generally impartial except when he is influenced by special requests.

## The Greeks (Achaeans, Argives, and Danaans)

**Achilles** (A-kil'-eez): Son of Peleus, King of Phthia, and Thetis, a sea goddess. Leader of the Myrmidons, the contingent from Phthia, and their fifty ships. Central character whose actions determine the course of the epic. *war rages between him and agamemnon over honor and a woman*

**Agamemnon** (A-ga-mem'-non): Son of Atreus and Aerope; brother of Menelaus; husband of Clytemnestra. Commander in chief of the Greek forces and leader of the contingent from Argos and Mycenae and their hundred ships. His quarrel with Achilles sets the plot in motion.

**Ajax** (Ay'-jax)(1): Son of Telamon and Periboea; half-brother of Teucer. Leader of the contingent from Salamis and their twelve ships. Also called Great Ajax and Telamonian Ajax. Since he is known as the greatest in battle next to Achilles, his ships guard the flank opposite that guarded by Achilles. To be distinguished from the lesser Ajax (2).

**Ajax** (2): Son of Oïleus and Eriopis. Leader of the contingent from Locris and their forty ships. He is called Little Ajax, Oïlean Ajax, or Locrian Ajax to distinguish him from Great Ajax (1).

**Antilochus** (An-ti'-lo-kus): Son of Nestor and Eurydice or Anaxibia. Brother of Thrasymedes and co-leader with him and their father of the contingent from Pylos and its ninety ships. Antilochus contributes significantly in combat throughout the epic.

**Automedon** (Aw-to'-me-don): Son of Diores. Charioteer of Achilles' immortal horses.

**Calchas** (Kal'-kas): Son of Thestor. The foremost Greek seer, consulted by the Greeks at key moments of the expedition to Troy.

**Diomedes** (Deye-o-mee'-deez): Son of Tydeus and Deïpyle. Leader with Sthenelus of the contingent from Argos and Tiryns and their *befriends Gracus on the battlefield* eighty ships. Known as one of the greatest Greek fighters and sometimes paired with Odysseus in exploits.

**Epeius** (E-pee'-us): Son of Panopeus. A Phocian fighter who participates in the funeral games as a boxing champion and is known elsewhere as the builder of the Trojan Horse, the war machine that eventually conquers Troy.

**Eumelus** (Yoo-mee'-lus): Son of Admetus and Alcestis. Leader of the Thessalian contingent from Pherae and their eleven ships. Known for his famous horses, he participates in the funeral games as a charioteer.

**Euryalus** (Yoo-reye'-a-lus): Son of Mecisteus. One of the leaders of the contingent from Argos under Diomedes. He participates in the funeral games as a boxer.

**Eurybates** (Yoo-ri'-ba-teez): A principal herald or official messenger of Agamemnon and the Greek forces; his name means "wide walker."

**Eurypylus** (Yoo-ri'-pi-lus): Son of Euaemon and Opis. Leader of one of the Thessalian contingents, with forty ships.

**Helen** (He'-len): Daughter of Zeus and Leda. Originally the wife of Menelaus of Sparta; in the *Iliad*, wife of Paris of Troy. According to ancient mythology, she was the most beautiful woman in the world. In spite of her married status, she was offered as a bride to Paris Alexander by the goddess Aphrodite, on the condition that he would award the Golden Apple of Discord to her. Helen then became known as the cause of the Trojan War, although other reasons for the war are mentioned in Homer and other versions of Helen's story exist in other sources. *So technically, Aphrodite is at fault too.*

**Idomeneus** (Eye-do'-men-yoos): Son of Deucalion. Leader of the contingent from the island of Crete and its eighty ships. One of the most prominent Greek fighters, although older than most.

**Leitus** (Lee'-i-tus): Son of Alectryon and Cleobule. Co-leader with Peneleos of the Boeotian contingent and its fifty ships.

**Leonteus** (Le-on'-tyoos): Son of Coronus. Co-leader with Polypoetes of the Lapith contingent and its forty ships. The two are instrumental in repelling the Trojans' attack on the ships.

**Machaon** (Ma-kay'-on): Son of Asclepius. Co-leader with his brother Podalirius of the Thessalian contingent from Tricca and Oechalia and its thirty ships. A Greek warrior best known, like his brother, for medical skills inherited from his famous father.

**Meges** (Me'-jeez): Son of Phyleus and Ctimene. Leader of the contingent from Dulichium and its forty ships.

**Menelaus** (Me-ne-lay'-us): Son of Atreus and Aerope; brother of Agamemnon, the commander in chief; husband of Helen, who was taken from his home by Paris. Leader of the Lacedaemonian contingent from the Peloponnese and its sixty ships. A prominent Greek warrior.

**Menestheus** (Me-nes'-thyoos): Son of Peteos. Leader of the Athenian contingent and its fifty ships.

**Meriones** (Me-reye'-o-neez): Son of Molus. Second in command under Idomeneus of the contingent from Crete and its eighty ships. A leading Greek warrior and a major participant in the funeral games.

**Nestor** (Nes'-tor): Son of Neleus and Chloris. Leader with his two sons, Antilochus and Thrasymedes, of the contingent from Pylos and its ninety ships. Although known principally as a wise counsellor to the Greeks and as the oldest among their warriors, Nestor still participates in battle to some degree.

**Odysseus** (O-dis'-yoos): Son of Laertes and Anticleia. Leader of the contingent from the island of Ithaca and its twelve ships. Odysseus serves as a prominent fighter, orator, and general troubleshooter for the Greeks. He is the hero of Homer's *Odyssey*, which tells of his return home.

**Patroclus** (Pa-tro'-klus): Son of Menoetius. Greek warrior with the Myrmidon contingent and best friend of Achilles, its leader. Patroclus is a key figure in the *Iliad* because of his decision to fight in Achilles' place. His death convinces Achilles to start fighting again.

**Peneleos** (Pee-ne'-lee-ohs): Son of Hippalcimus and Asterope. Co-leader with Leitus of the Boeotian contingent and its fifty ships.

**Phoenix** (Fee'-nix): Son of Amyntor. Greek warrior with the Myrmidons and friend and mentor of Achilles, whose father Peleus made Phoenix king of the Dolopians.

**Podalirius** (Po-da-leye'-ri-us): Son of Asclepius and Epione. Co-leader with his brother Machaon of the Thessalian contingent from Tricca and Oechalia and its thirty ships. A Greek warrior best known, along with his brother, for medical skills inherited from his famous father.

**Polypoetes** (Po-li-pee'-teez): Son of Peirithous and Hippodameia. Co-leader with Leonteus of the Lapith contingent and its forty ships. The two are instrumental in repelling the Trojans' attack on the ships.

**Sthenelus** (Sthen'-e-lus): Son of Capaneus and Evadne. A close friend of Diomedes and second in command under him of the contingent from Argos and its eighty ships.

**Talthybius** (Tal-thi'-bi-us): The principal herald, or official messenger, for Agamemnon and the Greek forces.

**Teucer** (Tyoo'-sur): Son of Telamon and Hesione. The illegitimate half-brother of Telamonian (or Great) Ajax, he accompanies the contingent from Salamis and is a notable Greek warrior, particularly with the bow.

**Thersites** (Thur-seye'-teez): Son of Agrius. A Greek warrior known for raucous and rebellious speeches in assemblies.

**Thrasymedes** (Thra-si-mee'-deez): Son of Nestor and Eurydice or Anaxibia. Brother of Antilochus and co-leader with him and their father of the contingent from Pylos. He was known as chief among the sentinels.

**Tlepolemus** (Tle-po'-le-mus): Son of the great hero Heracles and Astyocheia. Leader of the contingent from Rhodes and its nine ships.

## The Trojans (Dardanians) and Allies

**Aeneas** (Ee-nee'-as): Son of Anchises and the goddess Aphrodite. A Trojan fighter of repute who would survive to establish the ruling line of Rome.

**Andromache** (An-dro'-ma-kee): Daughter of Eëtion; wife of Hector; mother of Scamandrius, who was also called Astyanax ("city lord") for his father's glory. She lost her birth family to Achilles earlier in the war and fears losing her husband and child as well.

Loses everything to Achilles

**Antenor** (An-tee'-nor): Wise Trojan counsellor. Husband of the priestess of Athena, Theano, and father of many sons killed by the Achaeans.

**Astyanax** (A-steye'-a-nax): Infant son of the Trojan hero Hector and his wife Andromache. His given name is Scamandrius, but he is called Astyanax ("city lord") to honor his father. The child is the most likely heir to the Trojan realm and the subject of much concern on the part of his parents.

**Briseis** (Breye-see'-is): Daughter of Briseus. A war prize awarded to Achilles after he sacked Lyrnessus, she was subsequently taken away by Agamemnon.

**Cassandra** (Ka-san'-dra): Daughter of King Priam and Hecuba; sister of Hector, Paris, Helenus, and Deïphobus. Known elsewhere for her prophetic abilities and as an oracle who is never believed.

**Cebriones** (Se-breye'-o-neez): Illegitimate son of King Priam. Warrior and charioteer of his half brother Hector.

**Chryseis** (Kreye-see'-is): Daughter of Chryses. War prize awarded to Agamemnon as his share of the looting and subsequently ransomed by her father.

**Chryses** (Kreye'-seez): Priest of Apollo who comes to the Achaean camp to ransom his daughter Chryseis, war prize of Agamemnon.

**Deïphobus** (Dee-i'-fo-bus): Son of King Priam and Hecuba; brother of Hector, Paris, Helenus, and Cassandra. Trojan warrior who consults with Hector on strategy.

**Dolon** (Doh'-lon): Son of Eumedes. A Trojan sent to spy on the Achaean forces, he runs into the enemy with disastrous consequences.

**Euphorbus** (Yoo-for'-bus): Son of Panthous and Phrontis. Trojan warrior who wounds Patroclus.

**Glaucus** (Glaw'-kus): Son of Hippolochus. Co-leader with his cousin Sarpedon of the Lycians, Trojan allies. Glaucus is notable as well for his descent from Bellerophon, one of the great heroes of Greek mythology, who in other mythological versions performed glorious feats on the back of the winged horse Pegasus.

**Hector** (Hek'-tor): Oldest son of King Priam and Hecuba; brother of Paris, Helenus, Deïphobus, and Cassandra; husband of Andromache. Leader of the Trojans in battle and their foremost fighter; known as the defense of the city of Troy.

**Hecuba** (He'-kew-ba): Daughter of Dymas, King of Phrygia, and Eunoe. Official consort of King Priam of Troy and mother of many of his children, including Hector, Paris, Helenus, Deïphobus, Cassandra, and Laodice. Known as a prototype of the grieving mother who must face tragic losses in war.

**Helenus** (He'-le-nus): Son of King Priam and Hecuba; brother of Hector, Paris, Deïphobus, and Cassandra. A Trojan fighter and seer, he was awarded the gift of prophecy by Apollo. In other mythological versions, he is said to have become dissatisfied with the Trojans for various reasons and to have gone over to the Achaean side, helping them by means of his prophetic knowledge.

**Idaeus** (Eye-dee'-us): The principal herald, or official messenger, of King Priam and the Trojan forces.

**Laodice** (Lay-o'-di-see): Daughter of King Priam and Hecuba. Sometimes called the most beautiful of their daughters.

**Pandarus** (Pan'-da-rus): Son of King Lycaon of Lycia. Leader of the Troes and a bowman whose role in the *Iliad* is limited mainly to that of peacebreaker. In later mythology Pandarus' role is expanded considerably, although it generally involves the aspect of treachery.

**Paris** (Pa'-ris): Son of King Priam and Hecuba; brother of Hector, Helenus, Deïphobus, and Cassandra. Also called Alexander. A leading Trojan fighter, Paris is better known as the cause of the Trojan War through his seduction of Helen, wife of Menelaus of Sparta.

**Polydamas** (Po-li'-da-mas): Son of Panthous and Phrontis. A Trojan fighter who sometimes advises Hector on strategy.

**Priam** (Preye'-am): Son of Laomedon; husband of Hecuba; father of Hector, Paris, Helenus, Deïphobus, Cassandra, Laodice, and many others. The wealthy and aged ruler of Troy.

brave ,too for approaching
achilles, alone, for the body
of his son.

**Rhesus** (Ree'-sus): Son of Eïoneus. A Thracian king and ally of the Trojans who arrives late in the war with his famous snow-white horses to do battle with the Achaeans.

**Sarpedon** (Sar-pee'-don): Son of Zeus and Laodamia. Co-leader with his cousin Glaucus of the Lycians, allies of the Trojans. A notable warrior on the Trojan side and famous as progeny of Zeus.

**Theano** (Thee-ay'-no): Daughter of Cisseus, a king of Thrace; wife of Antenor and mother of his many sons. Priestess of Athena at Troy.

# CATALOGUE OF COMBAT DEATHS

Names in the left-hand column are of warriors (and in a sole instance, the god Ares) who conquer named warriors in the course of the epic. The right-hand column shows the names of the defeated with a line-number reference for each. The line number reference indicates the moment of death.

| | |
|---|---|
| Acamas | Promachus 14.488 |
| Achilles | Iphition 20.396; Demoleon 20.410; Hippodamas 20.419; Polydorus 20.432; Dryops 20.470; Demuchus 20.473; Laogonus 20.481; Dardanus 20.476; Tros 20.487; Mulius 20.490; Echeclus 20.495; Deucalion 20.502; Rhigmus 20.506; Areithous 20.509; many unnamed Trojans 21.25; Lycaon 21.125; Asteropaeus 21.190; Thersilochus 21.217; Mydon 21.217; Astypylus 21.218; Mnesus 21.218; Thrasius 21.218; Aenius 21.218; Ophelestes 21.219; many unnamed Trojans 21.537; Hector 22.403; twelve unnamed Trojans 23.192 |
| Aeneas | Crethon 5.584; Orsilochus 5.584; Aphareus 13.566; Medon 15.338; Iasus 15.338; Leocritus 17.352 |
| Agamemnon | Odius 5.49; Deicoön 5.581; Elatus 6.33; Adrastus 6.64; Bienor 11.94; Oïleus 11.102; Isus 11.105; Antiphus 11.105; Peisander 11.154; Hippolochus 11.158; unnamed Trojans 11.195 Iphidamas 11.263; Coon 11.282; unnamed Trojans 11.286 |
| Agenor | Elephenor 4.510; Clonius 15.347 |
| Ajax, Oïlean | Satnius 14.452; many unnamed Trojans 14.533; Cleobulus 16.352 |
| Ajax, Telamonian | Simoeisius 4.520; Amphius 5.666; Acamas 6.12; Dorycles 11.519; Lysander 11.521; Pyrasus 11.521; Pylartes 11.521; Epicles 12.403; Archelochus 14.478; |

|  | Hyrtius 14.524; Caletor 15.435; Laodamas 15.535; twelve unnamed Trojans assumed dead 15.797; many unnamed Trojans 17.239; Hippothous 17.301; Phorcys 17.319 |

Antilochus  Echepolus 4.496; Pylaemenes 5.622; Mydon 5.624; Ablerus 6.32; unnamed charioteer 13.417; Thoön 13.571; Phalces 14.526; Mermerus 14.526; Melanippus 15.605; Atumnius 16.335

Antiphus  Leucas 4.535

Ares  Periphas 5.897

Automedon  Aretus 17.538

Deïphobus  Hypsenor 13.428; Ascalaphus 13.544

Diomedes  Phegeus 5.23; Astynous 5.161; Hypeiron 5.161; Abas 5.169; Polyidus 5.169; Xanthus 5.174; Thoön 5.175; Echemmon 5.179; Chromius 5.179; Pandarus 5.320; Axylus 6.13; Calesius 6.19; Eniopoeus 8.128; Agelaus 8.263; Dolon 10.472; twelve unnamed Thracians 10.499; Rhesus 10.512; Thymbraeus 11.339; two unnamed sons of Merops 11.351; Agastrophus 11.360

Euryalus  Opheltius 6.21; Dresus 6.21; Aesepus 6.22; Pedasus 6.22

Eurypylus  Hypsenor 5.86; Melanthius 6.36; Apiason 11.613

Glaucus  Iphinous 7.17; Bathycles 16.631

Hector  Menesthes 5.658; Anchialus 5.658; Teuthras 5.760; Orestes 5.760; Oenomaus 5.761; Trechus 5.761; Helenus 5.762; Oresbius 5.762; Eioneus 7.11; unnamed warriors 8.350; Asaeus 11.317; Autonous 11.317; Dolops 11.319; Opheltius 11.319; Agelaus 11.320; Aesymnus 11.320; Orus 11.320; Hipponous 11.320; unnamed Greeks 13.152; Amphimachus 13.197; Stichius 15.335; Arcesilaus 15.335; Lycophron 15.449; Schedius 15.533; Periphetes 15.688; Epeigeus 16.612; Patroclus 16.896; Schedius 17.314; Coeranus 17.634

| | |
|---|---|
| Helenus | Deïpyrus 13.605 |
| Idomeneus | Phaestus 5.51; Othryoneus 13.389; Asius 13.411; Alcathous 13.461; Oenomaus 13.530; Erymas 16.372 |
| Leitus | Phylacus 6.35 |
| Leonteus | Hippomachus 12.196; Antiphates 12.198; Menon 12.200; Iamenus 12.200; Orestes 12.201 |
| Lycomedes | Apisaon 17.358 |
| Meges | Pedaeus 5.78; Croesmus 15.544; Amphiclus 16.331 |
| Menelaus | Scamandrius 5.57; Pylaemenes 5.622; Mydon 5.624; Peisander 13.645; Hyperenor 14.532; Dolops 15.567; Thoas 16.326; Euphorbus 17.48; Podes 17.592 |
| Meriones | Phereclus 5.66; Adamas 13.599; Harpalion 13.684; Morys 14.527; Hippotion 14.527; Acamas 16.365; Laogonus 16.639 |
| Odysseus | Democoön 4.548; Coeranus 5.730; Alastor 5.730; Chromius 5.730; Alcandrus 5.731; Halius 5.731; Noemon 5.731; Prytanis 5.731; Pidytes 6.30; Molion 11.340; Hippodamus 11.352; Hypeirochus 11.352; Deiopites 11.447; Thoön 11.448; Eunomus 11.448; Chersidamas 11.451; Charops 11.453; Socus 11.478 |
| Paris | Menesthius 7.9; Euchenor 13.705; Deiochus 15.348 |
| Patroclus | Pyraechmes 16.297; Areilycus 16.321; many unnamed Trojans 16.411; Pronous 16.434; Thestor 16.446; Erylaus 16.449; Erymas 16.451; Amphoterus 16.451; Epaltes 16.451; Echius 16.451; Tlepolemus 16.452; Ipheus 16.452; Pyris 16.452; Euippus 16.453; Polymelus 16.457; Thrasymelus 16.500; Sarpedon 16.535; Sthenelaus 16.619; Adrastus 16.726; Autonous 16.726; Echeclus 16.726; Perimus 16.727; Epistor 16.727; Melanippus 16.734; Elasus 16.728; Mulius 16.728; Pylartes 16.728; Cebriones 16.778; twenty-seven unnamed Trojans 16.825 |

| | |
|---|---|
| Peirus | Diores 4.572 |
| Peneleos | Ilioneus 14.510; Lycon 16.360 |
| Polites | Echius 15.346 |
| Polydamas | Prothoenor 14.652; Mecisteus 15.345; Otus 15.537 |
| Polypoetes | Astyalus 6.29; Damasus 12.192; Pylon 12.194; Ormenus 12.194 |
| Sarpedon | Tlepolemus 5.712; Alcmaon 12.413; Pedasus 16.504 |
| Teucer | Aretaon 6.31; Orsilochus 8.277; Ormenus 8.277; Ophelestes 8.277; Daetor 8.278; Chromius 8.278; Lycophontes 8.278; Amopaon 8.279; Melanippus 8.279; Gorgythion 8.309; Archeptolemus 8.320; Imbrius 13.184; Prothoön 14.528; Periphetes 14.528; Cleitus 15.465 |
| Thoas | Peirus 4.577 |
| Thrasymedes | Maris 16.342 |

# INDEX OF SPEECHES

to Hector 17.342; to Apollo (as Lycaon) 20.92; to Achilles 20.207

Agamemnon    to Chryses 1.34; to Calchas 1.112; to Achilles (argument with) 1.140, 1.183; to Nestor 1.301; to heralds 1.335; to elders 2.60; to all Greeks 2.119; to Nestor 2.400; to Zeus 2.441; to Zeus 3.295; to Trojans 3.482; to Menelaus 4.170, 4.204; to Talthybius 4.208; to troops (encouraging words) 4.250; to Idomeneus 4.274; to Ajaxes 4.305; to Nestor 4.336; to Odysseus and Menestheus 4.360; to Odysseus 4.381; to Diomedes and Sthenelus 4.394; to Greeks 5.570; to Menelaus 6.55; to Menelaus 7.114; to Idaeus 7.419; to Greeks 8.229; to Teucer 8.283; to Greeks 9.18; to Nestor 9.120; to Odysseus 9.697; to Menelaus 10.43; to Menelaus 10.64; to Nestor 10.88, 10.123; to Diomedes 10.243; to Peisander and Hippolochus 11.147; to Greek Commanders 11.297; to Nestor 14.39, 14.63; to Odysseus 14.100; to all Greeks 19.90; to Odysseus 19.197; to Zeus (prayers) 19.272

Agenor    to himself 21.571; to Achilles 21.606

Oïlean Ajax    to troops 12.278; to T. Ajax 13.72; to Idomeneus 23.494; to Greeks 23.809

Telamonian Ajax    to heroes 7.199; to Hector 7.237; to Idaeus 7.298; to Odysseus and Achilles 9.642; to troops 12.278; to Oïlean Ajax 12.380, 13.80; to Hector 13.853; to Polydamas 14.480; to Teucer 15.451, 15.489; to Greeks 15.521, 15.585, 15.777; to Menelaus 17.241, 17.644, 17.667, 17.730; to Odysseus 23.751

Alcimedon    to Automedon 17.485

Andromache    to Hector 6.427; to her women 22.500; to Hector (dead) 22.530; to Hector (dead) 24.777

Antenor    to Helen 3.219; to Trojans 7.362

Antilochus    to Achilles 18.19; to his horses 23.424; to Achilles 23.559; to Menelaus 23.605; to Greeks 23.814

to his men 5.650; to Athena 5.868; to Glaucus 6.124, 6.221; to Greek leaders 7.413; to Odysseus 8.99; to Nestor 8.108, 8.148; to Agamemnon 9.35, 9.722; to Nestor 10.171, 10.228; to Agamemnon 10.251; to Athena 10.297; to Dolon 10.384, 10.461; to Odysseus 11.335, 11.367; to Hector 11.382; to Paris 11.408; to Agamemnon and Odysseus 14.105

Dione          to Aphrodite 5.406, 5.415

Dolon          to Hector 10.334; to Odysseus and Diomedes 10.392, 10.405, 10.427, 10.441

Dream          to Agamemnon 2.27

Epeius          to Greeks 23.694

Euphorbus          to Menelaus 17.12, 17.32

Eurypylus          to Greeks 11.622; to Patroclus 11.864

Glaucus          to Diomedes 6.148; to Apollo 16.557; to Hector 16.570, 17.139

Greeks          to Zeus 7.211

Hector          to Paris 3.45; to Trojans 3.89, 6.112; to Hecuba 6.275; to Paris 6.342; to Helen 6.378; to servants 6.394; to Andromache 6.463; to Zeus 6.501; to Andromache 6.511; to Paris 6.549; to Greeks and Trojans 7.70; to T. Ajax 7.245, 7.302; to Diomedes 8.163; to Trojan troops 8.176; to horses 8.186; to troops 8.509; to Trojan leaders 10.318; to Dolon (swearing) 10.345; to Trojans 11.306; to Polydamas 12.239; to Trojans 12.463, 13.157; to Polydamas 13.792; to Paris 13.809; to T. Ajax 13.868; to Apollo 15.249; to Trojans 15.355, 15.439, 15.504; to Melanippus 15.577; to Trojans 15.758; to Patroclus 16.871, 16.899; to Glaucus 17.168; to Trojans 17.182, 17.222; to Aeneas 17.501; to Polydamas 18.306; to Trojans 20.373; to Achilles 20.445; to himself 22.114; to Athena (as Deïphobus) 22.260; to Achilles 22.277, 22.306; to himself 22.325; to Achilles 22.375, 22.395

Hecuba      to Hector 6.263, 22.91; to Hector (dead) 22.476; to Priam 24.214, 24.307; to Hector (dead) 24.802

Helen       to Priam 3.180, 3.214, 3.245; to Aphrodite 3.427; to Paris 3.456; to Hector 6.361; to Hector (dead) 24.815

Helenus     to Aeneas and Hector 6.78; to Hector 7.50

Hephaestus  to Hera 1.606, 1.619; to Charis 18.423; to Thetis 18.457, 18.499

Hera        to Zeus 1.573, 1.584; to Athena 2.172; to Zeus 4.33, 4.61; to Athena 5.767; to Zeus 5.809; to Greeks 5.839; to Poseidon 8.200; to Athena 8.359, 8.438; to Zeus 8.474; to Aphrodite 14.189, 14.197; to Sleep 14.232; to Zeus 14.305, 14.335, 15.38; to Themis 15.95; to gods 15.106; to Apollo and Iris 15.147; to Zeus 16.477, 18.389; to Poseidon and Athena 20.120; to Poseidon 20.316; to Hephaestus 21.341, 21.389; to Athena 21.432; to Artemis 21.493; to Apollo 24.61

Hermes      to Leto 21.512; to Priam 24.386, 24.403, 24.414, 24.435, 24.460, 24.488, 24.733

Hippolochus to Agamemnon 11.140

Housekeeper to Hector 6.400

Idaeus      to Priam 3.268; to Hector and T. Ajax 7.293; to Greek leaders 7.398; to Priam 24.378

Idomeneus   to Agamemnon 4.283; to Nestor 11.544; to Poseidon (as Thoas) 13.235; to Meriones 13.263, 13.273, 13.286, 13.322; to Othryaneus 13.390; to Deïphobus 13.463; to Greeks 13.503, 23.477; to Oïlean Ajax 23.502

Iris        to Priam 2.902; to Helen 3.132; to Athena and Hera 8.423; to Hector 11.216; to Poseidon 15.176, 15.203; to Achilles 18.181, 18.195, 18.208; to the Winds 23.223; to Thetis 24.96; to Priam 24.183

Lycaon      to Achilles 21.79

Paris                to Hector 3.64; to Helen 3.465; to Hector 6.349,
                     6.546; to Trojans 7.371; to Diomedes 11.403; to
                     Hector 13.815

Patroclus            to Achilles 11.644; to Nestor 11.691; to Eurypylus
                     11.858, 11.878, 15.412; to Achilles 16.23; to Myrmi-
                     dons 16.275; to Ajaxes 16.589; to Meriones 16.657;
                     boasting 16.780; to Hector 16.885; (dead) to Achil-
                     les 23.74

Peisander            to Agamemnon 11.140

Peneleos             to Trojans 14.514

Phoenix              to Achilles 9.446

Polydamas            to Hector and Trojan commanders 12.64; to Hec-
                     tor 12.218; to Hector 13.768; boasting 14.464; to
                     Trojans 18.272

Poseidon             to gods 7.461; to Hera 8.209; to Ajaxes 13.51; to
                     Greeks 13.97; to Idomeneus 13.231, 13.245; to Aga-
                     memnon 14.135; to Greeks 14.370; to Iris 15.187,
                     15.208; to Zeus 20.17; to Hera 20.137; to gods
                     20.298; to Aeneas 20.340; to Achilles 21.298; to
                     Apollo 21.448

Priam                to Helen 3.170, 3.193, 3.206, 3.242; to Greeks and
                     Trojans 3.326; to Trojans 7.382; to gatekeeper 21.548;
                     to Hector 22.45; to Trojans 22.460; to Hecuba 24.207,
                     24.232; to Trojans 24.255; to remaining sons 24.269;
                     to Hecuba 24.320; to Zeus 24.328; to Hermes 24.397,
                     24.411, 24.430, 24.450; to Achilles 24.520, 24.685;
                     to Trojans 24.768; to Trojan army 24.833

Sarpedon             to Hector 5.509; to Tlepolemus 5.700; to Hector
                     5.738; to Glaucus 12.320; to Lycians 12.430; to Tro-
                     jans (Lycians) 16.459; to Glaucus 16.527

Scamander            to Achilles 21.223; to Apollo 21.238; to Simois
                     21.319; to Hephaestus 21.367; to Hera 21.379

Sleep                to Hera 14.243, 14.275; to Poseidon 14.363

Socus                to Odysseus 11.457

# SUGGESTIONS FOR
# FURTHER READING

*Homeri Opera*. Ed. D. B. Monro and T. W. Allen. Vols. I and II. Oxford Classical Texts. London, 1920.

*The Iliad: A Commentary*. General Ed., G. S. Kirk. Vol. I: Books 1–4, Kirk. Cambridge, England, 1985. Vol. II: Books 5–8, Kirk, 1990. Vol. III: Books 9–12, J. B. Hainsworth; Vol. IV: Books 13–16, Richard Janko; Vol. V: Books 17–20, Mark W. Edwards; Vol. VI: Books 21–24, Nicholas Richardson.

Arnold, Matthew. "On Translating Homer." In *On the Classical Tradition*, ed. R. H. Super. Michigan University Press. Ann Arbor and London, 1960.

Austin, Norman. *Archery at the Dark of the Moon: Poetic Problems in Homer's Odyssey*. University of California Press. Berkeley, Los Angeles, and London, 1975.

Bespaloff, Rachel. *On the Iliad*. Trans. Mary McCarthy. New York, 1947.

Bowra, Sir Maurice. *Tradition and Design in the Iliad*. London, 1930.

Clarke, Howard. *Homer's Readers: A Historical Introduction to the Iliad and the Odyssey*. Newark, Del., 1981.

Edwards, Mark W. *Homer: Poet of the Iliad*. Johns Hopkins University Press. Baltimore, Md., and London, 1987.

Griffin, Jasper. *Homer on Life and Death*. Clarendon Press. Oxford, 1980.

Kirk, G. S. *The Songs of Homer*. Cambridge University Press. Cambridge, England, 1962.

Lamberton, R. and Keaney, J. J., eds.: *Homer's Ancient Readers: The Hermeneutics of Greek Epic's Earliest Exegetes*. Princeton University Press, 1992.

Lord, Albert. *The Singer of Tales*. Harvard University Press. Cambridge, Mass., 1960.

Lord, Albert. *The Singer Resumes the Tale*. Ed. M. L. Lord. Cornell University Press. Ithaca, N.Y., 1995.

Martin, Richard. *The Language of Heroes: Speech and Performance in the Iliad*. Cornell University Press. Ithaca, N.Y., 1989.

Moulton, Carroll. *Similes in the Homeric Poems*. Vandenhoeck und Ruprecht. Göttingen, Germany, 1977.

Mueller, Martin. *The Iliad*. Allen & Unwin. London, 1984.

Nagler, Michael. *Spontaneity and Tradition: A Study in the Oral Art of Homer*. University of California Press. Berkeley, Los Angeles, and London, 1974.

Nagy, Gregory. *The Best of the Achaeans: Concepts of the Hero in Archaic Greek Poetry*. Johns Hopkins University Press. Baltimore, Md., and London, 1979.

Owen, E. T. *The Story of the Iliad*. Reprint Bolchazy-Carducci. Wauconda, Ill., 1989.

Page, Sir Denys. *History and the Homeric Iliad*. Sather Classical Lectures, vol. 31. University of California Press. Berkeley, Los Angeles, and London, 1959.

Parry, Milman. *The Making of Homeric Verse: The Collected Papers of Milman Parry*. Ed. Adam Parry. Clarendon Press. Oxford, 1971.

Powell, Barry and Ian Morris, eds. *A New Companion to Homer*. Brill. Leiden, 1996.

Redfield, J. M. *Nature and Culture in the Iliad: The Tragedy of Hector*. University of Chicago Press. Chicago and London, 1975. Expanded edition: Duke University Press. Durham, N.C. and London, 1994.

Rutherford, R. B. *Homer*. Greece and Rome. New surveys in the classics, no. 26. Oxford University Press, 1994.

Schein, Seth L. *The Mortal Hero: An Introduction to Homer's Iliad*. University of California Press. Berkeley, Los Angeles, and London, 1984.

Segal, Charles. *The Theme of the Mutilation of the Corpse in the Iliad. Mnemosyne*, supp. vol. 17. Leiden, The Netherlands, 1971.

Shay, Jonathan. *Achilles in Vietnam: Combat Trauma and the Undoing of Character*. Athenaeum. New York, 1994.

Shive, David M. *Naming Achilles*. Oxford University Press. New York, 1987.

Silk, M. S. *Homer: The Iliad*. Cambridge University Press. Cambridge, England, 1987.

Slatkin, Laura M.: *The Power of Thetis: Allusion and Interpretation in the Iliad*. University of California Press. Berkeley, Los Angeles, and London, 1991.

Steiner, George, and Robert Fagles, eds. *Homer: A Collection of Critical Essays*. Ed. Maynard Mack. Twentieth Century Views. Englewood Cliffs, N.J., 1962.

Taplin, Oliver. *Homeric Soundings*. New York and London, forthcoming.

Vivante, Paolo. *Homer*. Ed. John Herington. Hermes Books. Yale University Press. New Haven and London, 1985.

Wace, Alan J. B., and Frank Stubbings. *A Companion to Homer*. London, 1962.

Wade-Gery, H. T. *The Poet of the Iliad*. Cambridge, England, 1952.

Weil, Simone. *The Iliad or The Poem of Force*. Trans. Mary McCarthy. Politics Pamphlet No. 1. New York, n.d. Reprint. Wallingford, Penn., n.d.

Whitman, Cedric H. *Homer and the Heroic Tradition*. Harvard University Press. Cambridge, Mass., and London, 1958.

Wright, John. *Essays on the Iliad: Selected Modern Criticism*. Indiana University Press. Bloomington, 1978.